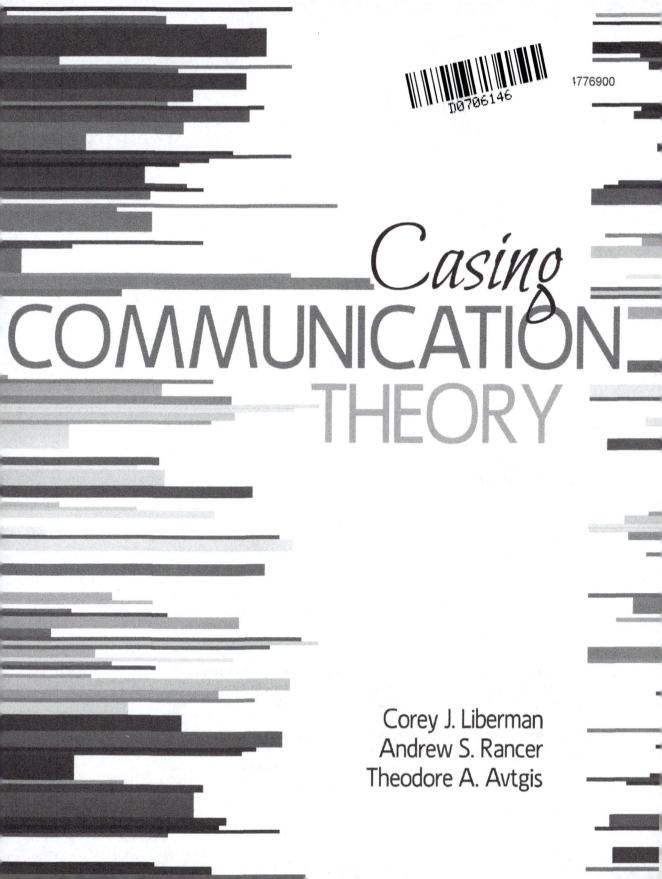

Casing
COMMUNICATION
THEORY

Corey J. Liberman
Andrew S. Rancer
Theodore A. Avtgis

Cover photos courtesy of Shutterstock.com

www.kendallhunt.com
Send all inquiries to:
4050 Westmark Drive
Dubuque, IA 52004-1840

DEDICATION

My wife, Sara; my kids, Hailey and Bradley; my grandfather, Kenneth, who is my perpetual and everlasting idol; my grandmother, Joan, who is an inspirational light; the late John Leustek, who I miss every day, and who has made me proud to be in this profession since I met him; and my stepfather, Martin, who was among my life's biggest mentors and role models

My wife, Kathi Dierks Rancer; my daughter, Aimee Rancer; and to the memory of a great communicator and friend, Kevin F. Greeley

My father, Dr. Alexander W. Avtgis, and my son, Aiden Alexander Avtgis

TABLE OF CONTENTS

CASING
COMMUNICATION THEORY
INTRODUCTION

Whether you are reading this as an instructor or a student, and whether this is your first time being introduced to communication theory or whether you are an experienced veteran, you are about to be exposed to some of the most cited, most prolific, most important theories within the field. The editors of this text are certain that, after having read the 24 case studies that follow, you, the reader, will be able to better understand the "there is nothing so practical as a good theory" quote, made popular by psychologist and theorist Kurt Lewin nearly 70 years ago. Before you begin your forthcoming case study journey, we find it important and necessary to define and clarify a few things for you.

First, what is a theory? Although this can be defined in a number of different ways (just like the word *communication*), we define theory as a general statement about the relationship between and among variables that has been tested and supported by research and that has the ability to *describe, explain, predict,* and *control.* All fields of study, whether they be in the social sciences, formal sciences, or natural sciences, have theories that undergird the major ideas, arguments, claims, theses, and paradigms within them. Without theories, our understanding of the world would be unguided. As an example, one of the theories to which you will be exposed within this book is Social Penetration Theory, a communication theory developed by psychologists Irwin Altman and Dalmas Taylor in 1973. Without this influential theory of interpersonal communication, social actors involved in relationships would not know, for example, that there is empirical evidence linking such variables as self-disclosure, breadth of communication, depth of communication, and reciprocal message-processing with effective relational progression outcomes. Another theory, about which there is a case study chapter in this volume, is Nonverbal Expectancy Violations Theory, first developed by communication scholar Judee Burgoon in 1975. Without this theory, one would lack the empirical knowledge necessary to know that the violation of expectations might produce positively-valenced outcomes in some situations and negatively-valenced outcomes in others. The key, of course, to understanding and appreciating theory is to understand that theory has practical value. To stop and reflect on a social experience, whether it be one that failed as a result of poor conflict management or one that succeeded as a result of effective persuasive strategizing, and to be able to make the claim that Problematic Integration Theory or the Communication

Theory of Identity or Relational Dialectics Theory or Action Assembly Theory (all covered in this text) can shed light on both the process and outcome of it, is an extraordinary thing.

Why do we *want* and/or *need* theories? Well…wouldn't it be nice to know why the person who takes your daily coffee order was not his usual, chipper self this morning? Wouldn't it be nice to know why a significant other did not respond favorably to an apology? Wouldn't it be nice to know why your friends did not laugh at your recent joke? Wouldn't it be nice to know why your group was inefficient and ineffective at making a recent group decision? Wouldn't it be nice to know why employees working in your department are so unlikely to communicate upward dissent? Wouldn't it be nice to know how to use computer-mediated communication to engage in effective dialogic exchange? Wouldn't it be nice to know how to best train a new group of incoming cadets? Let us save you the time and energy and cognition by answering the foregoing questions for you. The answers are all YES!

As mentioned, theories enable us, as social actors, to *describe, explain, predict,* and *control* social phenomena, such as those mentioned in the examples just highlighted. Theories *describe*, meaning that they answer the question *what?* What makes relational stability so difficult? What makes group decision-making so inherently problematic? What makes the communication of apology so antagonizing? Theories *explain*, meaning that they answer the question *why?* Why is it more difficult to express emotions to certain relational actors as compared to others? Why is it OK to tell an off-color joke to one person, but not appropriate to tell the same joke to another? Why is the sibling relationship potentially the most difficult, yet also most rewarding, relationship of all? Theories *predict*, meaning that they answer the question *when?* Fear appeals seem to work when doctors communicate with patients, but when is this most likely to work? Politicians are able to lobby individuals to support their party and their perspective, but under what parameters is this most likely? Marketers are more likely to sell their product if they use certain colors and not others, but under what conditions? Finally, theories *control*, meaning that they answer the question *now what?* As a result of communication theories, we now have more effective strategies for persuading people to become organ donors; we now have more efficient and productive ways of communicating to the public during times of risk and crisis; and we now have more fruitful strategies for communicating with young children about a forthcoming divorce.

This is why theories are so *important*. This is why theories are so *necessary*. They provide us with the information and data necessary to circumnavigate our social landscape. If you have ever been told that you are a good friend or a good work partner or an effective salesperson or a good listener or a good public speaker or a good group leader, it is because, believe it or not, you have enacted behaviors and outcomes associated with one or more of the theories within the field of communication, many of which are highlighted in this casebook.

Finally, before moving on to the 24 cases, we wanted to mention some of the prerequisites (or characteristics, if you will) of all theories. First, theories can be *questioned*. That is, we are not promising that you will agree with every claim made in every chapter within this text. It is absolutely OK to disagree. In fact, some of your professors might ask that you create an argument against the theory that you read. After all, one way to create a new theory is to disagree with one that current exists, right? Some scholars spend their entire careers not attempting to create new theories, but rather attempting to refute theories that already exist. Second, theories are *testable*. One of the theories about which you will read is called Cultivation Theory. In short, it argues that, as consumers of media content, certain social actors are more likely to be affected by exposure to media content as compared to others (i.e., heavy viewers versus light viewers). However, in order to know that this is, in fact, the case, we must be able to put this theory to the test. We must be able to determine, for example, that those who expose themselves to more mediated content (i.e., television) are less able to discern the cultural differences between the television world and the "real" world (as it were). Third, theories are *parsimonious*, which is another way of saying that theories are explaining the most, yet saying the least. Theories, by their very nature, can be quite complicated. For example, if you have ever attempted to learn about String Theory, among the pinnacles of Theoretical Physics, you might very well still be on a daily dose of aspirin. Theorists, however, are encouraged to explain even the most complicated, convoluted ideas as simply as possible.

Fourth, theories are *valid*, meaning that they truly explain what they claim to explain. For example, one of the theories represented within this casebook is Confirmation Theory, which argues that individuals are best served when co-interactants provide self-validating responses during the process of interpersonal interaction. The result of such self-validation is an increased likelihood in self-worth, resulting in a number of positive relational outcomes (i.e., recognition, acknowledgement, endorsement). This theory is valid to the extent that it truly explains why such outcomes result from the confirming, self-validating communication. Fifth, theories are *reliable*, meaning that, when put to the empirical test (based on the accruement of data), similar results surface. In the physical sciences, there exist laws (i.e., Newton's Laws of Motion; Laws of Thermodynamics; Law of Gravity). A law means that there is no way to disprove the claim. There are no laws in the social sciences. Why? Because of human variability. In other words, people are different. That is, there are no laws saying that using humor during post-mortem ceremonies will bring collective familial joy, because the same humor that might bring resolve for some might bring additional (if not more) pain for others. A reliable theory in the social sciences is one that is supported, through empirical investigation. Finally, theories are *useful*, meaning that they can somehow be applied to the practical world(s) in which we live. Since we operate, so often, in relationships, groups, and organizations, and in such contexts as families, doctor/patient, and superior/subordinate, there are communication theories that independently and collectively examine how communication seems to "work" in nearly each and every social environment one might imagine.

As you read the case studies to follow, think about the relationship between the theory embedded within the chapter and the case itself to see the mutual relationship between the two: how the theory comes to explain the case study and how the case study, in turn, comes to shape the theory. Determine whether and to what extent you agree with the major tenets of theory. Should anything be questioned? Reexamined? Restructured? Rethought? Might you have an idea for a new theory of communication in a particular social context? Does the theory effectively explain, describe, predict, and control the social phenomenon/phenomena about which you just read? It is our hope that you will begin to see how fun theory can actually be...and how and why theory contributes to our knowledge of the very principles of human communication.

AUTHOR BIOS

Josh Averbeck (Ph.D., University of Oklahoma, 2011) is an Associate Professor of Communication at Western Illinois University. His research interests include language use in persuasive messages, language expectations, health communication, and irony. He has published more than 25 articles and chapters, some of which have appeared in *Communication Monographs, Human Communication Research,* and *Journal of Communication.*

Theodore A. Avtgis (Ph.D., Kent State University, 1999) is president of Medical Communication Specialists (MCS), a consulting firm that focuses on communication training and development efforts for medical personnel and first responders. He has published dozens of peer-reviewed research articles, 13 books, 22 book chapters, and dozens of professional presentations. His research focuses on health communication, risk and crisis communication, and aggressive communication.

Austin Babrow (Ph.D., University of Illinois at Urbana-Champaign, 1986) is a professor in the School of Communication Studies at Ohio University, where he studies and teaches communication theory as well as health, environmental, and risk communication. He is also active in the movement to limit climate disruption (e.g., advocating for sustainable energy, working to halt fracking); to secure the right of local governance and freedom from corporate influence on policy and regulation, particularly as it relates to energy development; and to elect politicians who will work to mitigate climate change.

Peter Babrow (B.S., Ohio University, 2018) is a 2018 graduate of Ohio University with deep interests in social and cognitive psychology, culture, politics, and social justice. He is currently serving as an Americorps volunteer in Austin, TX. Peter did volunteer work in the 2012 and 2016 presidential election campaigns, canvassed in the 2018 campaign in Ohio, and volunteered in US Representative Beto O'Rourke's (D-TX) campaign for the US Senate.

Quinten S. Bernhold (M.A., University of California, Santa Barbara, 2016) is a Ph.D. candidate in the Department of Communication at the University of California, Santa Barbara. His research interests include intergenerational communication within families and successful aging.

Dawn O. Braithwaite (Ph.D., University of Minnesota, 1988) is the Willa Cather Professor and Chair of Communication Studies at the University of Nebraska-Lincoln. She is a specialist in interpersonal and family communication, studying how people in nontraditional personal and family relationships communicate to construct and navigate family change and challenges via dialectics of relating and rituals. She has authored 120 articles and is coeditor or coauthor of five books. She received the National Communication Association's Brommel Award for Outstanding Contributions in Family Communication, the University of Nebraska-Lincoln College of Arts & Sciences Award for Outstanding Research in Social Science, and named the Western States Communication Association Distinguished Scholar in 2014. Braithwaite is a Past President of WSCA and NCA and received NCA's Samuel L. Becker Distinguished Service Award in 2017.

Maria Brann (Ph.D., University of Kentucky, 2003) is an associate professor in the Department of Communication Studies at IUPUI and affiliate faculty with the Injury Control Research Center at West Virginia University. Dr. Brann explores the integration of health, interpersonal, and gendered communication. As a translational health communication scholar who studies health vulnerabilities, her primary research interests focus on the study of women's issues in health communication contexts and promotion of healthy lifestyle behaviors. She is the editor of *Contemporary Case Studies in Health Communication: Theoretical & Applied Approaches*. Additionally, her work has been published in numerous refereed journals such as *Health Communication, Journal of Applied Communication Research,* and *Patient Education and Counseling* and in several scholarly books including *Casing Persuasive Communication, Pregnancy Loss: A Narrative Collection,* and *Gender in Applied Communication Contexts.*

Diana Breshears (Ph.D., University of Nebraska-Lincoln, 2011) is a senior lecturer in the Communication Science department at University of the Free State, Qwaqwa Campus. She specializes in the fields of interpersonal and family communication. Through her research, Diana explores the social and familial experiences of people with nontraditional family identities. She is currently working on a research project investigating transracial adoption in South Africa.

Heather J. Carmack (Ph.D., Ohio University, 2008) is an associate professor of health communication in the Department of Communication Studies at the University of Alabama. Her research focuses on micro and macro communication practices impacting communication about patient safety, specifically medical errors. She also examines communication surrounding dying and death. Her research has been published in communication and interdisciplinary health journals, including *Health Communication, Management Communication Quarterly, Communication Studies,* and *Qualitative Health Research.*

Jeffrey T. Child (Ph.D., North Dakota State University, 2007) is a professor at Kent State University in the School of Communication Studies. His primary research explores privacy regulation, communication technology, and interaction. Most recently, his work has focused on how people manage their privacy and respond to breakdowns in privacy management when interacting on social media. His research has been published in journals like the *Journal of Family Communication, Computers in Human Behavior, Journal of the American Society for Information Science and Technology, Communication Quarterly,* and *Communication Studies,* among others.

Cristin A. Compton (Ph.D., University of Missouri, 2016) is an assistant professor in the School of Communication Studies at Kent State University. Her scholarship focuses on power, identity work, and organizing processes, specifically exploring how sexuality, gender, and power intersect to organize people and their lived experiences. Her current research continues her exploration of "co-sexuality," the process of communicatively constructing "normal" sexuality and adhering and diverging from that norm in different organizational contexts. She has been invited to present her scholarship at conferences including the International Communication Association, the National Communication Association, The Organization for Communication, Language, and Gender, and the Central States Communication Association. Her research has been published in journals such as *Journal of Communication* and *Management Communication Quarterly.*

Gregory A. Cranmer (Ph.D., West Virginia University, 2015) is an assistant professor of Sport Communication in the Department of Communication at Clemson University, a faculty fellow of the Robert H. Brooks Sports Science Institute, and a member of the Heterodox Academy. His research focuses on how individuals adjust within social groups (organizations and sport teams) and how leadership within these groups can effectively communicate with subordinates. He is also deeply passionate about promoting academic climates that value the diversity of ideas and the prioritization of understanding with those whom we disagree.

Rachel L. DiCioccio (Ph.D., Kent State University, 2001) is a professor in the Harrington School of Communication and Media and the Director of the Office of Innovation in General Education at the University of Rhode Island. She teaches undergraduate and graduate courses in humor, conflict management, family communication, and communication pedagogy, and in 2009 was awarded URI's Teaching Excellence Award for the College of Arts & Sciences. Her research interests include teasing, humor communication, and family argument processes during crisis decision-making. She has published numerous book chapters and articles in various journals including; *The Journal of Communication, Communication Reports, Human Communication,* and *The Review of Communication* and edited the scholarly text, *Humor Communication: Theory, Impact, and Outcomes.*

James Price Dillard (Ph.D., Michigan State University, 1983) is a Distinguished Professor of Communication Arts & Sciences at Penn State University. He is a former editor of *Human Communication Research* and coeditor of *The Persuasion Handbook* (with M. Pfau and L. Shen), a fellow of the International Communication Association, and the recipient of the first John E. Hunter Award for Meta-Analysis. Dillard's scholarly interests focus on how communication produces change in the opinions and behaviors of others with special emphasis on the role of emotion.

Thomas Feeley (Ph.D., University at Buffalo, 1996) is Professor of Communication and Chair of Media Studies at the University at Buffalo, The State University of New York. His research is at the intersection of theories of persuasion and understanding communication behavior in applied health/organizational contexts. He has published over 100 journal articles and book chapters and recently authored the book, *Research from the Inside-Out: Lessons from Exemplary Studies in Communication* (Routledge).

Kasey Foley (M.A., John Carroll University, 2016) is a Ph.D. candidate in the Communication Arts and Sciences Department at Pennsylvania State University. Her research examines interpersonal and health communication, with a focus on how advice functions within personal and professional interactions. She is currently conducting research examining medical advising between clinicians and patients.

Howard "Howie" Giles (Ph.D., University of Bristol, 1971) was previously Head of Psychology at the University of Bristol, and is now a Distinguished Research Professor of Communication at the University of California, Santa Barbara, and Honorary Professor in the School of Psychology at The University of Queensland, Brisbane, Australia. His research interests embrace many areas of intergroup communication. He has been the recipient of an array of awards, including the International Communication Association's Inaugural Career Productivity Award in 2000, is past president of the International Communication Association and the International Association of Language and Social Psychology, past editor of *Human Communication Research*, and founding editor of both the *Journal of Language and Social Psychology* and the *Journal of Asian Pacific Communication*. Giles now also works with the Santa Barbara Police Department as their Director of Volunteer Services.

John O. Greene (Ph.D., University of Wisconsin-Madison, 1983) is a professor in the Brian Lamb School of Communication at Purdue University. He is a former editor of *Human Communication Research* (2001–2003) and former book review editor of *Communication Theory* (1993–1996). He is a recipient of the National

Communication Association's Charles H. Woolbert Research Award (1994) and a two-time recipient of the Gerald R. Miller Book Award (2002, 2004).

Katy Harris (M.S., University of Tennessee, 2016) is a doctoral student at the University at Buffalo, The State University of New York, studying social influence techniques under Dr. Thomas Feeley. She earned her bachelor of arts and master of science degrees from the University of Tennessee, Knoxville.

Michael Hecht (Ph.D., University of Illinois, 1976) is a Distinguished Professor Emeritus of Communication Arts and Sciences at Penn State University and president of REAL Prevention, LLC. Dr. Hecht specializes in culturally grounded, narrative health message design and evaluation with diverse communities. His evidence-based "keepin' it REAL" (kiR) is a narrative, multicultural, school-based substance use prevention curriculum for elementary and middle school students that he cocreated with Dr. Miller-Day. Since its adoption by D.A.R.E. America, kiR is the most widely disseminated substance use prevention program in the world, reaching almost 1 million US youth as well as those in over 50 countries around the world. He also was involved in adaptations of the curriculum for use in rural US communities as well as for Nicaraguan youth. Other projects focus on using interactive video games for sex education, narrative HPV vaccination promotion, and an e-learning media literacy curriculum for substance use prevention. In addition to D.A.R.E., collaborators include Planned Parenthood and the 4-H Clubs of America. This work has been funded by the National Institutes of Health, Robert Wood Johnson Foundation, US Department of State, and the Nemours Foundation, among others. Hecht has served on NIH's Community-Level Health Promotion Review Group, including being selected as its chair, as well as on numerous editorial boards in communication and other fields. Hecht's work spurred the creation of Real Prevention LLC., a business that provides consulting, training, support, and evaluation services to organizations interested in adopting kiR or developing new interventions. Michael's teaching interests were interpersonal communication, intercultural communication, and communication theory.

Young Yun Kim (Ph.D., Northwestern University, 1976) is a professor in the Department of Communication at the University of Oklahoma. Born and raised in South Korea, she completed her B.A. degree in English at the Seoul National University. She came to the United States in 1970 under the sponsorship of East-West Center and completed her M.A. degree in speech communication at the University of Hawaii, followed by her Ph.D. degree in communication from Northwestern University in Evanston, Illinois. Professor Kim has published over 200 journal articles and book chapters, as well as 12 books including the three-volume *International Encyclopedia of Intercultural Communication* (2018). She is a Fellow of the International Communication Association and a recipient of the Top Scholar Award for Lifetime Achievement from the Intercultural Communication Division of the International Communication Association. She has served as Chair of the Intercultural Communication Division of the International Communication Association as well as of the National Communication Association, and as President of the International Academy for Intercultural Research. Professor Kim began her scientific investigation of cross-cultural adaptation as a graduate student at Northwestern University. Driven by a keen personal interest in understanding the adaptive struggles and successes that she and those around her were experiencing, her doctoral thesis addressed these issues through a survey among Korean immigrants in the Chicago area. She has subsequently conducted original studies among various groups of immigrants, refugees, and ethnic minorities in the United States including Japanese, Mexicans, Southeast Asians, and American Indians, as well as international students attending universities in Germany, Japan, Korea, and the United States. Since the 1990s, Professor Kim has broadened her research domain to include issues of ethnicity/race, ethnic identity, and interethnic communication within a society. She has carried out a research program examining key psychological, situational, and macroenvironmental factors, and their interrelationships with associative and dissociative communication behaviors in interethnic encounters. Her Contextual Theory of Interethnic Communication was published in 2005 in *Theorizing about Intercultural Communication* (ed. by W. Gudykunst). She is currently writing a book-length version of this theory. Professor Kim's enduring interest in her two interrelated research domains, cross-cultural adaptation and interethnic communication, is a natural outgrowth of her own personal evolution—from a newcomer to American society striving for excellence in her academic pursuits, to an insider seeking to make an intellectual contribution to the continuing national endeavor to reach for "a more perfect union."

Timothy R. Levine (Ph.D., Michigan State University, 1992) is Distinguished Professor and Chair of the Department of Communication Studies at the University of Alabama Birmingham (UAB). His research interests are diverse and include interpersonal communication, persuasion, research design and measurement, and deception. He has published more than 130 journal articles. Levine's research has been funded by the National Science Foundation, the US Department of Defense, and the US Department of Justice. His forthcoming book on Truth-Default Theory is due out in 2019 by the University of Alabama Press.

Corey Jay Liberman (Ph.D., Rutgers University, 2008) is an associate professor in the Department of Communication and Media Arts at Marymount Manhattan College. His research spans the interpersonal communication, group communication, and organizational communication worlds, and he is currently interested in studying the social practices of dissent within organizations, specifically the antecedents, processes, and effects associated with effective employee dissent communication. He is currently working on a book dealing with risk and crisis communication, as well as a case study book focusing on mediated communication.

Darren L. Linvill (Ph.D., Clemson University, 2008) is an associate professor in the Department of Communication at Clemson University. Dr. Linvill's research explores issues related civil discourse in society and, in particular, on college campuses. Dr. Linvill has written extensively about how students and institutions engage with difficult topics, both in the classroom and online.

Yu Lu (Ph.D., Pennsylvania State University, 2015) is a postdoctoral research fellow at the University of Texas Medical Branch. Her primary research interests are at the intersection of health and intercultural communication with a focus on health disparities and culturally appropriate health message design, specifically in the context of risk behaviors such as substance use and relationship violence. She is also interested in research methods particularly in the context of working with diverse cultural groups, such as accessing and gaining trust with minority populations and cross-cultural measure adaptation. She has taught various communication courses including intercultural communication, health communication, communication theory, group communication, interviewing, and research methods.

Erina MacGeorge (Ph.D., University of Illinois, 1999) is a social scientist whose research examines interpersonal and health communication, with a focus on social support and social influence. Her work includes the development of advice response theory, which explains advice outcomes for recipients as a function of message, advisor, situation, and recipient characteristics. Recent studies have examined advice between doctors and parents about childhood antibiotic use and breast cancer patients making surgical decisions with input from their social networks, as well as advice between college student friends coping with everyday problems. She recently edited the *Oxford Handbook of Advice*.

Roxana D. Maiorescu-Murphy (Ph.D., Purdue University, 2013) is an assistant professor in the Department of Marketing Communication at Emerson College, where she studies global public relations and social media. She is especially interested in employee communication, diversity, and organizational culture.

Jimmie Manning (Ph.D., University of Kansas, 2006) is Professor and Chair of Communication Studies at the University of Nevada, Reno. His research focuses on meaning-making in relationships. This research spans multiple contexts to understand how individuals, couples, families, organizations, and other cultural institutions attempt to define, support, control, limit, encourage, or otherwise negotiate relationships. He explores these ideas through three contexts: relational discourses, especially those about sexuality, gender, love, and identity; connections between relationships and efficacy in health and organizational contexts; and digitally mediated communication. His research has been supported by funding agencies such as the National Science Foundation and Learn & Serve America and has accrued over 90 publications in outlets including *Communication Monographs, Journal of Social and Personal Relationships,* and *Journal of Computer-Mediated Communication.* He recently coauthored the book *Researching Interpersonal Relationships: Qualitative Methods, Research, and Analysis* (Sage Publications) and has another solo-authored book, *Qualitative Research in Sexuality & Gender Studies* (Oxford University Press) forthcoming. He also serves as editor for the journal *Sexuality & Communication.*

Peter J. Marston (Ph.D., University of Southern California, 1987) is a Professor of Communication Studies at California State University, Northridge. His published scholarship has focused on the subjective experience and communication of romantic love and, more recently, the discourses of pseudoscience and the paranormal. His teaching centers around fundamental issues in the philosophy of communication, specifically the nature and potential of human understanding and the cultivation of agency and purpose in symbolic action.

Andrew S. Rancer (Ph.D., Kent State University, 1979) is Professor Emeritus in the School of Communication at the University of Akron. He is the coauthor of six books and numerous book chapters and journal articles in professional and scholarly journals. His research has focused primarily on the communication traits of argumentativeness and verbal aggressiveness with the goal of training individuals to engage in constructive conflict and avoid destructive conflict by understanding how these traits function during interpersonal and relational conflict. He has taught a variety of communication courses (e.g., persuasion, training methods in communication, nonverbal communication, interpersonal communication, communication research, communication theory) to undergraduate, graduate students, and adult learners for over 40 years.

Robert J. Razzante (M.Ed., Ohio University, 2016) is a Ph.D. student in the Hugh Downs School of Human Communication at Arizona State University. His research interests center on the link between communication, privilege, and marginalization in varying contexts. Rob's recent work explores intersectionality through the lens of co-cultural theory and dominant group theory. More specifically, he is interested in how the framework can encourage responsible users of privilege in varying organizational and community settings.

Sarah Tracy (Ph.D., University of Colorado, 2000) is a professor in the Hugh Downs School of Human Communication at Arizona State University. Sarah's scholarly work examines emotion, communication and identity in the workplace with particular focus on workplace bullying, emotional labor, compassion, leadership, and work-life wellness. Her award-winning research has resulted in over 65 monographs and two books, *Leading Organizations through Transition* and *Qualitative Research Methods*. She regularly provides academic and professional workshops related to her research, and favorite courses to teach include Being a Leader, Qualitative Methods, and Communication and the Art of Happiness.

Heather L. Walter (Ph.D., University at Buffalo, the State University of New York, 1999) is the Director of the School of Communication at the University of Akron. Her research is focused in the area of organizational communication and conflict, with a focus on communication networks. She has published many journal articles and chapters on this topic, including several case studies designed to show the applied nature of organizational communication. She has taught courses in research, theory, and organizational communication areas (e.g. small group communication, communication & conflict, and analyzing organizational communication). She enjoys working with undergraduate and graduate students and helping them see the relevance of communication theory to their everyday lives.

Charles J. Wigley III (Ph.D., Kent State University, 1986) is Professor Emeritus, Canisius College, Buffalo, NY. His primary research interests include verbal aggressiveness and the role of communication variables in the jury selection process. He has published numerous book chapters and articles in *Communication Monographs, Communication Quarterly, Communication Reports, Communication Research Reports*, and *Communication Currents*. He completed his doctoral studies under his former high school debate coach and coauthor, the late Dr. Dominic A. Infante.

Kevin B. Wright (Ph.D., University of Oklahoma, 1999) is a professor of health communication in the Department of Communication at George Mason University. His research focuses on social support processes and health outcomes, online health information seeking, health organizations, and the use of technology in provider-patient relationships and health campaign design.

Chapter 1

AAT: Action Assembly Theory/ Alice's Adventures in Theoryland

John O. Greene, Ph.D., *Purdue University*

At the outset it is important to note that the term "action assembly theory" is something of a misnomer in the sense that AAT is more appropriately viewed as a family of interrelated theoretical formulations. The common conceptual thread (the "DNA") that runs through all of the members of this family is the basic idea that thoughts and overt actions are formulated by combining elemental units of information stored in long-term memory. Among the members of this extended family, then, are the original formulation of the theory (AAT; Greene, 1984) and "second generation Action Assembly Theory" (AAT2; Greene, 1997). Other family members include the "Theory of Transcendent Interactions" (TTI; Greene & Herbers, 2011), and the newest addition, the theory of "Adult Communicative Play" (ACP; Greene & Pruim, 2018).

The AAT program of theory development is the product of attempts to address certain foundational questions regarding communication processes. Among these questions are the following:

- It is commonly recognized that communication is an inherently creative endeavor, but how is it possible for a person to think, or say, or do, something that he or she has never heard, thought, said, or done before?
- It should be obvious that interpersonal interaction is a skilled activity (that it can be done well or poorly), but what is the nature of the processes that underlie more (and less) skillful communicative behavior?
- Social interactions can be arrayed along a continuum defined at one end by experiences of connection, understanding, and interpersonal coordination, and, as one moves away from this "ideal," by interactions that are uninteresting, stilted, strained, or worse. But what factors and processes determine where along this continuum a particular interaction will fall?

In pursuit of these, and other related questions, Action Assembly Theories have been brought to bear in studying a variety of phenomena including communication skill deficits (Greene & Geddes, 1993) and communication skill acquisition (see Greene, 2003), message planning (e.g., Greene, 1995a; as well as Goals—Plans—Action theorizing; Greene, 2000), listening (Geiman & Greene, 2019), communication apprehension (e.g., Greene & Sparks, 1983), "creative facility" (see below; e.g., Dorrance Hall, et al., 2017), deceptive message production (Greene, O'Hair, Cody, & Yen, 1985; see also Greene, 2014), attempts to accomplish multiple, contradictory message goals (see Greene, 1995b), and even the nature of the self (Greene & Geddes, 1988).

AAT has its roots in cognitive functionalist approaches to theorizing wherein explanatory accounts involve specifying the mental structures and processes that give rise to the phenomena of interest (see Greene & Dorrance Hall, 2013). In other words, theories of this sort seek to describe the nature of the information represented in the mind (i.e., issues of structure) and how that information is accessed and utilized (i.e., issues of process) to produce the behavioral patterns of interest to the theorist. At its most basic level, AAT specifies just two structures (procedural records and the output representation) and two processes (activation and assembly) to account for the entire sweep of an individual's verbal and nonverbal behaviors.

The concept of a "procedural record" in AAT stems from the observation that even the simplest movement must, in fact, involve the interplay of a great many action specifications, at various levels of representational abstraction (i.e., from high level conceptual specifications such as "flip to the 'Interview with the Caterpillar' at the end of this chapter," to the motor programs for actually moving your wrist and fingers to carry out that action). AAT, then, posits that these action features are linked in long-term memory to the results, or outcomes, associated with manifestation of particular actions (e.g., pressing the accelerator makes the car go faster). And, because an action—outcome relationship that holds in one situation may not apply in another (e.g., what works in securing compliance from one roommate doesn't work with the other), memory comes to preserve action—outcome—in situation relationships; i.e., "procedural records"—the basic "building blocks" of thought and action.

According to AAT, if an individual possesses many hundreds of thousands of procedural records, then there must be some process for accessing the relatively small subset (think thousands) of records that are most relevant to his or her current goals and situational constraints. This is where the activation process comes in. AAT posits that every procedural record is characterized at any moment by some level of activation, a continuous quantity that is incremented above resting levels when the outcome features in a record correspond with a person's goals and/or current situational features are similar to those represented in the record.[1] The upshot is that the most highly activated action features will be those that are most relevant in the moment.

But activation of relevant action features alone cannot stand as a theoretical account of verbal and nonverbal message production. As a simple illustration of this point, consider that if a person wished to convey the ideation "my automobile won't start," any number of potential word entries to fill the lexical slot for the concept "automobile" (e.g., "car," "clunker," "lemon") would likely be highly activated. It is here that the assembly process comes into play. Assembly is somewhat akin to fitting the pieces of a jigsaw puzzle together, but with the twist that time and size matter. The activation level of an isolated action feature is thought to be extremely fleeting (fractions of a second), but action features (puzzle pieces) that coalesce to form larger configurations of behavioral specifications reinforce each other and remain activated for longer spans, thereby increasing the likelihood that they will be manifested in overt behavior.

This image of coalitions of action features, forming and fragmenting on time-scale faster than an eye-blink, constitutes the essence of the second fundamental structure in AAT, the output representation. At root, the output representation is the momentary constellation of coalitions of action features that comprise a person's thoughts (conscious and otherwise) and overt behaviors as they unfold toward the ever-extending event horizon.

The basic conceptual framework of AAT, despite the fact that it is founded on conceptions of just two theoretical structures and two processes, affords insights about a wide range of communicative phenomena. As was noted at the outset of this chapter, there is an inherent novel, creative character to behavior—and this is true of even the simplest motor behaviors. If you repeat the same familiar phrase over and over again, there will be variations in movement parameters of your vocal apparatus from trial to trial. Of greater interest to communication scholars is that people constantly think and say new things. From the perspective of AAT, this capacity for creativity is the inevitable result of the operation of the assembly process that functions to produce novel configurations of action features—just as the 88 keys on a piano can be used to produce an infinite number of novel compositions—except, of course, the number of procedural records in long-term

---

[1] An important extension of this element of AAT theorizing is given in TTI (Greene & Herbers, 2011) where the principle of "direct feature activation" suggests that, in addition to goals and situational features, elements of a person's interlocutor's behavior will serve to increment the activation level of his or her own corresponding action features.

memory and the fact that they code action features in multiple representational formats (again, from high level, abstract conceptions of what one is doing to low level motor programs) affords exponentially more combinatorial possibilities and complexities than even that of the piano.

A particularly important line of theorizing prompted by AAT centers on the notion of *assembly difficulties*. Returning to the analogy of fitting puzzle pieces, consider what might happen when activated action features don't mesh, as, for example, when things a person might say to accomplish one goal, like giving an honest assessment of a friend's violin recital performance, can't be reconciled with not wanting to hurt his feelings. Assembly difficulties of a different sort arise when an individual has an abstract conception of what she wants to say, but is unable to find an appropriate word for expressing that ideation, or when someone has a "picture in his head" of executing a graceful tango step, but simply lacks the motor skills to do anything more than step on the feet of his dance partner.

An important component of the AAT program of work from the very outset has been the development of empirical methods for testing various theoretically derived hypotheses. Several of these research paradigms involve examining speech fluency (especially speech-onset latency [i.e., the time it takes a person to begin speaking] and silent pauses [i.e., periods after the onset of speech when there is no phonation]) as an index of assembly difficulties—the idea being that speech production will falter when a person encounters problems in forming coherent coalitions of action features. And what makes such measures of speech fluency doubly interesting is that not only do they provide a window on underlying cognitive processes, they also play an important role in social perception (consider for example, the sorts of impressions we form about the credibility and expertise of slow, halting speakers). The basic insight that assembly difficulties lead to diminished speech fluency has been substantiated in numerous studies (see Greene, 1995a, 1995b), but the AAT framework also specifies factors and conditions that can, at least to some extent, offset such effects.

According to AAT, one of the ways of overcoming assembly difficulties is by advance planning—in effect, resolving problems by assembling portions of the output representation before they are actually implemented. We typically imagine that criminals work to "get their story straight" before being questioned, and closer to home, most students understand the advantages of thinking about what to say long before they arrive at their professors' offices to argue for a grade change.

A second line of theorizing relevant to the time-course of assembly focuses on the effects of repetition or practice. Just as the theory holds that, through experience, people form links in memory between features of actions, outcomes, and situations, so too, do they come to link multiple action features when those features are repetitively concurrently or sequentially activated and assembled. The implication is that rather than individual action features that must be integrated anew each time, "unitized assemblies" of features afford ready-made solutions to recurrent goal—situation configurations. Moreover, these larger complexes of pre-assembled action features are "strengthened" each time they are activated such that their implementation becomes increasingly reliable, rapid, and error-free.

This component of theorizing in AAT prompted a series of studies (see Greene, 2003) on the effects of practice on adult communication skill acquisition, including those factors that differentiate the message behavior of experts and novices (e.g., newly hired sales reps versus their more experienced counterparts). These studies indicated that, among other things: (a) people do become more fluent with practice, (b) the course of performance improvement is described by a general power function (i.e., large improvements in the early stages of skill acquisition, followed by smaller performance increments as practice continues), (c) various individual-difference factors (e.g., working memory capacity) affect the time-course of skill acquisition, and (d) skill-acquisition curves for younger and older adults differ in systematic ways.

Beyond the effects of advance planning and experience in overcoming assembly difficulties, a third possibility emerged as a serendipitous outcome of a research program originally focused on examining other aspects of the theory. As alluded above, the theoretical developments in AAT have been paralleled at each turn by the introduction of new research paradigms to test various theoretically derived hypotheses (e.g., ways of creating assembly difficulties, of controlling opportunity for advance planning, of examining the time-course of acquisition of an entirely new skill over hundreds of trials, etc.). Because assembly (or more appropriately, coalition formation) is typically exceedingly rapid, a laboratory technique was developed to slow certain parts of it down enough to "get a look at it." One of the unanticipated insights to emerge from the initial application of this paradigm (essentially, a new way of manipulating assembly difficulties) was that some people were consistently faster than others in formulating messages to address those difficulties. This individual-difference variable, termed "creative facility," refers to a person's ability to produce fluent, appropriate messages—think of it as the ability to "think on one's feet" or come up with a "snappy comeback"—and contrast that ability with the person who thinks of the perfect rejoinder, but does so only hours after the fact. Subsequent studies have shown that creative facility is not related to likely personality traits like extroversion, but that it does appear to be associated with family communication patterns during one's formative years (see Dorrance Hall et al., 2017).

To this point this chapter has focused primarily on theoretical and empirical developments driven by the original formulation of the theory (Greene, 1984) and the subsequent "second generation Action Assembly Theory" (AAT2; see Greene, 1997, 2000, 2006). These facets of the broader AAT approach to thinking about and studying human communication are, for the most part, concerned with intra-individual processes, including the nature and role of consciousness, message planning and editing, and, of course, overt verbal and nonverbal message production. But other lines of work grounded in the AAT perspective are more fully focused on inter-individual mentation and action (i.e., the socially interactive nature of thought and talk).

In this vein, the Theory of Transcendent Interactions (TTI; Greene & Herbers, 2011) was developed as an account of occasions of exceptional interpersonal absorption, connection, and insight—interactions that are exciting, immersive, and memorable. But, although such experiences may be rare, according to TTI, they represent the endpoint of a continuum along which all interpersonal interactions, even those that are disjointed and difficult, can be arrayed, and in this sense TTI affords insights about even the most mundane of our everyday encounters.

The foundational premise of TTI is the notion that one's conversational partner can act to both pose, and assist in resolving, assembly difficulties. The upshot is that the "best" experiences of connection and mutuality don't come from interactions that are completely predictable, or from those in which what the other says and does is difficult to follow, but rather from a special "midrange" where both people's conversational contributions spur new understandings and insights. The theory, then, goes on to specify conditions (e.g., shared interests and knowledge; interpersonal trust versus threat) that are more likely to foster such exchanges.

Building on the conceptual foundations of AAT, and as an extension of TTI, the theory of Adult Communicative Play (ACP; Greene & Pruim, 2018) focuses on the dynamics of occasions of affectionate teasing, puns, sharing "inside jokes," re-tellings and collaborative elaborations of humorous stories, and so on. In essence, the theory is concerned with explicating the nature of the processes that give rise to such (sometimes raucous, sometimes poignant) conversational moments. ACP, then, posits a conception of "quintessential play" (i.e., the very best instances of interpersonal coordination and enjoyment, deriving from the juxtaposition of pattern and novelty) and goes on to specify various person factors (e.g., dispositional playfulness), relationship factors (e.g., affection), and contextual factors (e.g., social rules and norms) that play a role in fostering quintessential play.

And now, won't you please join my friend Alice and me for an afternoon adventure? You'll be able to recognize me as the Cheshire Cat, and you'll be perfect just as you are, but let us see if we can discern what's up with the other characters we encounter.

AAT: Alice's Adventures in Theoryland

Despite its apparent tiny size, the doorway at the end of the long hall opened on a beautiful garden in late-summer, late-afternoon splendor. Across the lawn came running a White Rabbit, clad in a waistcoat, and always watching the time, but he paused just long enough to pose to Alice: "Knock-knock." And Alice, ever-eager to join in the fun of play, conversational and otherwise, helpfully responded, "Who's there?" "To," came the reply. "To, who?" At which point, the Rabbit, in a rather impatient tone, responded, "No, to WHOM," as he scurried away.

As we stared after the Rabbit, the Queen of Hearts, speaking quite rapidly, rushed past, repeating, *"Collar that Dormouse!   Behead that Dormouse!   Turn that Dormouse out of court!   Suppress him!   Pinch him!   Off with his whiskers!..."* [2] until her voice was lost in the distance.

Strolling about the grounds we encountered a very odd pair, two footmen, dressed in livery, one looking very much like a fish, and the other like a frog, and both in powdered wigs. The Fish-Footman, proceeded to read, in an official tone, *"An invitation!"* To which the Frog-footman responded, "An invitation!" And his companion continued, *"From the Queen!"* and the Frog-footman echoed, "From the Queen!" And so they continued, *"To play croquet!"* "To play croquet!" Exasperated at their redundancy, Alice asked, "Why must you simply repeat what you read and hear?" The Fish-footman, still reading from the invitation, and handing Alice a sheet of paper, continued, "All guests are required to strictly adhere to their scripted lines!" Followed by "All guests are required to strictly adhere to their scripted lines!" Alice, crumpling the paper, turned on her heel and strode away, saying "This will never do!" Followed by the footmen: "This will never do!" "This will never do!"

Spying a long table set for tea beneath a spreading tree,

Alice suggested that we join the March Hare, the Hatter, and the Dormouse in the afternoon lea.

The Hare and the Hatter were mildly dismayed

by the events of the entire matter (the Dormouse was quite asleep),

---

[2] All lines in italics are from Lewis Carroll's *Alice's Adventures in Wonderland*.

and the Hatter only partly in jest,

demanded of Alice, *"Why is a raven like a writing-desk?"*

Now Alice, being quite quick-witted, and recognizing at once that the Hatter no answer,

eschewed the obvious (bills and legs) and responded, "Because both of them, except for one, cavorts with cocky canter."

At this, the Hatter could only look at his watch—

it always showed six o'clock—

and, an opening at hand, we used the chance,

and anon, came upon, the most remarkable dance.

On the shore of the sea, the Mock Turtle and the Gryphon were engaged in a most intricate quadrille (at least insofar as THAT can be done by two!). And, just as their steps, their thoughts entwined in sublime coordination. "How green is the sea!" "Yes, how beautiful!" "I see glimmers of celadon… and Eton blue." "Indeed, I see them, too, and look there… Arcadian green… and there, laurel!"

At this point, over a low dune came the Queen, running not as fast as before, but speaking even more rapidly, *"Collar that Dormouse! Behead that Dormouse! Turn that Dormouse out of court! Suppress him! Pinch him! Off with his whiskers!..."* until her voice was again lost in the distance.

As we stared after her, the Gryphon continued, "A resplendent day such as this makes me think of the way the sun shimmers on the sea when seen from a great height" (for the Gryphon could fly). "Oh, you must tell me more of what you have seen of the sea!" said the Mock Turtle; and the Gryphon, "And I am most curious to learn about your immersive experiences." They continued their conversation, oblivious to the passage of time (for it was not perpetually six o'clock here), and we took our leave of their company.

Across the links came a cry, *"The trial's beginning!"* This caused considerable commotion in the garden, and we followed along with the growing procession to see what might happen. In the courtroom, the Knave of Hearts stood accused of stealing the Queen of Hearts' tarts. But this charge was quite curious because the large tray of tarts was in plain sight! Thus, the Knave faced a dire conundrum: To absolve himself he could point out that the tarts were never stolen, but to do so he ran the risk of incurring the wrath of the King who had charged him. At this point the King said *"Consider your verdict,"* but no evidence had yet been given!

Called to the stand, the Hatter tried to recount events, but even though he had a story in mind, could find no words to express it, and so he simply said, *"I cannot remember."* The King replied, *"Give your evidence, or I'll have you executed, whether you're nervous or not."* The Hatter, on one knee, said *"I am a poor man, your Majesty."* *"You are a* very *poor speaker,"* replied the King.

As the trial descended into chaos, the King invoked *"Rule 42"* (the *"oldest rule in the book"*), the Queen, with nary a pause for breath, shouted, *"CollarthatDormouse!BeheadthatDormouse!TurnthatDormouseoutofcourt!Suppresshim!Pinchhim!Off with his whiskers!..."* At this, Alice wakened from her afternoon slumber; and you, my companion for the hour, turned to other things. As for the Cat, he gradually faded from view, until only his grin remained.

Discussion Questions

1. Can you draw a diagram of a "procedural record"?

2. Every person's behavior is characterized by repetitive patterns (we all have a working vocabulary of words and phrases that we use over and over, and we also have patterns of nonverbal behaviors [e.g., mannerisms, facial expressions] that our friends would immediately recognize as being "us"). But, as this chapter notes, even though our behavior is patterned, it is also creative in the sense that we never do exactly the same thing twice. How does AAT account for the patterned nature of behavior? How does AAT account for the creative nature of behavior?

3. Can you think of a recent situation where you encountered an "assembly difficulty"? Would an observer have been able to tell that you were experiencing that difficulty? How so?

4. How does AAT account for the fact that communication performance (e.g., giving a speech, answering questions in a job interview) improves with practice?

5. Based on the concept of "creative facility" discussed in the chapter, can you identify people you know who are probably (a) high and (b) low in creative facility? Where along this dimension would you rate yourself and why?

6. Can you recall a conversation where you just seemed to "click" with another person; where the two of you just seemed to be completely "in synch"? Looking back, what factors do you think contributed to such a sense of engagement and connection?

REFERENCES

Dorrance Hall, E., Greene, J.O., Anderson, L.B., Hingson, L., Gill, E., Berkelaar, B.L., & Morgan, M. (2017). The family environment of "quick witted" persons: Birth order, family communication patterns, and creative facility. *Communication Studies, 68,* 493–510.

Geiman, K. L., & Greene, J. O. (2019). Listening and experiences of interpersonal transcendence. *Communication Studies, 70,* 114–128.

Greene, J.O. (1984). A cognitive approach to human communication: An action assembly theory. *Communication Monographs, 51,* 289–306.

Greene, J.O. (1995a). An action assembly perspective on verbal and nonverbal message production: A dancer's message unveiled. In D.E. Hewes (Ed.), *The cognitive bases of interpersonal communication* (pp. 51–85). Hillsdale, NJ: Lawrence Erlbaum.

Greene, J.O. (1995b). Production of messages in pursuit of multiple social goals: Action assembly theory contributions to the study of cognitive encoding processes. In B.R. Burleson (Ed.), *Communication yearbook 18* (pp. 26–53). Thousand Oaks, CA: Sage.

Greene, J.O. (1997). A second generation action assembly theory. In J.O. Greene (Ed.), *Message production: Advances in communication theory* (pp. 151–170). Mahwah, NJ: Lawrence Erlbaum.

Greene, J.O. (2000). Evanescent mentation: An ameliorative conceptual foundation for research and theory on message production. *Communication Theory, 10,* 139–155.

Greene, J.O. (2003). Models of adult communication skill acquisition: Practice and the course of performance improvement. In J.O. Greene & B.R. Burleson (Eds.), *Handbook of communication and social interaction skills* (pp. 51-91). Mahwah, NJ: Lawrence Erlbaum.

Greene, J.O. (2006). Have I got something to tell you: Ideational dynamics and message production. *Journal of Language and Social Psychology, 25,* 64–75.

Greene, J.O., & Dorrance Hall, E. (2103). Cognitive theories of communication. In P.J. Schulz & P. Cobley (Eds.), *Handbooks of communication science. Vol 1: Theories and models of communication* (pp. 181–198). Berlin, GR: Mouton de Gruyter.

Greene, J.O. (2014). Just looking around. *Journal of Language and Social Psychology, 33,* 398–404.

Greene, J.O., & Geddes, D. (1988). Representation and processing in the self-system: An action-oriented approach to self and self-relevant phenomena. *Communication Monographs, 55,* 287–314.

Greene, J.O., & Geddes, D. (1993). An action assembly perspective on social skill. *Communication Theory, 3,* 26–49.

Greene, J.O., & Herbers, L.E. (2011). Conditions of interpersonal transcendence. *International Journal of Listening, 25,* 66–84.

Greene, J.O., O'Hair, H.D., Cody, M.J., & Yen, C. (1985). Planning and control of behavior during deception. *Human Communication Research, 11,* 335–364.

Greene, J.O., & Pruim, D.E. (2018, May). *Grown-ups at play: Theorizing quintessential experiences of interpersonal connection, novelty, and mirth.* Paper presented at the annual meeting of the International Communication Association, Prague, Czech Republic.

Greene, J.O., & Sparks, G.G. (1983). Explication and test of a cognitive model of communication apprehension: A new look at an old construct. *Human Communication Research, 9,* 349–366.

Interview with the Caterpillar

Q: "What are we to make of all this? The whole thing does seem a little outlandish."

A: "Tut tut—it's really quite simple—as long as we keep our theory-wits about us."

Q: "Then what about the White Rabbit and the knock-knock joke?"

A: "Ah, that's perfectly sensible, just remember the Theory of Adult Communicative Play: Play involves the juxtaposition of pattern and novelty! Every child knows THAT pattern; the fun comes from the "new" part. And, I'll tell you one more thing while we're on the topic: ACP tells us that some people are more likely to play than others, and where could we find a better example of dispositional playfulness than our friend Alice?"

Q: "Alright, but what's up with the Queen of Hearts? She keeps showing up, shouting about the Dormouse… And what's a dormouse, anyway?"

A: "Alice, the Cat, and her friend encountered the Queen three times, and every time she was saying the same thing, but her speech rate got ever-faster. And, of course, AAT tells us that, because of unitized assemblies, repetition and practice lead to more rapid performance. As for your second question, this is a book about *communication* theory, not mammalogy."

Q: "Um, okay, I guess, but what's the deal with the Fish-Footman and the Frog-Footman?"

A: "Ah, a good question! Remember that AAT is concerned with explaining how it is possible for people to think, and say, and do things they have never thought, said, or done before. But in the case of the unfortunate Footmen we get a glimpse of what things might be like if we could only read or repeat. I think you'll agree that it's better not to be in their situation."

Q: "Mmm… what about the tea party, then? And the riddle about ravens and writing desks?"

A: "One of my favorite parts of the story… *creative facility, creative facility*—the Hatter had no answer to his own riddle, but Alice assembled a snappy comeback in a flash. Some people really can think on their feet."

Q: "I think I'm starting to get the hang of this! The part about the Mock Turtle and the Gryphon—that must be about transcendent interactions!"

A: "Indeed, remember that 'their thoughts entwined in sublime coordination.' The Mock Turtle and the Gryphon had in common a knowledge base and vocabulary that allowed them to connect in a deep way, but because one could fly above the ocean and the other could swim beneath the waves, they each could bring something unique to their conversation."

Q: "And the trial... assembly difficulties, right?"

A: "Quite right—the Knave was faced with trying to accomplish contradictory goals, and the Hatter could not find words to express his thoughts. And of course, as the King observed of the Hatter, his speech fluency suffered. And, now I really must go... there are pressing matters that I need to discuss with the Cat."

Chapter 2

A Goals-Plans-Action Theory of Communication: Ravi and Joe Battle over Cleaning the Apartment

James Price Dillard, Ph.D., *Pennsylvania State University*

Why do people say what they say? The answer given by Goals-Plans-Action Theory is that usually individuals craft messages that they believe will help them to achieve whatever they are trying to accomplish. Goals-Plans-Action (GPA) is a theory of message production that has its roots in the study of interpersonal influence. But, the principles around which the theory is built are general ones that can be used to understand many different forms of communication. This chapter begins by examining the most basic features of the theory, then moves on to a close inspection of the concepts and processes that define it, and culminates in a case intended to illustrate how Goals-Plans-Action Theory can shed light on human interaction.

Assumptions

Goals-Plans-Action is a theory of purposeful behavior (Dillard, 1990). It assumes that individuals make choices about the messages that they create and that they do so with some degree of mindfulness. This does not mean that individuals are knowledgeable about all available options, nor that they are thinking about every part of the message production process. It *does* mean that *people have some control over their behavior*. This is the agency assumption. And Goals-Plans-Action contends that *people usually know what they are doing*. This is the awareness assumption. Both points may seem obvious, but consider the alternatives. Some actions, such as screaming when you find a spider crawling across your hand, are more like reflexes than planned behavior. In such circumstances, behavior is not under conscious control. But, even when people think they are guiding their own behavior, they may be susceptible to outside influence. For instance, people tend to eat more when larger portions of food are put in front of them (Rolls, Morris, & Roe, 2002), though not apparently as the result of making a deliberately informed decision.

Core Process and Concepts

Goals-Plans-Action Theory views message production as a three-part sequence. The first step involves *goals*, which are future states of affair that an individual is committed to achieving or maintaining (Dillard, 1997). Goals represent what people are trying to do. They motivate plans, the second component in the model. *Plans* are mental representations of messages and message sequences that are intended to enable goal attainment (Berger & diBattista, 1993). The final step includes *actions*, or the messages that people actually utter in their efforts to realize a goal. So, when someone has the goal of borrowing class notes from a fellow student, that prompts a plan (i.e., Thought: "I could just ask Bill") and, possibly, an action (i.e., Utterance: "Could I borrow your notes?"). That seems simple and straightforward. But, consider all of the times that you wanted to say something, yet didn't know what to say, and, consequently, said nothing at all. Or the times that you didn't know what to say at first, but later figured something out, which may or may not have done the job. Goals-Plans-Action is concerned with all of those moments when you clutch up or finally say something, when you have failures or partial successes, and those moments when you confidently express yourself and all goes as planned.

Elaborating Goals

Types of Influence Goals. It might seem that there is an infinite number of reasons to influence others, but Dillard, Anderson, and Knobloch (2002) suggest that they can all be boiled down to a list of just eight. Four of the most common are the following:

- *Gain assistance goals* focus on obtaining resources from others for the benefit of one's self. Borrowing class notes is one example, but this goal can also include nonmaterial resources such as information.
- *Give advice goals* are concerned with helping another person with some perceived problem. These often involve the other person's health, such as when one's roommate is drinking too much, too often, or their relationships, such as when one encourages a friend to get out of a bad relationship.

- *Change relationship goals* explicitly focus on making alterations to the source-target relationship. This might include going from acquaintance to friend, from friend to lover, from dating partners back to just friends, or from friends to enemies.
- *Enforce rights/obligations goals* represent efforts to compel the target to fulfill his or her commitments or meet role requirements. One common issue among college students revolves around what roommates owe one another by virtue of their being roommates.

Primary Goals. The goals just described are influence goals, but they are also known in Goals-Plans-Action parlance as primary goals. They were given this name because they are special in several respects. For one, primary goals lie at the beginning of the goals-plans-action sequence. They are primary in the sense that they initiate the processes that result in message production. This is the *motivational function* of goals. Second, it is useful to think of human interaction as a stream of interlocking behaviors. The speaker says something, the hearer responds, the speaker responds to that, and so on. Primary goals allow individuals to segment that stream into meaningful units. They enable people to answer the question "What is this interaction about?" This is the *social meaning function* of primary goals. Finally, primary goals direct mental operations. By providing an understanding of the purpose of an interaction, goals determine which aspects of a situation are perceived and which are not. A person who feels threatened may pay close attention to the speaker's size and emotional state, while giving little thought to the other's hair style or wardrobe. Thus, primary goals serve a *guidance function* that results in some perceptions, memories, and thoughts becoming more salient and others becoming less so.

Secondary Goals. Pursuing, or planning to pursue, a primary goal may give rise to other concerns. For example, one college student who hopes to initiate a romantic relationship with another (Goal 1) might recognize the risk of rejection and wish to avoid feeling hurt (Goal 2) or making the target of the change feel uncomfortable (Goal 3). Such concerns are called *secondary goals* because they follow logically from the adoption of a primary goal. You don't have to worry about being rejected unless you are willing to take a chance on the relationship goal in the first place. More formally, the source holds a secondary goal only because he or she is attempting to influence the target. It is the desire to achieve the primary goal that brings about consideration of one or more secondary goals (Dillard, 1990).

Research supports the existence of five secondary goals (Dillard, Segrin, & Harden, 1989), though not every goal will be relevant to every situation.

- *Identity goals* focus on ethical, moral, and personal standards for behavior. They arise from individuals' principles and values and, at the broadest level, individuals' conceptions of self. For instance, a child who wants a piece of chocolate cake might think nothing of knocking down a sibling and taking the piece of cake away. Most adults would reject that strategy on ethical grounds.

- *Conversation management* goals involve concerns about making the interaction work. Although there are exceptions, individuals usually prefer that interactions proceed smoothly, rather than awkwardly, and that neither interactant threatens the identity of the other. Thus, while conversation management goals may have implications that extend beyond the conversation, they also have a relatively short time horizon (i.e., typically the duration of the conversation). In this vein, when one person asks "What did you mean by that?" the other person usually offers some explanation of his or her behavior, rather than simply ignoring the question. Playing by the rules of conversation helps individuals create mutual understanding of what the conversation is about (Grice, 1975).

- *Relational resource goals* focus on relationship management. These goals are manifestations of the value that individuals have for social and personal relationships. It is most often the case that people try to maintain or improve their relationships with others, but in certain circumstances, individuals may seek to ostracize or insult others. Of course, relationship resource goals do not really come into play unless one has a preexisting relationship with the hearer or hopes to establish one. Relational resource goals focus on the benefits that flow to the source because of the relationship itself (i.e., I feel good when I'm with him; I need to get along with him because he is part of our group). Relational resource goals have a longer time horizon than conversation management goals (Dillard, 1989)

- *Personal resource goals* reflect the physical, temporal, and material concerns of the communicator. They arise from the desire to maintain or enhance one's physical well-being, temporal resources, finances, and material possessions. The statement "When I realized that I was wasting my time, I just left the interview" illustrates concern for the temporal aspect of personal resources. The desire to behave efficiently can be seen as a personal resource goal, although Goals-Plans-Action Theory does not suppose that individuals always prefer a high level of efficiency. In fact, some people take pleasure in going with the flow, rather than having everything organized. These different approaches to life result in different goals in specific conversations. As with any of the secondary goals, personal resource goals will not be relevant to every interaction, but when they are relevant, they can be important to determining how messages are created and uttered.

- Finally, by identifying *affect management goals*, the theory posits that individuals try to regulate their emotions. This is not as simple as wishing to enjoy positive feelings and avoid negative ones. Sometimes people try to increase their level of anxiety because it motivates them to perform well on an exam or speech. But, people who are naturally prone to anxiety may have the opposite goal. They need to work hard to tamp down feelings of nervousness, especially prior to a public speech.

Relationships Among Goals. The most basic decision that one can make about communication is whether or not to engage another person in interaction. The interplay of primary and secondary goals can help to understand this choice point in the message production process. To simplify, assume a primary goal and just one secondary goal, then evaluate the degree of compatibility between the two. There are just three possibilities, the first of which being that the two goals are *incompatible*. Imagine someone who intends to end a long-term romantic relationship but not hurt the other person's feelings. Sometimes people stay in relationships longer than they should because it is difficult to articulate, "We are over."

Second, the secondary goal may be *irrelevant* to the primary goal. For example, concern for one's physical well-being is not often an issue when asking a friend to see a film. In this circumstance, some of the secondary goals may not even come to mind. There are some situations, probably very few, in which none of the secondary goals are relevant. Emergencies are one example. Imagine that you are crossing the street when you see an out-of-control car speeding toward a friend who is lost in the music of his iPhone. Because you need to warn him and to do so quickly, you probably won't be too concerned about how to be polite (conversation management) or how saving his life might make you late to class (personal resource goal) or how the situation might create anxiety for you (affect management). Instead, you'll be focusing on just one goal, the primary/influence goal, which is how to create immediate behavior change in your friend.

The third possibility is that the primary and secondary goals are *compatible*. This is akin to "killing two birds with one stone." Although desirable, it occurs less frequently than one might hope. Initiating a relationship illustrates one context in which this might occur. The norm of reciprocity demands that individuals repay favors provided to them by others. When one person asks another for help that he or she cannot immediately repay (i.e., a ride to the grocery store), the message source is signaling a willingness to enter into a relationship in which reciprocity will occur over time. This willingness is a defining feature of friendships. Thus, the speaker may obtain a ride and, in so doing, also enhance a budding relationship.

The concept of secondary goals has at least one major implication for how we conceive of interpersonal influence. It suggests that most interactions involve multiple goals that individuals try to achieve more or less simultaneously. Every interaction has a primary goal and most interactions have one or more secondary goals (Dillard, 1990). Because people are usually trying to achieve more than one goal in a conversation, interpersonal communication can be a complicated task. On the other hand, it is worth emphasizing that not every interaction will activate consideration of all five secondary goals. If secondary goals are to shape message production, however, they must be at least minimally relevant. After passing that threshold, the more important they are, the greater their impact.

Elaborating Plans and Actions

Communicative plans are mental guidelines for the production of verbal and nonverbal behaviors. With regard to influence specifically, most people understand that there are a variety of ways that they might try to influence others: threats, warnings, rewards, promises, explanation, social pressure, liking, and so on. As researchers, we can't directly measure plans, but we can infer what they look like by examining people's behavior. Research on the perception of *influence actions* suggests that four dimensions are particularly important to consider (Dillard, Wilson, Tusing, & Kinney, 1997).

The first of these dimensions, *explicitness*, is the degree to which the source makes her or his intentions transparent in the message itself. When one roommate says to another "I would like for you to come to the gym with me," the speaker's desire is clear. But, if the same person were to say "Hey, I'm going to the gym," the other roommate has to read between the lines to interpret the speaker's intention.

Dominance, the second dimension, refers to power of the source compared to the target as expressed in the message. Consider the following two requests: "You said that you wanted to work out...so get off your butt and do it" and "I would really, really appreciate it if you worked out with me." Depending on the source-target relationship, the first message might be seen as a little aggressive. It seems as if the source is implicitly saying that she/he has the right to boss the target around. In contrast, the second message is beseeching. It leaves the decision up to the target and puts the source in a more submissive position. Of course, messages that convey equality are possible too: "I'm thinking about working out later today. Wanna come?"

The third dimension is *argument*, which references the extent to which some rationale for the sought-after action is present in the message. The utterance, "I sleep a lot better when I work out…I'll bet that you would, too," suggests what the source wants the target to do, and it provides a reason for the source's wants. In contrast, the message, "We should go work out," is clear, but it lacks any justification. Argument refers to whether the message *includes* a reason, not whether you think the reason is a good one.

Control over outcomes is the final dimension. This refers to the extent to which the source has control over the reasons for compliance. This distinction makes clear the difference between a threat (i.e., I will hurt you if…) and a warning (i.e., You could be harmed if…). Reward messages vary in control, too. Note the difference between "I will pay you to vote for Smith" versus "Smith will help you…you should vote for him."

Message Production

With the preceding concepts in mind, we are now in a position to discuss message production in closer detail. The Goals-Plans-Action model suggests that there are two paths that one might take to forming an utterance. These options, along with some additional concepts, are illustrated in Figure 1. First, let's trace the process

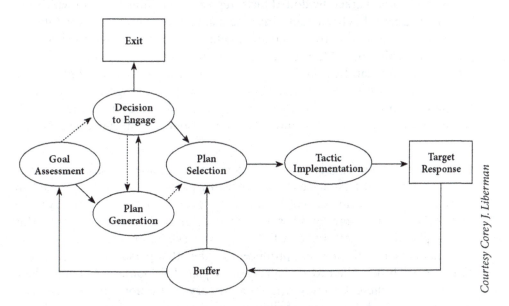

Courtesy Corey J. Liberman

Figure 1. The Goals-Plans-Action Model of Message Production

represented by the solid lines. When the desire to influence another person arises and triggers consideration of potential secondary goals, individuals have to assess the relationships among the primary and secondary goals (the *Goal Assessment* oval). Next, they engage in *Plan Generation*. The term "generation" is used broadly to mean a process that ranges from simply remembering a preexisting plan to creating something completely novel. If no plan is available that is judged to be both feasible and effective, the actor may decide not to engage the other. Conversely, if an available plan is seen as likely to succeed and the actor believes that she or he can execute it, then she or he makes the *Decision to Engage* and then moves toward translating it into action (the *Tactic Implementation* oval). Of course, translation involves a great many lower-level cognitive processes that must operate in unison if a plan is to be successfully converted into behavior. For example, a plan that depends on flattering the target might fail because the speaker cannot find a way to deliver a compliment that does not sound insincere. This illustrates a distinction between *strategy-level* plans (more abstract) and *tactic-level* plans (less abstract). Most teenagers have a pretty good idea about how to drive a car (analogous to *Plan Generation*), but actually coordinating all of one's actions so that the car goes where one wants it to go is a different level of knowledge (analogous to *Tactic Implementation*). Knowing that pushing on the brake pedal will stop the car is different that knowing how hard to push and for how long.

The second path, marked by dotted lines, represents circumstances in which the *Decision to Engage* has been made. Imagine that your boss has called you into her office for the purpose of firing you. You might wish to change her mind on that point, but whether or not the conversation occurs is not your choice. In preemptory fashion, you can *Exit the Interaction* by not trying to influence her at all or you can *Engage* with whatever you can come up with on the spot. In other cases, the *Decision to Engage* can be driven by a potent primary goal. Seeing an adult strike his child in grocery store might demand a response from you, consequences be damned.

Once the decision to engage has been made, actors consider the available means of persuasion. To the extent that the preexisting plans are judged to be less than satisfactory and the primary goal is viewed as important, individuals will try to (a) make existing plans more complete or more complex, or (b) create new plans. This kind of planning is constrained by the fact that successful interaction depends on the other person. If the message producer sees the other person as unpredictable, he or she will be less likely to go to the effort of plan development. Although there may be many different ways to achieve a primary goal if none of the secondary goals are activated, it is more challenging to devise a plan that will satisfy the competing desires that are present when the set of primary and secondary goals is complex. Students working in group projects may find themselves needing to tell one of the group members that he or she is not making a fair contribution to the workload. This becomes more complicated when the slacker is a roommate or good friend. Achieving two goals simultaneously (i.e., changing behavior and not damaging the relationship) is more complicated than achieving either goal alone.

When multiple plans are available, the source must choose among them. People do this by assessing the degree to which each plan satisfies the combination of primary and secondary goals. This can happen very quickly and often does, as the Goals-Plans-Action process typically moves at the speed of conversation. At other times, people will carefully weigh the message options available to them, vacillate about whether or not to engage, perhaps settle on an influence strategy, then rehearse delivery of the message, all in advance of actually saying anything.

From Action to Interaction

Thus far, we have considered the process by which one individual produces a string of words that is intended to influence the other. Obviously, conversation is more than that. To model interaction, we can think of each of the participants going through the process depicted in Figure 1. In an influence interaction, the source produces an utterance designed to change the other's opinion(s) or behavior(s). The target of influence goes through a similar process of generating goals and plans prior to creating a string of words that indicate compliance or resistance, or some other action that is equivalent to exit. With these pieces of the theory in mind, it may help to consider an extended example.

Case: Ravi and Joe Confront Keeping the Apartment Clean

During their first year at Miller University, Ravi and Joe lived on the same floor of the dormitory named Boster Hall. They hung out with the same group of people and, after a while, became pretty good friends. They shared a liking for basketball, which meant plenty of court time for themselves, as well as time spent keeping a close eye on the college teams. Ravi came to admire Joe for his spontaneity and humor. Joe thought that Ravi's calm, methodical approach to living was something that he needed more of in his own life. During spring semester, they agreed that it would be a good idea to share an apartment the following year. But, now, after several months of living together they are discovering unexpected differences.

001: Ravi: Hey, dude, I've been putting off talking to you about this thing, but it's bugging me. So, I'm gonna—I gotta say something now. It's, well, like, things are a mess around here *(sweeping his hand to indicate the living room and kitchen area of the apartment)*. The table is always covered with cans and plates, the sink is overflowing with dirty dishes, the trash can is stuffed to the gills, and the stuff in the refrigerator has turned into a freakin' science project.

002: Joe: I guess that things are pretty messy. Doesn't really both me.

003: Ravi: That's the thing. It *does* bother me. I spend a lot of time cleaning up because there is no place to set a drink on the table. Seems like I'm the only one who ever takes the trash out or does the dishes. I have to clean the place up before I can study or relax.

004: Joe: Yeah, well, hmmm.

005: Ravi: So, I would appreciate it if you could pick up after yourself. You know, carry some of the load on keeping this place clean.

006: Joe: Ok, I'll give it try. But don't worry so much OK?

In Ravi's first speaking turn (001), we see that he has been thinking about the cleaning issue for some time, but only recently has it become important enough for him to choose to raise the issue. From the Goals-Plans-Action perspective, he has formed an *influence goal*. This is a *gain assistance goal* because what he wants will primarily benefit him. We can also see, from his hesitance about broaching the topic, that he might be experiencing goal conflict. Asking a roommate to clean up carries certain risks, one of which is implying that the roommate isn't living up to expectations. That could be interpreted as a criticism or a threat to Joe's identity, thereby creating possible damage to the relationship. Moreover, asking anyone to do anything always carries the risk that the request will be seen as interfering with their desire to govern their own actions (another aspect of the hearer's identity).

In this conversation it appears that Ravi's plan involves two parts. The first one focuses on describing the problem (turns 001 and 003), which is then followed by a request/solution (turn 005). The request is high in explicitness because Ravi says exactly what he wants Joe to do. But, it is low in dominance; Ravi is respectful of Joe and couches the request as something he would appreciate, rather than something he is demanding. It is also high in logic: Ravi provides multiple reasons for why he is asking Joe to change his behavior. In contrast to Ravi's explicitness, Joe is vague and noncommittal. He does agree, sort of, to do what Ravi wants (turn 006), but he is so inexplicit (turns 002 and 004) it is not clear that Joe concurs with the claim that there is a problem. Still, the episode ends with what appears to be compliance. Two weeks later, the issue surfaces again, when they gather in front of the TV to watch the Roloff College Warriors go up against the Seibold University Wolves:

007: Ravi: Hey, can you move this crap off the table so that I have a place to put the pizza?

008: Joe: Yeah, sure *(pushing the dirty plates, empty cans, and used glasses to the far side of the table).*

009: Ravi: No, I mean actually clean up.

010: Joe: The game's about to start. I'll do it later, after the game.

011: Ravi: You said that you were going to take some responsibility for keeping the place clean. I'm not seeing it.

012: Joe: Please. Let's talk after the game.

013: Ravi: *(eye roll)*

This episode begins with a request (turn 007), one that is focused on a concrete problem that requires immediate attention. The utterance is high in explicitness, moderate in dominance (it seems to express irritation), and high in logic (a reason is given). Ravi's intent seems to be even more explicit and a bit more dominant when he repeats the request in turn 009. This is a small, low-stakes issue, which produced an utterance that probably was not the result of careful planning. But, it quickly segues into the larger issue of Joe's earlier agreement to work on keeping the apartment clean (011), an issue that involves several different kinds of behavior for Joe in addition to the table (i.e., trash, dishes, refrigerator). Regarding the larger issue, Ravi's communicative strategy seems to revolve around a consistency demand, a persuasive strategy that calls for people to behave in accordance with commitments made in prior utterances. Most people have this strategy as part of their repertoire, so it is likely that Ravi simply recalled the strategy from memory and implemented it without much forethought or planning.

It appears that Joe's goal is to deflect or delay conversation about the cleaning issue so that he can focus his attention on the basketball game. His effort to avoid making the interaction about cleaning is pretty explicit. He goes to bed immediately after the game and, in so doing, avoids the topic altogether, until the following week when Ravi broaches it at breakfast:

014: Ravi: OK, a**hole. Look around. I've dealt with the trash for the last four weeks. The fridge is a nightmare and your dishes are piled up in the sink. I've had it.

015: Joe: Wooo, man. Chill a bit. This isn't worth getting worked up over.

016: Ravi: That's where you are wrong. Since we moved in here, I'm the only one doing any kind of clean up. The place is a pig sty and you just sit around waiting for me to take care of things for you. I'm not your mother.

017: Joe: You insult me?

018: Ravi: You bet I do! You deserve it, you slob. I'm looking for a new place to live. I'm breaking the lease at the end of the semester, then I'm outta here. You can find another roommate who doesn't mind living in filth.

Ravi's first utterance makes it plain that he has abandoned the goal of changing Joe's behavior. Indeed, the odds of successfully achieving that goal seem pretty slim at this point. But, Ravi is not without a goal. He has replaced the *influence goal* with what would otherwise be considered *secondary goals*. To the extent that we can guess his thoughts from his utterances, it appears that his aim is to express his anger, an *affect management goal*. Although it might be tempting to think that affect management means reducing negative emotions and increasing positive feelings, that is not always the case. In some circumstances, people seek to ramp their negative affect.

Another goal of Ravi's might be to demean Joe, a *relational resource goal*. Usually we strive to maintain or enhance relationships. Ravi showed evidence of this in the first episode. A relational resource goal can also be turned on its head when people take active steps to harm a relationship. As is true in the talk above, this often means insulting and undermining the other. In this last episode, Ravi makes explicit, dominating comments that are designed to attack Joe's identity and perhaps make him feel guilty or inadequate. What began as an attempt at interpersonal influence has become a full-blown conflict.

Conclusion

Understanding why people say what they say is not a simple problem. Goals-Plans-Action may not provide a complete solution, but it does offer some ideas about how to view the process of message production that others have found useful. To give a just a few examples, Goals-Plans-Action has been used to understand how undergraduates try to get their grades changed (Sabee & Wilson, 2005), how students confront other students who have committed academic misconduct (Henningsen, Valde, & Denbow, 2013), and how young adults try to abstain from sexual intercourse (Coffelt, 2017). If the theory has also given you a new way to see communication, then it has done what it was created to do.

Discussion Questions

1. What is the role of awareness as it relates to Goals-Plans-Action Theory? Do people always plan what they will say thoughtfully, or it is possible to say something without consciously thinking about it first? Reflect on your own experience to help answer this question.

2. The Goals-Plans-Action Theory has been criticized as portraying all behavior as purely self-interested. Is that accurate or can goals be altruistic too? Consider the examples of goals that are given in the chapter.

3. Another criticism of the theory is that it assumes that people enter conversations with one or more goals and they remain active throughout the conversation without changing. Review the case study, then decide if that criticism is valid. Compare your answer to your own experience.

4. Is it possible for a secondary goal to become more important than a primary goal? Did you see this happen in the case study? Can you identify specific examples of this kind of change either in the case study or your own life?

REFERENCES

Berger, C. R., & diBattista, P. (1993). Communication failure and plan adaptation. If at first you don't succeed, say it louder and slower. *Communication Monographs, 60,* 220–238. doi: 10.1080/0367759309376310

Coffelt, T. A. (2017). Sexual goals, plans, and actions: Toward a sexual script emerging adults use to delay or abstain from sexual intercourse. *Western Journal of Communication, 82,* 416–438. doi: 10.1080/10570314.2017.1400095

Dillard, J.P. (1989). Types of influence goals in close relationships. *Journal of Personal and Social Relationships, 6,* 293–308.

Dillard, J. P. (1990). A goal-driven model of interpersonal influence. In J. P. Dillard (Ed.), *Seeking compliance: The production of interpersonal influence messages* (pp. 41–56). Scottsdale, AZ: Gorsuch Scarisbrick.

Dillard, J. P. (1997). Explicating the goal construct: Tools for theorists. In J. O. Greene (Ed.), *Message production: Advances in communication theory* (pp. 47–69). Mahwah, NJ: Erlbaum.

Dillard, J. P., Anderson, J. W., & Knobloch, L. K. (2002). Interpersonal influence. In M. Knapp & J. Daly (Eds.), *The handbook of interpersonal communication* (pp. 423–474). Thousand Oaks, CA: Sage.

Dillard, J. P., & Schrader, D. C. (1998). Reply: On the utility of the goals-plans-action sequence. *Communication Studies, 49,* 300–304.

Dillard, J. P., Segrin, C., & Harden, J. M. (1989). Primary and secondary goals in the interpersonal influence process. *Communication Monographs, 56,* 19–38.

Dillard, J. P., Wilson, S. R., Tusing, K. J., & Kinney, T. A. (1997). Politeness judgments in personal relationships. *Journal of Language and Social Psychology, 16,* 297–325.

Grice, H. P. (1975). Logic and conversation. In P. Cole & J. L. Morgan (Eds.), *Syntax and semantics* (Vol. 3, pp. 41–58). New York, NY: Academic Press.

Henningsen, M. L. M., Valde, K. S., & Denbow, J. (2013). Academic misconduct: A Goals-Plans-Action approach to peer confrontation and whistle-blowing. *Communication Education, 62,* 148–168.

Rolls, B. J., Morris, E. L., & Roe, L. S. (2002). Portion size of food affects energy intake in normal-weight and overweight men and women. *The American Journal of Clinical Nutrition, 76,* 1207–1213. doi.org/10.1093/ajcn/76.6.1207

Sabee, C. M., & Wilson, S. R. (2005). Students' primary goals, attributions, and facework during conversations about disappointing grades. *Communication Education, 54,* 185–204.

Chapter 3

Communication Accommodation Theory as a Lens to Examine Painful Self-Disclosures in Grandparent-Grandchild Relationships

Quinten S. Bernhold, M.A., *University of California, Santa Barbara*
Howard Giles, Ph.D., *University of California, Santa Barbara*

Communication Accommodation Theory (CAT; e.g., Giles, 2016a) has emerged as a key interpersonal and intergroup theory, and has been studied across an array of languages, cultures, and applied settings (Soliz & Giles, 2014). This chapter, with its illustrative case accounts, focuses on one domain of CAT research, namely problematic communication in grandparent-grandchild (GP-GC) relationships. GP-GC communication is often a source of satisfaction for both parties (Lin, Harwood, & Bonnesen, 2002; Mansson, 2013), yet such communication is not always pleasant. Several communication patterns exacerbate frustrations or discomfort for one or both parties. For example, grandparents feel particularly frustrated when they perceive grandchildren as disinterested in them or not investing in the GP-GC relationship (e.g., Bangerter & Waldron, 2014). Grandchildren also experience declines in closeness when they perceive their grandparents as deceiving or judging them (Holladay et al., 1998).

Although several communication patterns may erode relational quality, grandparents' painful self-disclosures (PSDs) to grandchildren are one of the most frequently studied. PSDs consist of disclosures about bereavement, immobility, poor health, loneliness, or other topics the listener perceives as uncomfortable and underaccommodative (Coupland, Coupland, Giles, & Henwood, 1991; Coupland, Coupland, & Giles, 1991). Sociolinguistic data of intergenerational interactions suggest that PSDs from older to younger interactants are much more common than younger-to-older PSDs (Coupland, Coupland, Giles, Henwood, & Wiemann, 1988). Similar to interactions with unrelated older adults, PSDs are also uncomfortable in GP-GC conversations under certain circumstances, such as when grandchildren perceive grandparents are disclosing uncomfortable information in order to get grandchildren to do favors or other tasks they otherwise might not be inclined to do (e.g., Barker, 2007).

This chapter explores PSDs in GP-GC relationships as an illustrative case of underaccommodative communication (see Gasiorek, 2016a). We begin by reviewing the importance of CAT and defining key concepts. We then discuss general principles and processes stipulated by CAT, as well as how these principles have manifested in past research on PSDs. Third, we present actual, open-ended accounts from grandchildren about underaccommodation they receive from grandparents in the form of PSDs that constitute our case study. We use these accounts as a foundation for outlining ways future researchers can advance the study of underaccommodation in GP-GC relationships, as well as discussing practical implications for grandparents and grandchildren.

The Importance of CAT

CAT explains how and why people adjust (i.e., accommodate) or fail to adjust their communication to an interaction partner, as well as the consequences of such adjustments. Although CAT is not the only theory to consider accommodation and nonaccommodation, its treatment of these constructs is, arguably, more comprehensive than the treatments of other theories (for a review, see Gasiorek, 2016b). CAT goes further than other perspectives by proposing speaker-oriented *and* listener-oriented versions of accommodation and nonaccommodation. From speakers' perspectives, *accommodation* refers to adjustments designed to regulate social distance or comprehension. Speakers' adjustments to decrease social distance (often, to establish a common ingroup identity with the listener) and/or facilitate comprehension often manifest as *convergence*, or becoming more similar to interaction partners. From listeners' perspectives, *accommodation* refers to perceptions that speakers' behavior is appropriately adjusted (Gasiorek, 2015).

Nonaccommodation can also be considered from both parties' perspectives. Speakers engage in nonaccommodation when they wish to increase social distance or decrease comprehension. For example, they can *diverge* by making their behaviors more distinct from those of their partners (Thakerar, Giles, & Cheshire, 1982). Listeners can perceive nonaccommodation as *overaccommodative* (i.e., perceiving that speakers have gone too far in the adjustment necessary for appropriate interaction) or *underaccommodative* (i.e., perceiving that speakers have not gone far enough in the adjustment necessary for appropriate interaction) (Coupland,

Coupland, Giles, & Henwood, 1988). The common thread behind these versions of nonaccommodation is that distinctiveness, disaffiliation, or disconfirmation is intended, communicated, or interpreted (Gasiorek, 2016a). Put differently, nonaccommodation occurs when speakers want to establish their personal or social identities as different from (and perhaps superior to) those of the listener, thereby removing themselves from any shared connection with the listener. Nonaccommodation also occurs when speakers' actual behaviors suggest they are different from the listener (e.g., speakers adopting and emphasizing a contrasting accent than the listener's accent), or when listeners interpret speakers' behaviors as establishing a lack of shared social connection or understanding. Speaker- and listener-oriented versions of accommodation and nonaccommodation, therefore, allow for diverse foci when studying communication, including speakers' intentions, objective communication, and listeners' perceptions (Gallois, Gasiorek, Giles, & Soliz, 2016).

Additional aspects of CAT's importance include its large body of international scholarship, its interpersonal *and* intergroup focus, and the array of contexts amenable to study from a CAT perspective. Of all the frameworks addressing how and why interaction partners adjust to each other's communication styles, CAT has arguably generated the most interdisciplinary and international research (Giles & Ogay, 2006; Soliz & Giles, 2014). Moreover, CAT simultaneously adopts an interpersonal and intergroup focus (Dragojevic & Giles, 2014; Palomares, Giles, Soliz, & Gallois, 2016). The communication discipline has traditionally treated interactions in a dichotomy of either interpersonal or intergroup, which is problematic because idiosyncratic and relationship-specific preferences may work in tandem with larger social identities to shape the unfolding of interactions and relational outcomes (for a review, see Gangi & Soliz, 2016).

Bridging the dichotomy, CAT allows for an examination of how both interpersonal and intergroup forces can shape relational outcomes, a dual focus that has been applied to the GP-GC domain (Bernhold & Giles, 2017). To illustrate the importance of this dual focus when studying GP-GC relationships, Soliz, Thorson, and Rittenour (2009) invoked CAT and found that multiethnic grandchildren's perceptions of their parents' and grandparents' supportive communication, ethnic-specific identity accommodation (e.g., encouragement of grandchildren to learn more about their ethnic heritage), and reciprocal self-disclosure between grandchildren and older generations positively predicted grandchildren's relational satisfaction. This work illustrates how relational outcomes are simultaneously a function of interpersonal (e.g., grandparents' accommodative and reciprocal self-disclosures about thoughts and feelings with grandchildren) and intergroup (e.g., grandparents' accommodations toward multiethnic grandchildren by encouraging grandchildren to learn more about their cultural customs, despite the grandparents not sharing the same heritage and culture) phenomena. Practically, this suggests that family members must be attuned to and respond appropriately to aspects that make other family members unique individuals as well as aspects that make them part of broader social collectives in order to foster fulfilling relationships with those family members. At times, this might be challenging, as people might not share the same idiosyncratic preferences and broader social identities that other family members share (as is the case, for example, when family members disagree about religious values; Colaner, Soliz, & Nelson, 2014).

Finally, CAT applies to a variety of contexts (Giles, 2016a; McGlone & Giles, 2011). Early research was grounded in intercultural and interethnic settings. These studies found that observers judged speakers with more prestigious accents as conveying higher-quality persuasive arguments, as well as judged bilingual speakers more favorably when they perceived the speakers were trying to accommodate to the observers' preferred language (e.g., Giles, 1973; Giles, Taylor, & Bourhis, 1973). In the late 1980s and 1990s, CAT scholars began focusing on intergenerational communication and health. The Communication Predicament of Aging model (CPA model: Ryan, Giles, Bartolucci, & Henwood, 1986) showed how the overaccommodation older adults receive from younger adults (i.e., patronizing talk) may constrain older adults' opportunities for communication, reduce their self-esteem and sense of control, and ultimately contribute to physiological and psychological declines. More recently, scholars have applied CAT to the law enforcement domain, showing how perceptions of police officers' accommodation can foster civilians' trust in police officers, with the latter in turn increasing civilians' intentions to comply with police requests (e.g., Barker et al., 2008). Post-2000 CAT research has also examined a variety of family relationships, including stepparent-stepchild relationships (Speer, Giles, & Denes, 2013) and parent-child relationships in interreligious families (Colaner et al., 2014). Although not exhaustive of all contexts in which CAT has been interpretively invoked and applied, these domains illustrate the theory's heurism across many settings.

While CAT research on intragenerational and intergenerational communication has yielded rich insights over the decades, there has regrettably been "a notable decline" in such research since 2011 as other contexts have increased in prominence (Soliz & Bergquist, 2016, p. 64). In part, this chapter is intended to serve as a call for a renewed focus on intragenerational and intergenerational communication more generally, and PSDs in GP-GC relationships more specifically.

Principles and Processes Stipulated by CAT

A set of propositions summarizes CAT's logic and guides research predictions. These propositions are refined on an ongoing basis to reflect the current state of scholarship. The most recent set of propositions is as follows (see Dragojevic, Gasiorek, & Giles, 2016; Gallois, Weatherall, & Giles, 2016):

- Communication accommodation is a foundational aspect of interaction that facilitates comprehension or regulates social distance (i.e., affiliation).

- Interpersonal and intergroup histories, individual preferences, and contextual factors influence interaction partners' expectations about what constitutes appropriate accommodation.

- Interaction partners' motivation and ability to adjust influence the degree and quality of their accommodation.

- Speakers increasingly accommodate to listeners the more they wish to affiliate with listeners or increase listeners' comprehension.

- Listeners' perceptions of speakers' accommodation decrease social distance while increasing comprehension, conversation satisfaction, and favorable evaluations of speakers.

- Speakers engage in nonaccommodation the more they wish to increase social distance or hinder comprehension.

- Listeners' perceptions of speakers' nonaccommodation increase social distance while decreasing comprehension, conversation satisfaction, and favorable evaluations of speakers, yet listeners' perceptions of speakers' motives may moderate these associations.

- Interactional dynamics and the turn-by-turn unfolding of conversations influence the degree and quality of accommodation.

As the seventh proposition suggests, CAT allows for listener-oriented versions of nonaccommodation. Listeners' evaluations of speakers' nonaccommodation seem more influential in shaping interaction outcomes than are speakers' evaluations (Soliz & Bergquist, 2016). Thus, it is important to understand what factors influence listeners' evaluations of speakers' behavior. One factor garnering an increased amount of research attention of late involves *inferred motives* that are the substance and valence that listeners assign to speakers' intentions (Gasiorek & Giles, 2012). Attributing negative motives to underaccommodative speakers predicts listeners stopping the interaction and expressing negative affect nonverbally, which are two conversational moves likely to exacerbate conflict (Gasiorek, 2013). Moreover, in the face of *accumulated* underaccommodation, listeners make increasingly unfavorable evaluations of speakers' motives, with these unfavorable attributions then reducing communication satisfaction (Gasiorek & Dragojevic, 2017). However, unfavorable attributions of speakers' motives may be alleviated when listeners engage in perspective-taking (i.e., putting themselves in speakers' "shoes" and trying to understand why speakers are conversing the way they are). Gasiorek (2015) found that when recalling nonaccommodative conversations, listeners attributed less negative motives to speakers when listeners engaged in perspective-taking. One task for future researchers is to further probe how perspective-taking alleviates unfavorable attributions of speakers' motives, and perhaps indirectly predicts more favorable evaluations of the speakers and interaction via these more favorable attributions of motive.

Perceptions of older adults' PSDs, as well as attributions of older adults' motives for engaging in PSDs, have predicted various outcomes. Young adults have judged nonfamily older adults who engage in PSDs as self-centered and embodying negative substereotypes (e.g., despondent); they have also judged PSDs as less appropriate than other forms of talk (Bonnesen & Hummert, 2002; Coupland, Henwood, Coupland, & Giles, 1990). In the GP-GC domain, grandparents' PSDs have positively predicted grandchildren's awareness of grandparents' age, as well as negatively predicted relational closeness (Harwood, Raman, & Hewstone, 2006). PSDs are especially likely to invoke discomfort when grandchildren attribute control motives to grandparents (i.e., perceiving that grandparents communicate in order to get grandchildren to do something) (Barker, 2007). Such communication patterns are not uniformly negative, however. PSDs invoke less discomfort when grandchildren assign their grandparents identity motives (i.e., perceiving that grandparents communicate in order to let them know more about who they are as people) or positive affect motives (i.e., perceiving that grandparents communicate in order to be role models and show them how to navigate difficult life circumstances) (Barker, 2007). The larger communicative environment may also play a role, as grandchildren who come from conversation-oriented families have reported less discomfort with grandparent PSDs compared to grandchildren whose families do not discuss topics openly (Fowler & Soliz, 2010).

This research suggests that although PSDs are often construed as underaccommodative and linked to negative outcomes, they are not always perceived as such. Thus, one overarching question is the following: under what conditions are PSDs linked to negative personal, relational, and interactional outcomes, and under what conditions are PSDs not detrimental? The cases that follow come from grandchildren's open-ended accounts detailing what painful topics their grandparents disclose, the reasons why such disclosures are uncomfortable, and their responses to the PSDs. All cases are reported verbatim, allowing for minor editing of mechanical issues. These cases suggest ways CAT scholars can continue addressing the overarching questions stated above, as well as provide practical recommendations for grandparents and grandchildren.

Illustrative Cases

The following cases come from a larger data set in which grandchildren reported on their grandparents' self-disclosures and affectionate communication. The data set included open-ended descriptions from grandchildren about what parts of their grandparents' disclosures were comfortable and uncomfortable, as well as closed-ended questions about the variety of ways grandparents communicate affection to grandchildren. The closed-ended data on affectionate communication are the subject of a different study (Bernhold & Giles, 2019). As we were reading the open-ended descriptions of self-disclosures, we were struck by the diversity in the existence and severity of PSDs. Given this diversity, we decided to showcase a series of cases in this chapter rather than focusing on a single case. Some grandchildren noted that their grandparents' PSDs were extremely disconcerting. Participant 299 wrote the following about his maternal grandmother:

> The only things she talks about that make me uncomfortable are when she talks about her experiences with cancer, and when she talks about her death. Both of these topics make me extremely uncomfortable. This doesn't make me uncomfortable because I can't deal with death or cancer. The thought of losing my grandmother is just extremely unbearable … It makes me so sad it almost brings me to tears whenever we talk about it. I don't like thinking about or visualizing the death of my grandmother, one of my childhood best friends … I usually don't say much. I try to put it off by changing or avoiding the subject altogether when it gets brought up, but if we must talk about it I am usually quiet, not saying much at all. I often try to comfort her when she talks and tell her it's going to be okay, she's going to be fine, etc.

In addition to conveying the grandson's distress, the response is noteworthy in its description of the grandson's responses to the grandparent. *Lowly person-centered messages* deny, invalidate, or criticize the partner's feelings, whereas *moderately person-centered messages* acknowledge the partner's feelings and express sympathy and condolence. *Highly person-centered messages* acknowledge the partner's feelings, allow the partner to explore reasons why they are feeling that way, and help the partner contextualize feelings in a broader context (Burleson, 2010; Burleson et al., 2011). The grandson's attempts at changing the subject fall under low person-centeredness, whereas his attempts to reassure the grandparent (e.g., "it's going to be okay") qualify as moderate person centeredness.

Relatedly, Coupland et al. (1988) proposed a taxonomy of receiver responses to PSD that vary in the degree to which they encourage further disclosure. At one end of the spectrum, the hearer could change the subject, thereby preempting further disclosures at the risk of invaliding the older person's feelings. In the middle of the spectrum, the hearer could respond neutrally ("mm") or with sympathy ("oh dear"). At the other end of the spectrum, the recipient could ask for more information and help the discloser evaluate the painful event. In the above case, we do not know how the grandmother interprets the grandson's minimal responses. More broadly, we are not aware of any research (qualitative or quantitative) examining grandparents' perceptions of their grandchildren's responses to PSDs, nor how such perceptions are linked to grandparent well-being (both mental and physical). Other research has shown that grandparents' perceptions of their grandchildren's accommodation (e.g., complimenting and showing affection for the grandparent, being attentive to the grandparent) are especially important predictors of relational solidarity (Harwood, 2000), but this work did not directly focus on grandchildren's responses to PSDs. We would argue that the time is long overdue to examine grandparents' evaluations of their grandchildren's responses to PSDs in order to better inform grandchildren on the types of responses grandparents perceive as most helpful. In the meantime, grandchildren might heed findings from the social support literature suggesting that distressed people perceive lowly person-centered messages as least helpful (e.g., Burleson et al., 2011; Holmstrom et al., 2015).

The example also illustrates CAT's attention to the multiple vantage points from which nonaccommodation can be studied (in this case, from the speaker's perspective versus from the listener's perspective), and, as such, potential disconnects between speaker intentions and listener interpretations. Although we do not know the grandmother's intentions, she may have been disclosing her experiences with cancer and death in order to elicit high-quality comfort from her grandson, whereas her grandson assessed her communication as extremely uncomfortable and did not provide such comfort. Using dyadic data, future CAT researchers might explore whether dyads with greater *disconnects* between speakers' intentions for engaging in PSDs and listeners' interpretations predict less relational satisfaction, less relational closeness, and reduced likelihood of grandchildren to care for grandparents during times of need or ill health, for example.

Another observation involved some grandchildren saying they are not uncomfortable with any information their grandparent discloses. Participant 199 recounted the following about his paternal grandmother: "My grandmother does not disclose information to me that would otherwise not be important or I would be uninterested in hearing. She knows the boundaries of what would make me uncomfortable. Even when she asks me about girlfriends I do not become uncomfortable." Similarly, Participant 289 noted the following, "My grandpa doesn't share any information that makes me feel uncomfortable. He is a very respectful and reserved person and does not say anything that makes me feel awkward." The pithy reply of Participant 333 perhaps best shows how PSDs are not problematic for all GP-GC relationships:

> My grandma does not share anything that makes me feel uncomfortable. She is a flat out baller that knows what to say and when. Even in her old age, she is wise beyond her years. I also firmly believe that something can only become awkward if you make it awkward. In most settings, there are multiple ways to go about things and awkward is never one that occurs.

As these responses illustrate, some grandchildren do not even perceive PSDs to exist in their grandparents' communication, much less finding these disclosures troublesome. We suspect that cognitive complexity underlies these responses. *Cognitive complexity* refers to the sophistication with which people process incoming information; people with more cognitive schemas to label thoughts, feelings, and behaviors during interaction are more cognitively complex than people with fewer schemas (Burleson, 2007; Youngvorst & Jones, 2017). Participants 199, 289, and 333 referred to their grandparents' wisdom in discerning appropriate boundaries. Participant 333 also discussed how there are multiple ways to interpret a conversation, and awkward interpretations do not occur during cognitive processing of his grandmother's communication. Although we did not measure it, grandchildren and grandparents in these dyads may exhibit high cognitive complexity, which may benefit their relational health (see also, the Age Stereotypes in Interactions model, which posits that young adults' cognitive complexity may buffer them from negatively stereotyping and patronizing older adults) (e.g., Hummert, Garstka, Ryan, & Bonnesen, 2004). Practically speaking, grandchildren might be advised on multiple ways to interpret grandparents' disclosures, and reframing PSDs might be helpful in reducing some grandchildren's distress.

Theoretically, these examples illustrate how future researchers may benefit from formally incorporating cognitive complexity as a construct in GP-GC PSD research. This relates to the seventh proposition of CAT about how it is listeners' perceptions of speakers' communication that guide listener responses. More cognitively complex grandchildren may be less likely to attribute negative motives (e.g., egotism) to their grandparents' PSDs, perhaps orienting these grandchildren to respond in more favorable ways. Researchers can look to related CAT work on inferred motives and perspective-taking (e.g., Gasiorek, 2015) as guidance when designing future studies to test these ideas in GP-GC relationships.

Finally, we wish to note that grandchildren often discussed how their grandparents disclosed uncomfortable information about third parties (usually family members not present). Such information made grandchildren feel as if they had to "choose sides" in family disputes. Participant 44, for instance, felt as if her grandmother pitted her against her father:

> Sometimes when my grandmother talks about my father (who is divorced from my mother), it makes me uncomfortable because she obviously really doesn't like him anymore because he hurt my mom. I feel uncomfortable because her opinion is biased and he's still my father so I don't like to hear bad things about him, especially from her because her hurt and pain is very real toward him so it sometimes makes me resent him for hurting my mom ... It makes me feel uncomfortable because I do not want to hear bad stories or words spoken about my father because he's my father! I love him and have worked hard to forgive him for cheating on my mother, and when my grandmother brings him up, it kind of opens up an old wound that does not need to be opened at that time.

This response illustrates the receiver-oriented nature of underaccommodation. Although the grandmother may have only wanted to support her daughter's side and may not have intended to reopen old wounds, the granddaughter nevertheless perceived the grandmother as insufficiently adjusting her communication to meet the granddaughter's preferences. We also found the negative revelations about third-party family members noteworthy because past research has found grandparents to be crucial sources of social support for grandchildren during family conflicts such as parental divorce (Soliz, 2008). Although these responses did not contain personal information about grandparents themselves, they involved quite negative information about third parties.

Researchers might explore this theme of negative revelations about third parties more systematically by borrowing from the literature on parents' inappropriate disclosures during divorce (e.g., Afifi, McManus, Hutchinson, & Baker, 2007). Inappropriate disclosures about third parties might be potent forms of underaccommodation in the aftermath of family conflict. Practically speaking, grandparents might be advised to be more conscientious of the information they reveal about third parties so that their grandchildren do not feel as if they have to choose sides or look down on other family members. Theoretically, the example reiterates some of the ideas discussed previously with respect to CAT's seventh proposition, namely how it is listeners' perceptions of speaker behavior that guide listener responses. The example also suggests that dyadic data about grandparents' motives for revealing negative information about third parties and grandchildren's interpretations of such negative information might reveal a disconnect between both parties' perspectives, and this disconnect may predict a host of adverse outcomes such as less relational satisfaction and less willingness on the part of grandchildren to help care for grandparents during times of need.

Summary and Conclusions

Taken together, the case studies illustrate several aspects of CAT and suggest opportunities for future research. In line with the theory's seventh proposition, the wide variety of responses to PSDs—ranging in severity from extreme discomfort to no distress at all—highlights that PSDs do not uniformly invoke a singular judgment of inappropriateness in all grandchildren. Rather, grandchildren's perceptions of PSDs vary widely and may be the product of factors such as cognitive complexity. One opportunity for further CAT development involves a need for more dyadic research on how relational partners influence one another (Pitts & Harwood, 2015; Soliz & Bergquist, 2016). Applied to PSDs in GP-GC relationships, we believe one opportunity ripe for future research involves examining how grandparents' motives for engaging in PSDs, grandchildren's perceptions of grandparent motives, grandchildren's perceptions of their own responses to grandparents' PSDs, and grandparents' perceptions of their grandchildren's responses to PSDs interrelate with one another and predict noteworthy outcomes such as relational satisfaction and grandchildren's provision of emotional, instrumental, and other types of care to grandparents experiencing health problems or other difficulties.

By incorporating the perspective of grandparents, future dyadic research on these questions will also shed light on CAT's fourth proposition. The fourth proposition states that speakers will increasingly accommodate the more they wish to affiliate with the listener or facilitate the listener's comprehension (Dragojevic et al., 2016). Some grandparents may perceive their PSDs as accommodative and appropriate moves undertaken with an aim of affiliating with grandchildren and establishing a shared sense of solidarity against life's hardships. Conversely, other grandparents may perceive PSDs as nonaccommodative moves undertaken with the egotistical goal of obtaining emotional comfort from their grandchildren, even if they are aware that such PSDs will be uncomfortable for grandchildren. Future researchers can assess the extent to which these competing perceptions and motives resonate with grandparents' experiences and bear consequences for GP-GC interactions and relationships.

More broadly, the chapter addressed three objectives. First, it established CAT's importance by discussing the theory's breadth, international scholarship, focus on interpersonal *and* intergroup phenomena, and utility in a variety of applied contexts. It then outlined the principles and processes stipulated by CAT, as well as discussed how these principles overlap with PSD research. Third, it presented real-life accounts from grandchildren about the PSDs they receive from grandparents. These accounts illustrate how grandchildren perceive their grandparents' communication as underaccommodative or accommodative. They also suggest ways to advance the study of PSDs, such as by exploring how *grandparents* perceive grandchildren's responses to PSD. We hope these insights serve as a springboard for future research on the intricacies of PSDs in GP-GC relationships.

Discussion Questions

1. Explain how accommodation and nonaccommodation can be studied from a variety of vantage points. Whose perspective do researchers usually consider when studying PSDs?

2. What are some ways in which CAT is a unique social scientific theory? How might you capitalize on these unique characteristics when designing a study on family communication (either in GP-GC relationships or other types of family relationships)?

3. Are grandparents' disclosures about poor health and other difficulties always negative? What are some factors that might qualify how grandchildren and other family members interpret such disclosures?

4. Is the study of PSDs in GP-GC relationships too one-sided? How might grandchildren engage in nonaccommodation toward their grandparents? How might grandparents accommodate to their grandchildren?

REFERENCES

Berger, C. R., & diBattista, Afifi, T. D., McManus, T., Hutchinson, S., & Baker, B. (2007). Inappropriate parental divorce disclosures, the factors that prompt them, and their impact on parents' and adolescents' well-being. *Communication Monographs, 74,* 78–102. doi: 10.1080/03637750701196870

Bangerter, L. R., & Waldron, V. R. (2014). Turning points in long-distance grandparent-grandchild relationships. *Journal of Aging Studies, 29,* 88–97. doi: 10.1016/j.jaging.2014.01.004

Barker, V. (2007). Young adults' reactions to grandparent painful self-disclosure: The influence of grandparent sex and overall motivations for communication. *International Journal of Aging and Human Development, 64,* 195–215. doi: 10.2190/ktnu-0373-20w7-4781

Barker, V., Giles, H., Hajek, C., Ota, H., Noels, K. A., Lim, T.-S., & Somera, L. (2008). Police-civilian interaction, compliance, accommodation, and trust in an intergroup context: International data. *Journal of International and Intercultural Communication, 1,* 93–112. doi: 10.1080/17513050801891986

Bernhold, Q. S., & Giles, H. (2017). Grandparent-grandchild communication: A review of theoretically informed research. *Journal of Intergenerational Relationships, 15,* 368–388. doi: 10.1080/15350770.2017.1368348

Bernhold, Q. S., & Giles, H. (2019). Paternal grandmothers benefit the most from expressing affection to grandchildren: An extension of evolutionary and sociological research. *Journal of Social and Personal Relationships, 36,* 514–534. doi: 10.1111/0265407517734657

Bonnesen, J. L., & Hummert, M. L. (2002). Painful self-disclosures of older adults in relation to aging stereotypes and perceived motivations. *Journal of Language and Social Psychology, 21,* 275–301. doi: 10.1177/0261927x02021003004

Burleson, B. R. (2007). Constructivism: A general theory of communication skill. In B. B. Whaley & W. Samter (Eds.), *Explaining communication: Contemporary theories and exemplars* (pp. 105–128). Mahwah, NJ: Erlbaum.

Burleson, B. R. (2010). Explaining recipient responses to supportive messages: Development and tests of a dual-process theory. In S. W. Smith & S. Wilson (Eds.), *New directions in interpersonal communication research* (pp. 159–179). Thousand Oaks, CA: Sage.

Burleson, B. R., Hanasono, L. K., Bodie, G. D., Holmstrom, A. J., McCullough, J. D., Rack, J. J., & Rosier, J. G. (2011). Are gender differences in responses to supportive communication a matter of ability, motivation, or both? Reading patterns of situation effects through the lens of a dual-process theory. *Communication Quarterly, 59*, 37–60. doi: 10.1080/0146.3373.2011.541324

Colaner, C. W., Soliz, J., & Nelson, L. R. (2014). Communicatively managing religious identity difference in parent-child relationships: The role of accommodative and nonaccommodative communication. *Journal of Family Communication, 14*, 310–327. doi: 10.1080/15267431.2014.945700

Coupland, J., Coupland, N., Giles, H., & Henwood, K. (1991). Formulating age: Dimensions of age identity in elderly talk. *Discourse Processes, 14*, 87–106. doi: 10.1080/01638539109544776

Coupland, N., Coupland, J., & Giles, H. (1991). *Language, society and the elderly: Discourse, identity, and aging.* Oxford, UK: Blackwell.

Coupland, N., Coupland, J., Giles, H., & Henwood, K. (1988). Accommodating the elderly: Invoking and extending a theory. *Language in Society, 17*, 1–41. doi: 10.1017/s0047404500012574

Coupland, N., Coupland, J., Giles, H., Henwood, K., & Wiemann, J. (1988). Elderly self-disclosure: Interactional and intergroup issues. *Language and Communication, 8*, 109–133. doi: 10.1016/0271-5309(88)90010-9

Coupland, N., Henwood, K., Coupland, J., & Giles, H. (1990). Accommodating troubles-talk: The management of elderly self-disclosure. In F. McGregor & R. S. White (Eds.), *Reception and response: Hearer creativity and the analysis of spoken and written texts* (pp. 112–144). London, UK: Croom Helm.

Dragojevic, M., Gasiorek, J., & Giles, H. (2016). Accommodative strategies as core of the theory. In H. Giles (Ed.), *Communication accommodation theory: Negotiating personal relationships and social identities across contexts* (pp. 36–59). Cambridge, UK: Cambridge University Press.

Dragojevic, M., & Giles, H. (2014). Language and interpersonal communication: Their intergroup dynamics. In C. R. Berger (Ed.), *Handbook of interpersonal communication*. Berlin, Germany: De Gruyter Mouton.

Fowler, C., & Soliz, J. (2010). Responses of young adult grandchildren to grandparents' painful self-disclosures. *Journal of Language and Social Psychology, 29,* 75–100. doi: 10.1177/0261927X09351680

Gallois, C., Gasiorek, J., Giles, H., & Soliz, J. (2016). Communication accommodation theory: Integrations and new framework developments. In H. Giles (Ed.), *Communication accommodation theory: Negotiating personal relationships and social identities across contexts* (pp. 192–210). Cambridge, UK: Cambridge University Press.

Gallois, C., Weatherall, A., & Giles, H. (2016). CAT and talk in action. In H. Giles (Ed.), *Communication accommodation theory: Negotiating personal relationships and social identities across contexts* (pp. 105–122). Cambridge, UK: Cambridge University Press.

Gangi, K., & Soliz, J. (2016). De-dichotomizing intergroup and interpersonal dynamics: Perspectives on communication, identity, and relationships. In H. Giles & A. Maass (Eds.), *Advances in intergroup communication* (pp. 35–50). New York, NY: Peter Lang.

Gasiorek, J. (2013). "I was impolite to her because that's how she was to me": Perceptions of motive and young adults' communicative responses to underaccommodation. *Western Journal of Communication, 77,* 604–624. doi: 10.1080/10570314.2013.778421

Gasiorek, J. (2015). Perspective-taking, inferred motive, and perceived accommodation in nonaccommodative conversations. *Journal of Language and Social Psychology, 34,* 577–586. doi: 10.1177/0261927X15584681

Gasiorek, J. (2016a). The "dark side" of CAT: Nonaccommodation. In H. Giles (Ed.), *Communication accommodation theory: Negotiating personal relationships and social identities across contexts* (pp. 85–104). Cambridge, UK: Cambridge University Press.

Gasiorek, J. (2016b). Theoretical perspectives on interpersonal adjustments in language and communication. In H. Giles (Ed.), *Communication accommodation theory: Negotiating personal relationships and social identities across contexts* (pp. 13–35). Cambridge, UK: Cambridge University Press.

Gasiorek, J., & Dragojevic, M. (2017). The effects of accumulated underaccommodation on perceptions of underaccommodative communication and speakers. *Human Communication Research, 43,* 276–294. doi: 10.1111/hcre.12105

Gasiorek, J., & Giles, H. (2012). Effects of inferred motive on evaluations of nonaccommodative communication. *Human Communication Research, 38,* 309–331. doi: 10.1111/j.1468-2958.2012.01426.x

Giles, H. (1973). Communicative effectiveness as a function of accented speech. *Speech Monographs, 40,* 330–331. doi: 10.1080/03637757309375813

Giles, H. (Ed.). (2016a). *Communication accommodation theory: Negotiating personal relationships and social identities across contexts.* Cambridge, UK: Cambridge University Press.

Giles, H. (2016b). The social origins of CAT. In H. Giles (Ed.), *Communication accommodation theory: Negotiating personal relationships and social identities across contexts* (pp. 1–12). Cambridge, UK: Cambridge University Press.

Giles, H., & Ogay, T. (2006). Communication accommodation theory. In B. Whaley & W. Samter (Eds.), *Explaining communication: Contemporary theories and exemplars* (pp. 293–310). Mahwah, NJ: Erlbaum.

Giles, H., Taylor, D. M., & Bourhis, R. (1973). Towards a theory of interpersonal accommodation through language: Some Canadian data. *Language in Society, 2,* 177–192. doi: 10.1017/s0047404500000701

Harwood, J. (2000). Communicative predictors of solidarity in the grandparent-grandchild relationship. *Journal of Social and Personal Relationships, 17,* 743–766. doi: 10.1177/0265407500176003

Harwood, J., Raman, P., & Hewstone, M. (2006). The family and communication dynamics of group salience. *Journal of Family Communication, 6,* 181–200. doi: 10.1207/s15327698jfc0603_2

Holladay, S., Lackovich, R., Lee, M., Coleman, M., Harding, D., & Denton, D. (1998). (Re)constructing relationships with grandparents: A turning point analysis of granddaughters' relational development with maternal grandmothers. *International Journal of Aging and Human Development, 46,* 287–303. doi: 10.2190/00GV-5PWF-UDNH-EHDV

Holmstrom, A. J., Bodie, G. D., Burleson, B. R., McCullough, J. D., Rack, J. J., Hanasono, L. K., & Rosier, J. G. (2015). Testing a dual-process theory of supportive communication outcomes: How multiple factors influence outcomes in support situations. *Communication Research, 42,* 526–546. doi: 10.1177/0093650213476293

Hummert, M. L., Garstka, T. A., Ryan, E. B., & Bonneson, J. L. (2004). The role of age stereotypes in interpersonal communication. In J. Coupland & J. F. Nussbaum (Eds.), *Handbook of communication and aging research* (pp. 91–114). Mahwah, NJ: Erlbaum.

Lin, M-C., Harwood, J., & Bonnesen, J. L. (2002). Conversation topics and communication satisfaction in grandparent-grandchild relationships. *Journal of Language and Social Psychology, 21,* 302–323. doi: 10.1177/0261927X02021003005

Mansson, D. H. (2013). The Grandchildren Received Affection Scale: Examining affectual solidarity factors. *Southern Communication Journal, 78,* 70–90. doi: 10.1080/1041794X.2012.729124

McGlone, M. S., & Giles, H. (2011). Language and interpersonal communication. In M. L. Knapp & J. A. Daly (Eds.), *The SAGE handbook of interpersonal communication* (4th ed., pp. 201–238). Thousand Oaks, CA: Sage.

Palomares, N. A., Giles, H., Soliz, J., & Gallois, C. (2016). Intergroup accommodation, social categories, and identities. In H. Giles (Ed.), *Communication accommodation theory: Negotiating personal relationships and social identities across contexts* (pp. 123–151). Cambridge, UK: Cambridge University Press.

Pitts, M. J., & Harwood, J. (2015). Communication accommodation competence: The nature and nurture of accommodative resources across the lifespan. *Language and Communication, 41,* 89–99. doi: 10.1016/j.langcom.2014.10.002

Ryan, E. B., Giles, H., Bartolucci, G., & Henwood, K. (1986). Psycholinguistic and social psychological components of communication by and with the elderly. *Language and Communication, 6*, 1–24. doi: 10.1016/0271-5309(86)90002-9

Soliz, J. (2008). Intergenerational support and the role of grandparents in post-divorce families: Retrospective accounts of young adult grandchildren. *Qualitative Research Reports in Communication, 9*, 72–80. doi: 10.1080/17459430802400373

Soliz, J., & Bergquist, G. (2016). Methods of CAT inquiry: Quantitative studies. In H. Giles (Ed.), *Communication accommodation theory: Negotiating personal relationships and social identities across contexts* (pp. 60–78). Cambridge, UK: Cambridge University Press.

Soliz, J., & Giles, H. (2014). Relational and identity processes in communication: A contextual and meta-analytical review of communication accommodation theory. In E. Cohen (Ed.), *Communication yearbook 38* (pp. 108–143). Thousand Oaks, CA: Sage.

Soliz, J., Thorson, A. R., & Rittenour, C. E. (2009). Communicative correlates of satisfaction, family identity, and group salience in multiracial/ethnic families. *Journal of Marriage and Family, 71*, 819–832. doi: 10.1111/j.1741-3737.2009.00637.x

Speer, R. B., Giles, H., & Denes, A. (2013). Investigating stepparent-stepchild interactions: The role of communication accommodation. *Journal of Family Communication, 13*, 218–241. doi: 10.1080/15267431.2013.768248

Thakerar, J. N., Giles, H., & Cheshire, J. (1982). Psychological and linguistic parameters of speech accommodation theory. In C. Fraser & K. R. Scherer (Eds.), *Advances in the social psychology of language* (pp. 205–255). Cambridge, UK: Cambridge University Press.

Youngvorst, L. J., & Jones, S. M. (2017). The influence of cognitive complexity, empathy, and mindfulness on person-centered message evaluations. *Communication Quarterly, 65*, 549–564. doi: 10.1080/01463373.2017.1301508

Chapter 4

Call It Intuition: Moral Foundations Theory and Understanding Political and Social Disagreement in a Contentious Society

Gregory A. Cranmer, Ph.D., *Clemson University*

Darren Linvill, Ph.D., *Clemson University*

Today's political and social landscape is unarguably contentious. Moreover, the discourse around such topics has devolved into an unproductive pattern of ad hominem attacks and motivated reasoning that prioritizes justifying one's own positions more than developing an understanding of another's position. In other words, many individuals are passionately committed to defending their stances on social issues: even more so than understanding or appreciating the positions of others. According to a Pew Research Center survey, nearly half of all Democrats and Republicans in the United States report feeling fear, anger, and frustration regarding individuals in the differing political party (Pew Research Center, 2016). It is arguable that we, as a society and academic community, are witnessing a meaningful breakdown in productive communication and dialogue about a host of economic, civic, and social issues. For instance, one would not have to try very hard to find arguments within social discourse, especially on social media, that frame contrary viewpoints (regardless of topic or one's own position) as the result of evil, unintelligent, or, at best, ignorant people.

There are potential explanations for why individuals may disagree so profoundly on the fundamental issues that confront our society and why some may have difficulty understanding the viewpoints of others. One such explanation posits that the breakdown in productive discourse may stem from the root of our disagreements being deeply engrained not only in our worldviews, but within our intuitions. Jonathan Haidt—a noted psychologist and creator of moral foundations theory (MFT)—argues that these intuitions guide how we come to understand

and respond to stimuli. Subsequent evidence has demonstrated that these intuitions are associated with our worldviews and political orientations, personality and communication traits, and how we respond to messages.

Assumptions & Applications of MFT

Ethics and morality have been topics of academic inquiry for centuries. Traditionally, social scientists argue that moral decision-making is often the result of cognitive reasoning and that morality explains human behavior and interaction (Gilligan, 1982; Kohlberg, 1969). Moral foundations theory, which builds upon the Social Intuitionist Model (Haidt, 2001), explains human behavior and interaction as a function of instinctive and impulsive reactions to relevant, moral stimuli (Graham et al., 2013). These stimuli include a variety of evolutionary and culturally relevant issues that span the well-being of individuals, issues of social justice, group dynamics, proper sources of authority, and concerns for purity (Haidt & Joseph, 2004). In other words, moral foundations theory is a descriptive, moral theory that takes a *pluralist* (i.e., recognizes multiple distinct aspects of morality) approach to understanding moral decision-making, which views moral reasoning as *intuitive* (i.e., moral decisions and related behavior are often gut reactions). Graham et al. (2013) argued that moral foundations theory can be understood via the framework of four basic assumptions.

MFT Assumptions

The first assumption of moral foundations theory is that morality is initially formed prior to human experience (Haidt, 2001). In other words, each individual possesses innate, moral dispositions that are determined by genetics and wired into their neurological functioning from conception to childhood. This assumption is rooted in evolutionary psychology, which puts forward the idea that humanity has historically faced recurrent problems. As such, predispositions that allow humans to respond to those problems are advantageous to human survival and, thus, are encouraged through selection and passed on to offspring. Although moral foundations theory articulates that moral intuitions are initially set by biology, it does not exclude the influence of social forces (Haidt & Joseph, 2004).

The second assumption of moral foundations theory is that morality is also shaped through the milieu in which individuals are socialized. This assumption acknowledges that humans are capable of learning attitudes, information, appraisals, schemas, and modes of interacting that may be specific to particular social groups (Haidt & Joseph, 2004). In this way, people morally develop—at least in part—based on their social surroundings. In other words, two individuals from different cultures can be born with the same initial moral dispositions but ultimately differ from each other because of different social influences. This reality is underscored by the variability in morality across cultures. If morality was entirely determined by the biological characteristics of people, the variation between cultures would not exist (Haidt, Koller, & Dias, 1993). In relation to the biological influence of morality, learning and culture are subsequent influences that occur in childhood and into adulthood. Graham, et al. (2013) use the metaphor of written works to explain this relationship, with the biological disposition being a first draft (i.e., a starting point) that is revised to varying degrees based on social influence. Together, biology and learning shape how individuals interact with each other and make decisions.

The third assumption of moral foundations theory is that the influence of morality on decision-making and interactions occurs primarily as a result of intuitive responses (Haidt, 2001, 2012). An intuitive response is an incredibly quick and evaluative feeling (i.e., correct-wrong, good-bad) that occurs without deliberative contemplation. More simply, Haidt (2001) described intuition as a gut reaction. The advocating of an intuitive process of evaluating stimuli along moral grounds is in stark contrast to historical models, which argue that morality is a rational, well-reasoned, or learned state (e.g., Gilligan, 1982; Kohlberg, 1969). Within moral foundations theory, rationalization and reason often follow intuitive responses and serve a means of justification for already made decisions or behaviors. To put it differently, people engage in moral reasoning, but this reasoning often is in an effort to justify or defend responses that have already occurred—not to proactively determine what those responses should be. As such, Haidt and colleagues position the intuitive response as a product of biology and culture and the reasoning/justification for that response as a process that is meant to address social attempts to enforce accountability for actions and decisions (Graham et al., 2013; Haidt, 2012).

The fourth assumption of moral foundations theory is that morality is comprised of multiple foundations (Haidt & Joseph, 2004). This pluralistic view of morality is based on the notion that humanity has endured numerous and varied challenges throughout its history (i.e., individual suffering, neediness of children, external threats, organizing social groups) and that the mental structures associated with morality have, likewise, produced multiple means to resolve those problems (Haidt, 2012). In other words, the challenges that humanity has encountered are diverse, as are the cognitive systems that work together to address those challenges. Each foundation within the theory coincides with a particular threat or concern that accompanies managing social collectives. An individual's predispositions toward each foundation determines what threats they prioritize and how they might respond. To date, five foundations are widely accepted and a sixth foundation is under consideration. However, Haidt (2012) cautioned that the current breadth of foundations is not definitive and that additional foundations may exist.

Overall, these assumptions forward that biology, socialization, culture, and experiences influence the salience of individuals' moral foundations. Despite cultural or individual variations in moral intuitions, the influence of salient foundations is consistent. This influence manifests via a fast-paced, innate cognitive process that prompts an instinctual reaction to stimuli. This process is quicker than individuals can cognitively reason, leading to a powerful "gut" reaction that influences behavior, attitudes, and communication. Subsequently, individuals defend this gut reaction with reasoning, which serves the function of answering social accountability rather than aiding in decision-making. However, the manner in which individuals respond to stimuli is determined by a set of multiple foundations. The salience of each foundation ranges on a continuum and varies by individual, with salient foundations being most predictive of behaviors, attitudes, and communication.

Moral Foundations

Moral foundations theory argues that moral foundations developed in humans in response to fundamental issues that were consistently faced during human development and threatened the existence of social collectives. These issues are triggered by a variety of stimuli. Moral foundations are meant to serve as innate, heuristic responses to these stimuli. Additionally, these foundations coincide with culturally relevant virtues and are accompanied by the experience of corresponding emotions. Within moral foundations theory, morality was originally theorized to be comprised of five foundations: harm/care, fairness/cheating, loyalty/betrayal, authority/subversion, and purity/sanctity (Haidt & Joseph, 2004). Some researchers categorize the foundations into two groups: individualizing foundations that recognize the rights and welfare of the individual (i.e., harm/care and fairness/cheating) and binding foundations that serve group functioning and cohesion (i.e., loyalty/betrayal, authority/subversion, and purity/sanctity) (Smith, Alford, Hibbing, Martin, & Hatem, 2017). Haidt (2012) forwarded a sixth potential foundation: liberty/oppression. We discuss the six foundations individually in an attempt to capture Haidt's (2012) initial understandings of moral foundations theory and provide the most nuanced accounting of the theory as possible.

Harm/Care. The foundation of harm/care encompasses intuitive responses of being sensitive to the needs of others, disliking the suffering of others, and having the potential to feel compassion. This foundation corresponds with the social virtues of caring and kindness. Harm/care stems from the need for all species to protect and care for their offspring. Haidt and colleagues argue that this adaptive challenge is especially salient for humans because young children are extremely dependent on their parents for an extended period of time (Graham et al., 2013; Haidt & Joseph, 2004). As such, this foundation is deeply engrained within human intuitions and culture, and those whose minds are structured to respond to these needs before they are experienced are advantaged. Triggers of harm/care reactions include stimuli that signal distress, suffering, or neediness of others, especially those viewed as vulnerable others. Responses grounded in a harm/care foundation include emotions of compassion, kindness, sympathy, and empathy for the vulnerable other, as well as anger and hostility toward the transgressor.

Fairness/Cheating. The foundation of fairness/cheating consists of concern for reciprocal interactions and mutual benefit within human collaboration. This foundation corresponds with the social virtues of justice, trustworthiness, and proportionality of rewards (i.e., receiving what you earn). Fairness/cheating is derived from the adaptive challenge of ensuring that collaborations and partnerships between individuals are productive or beneficial for those involved, while also deterring cheaters or slackers. Those who have intuitive structures in place to ensure degrees of reciprocity within collaboration, and to hold others accountable regarding their contributions to a collective, are advantaged in their ability to form continued and beneficial relationships within social groups. This foundation is triggered by observations of cheating, cooperation, deception, or disproportional distributions of resources. Those who are triggered to engage within a fairness/cheating response experience the emotions of anger, guilt, or gratitude depending on the outcome of a given interaction and their role within it.

Loyalty/Betrayal. The foundation of loyalty/betrayal consists of concern for group affiliations and shifting coalitions among social groups. The relevant social virtues for the loyalty/betrayal foundation include loyalty, patriotism, self-sacrifice, and heroism. This foundation arises from the challenge of humans needing to form and maintain cohesive collectives to maximize their chances of survival. A central means through which this survival is assured is through successful competition against other social groups. Those who have moral structures in place that allow them to form cohesive collectives increase their likelihood of being members of successful social groups that may aid in their survival. Loyalty/betrayal responses may be triggered by threats (real or perceived) to a social group to which one belongs. In other words, this foundation arises from the felt needs for protection of one's own group or fears of domination from outside groups. Those triggered along this foundation can experience emotions that range from pride or trust in those within their own group to anger or distrust of members from other groups.

Authority/Subversion. The foundation of authority/subversion concerns the proper responses to, and identification of, sources of authority. The social virtues associated with the authority/subversion foundation include respect, duty, obedience, or deference. This foundation coincides with the challenge of navigating the dominance hierarchies that form within social groups. Those who have the moral structures that facilitate the formation of beneficial relationships with those above and below them within a hierarchy, without disrupting that structure, are advantaged when operating in complex social systems. Engaging in an authority/subversion response is triggered by needs for protection, fears of domination, and respect for tradition. This foundation can manifest in emotions of awe, respect, or admiration for perceived legitimate sources of authority or the symbols of that authority.

Purity/Sanctity. The foundation of purity/sanctity involves perceptions of social or physical contamination. Purity/sanctity taps into the cultural virtues of chastity, purity, temperance, and cleanliness. This foundation arises from the biological and viral challenges and dangers (i.e., pathogens, parasites) that threatened humans as they began to live in larger groups and novel environments. In this manner, those who have cognitive structures organized around avoiding potential sources of contamination or illness have an evolutionary advantage, likened to a behavioral immune system. Purity/sanctity is triggered by issues related to bodily contamination, cultural or religious taboos, threats of disease, or deviant sexual behaviors. The triggering of this foundation is often accompanied by the emotion of disgust toward the violator of this foundation.

Liberty/Oppression. The newest foundation of liberty/oppression centers on the issues associated with rights, coercion, and use of power. Liberty/oppression is consistent with cultural values of autonomy, independence, and equality of rights. This foundation stems from the notion that early groups of humans were egalitarian, meaning that shared influence and resources were central to social dynamics. However, egalitarian forms of organizing became increasingly difficult to maintain as human groups grew in size of membership (Haidt, 2012). Further, the existence of dominant individuals threatens the access to resources for the majority of nondominant members of groups. With this in mind, those who have the intuitive systems to work together with others to ensure that dominant individuals cannot restrict the access to resources are advantaged for survival. This foundation is triggered by issues related to individuals' rights (or sometimes outcomes) or their desires to avoid being infringed upon. The liberty/oppression foundation is centrally associated with anger toward those labeled oppressors.

Communication Implications of MFT

Although moral foundations theory was developed within moral psychology literature, it is quite applicable to communication research because it provides a descriptive framework for understanding how individuals process and respond to stimuli and those around them. Thus, the theory naturally can show how receivers process messages and, potentially, how they respond as well. In particular, three bodies of moral foundations theory research warrant particular attention within a communicative context: trait research, media research, and political research.

Trait Research. The first relevant area of moral foundations theory research is the relationship among moral foundations, personality, and communicative traits. This body of research is based on the notion that moral foundations and traits are deeply ingrained dispositions that are rooted within biology, but also shaped through environmental and cultural features (Haidt, 2001; McCroskey, Daly, Martin, & Beatty, 1998). As such, both psychologists and communication scholars have framed moral foundations theory as a potential mechanism of personality and communicative dispositions. In other words, the innate sense of morality that is embedded within individuals is argued to shape various characteristics that are relevant for how they interact with others. For example, Lewis and Bates (2011) demonstrated that moral foundations are moderately related to personality traits using the Five Factor Model of Personality (Tupes & Christal, 1961). This research has demonstrated that those who value the individualizing foundations of harm/care and fairness/cheating are also more likely to have the personality traits of agreeableness (i.e., be compassionate and cooperative) and openness (i.e., be curious and appreciative of unusual ideas). Further, those who value harm/care also are more likely to be high on the neuroticism trait variable (i.e., experience negative emotions) and extraversion (i.e., be positive and seek interaction). The binding foundations of loyalty/betrayal, authority/subversion, and purity/sanctity were found to be associated with less openness. Loyalty/betrayal is also associated with greater degrees of extraversion (Lewis & Bates, 2011).

Given personality traits are recognized as a potential mechanism behind communication (Daly & Bippus, 1998). Cranmer and Martin (2015) attempted to begin to address the associations between morality and communication by examining the relationship among moral foundations and aggressive and adaptive communication traits among 205 young adults. These traits, in particular, were noted as germane to the moral context, given that they center on "issues of violating others' self-concepts, defending beliefs, having concern for others, and being open to alternative ways of thinking and behaving" (p. 361). For aggressive traits, the prioritization of individualizing foundations were associated with decreased verbal aggression, which is the tendency to attack others' self-concepts. In contrast, binding foundations were found to be lower in argumentativeness, which is the tendency to contemplate and debate ideas. For adaptive traits, individualizing foundations were associated with responsiveness to the communicative needs of others and cognitive flexibility to think about issues from multiple perspectives. However, those who valued the binding foundations were less cognitively flexible. Taken together, trait research demonstrates that personality traits associated with novelty, creativity, and concern for the feelings of others are more common with individualizing moral intuitions, whereas concerns for maintaining social or ideological systems is more common binding foundations. The trait literature reinforces the central notions of moral foundations theory that foundations are predispositions that are associated with how individuals view and interact with the world around them.

Media Research. Moral foundations theory research has also been utilized to understand how humans behave in regard to mediated content. These scholars frame moral foundations as a mechanism that determines the preferences and reactions to particular forms of media (Tamborini, 2011). For example, Tamborini, Eden, Bowman, Grizzard, and Lachlan (2012) demonstrated that the salience of harm/care is associated with the sensitivity that individuals have toward graphic violence within film. Thus, those who value the well-being and safety of vulnerable others find mediated violence less appealing. Subsequent research has expanded upon these notions through demonstrating that moral foundations are a mediator that explains indirect effects of national cultures on media preferences (Bowman, Joeckel, & Dogruel, 2012). In particular, this research found that American culture places greater emphasis on binding foundations, whereas German culture places great emphasis on individualizing foundations. Across these cultures, however, moral dispositions shaped preferences for select film and television genres. Specifically, prioritizing individualizing foundations fosters interest in media that emphasize the well-being of others (i.e., television news, drama films), whereas valuing binding foundations creates appreciation for media that emphasizes themes of patriotism, foreign enemies, or "us versus them" cultures (i.e., sports events, action films).

Additionally, moral intuitions influence reactions to media and decisions that people make within mediated environments. For instance, the harm/care foundation has been associated with which game path (i.e., a character's role within the plot of the game) video gamers take within role-playing video games (Boyan, Grizzard, & Bowman, 2015). Further, the specific decisions that gamers make within mediated environments result from their moral intuitions. When gamers encounter game scenarios that trigger the foundations that they hold salient, they intuitively respond (a gut reaction) as they would to real world stimuli (i.e., in accordance with their moral foundations). However, when a scenario does not engage morality, gamers determine their actions based on game strategy or as part of a virtual experience (a game reaction) (Joeckel, Bowman, & Dogruel, 2012). Together, media research dealing with moral foundations theory reveals that moral intuitions guide media consumption and, under the right conditions, influence how humans respond to fictional environments and stimuli in mediated environments. The media literature supports the tenets of moral foundations theory regarding individuals' reliance on foundations for decision-making and their intuitive responses toward violations of salient foundations.

Political Research. The field of political communication addresses the use of communicative strategies to influence the public's knowledge, beliefs, and actions (Swanson & Nimmo, 1990). It is the way in which communication can be employed to influence beliefs that moral foundations theory has the potential to be a particularly valuable tool. Communication scholars have, for instance, begun to examine the issue of growing political polarization in society (Robison & Mullinix, 2016). Using the traditional liberal/conservative ideological continuum to explore such social issues, however, has been shown to be a frequently flawed approach, as participants are often incapable of defining the meaning of either "liberal" or "conservative" (Luttbeg & Gant, 1985). If scholars, instead, approach research exploring the communication of political values and beliefs through the lens of moral foundations theory, there is the potential to give insight that is both more nuanced and comprehensive. As an example, Graham, Haidt, and Nosek (2009) found that liberal individuals are more likely to agree with statements grounded in the harm/care and fairness/cheating foundations, whereas conservatives are more likely to agree with messages grounded in all five foundations, including the loyalty/betrayal, authority/subversion, and purity/sanctity foundations. Building upon this knowledge, Day, Fiske, Downing, and Trail (2014) framed persuasive political messages within a moral frame consistent with participants' political ideology, and found that congruent messages are most influential and reinforce entrenched beliefs. The political literature demonstrates that individuals rely on their salient foundations to process information and advocate positions regarding how their societies should be structure—central notions of moral foundations theory.

Case Study

On March 2, 2017, the controversial writer and political scientist Charles Murray was on the campus of Middlebury College, a private liberal arts college in Middlebury, Vermont. Murray is well known for his divisive best seller, *The Bell Curve:*

Intelligence and Class Structure in American Life, which some scholars and activists argue promotes social theories grounded in racist ideologies that disparage African American and Hispanics' intellectual abilities. In early 2017, Murray was invited to Middlebury College, by a student group affiliated with the American Enterprise Institute: a conservative think tank at which Murray is a scholar. The intended purpose of his speech was to discuss his more recent book on cultural research. His talk did not take place as planned.

Prior to the speech, the large group of students gathered for the Murray event were warned that students who attempted to disrupt the talk would be in violation of campus policies (for a video of the full event, see Jaschik, 2017). Middlebury College President Laurie Patton invited "nondisruptive protest," but also argued that "the very premise of free speech on campus is that a speaker has a right to be heard." When Murray took the stage to begin his talk, however, between 100 and 150 students stood up, turned their backs on him, and began loudly chanting. These chants included statements such as "Racist, sexist, antigay, Charles Murray, go away," as well as "Your message is hatred…we cannot tolerate it" and also "Charles Murray, go away. Middlebury says no way." It is worth noting, for the purposes of context, that Allison Stanger, a left-leaning Middlebury College faculty member moderating the night's talk, has suggested that many of these protesters were operating on assumptions made of Murray's work without having read or engaged with his ideas directly (Stanger, 2017). In other words, it seems likely that many students made decisions regarding how to view and react to Murray intuitively and not through lengthy, internal deliberation.

After several minutes of student chanting, college officials announced that Murray would go to an unnamed location on campus to have a discussion with Stanger, which would be livestreamed back to the lecture hall. Soon after the move, students were able to identify the location of the livestreamed talk. This event was also disrupted, as students pulled fire alarms and banged on windows in the building. When Murray eventually moved to leave campus, masked protesters pushed and shoved him and Professor Stanger, grabbing Stanger's hair and injuring her neck before she and Murray were able to reach their vehicle. In total, 67 Middlebury College students eventually faced disciplinary action for their involvement in the protest (for further discussion, see Jaschik, 2017; Saul, 2017). Although the event has garnered considerable public attention, the night of March 2 in Vermont is not an isolated incident. As such, understanding these events from multiple perspectives has importance for social discourse and the free exchange of ideas.

Practical Implications

If we examine the events at Middlebury College using moral foundations theory as a theoretical lens, we can better understand the actions of the student protestors (i.e., the aim of descriptive theories). Using moral foundations theory, what is clearly questionable, and even troubling, behavior from the perspective of someone operating from one moral foundation can be viewed as consistent, and even necessary, from the perspective of someone operating primarily from another. It should be noted, regarding the discussion below, however, that an individual would not likely be motivated by only a single moral foundation; each person has, within him/her, every foundation which influences that person simultaneously but to differing degrees.

Students operating primarily from the harm/care foundation, for instance, appear to have been concerned for their fellow students, particularly those who they perceived as members of marginalized communities (i.e., women, minorities, LGBTQ students). This foundation is based upon the innate desire to protect those deemed vulnerable, arguably a good intention. Naturally, the violation of this foundation results in emotions of hostility and anger toward someone viewed as a transgressor (i.e., Charles Murray in this scenario). Under such circumstances, student protesters acted upon their desires to protect fellow students, and likely their emotions, and reacted with shouting and violence. In summary, if students viewed Murray's ideas as having the potential to harm vulnerable members of the Middlebury College community (whether justified or not), a conceivable reaction rooted in the harm/care foundation may be to aggressively defend those community members through protest.

Students operating from a fairness/cheating foundation may have had concerns regarding social inequality. Those students who believed resources in society are distributed unevenly, and that this inequality manifests itself through socially defined categories of persons, may have believed Murray's ideas, themselves, were unjust and, in fact, contribute to maintaining an inequitable status quo. Murray has proposed that a great deal of inequality exists due to gaps in intelligence. Students who believed, instead, that inequality was related to issues of race, gender, and sexual preference, would view these ideas as inherently unfair and react to them with anger. The belief that Murray's ideas contribute to social inequality would also possibly result in students focused on the fairness cheating foundations to have a desire to protest for what they view as justice.

Students operating from a loyalty/betrayal foundation could have reasonably reacted either in opposition to Murray's presence or for it, depending on their personal political affiliations and group identity. Those part of the student group which invited Murray, a group affiliated with the American Enterprise Institute, would have seen him as part of their social group and likely invited him, in part, for that very reason. In President Patton's own words prior to the event, however, Middlebury College has a predominately left-leaning, progressive student body. Many Middlebury College students operating from a loyalty/betrayal foundation would have likely viewed Murray as an outsider and acted with distrust, resulting in a desire to protest his speech.

Students operating from an authority/subversion foundation would have been concerned with obedience to appropriate hierarchy. It therefore seems unlikely that they would have been among those protesting the talk. Respect and deference are important values for these individuals. President Patton's words regarding the value of free speech, along with earlier threats of disciplinary action, would have worked to dissuade students operating from this foundation from actively protesting. It is also possible that respect and admiration for Murray's age, position as a scholar, and/or his status of invited guest of the college would have encouraged these students to be among those waiting to hear the talk, rather than protest it.

Students operating from a purity/sanctity foundation may have had concerns about the potential for deviant ideas being expressed within their campus community. In essence treating the campus as a pure site and Murray and his ideas as unclean and threatening their sanctuary. As part of a relatively ideologically homogenous, left-leaning student body, some Middlebury College students may have been unused to differing viewpoints and viewed Murray's ideas as dangerously divergent from those of the group. Such views would likely be worthy of disgust from the perspective of a student operating from the purity/sanctity foundation and such a view would conceivably result in the desire to remove such unclean views from the community through protest.

Like the authority/subversion foundation, it seems similarly unlikely that a student operating from a liberty/oppression foundation would act to protest Murray. It seems likely that these students would be concerned with Murray's individual autonomy, regardless of their thoughts on his views. These students would most likely reject the idea of using coercive power to stop the talk from taking place, regardless of the content of the talk. President Patton's argument that Murray had the "right" to be heard would have likely been met with approval from these students. A student operating from a liberty/oppression foundation would likely feel that to protest Murray's speech would infringe on his individual self-determination, and this would be unacceptable. It is possible that they might view a challenge to Murray's individual freedoms as a simultaneous challenge to their own.

It is clear that by applying Moral Foundation Theory to the Middlebury case we can better appreciate the grounding of various viewpoints regarding these events. The theory provides a lens to understand the frameworks through which individuals engage with their moral judgements. It is important to recognize that understanding a viewpoint and agreeing with that viewpoint are not the same. That said, it is our hope that understanding can lead to better, more informed dialogue which does not devolve into negativity or, as in the case of Middlebury, violence. Moral Foundation Theory can facilitate this dialogue.

Discussion Questions

1. How can we best facilitate meaningful dialogue between two individuals who disagree on a subject when that disagreement is based on differing moral foundations?

2. Name a political issue on which political parties seem to fundamentally disagree. How can moral foundations theory help us better understand this disagreement?

3. What beneficial role in society can each foundation of moral foundations theory play? What destructive role?

4. Think of a social or political issue on which you strongly hold a position. Examine the issue from each foundation. How might your position on the issue and rationale for that position change within the framework of each foundation?

5. Part of the explanatory framework of moral foundations theory is that violations of foundations trigger strong, innate reactions that are often tied to our emotions. How might this knowledge help individuals have more logical, reasoned discussions about difficult issues?

REFERENCES

Bowman, N. D., Joeckel, S., & Dogruel, L. (2012). A question of morality? The influence of moral salience and nationality on media preferences. *Communications: The European Journal of Communication Research, 37,* 345–369.

Boyan A., Grizzard, M., & Bowman, N. D. (2015). A massively moral game? Mass effect as a case study to understand the influence of players' moral intuitions on adherence to hero or antihero play styles. *Journal of Gaming and Virtual Worlds 7,* 41–57.

Cranmer, G. A., & Martin, M. M. (2015). An examination of aggression and adaption traits with moral foundations theory. *Communication Research Reports, 32,* 360–366. doi:10.1080/08824096.2015.1089848

Day, M. V., Fiske, S. T., Downing, E. L., & Trail, T. E. (2014). Shifting liberal and conservative attitudes using moral foundations theory. *Personality and Social Psychology Bulletin, 40,* 1559–1573. doi:10.1177/0146167214551152

Gilligan, C. (1982). *In a different voice: Psychological theory and women's development.* Cambridge, MA: Harvard University Press.

Graham, J., Haidt, J., Koleva, S., Motyl, M., Iyer, R., Wojcik, S. P., & Ditto, P. H. (2013). Moral foundations theory: The pragmatic validity of moral pluralism. *Advances in Experimental Social Psychology, 47,* 55–130. doi:10.1016/B978-0-12-407236-7.00002-4

Graham, J., Haidt, J., & Nosek, B. A. (2009). Liberals and conservatives rely on different sets of moral foundations. *Journal of Personality and Social Psychology, 96,* 1029–1046. doi:0.1037/a0015141

Haidt, J. (2001). The emotional dog and its rational tail: A social intuitionist approach to moral judgment. *Psychological Review, 108,* 814–834. doi:10.1037/0033-295x.108.4.814

Haidt, J. (2012). *The righteous mind: Why good people are divided by politics and religion.* New York, NY: Pantheon Books.

Haidt, J., & Joseph, C. (2004). Intuitive ethics: How innately prepared intuitions generate culturally variable virtues. *Daedalus, 133*(4), 55–66. doi:10.1162/001152604236555

Jaschik, S. (2017, March 3). Shouting down a lecture. Inside Higher Ed. Retrieved from https://www.insidehighered.com/news/2017/03/03/middlebury-students-shout-down-lecture-charles-murray

Joeckel, S., Bowman, N. D., & Dogruel, L. (2012). Gut or game? The influence of moral intuitions on decisions in video games. *Media Psychology, 15,* 460–485.

Kohlberg, L. (1969). Stage and sequence: The cognitive-development approach to socialization. In D. A. Goslin (Ed.), *Handbook of socialization theory and research.* Chicago: Rand McNally.

Lewis, G. J., & Bates, T. C. (2011). From left to right: How the personality system allows basic traits to influence politics via characteristic moral adaptations. *British Journal of Psychology, 102,* 546–558. doi:10.1111/j.2044-8295.2011.02016.x

Luttbeg, N. R., & Gant, M. M. (1985). The failure of liberal/conservative ideology as a cognitive structure. *Public Opinion Quarterly, 49,* 80–93. doi:10.1086/268902

Pew Research Center (2016). Partisanship and political animosity in 2016. Retrieved from http://www.people-press.org/2016/06/22/partisanship-and-political-animosity-in-2016/

Robison, J., & Mullinix, K. J. (2016). Elite polarization and public opinion: How polarization is communicated and its effects. *Political Communication, 33,* 261–282. doi:10.1080/10584609.2015.1055526

Saul, S. (2017, May 25). Middlebury disciplines student protesters. *The New York Times*, p. 15A.

Stanger, A. (2017, March 13). Understanding the angry mob at Middlebury that gave me a concussion. *The New York Times.* Retrieved from https://www.nytimes.com/2017/03/13/opinion/understanding-the-angry-mob-that-gave-me-a-concussion.html

Swanson, D. & Nimmo D. (1990). New directions in political communication: A resource book. Thousand Oaks: Sage.

Tamborini, R. (2011). Moral intuition and media entertainment. *Journal of Media Psychology, 23,* 39–45. doi:10.1027/1864-1105/a000031

Tamborini, R., Eden, A., Bowman, N. D., Grizzard, M., & Lachlan, K. A. (2012). The influence of morality subcultures on the acceptance and appeal of violence. *Journal of Communication, 62,* 136–157. doi: 10.1111/j.1460-2466.2011.01620.x

Chapter 5

Millennials in the Age of President Trump: An Application of Problematic Integration Theory

Austin S. Babrow, Ph.D, *Ohio University* | Peter A. Babrow, B.A., *Athens, Ohio*

In this chapter, we explain Problematic Integration Theory, its importance, and its relevance for and application to communication processes and practices. We then present a vignette describing the theory as it relates to the experience of millennials following the election of President Donald Trump, highlight several examples, and invite further reflection on this significant time in the evolution of the millennial generation.

Why the Theory Is Important

Problematic Integration (PI) Theory focuses on communication in situations where meanings are troubled in one or another of several distinctive ways (Babrow, 1992, 2007, 2016). Its importance lies in the significance of communication in these specific situations. Communication's importance grows in proportion to the extent to which our beliefs or expectations are inconsistent with our desires or values or, more generally, its importance lies in the significance of the desires or values at stake in a situation. The theory illuminates dynamics in these troubled meanings and the ways that communication contributes to their construction and reconstruction.

As we achieve greater understanding of these dynamics, we increase our potential for empathy and compassion. In other words, studying the theory teaches us that troublesome meanings are common, in that it is often hard to make sense of situations, to know what to believe or value, or to decide how to speak or act in our own best interests or on others' behalf. Greater awareness of these common problems, and insight into their nature, fosters empathy and compassion; we realize that "these struggles largely define our humanity, which is why so many of the world's great spiritual and religious wisdom traditions hold compassion as a central value" (Babrow & Striley,

2014, p. 106). In addition, the more thoroughly we understand these dynamics, the greater the likelihood we will see alternative ways of understanding troubled meanings and communicating about them. "As we learn more about PI's dynamics and communicative implications, we frequently come to realize our thoughts, feelings, and actions have far greater scope than we [at first] realized; we feel less constrained or stuck as we [think of] alternative constructions" (Babrow & Striley, 2014, p. 106). In turn, learning to recognize and understand the dynamics and possibilities illuminated by the theory should make us more sophisticated *and* cosmopolitan communicators (Babrow & Striley, 2014; also see Pearce, 1989).

PI Theory's Relevance for and Application to Communication Practices and Processes

PI Theory is a very general perspective on communication. It is relevant whenever we face and wrestle with troublesome meanings. These can be meanings of the past, present, or future. In this chapter, we focus on meanings of the present and future, touching only implicitly on the ways that communication contributes to our constructions of troubled meanings of the past.

The framework developed as a way to shift the focus of communication theories that emphasized psychological structures, processes, and content (see Greene, 1984) to the meaning of communication, particularly communication around problematic meanings. At the time the theory was developed, researchers were moving beyond conceptions of people as rational information processors, decision makers, and actors. The most substantial examples of this are dual-process theories. Collectively, these perspectives assert that our mind is a blend of two sorts of cognitive processes. One is characterized by slow, relatively conscious reasoning, such as that described by older theories of rational decision and action. The other is fast, operating outside consciousness and, hence, beyond conscious, rational control, and reliant on a variety of more rudimentary psychological processes (for a fascinating review, see Kahnemann, 2011).

PI Theory developed out of a more direct critique of the elements of rational choice and information processing models (Babrow, 1992). Its aim was to problematize the basic elements of these theories by focusing on troublesome meanings. The theory springs from the widely accepted idea that intentional actions are guided by beliefs that link a contemplated act with likely consequences and evaluations of those consequences (Fishbein & Ajzen, 1975). In other words, we intend to perform actions we expect will have mostly positive outcomes, and we avoid acts we expect will have largely negative consequences. PI Theory contends that these beliefs and values comprise important dimensions of the conscious meanings of our behavior. In the terms of the theory, we would say that thoughtful action requires a synthesis or *integration of expectations* and *evaluations* of consequences.

Much of the time, untroubled integration of expectations and desires guides our behavior: when what we want is what we can reasonably expect, or what we want to avoid is unlikely or impossible. With repeated experience, such behavior becomes habitual, or relatively mindless. However, often enough, integration is troublesome or problematic (hence, "problematic integration"). Communication is largely the construction, negotiation, and reconstruction of these expectations and evaluations and their (problematic) integration (Babrow, 1992, 2007).

The theory describes several basic forms of PI. First, we often face *uncertainty* about the outcomes of our actions; the hazier the likelihood of an outcome, and the more valuable it is (positively or negatively), the more likely we are to fret and communicate about the situation (Babrow, 2007; Babrow & Matthias, 2009). Second, even if the likelihood of an outcome is very clear to us, we are troubled when (a) the likelihood is very low and the outcome highly desirable, or (b) the outcome is both highly likely and highly undesirable (Babrow, 1992). In terms of the theory, this *divergence* of expectation and desire is troubling and stirs up rumination and communication as we worry, yearn, complain, or commiserate. Third, meanings are troublesome when we are *ambivalent*; believing that an act will result in both highly desirable and highly undesirable outcomes provokes hesitation, troubled thought, and communication (Babrow, 1992). Fourth, and finally, the meaning of action is troublesome and evokes thought and communication to the extent that we want something to be true that we know is *impossible*, or to the extent we want to avoid something and know it is *certain* to be or to occur (Babrow, 1992).

In addition to identifying the major forms of problematic meanings, or PI, noted above, the theory illuminates the role of communication in grappling with these difficulties. For one, it postulates that communication is a fundamental *medium* through which we learn about the world and its frequently problematic meanings (Babrow, 1992, 1995). As such, communication itself can be a source of PI. For example, we might worry (i.e., experience uncertainty or divergence) or be certain that something we must say will cause the message receiver pain. Alternatively, we might experience ambivalence in speaking, such as when what we have to say is very helpful for our self, but painful for the person we address. Fortunately, communication is also perhaps our most important *resource* for coping with PI. We use communication to inform, persuade, council, confess, forgive, comfort, console, commiserate, cooperate, negotiate, reframe, reconstruct, create, and much, much more, when faced with troublesome meanings. This extraordinary, and potentially unlimited, range of communicative responses reflects the likelihood that, even in the most trying circumstances, there are ways to cope with PI that we have not yet thought of. In other words, there are possibilities available to us if we can see beyond our habits of thought and the limitations of responses suggested by our group or culture. And, finally, the theory recognizes that some problematic meanings are irresolvable, irreducible challenges of human being (e.g., human fallibility, innocent suffering, conflicts between profoundly important values). In view of these existential challenges, communicating with humility and compassion takes on greater importance. The following illustrates some of these aspects of the theory through a millennial's reflection on the advent of Donald Trump's presidency.

Millennials in the Age of President Trump: Problematic Integration Theory's

Practical Implications for Communication

The context. By many accounts, the 2016 US presidential campaign was extraordinary. The primary season featured an unusually large slate of 17 Republican candidates participating in the primaries or at least one debate (Republican Party, 2016). And, of course, the primary contests culminated in the nomination of Donald Trump, a surprisingly self-assured candidate given that he had no previous experience in government; with considerable acumen, he reconstructed the meaning of this inexperience by positioning himself as a Washington outsider at a time when many citizens were unhappy with the federal government. On the Democratic side, the primaries quickly whittled 12 candidates down to two: Secretary of State Hillary Clinton and Senator Bernie Sanders. Many considered Clinton among the best qualified candidates for president in the nation's history. By contrast, "(m)any journalists and observers regarded Sanders, who was 74 years old, a self-described democratic socialist, and not even a formal member of the Democratic Party for most of his career, as an unlikely challenger to Clinton" (Shelley & Hitt, 2016, p. 272). And yet, Sanders won 23 primary contests to Clinton's 34.[1]

Historically, young adults have been the least likely to vote of all age groups. However, in the 2016 election, millennials were the only age cohort that increased voter turnout over the previous election. In all, analysts estimated that 46–50% of eligible voters under 30 years old cast a ballot (File, 2017). Exit polling by Tufts University's Center for Information and Research on Civic Learning and Engagement (CIRCLE) found that 55% of these voters cast their ballot for Clinton, whereas 37% reported voting for Trump (Youth Voting, n.d.). However, this apparently

---

[1] The numbers include primaries in 50 states, the District of Columbia, US territories, and a category of "citizens abroad."

lopsided preference is small in comparison to primary voting results. During the primaries, millennials expressed enormously greater support for Sanders than the other two front-runners. CIRCLE's analysis of 21 state primaries for which there was exit polling data, and that held primaries before June 1 (primaries ended on June 14), found that over two million people aged 17–29 reported voting for Sanders.[2] By contrast, less than 1.6 million young people voted for Clinton and Trump, combined.

Being a millennial in the age of President Trump: A narrative. Like many of my fellow millennials, I (P.B.) was an enthusiastic Sanders supporter. However, when Clinton won the nomination, I supported her. Indeed, I canvased for the Democratic candidates during the primaries and general presidential election, knocking on voters' doors in Athens and Nelsonville, Ohio. On the evening of the election, I watched the returns with my roommates, all but one of whom supported Clinton. However, when it looked like the vote would be close, we began to experience an anxious divergence of our expectations and desires: Clinton's chances of winning began to shrink as Trump's chances increased. Communication, in this case the election coverage, served as a conduit or medium through which we learned distressing news about the vote. As the evening wore on, the returns suggested an ever greater possibility that what we desired would be lost and that what we dreaded would become reality. We alternated between reassuring one another (and ourselves) that the tide would turn again and predictions of catastrophe. As the evening wore on, our expectations diverged ever more from our desire, until the catastrophe looked certain. As certainty approached, we could not bear the experience any more, at which point, using communication as a resource for coping with the mounting PI, we turned off the news coverage and sought escape by watching *Arrested Development*, trying not to think of the irony of the title at this moment in history.

It was a hell of a thing to experience the collective hope of a generation come crashing down on election night, 2016. Like many other millennials, I was paralyzed with shock and gloom when it became clear that Donald Trump would be the next president. The majority of my generation felt deeply betrayed. How could the country that raised us to expect so much have just elected the least qualified candidate to lead us? On issue after issue, the future we hoped for was in doubt (uncertainty) or seemed much less likely (divergence). In bleakest moments, we gave in to despair in the certainty of loss. To cope, we relied on communication, gathering for discussion in the coffee shops of our generation: social media. As the painful divergence increased, as bleak certainties gained ground in our imaginations, our online communication was flooded with proclamations of anger and

---

[2] In over 20 states and the District of Columbia, 17-year olds can vote in primaries if they will be 18 by the general election (Primary voting at age 17, n.d.).

disgust, disgruntled memes, and links to apocalyptic news articles. The more privileged among us could not reconcile with what had just happened (for powerful alternative responses among African Americans, see Coates, 2017; Saturday Night Live, 2016). It felt as if finding the right meme or article, finding the right words to share or say, could somehow magically undo the election, could somehow redeem our values and rescue the future. Maybe the new president would finally say something so undeniably awful, it would penetrate the adoration and grim acceptance that had won him the electoral college (although not the popular election) and stiffen public resistance. But each outrageous utterance was met with applause or the most charitable interpretations by his generally older supporters. Our sour disappointment increased as his foolhardy failure of a plan for governance took shape. For many of us, problematic integration—diverging expectations and desires, alternating with deeply unpleasant uncertainties and certainties—became the everyday grind.

Our collective online chatter, coupled with my own small-town setting, had created an echo chamber of nihilistic despair. Everywhere I went, every post I saw, every article I read, and every person I talked to confirmed that we had arrived at the other end of the kaleidoscope. Fellow anti-Trumpers and I could do nothing but lament the state of the union, while Trump's supporters celebrated in ways that reminded us why we were wallowing in the first place. I had repetitive arguments with my one pro-Trump roommate, neither of us budging an inch. I clung to diverging expectation and desire alternating with cataclysmic certainty that our country's future now lay in the hands of a malignant narcissist (Lee, 2017). At the same time, my roommate embodied nonproblematic integration of expectations and desires: reveling in joyous anticipation of a reclaimed Washington swamp, expulsion of illegal alien murderers and rapists, and an America returned to greatness. Invariably, I wanted to push the argument, but my roommate would end it with a reminder of who won the election and his inalienable right to tell me to "F— off."

But most of my cohort, most of those closest to me, felt lost in PI, floating aimlessly in a world without justice or dignity. We had been defanged, and worse. Not only was Trump advocating policies likely to gut our future (e.g., withdrawing the US from the Paris Climate Agreement, overturning the Affordable Care Act), he and his cronies were also eroding the distinction between fact and fantasy, and between groundless, flamboyant assertion and careful argument. How could anyone reasonably form and adjust beliefs and desires, and how could anyone rationally cope with diverging expectation and desire, uncertainty, and the like, in such times? In iconic representations of this challenge, Oxford Dictionaries identified "post-truth" as its word of the year (Flood, 2016), and, with apparent seriousness, Trump presidential advisor Kellyanne Conway introduced "alternative facts" into public discourse (in an episode of *Meet the Press* that aired on January 22, 2017).

The latter became almost a flashbulb memory for many millennials. If we had truly entered a post-truth era, if "alternative fact" was not an oxymoron, how could communication be a resource for coping with PI—other than creating a parallel universe into which only the wishful and delusional could escape?

In a world in which facts are irrelevant, proof is heresy, and insult is applauded, only angry passion is noble. In such a world, malevolent ignorance rules. Millennial Sanders supporters felt powerless. Even truly inspirational protests, such as the Women's March the day after Trump's inauguration, seemed to cause only the slightest dents in his chainmail.[3] And so, the first half of 2017 was a perfect storm of divergence, ambivalence, and alternating uncertainty about the future and certainty that we were lost; our generation was plagued by problematic integration and cursed with social and political immobility. Our only relief from unrelenting PI was communication: commiserating among our friends about outrageous tweets and mocking the president along with the comedic news on *Last Week Tonight*, *The Daily Show*, and *Full Frontal with Samantha Bee*. Aside from the most minute and personal forms of resistance and the collective sarcasm, there seemed to be little we could do, and we felt hesitant to do much.

In the second half of 2017, however, we started to come alive. We felt bolstered by the investigation into Russian meddling in the US election, but what, to me, has been most personally rousing was watching the meteoric rise of the Parkland survivors. Here were members of my own generation sticking it to cynicism and matching the ferocity of guns-for-all media bullies. The Parkland activists had taken the very platform that I had relegated to commiserating with the Bernie-minded and smack-talking to Trumpers and used it to start a fire under the rear of every politician and media outlet that attempted to undermine them. These young people were utterly inspiring. Finally, progressive liberals were stepping up to demand better government. Between the Parkland survivors and the snowballing Russia investigation, we were buzzing again. PI was giving way to renewed hope.

In the first half of 2017, I was wrought by lethargic pessimism. My friends and I complained about what was going on, but political discourse had become nothing more than commiseration. Now, later in the year, another roommate and I were excitedly swapping news stories and links to the explosion of ever bolder satirical send-ups of the Trump White House. The discussions, once dominated by grievance over the impossibility of our dreams, began to morph into possibility, into

---

[3] We (P.B. and A.B.) attended the D.C. march with a childhood friend, a young woman, and her parents, where we carried and saw signs with forceful expressions of converging beliefs and values: "Women's Rights Are Human Rights," "Love Still Trumps Hate," "Women Are The Wall," "Make America Think Again," and "The First Female President Is Watching."

what could be and what was being done. My values seemed once again realizable as I was turned on to fabulous news outlets and grass roots voices through *The Nation* (a magazine my family had always subscribed to but that I was now reading), *Pod Save America,* and *Majority 54.* I began enthusiastically sharing this information with friends and Facebook followers, encouraging them to do the same.

The slivers of hope afforded to us by each new indictment and conviction in the Russia investigation and message from the Parkland survivors had blown the doors wide open. The impossible was not so impossible anymore. The certainty of a lost future gave way to uncertainty, and from there to hope. Gears had started to turn, and we were preaching the gospel everywhere we could: in the privacy of our homes, in classrooms, at parties, through the Internet. My generation has often been characterized as over-reliant on mediated social networks. But now we were using this defining feature of "connectedness" to fight back. The "powers that be" wanted us to feel that things are the way that they are (youth have no power), and that they are that way because they cannot be changed (youth power is impossible). But we were coming to a real truth of the universe: the actual fact that the only constant is change. We had awoken to the undeniable fact that we are that change.

Observations to Prompt Conversation

The preceding narrative is replete with examples of PI and its interplay with communication. Here we will point out a few illustrations in the hope of stimulating further reflection and discussion. To begin, communication on election eve was nonproblematic, as expectations appeared to be converging with desires. Millennial Clinton supporters believed she would win the election, election news was simply the medium through which we received information confirming that expectation, and talk between friends anticipated celebration. However, voting coverage eventually was a medium through which expectant millennials began to see the election tide turn in Trump's favor. Millennials then began to experience diverging expectation and desire, which ratcheted up as the apparent possibility of a Trump victory increased. Communication then became a resource in coping with the mounting PI, as millennials commiserated and reassured one another. Indeed, the theory recognizes that, the more important the values at stake, the greater the PI, and the more important communication becomes in efforts to deal with troubled meaning (Babrow, 1992).

Eventually, as the news brought more and more evidence that Trump might be elected, many of us could not bear to watch our worst fear become reality. Some could no longer talk, as we were beset by ambivalence: we felt strongly inclined to use interaction with friends as a resource for coping with PI, but we could say nothing that was not painful. Communication itself had become a source of PI.

In the immediate aftermath of the election, millennial Sanders and Clinton supporters experienced the certainty of loss, uncertainty about the future, and diverging expectations and desires about all sorts of specific issues. For example, although President Trump is a climate science denier, many millennials understand the evidence that he either does not know or ignores. Literally thousands of studies, conducted and reviewed by researchers from 197 countries (Intergovernmental Panel on Climate Change, 2014), support the conclusion that "human activities, especially emissions of greenhouse gases, are the dominant cause of the observed" fact that we are living in the warmest period "in the history of modern civilization" (US Global Climate Research Program, 2017). These millennials know that, as a result, the planet is on the brink of numerous catastrophic climate tipping points: thresholds in the climate's homeostatic mechanisms beyond which incremental, linear change becomes catastrophic nonlinear transformation. Many also know that we appear to be in the midst of the sixth major planetary extinction event, this one caused not by an asteroid hitting the earth but by humans, that "weediest of species" (Kolbert, 2014, p. 6). And many millennials understand that the changes currently underway in the natural world will soon become irreversible if we do not act (Humphrey, 2006; IPCC, 2014). Hence, the diverging expectations and desires, intermingling with alternating uncertainty and certainty of a bleak future. Hence, the obsessive turn to social media to commiserate and complain, the sense of hopelessness, the nihilistic despair, and the wishful search for some magical meme or (re)tweet that might rescue hope. Hence, the grace and power of the righteous demand for a government and society that respects the urgent need for evidence, careful argument, judicious weighing of competing values, and the demand for appropriate action. Hence, our gratitude for the courage of climate scientists like Katharine Hayhoe, James Hansen, and Michael Mann, and the courage of the students leading the March for Our Lives.

In short, Problematic Integration Theory encourages us to search for possibilities available to us if we can see beyond our habits of thought and those of our group or culture. Applying the theory to the experience of millennials in the age of President Trump illuminates a generation at first gripped by despair when it accepted the age-old belief that the young have no power, and then finding its power when it saw beyond this dangerous but fragile construction. Of course, seeing beyond deeply engrained beliefs and values is difficult in itself, and it is even more challenging because troubling meanings evoke both strong emotion and complex weaves of uncertainty and inconsistency, both within our own mind and in interacting with others. For these reasons, the theory urges us to temper the immediacy of thought and feeling with the understanding that there is always more than meets the eye. This is no easy task, but the likelihood we will accomplish it grows with our willingness to observe, listen, learn, and speak. Finally,

PI theory reminds us to be humble and compassionate in facing these struggles, both in dealing with ourselves and in communicating with others, because everyone must grapple with the challenges of divergence, ambivalence, uncertainty, and impossibility. All humans tread this path. All humans rely on communication at every turn. Indeed, this is what makes us human. Recognizing these truths may be our best chance of reaching across the divides that threaten not only our nation, but also the web of life as we know it. In the face of the uncertainties and diverging expectations and desires that millennials are inheriting from parents and grandparents, love must trump hate if we are to deal with the deeply problematic meanings that will constitute our future.

Discussion Questions

1. What are some examples of specific forms of problematic integration that millennials experienced when Trump was elected: examples of diverging expectation and desire, ambivalence, uncertainty, and impossibility (or unpleasant certainty)? Use the case study as well as your own personal experiences and observations to answer this question and those that follow.

2. How have some of the specific problematic integrations identified in answer to the previous question created difficulties for millennials as they think about their trust in the country, the electoral process, and their future? What feelings have been aroused? How might these thoughts and feelings make it difficult to decide how to react to the election and act to achieve their desires?

3. Problematic integration often compels us to communicate, but it can also make communication difficult. How did millennials experience the drive to communicate in the aftermath of the election? What made this communication difficult? How did you experience these troublesome communication dynamics? How might they be overcome?

4. The author of the narrative about being a millennial when Trump was elected president eventually found inspiration and hope through witnessing the actions of the Parkland students. How did the Parkland students' example change the narrator's outlook? How might the narrator, other millennials you know, or you yourself have used communication to regain a sense of hope for the future, and how can millennials sustain this hopefulness and sense of power?

5. In what ways might humility and compassion be necessary for effective communication at this difficult time in the coming of age of millennials?

REFERENCES

Babrow, A. S. (1992). Communication and problematic integration: Understanding diverging probability and value, ambiguity, ambivalence, and impossibility. *Communication Theory, 2,* 95–130.

Babrow, A. S. (1995). Communication and problematic integration: Milan Kundera's "Lost Letters" in *The Book of Laughter and Forgetting. Communication Monographs, 62,* 283–300.

Babrow, A. S. (2007). Problematic integration theory. In B. B. Whaley & W. Samter (Eds.), *Explaining communication: Contemporary theories and exemplars (pp. 181–200).* Mahwah, NJ: Lawrence Erlbaum.

Babrow, A.S. (2016). Problematic integration theory. In C. Berger & M. Roloff (Eds.), *International encyclopedia of interpersonal communication* (pp. 1387–1395). Hoboken, NJ: Wiley-Blackwell.

Babrow, A. S., & Matthias, M. S. (2009). Generally unseen challenges in uncertainty management: An application of problematic integration theory. In T. Afifi &. W. Afifi (Eds.), *Uncertainty, information management and disclosure decisions: Theories and applications* (pp. 9–25). London: Routledge.

Babrow, A.S., & Striley, K.M. (2014). Problematic integration theory and uncertainty management theory. In D.O. Braithewaite & P. Schrodt (Eds.), *Engaging theories in interpersonal communication* (2nd ed., pp. 103–114). Los Angeles, CA: Sage.

Coates, T. (2017, October). The first white president. *The Atlantic.* Retrieved from https://www.theatlantic.com/magazine/archive/2017/10/the-first-white-president-ta-nehisi-coates/537909/.

File, T. (2017). Voting in America: A look at the 2016 presidential election. United States Census Bureau. Retrieved from https://www.census.gov/newsroom/blogs/random-samplings/2017/05/voting_in_america.html.

Fishbein, M., & Ajzen, I. (1975). *Belief, attitude, intention, and behavior: An introduction to theory and research.* Reading, MA: Addison-Wesley.

Flood, A. (2016, November 15). "Post-truth" named word of the year by Oxford Dictionaries. *The Guardian.* Retrieved July 11, 2018, from www.theguardian.com.

Greene, J.O. (1984). Evaluating cognitive explanations of communication phenomena. *Quarterly Journal of Speech, 70,* 241–254.

Humphrey, M. (2006). Democratic legitimacy, public justification and environmental direct action. *Political Studies, 54(2),* 310–327. doi. org/10.1111/j.1467-9248.2006.00602.x

Intergovernmental Panel on Climate Change. (2014). *Climate change 2014 Synthesis report summary for policymakers.* Retrieved from http://www.ipcc. ch/pdf/assessment-report/ar5/syr/AR5_SYR_FINAL_SPM.pdf.

Kahneman, D. (2011). *Thinking fast and slow.* New York: Farrar, Straus, and Giroux.

Kolbert, E. (2014). *The sixth extinction.* New York, NY: Henry Holt.

Lee, B. (2017). *The dangerous case of Donald Trump: 27 psychiatrists and mental health experts assess a president.* New York, NY: Thomas Dunne Books.

Pearce, W.B. (1989). *Communication and the human condition.* Carbondale: Southern Illinois Press.

Primary voting at age 17. (n.d.). *Fair vote.* Retrieved from http://www.fairvote. org/primary_voting_at_age_17#facts_17_year_old_primary_voting.

Republican Party presidential candidates. (2016). Retrieved from https://en.wikipedia.org/wiki.

Saturday Night Live Election Eve 2016. (Nov. 11, 2016). Retrieved from https://www.youtube.com/watch?v=SHG0ezLiVGc.

Shelley, F.M., & Hitt, A.M. (2016). The millennial vote in 2016 Democratic primary elections. *Southeastern Geographer, 56,* 272–282.

US Global Climate Research Program. (2017). *Climate science special report (NCA4): Executive summary.* Retrieved from https://science2017. globalchange.gov/chapter/executive-summary/.

Youth Voting. (n.d.). Center for information & research on civic learning and engagement. Retrieved from https://civicyouth.org/quick-facts/ youth-voting/.

Chapter 6

A Communication Privacy Management Analysis of an End of Life Admission

Jeffrey T. Child, Ph.D., *Kent State University* | Cristin A. Compton, Ph.D., *Kent State University*

As individuals age, privacy concerns adapt and change, in conjunction with developmental and life-course changes (Petronio, 2002). Some of these changes can be identity-threatening and hard to talk about for aging seniors. For example, having to rely more on family for finances and bill payment, transportation, healthcare, personal care, and daily life issues can be difficult to discuss because they often result in adjustments to family disclosure norms and shifts in the kinds of private information that gets shared within a family (Egbert, Child, Lin, Savery, & Bosley, 2017). This case study applies Communication Privacy Management (CPM) Theory to understand the mutual needs of privacy and disclosure in the context of deathbed disclosures and unfinished privacy management business. We first highlight the Communication Privacy Management theoretical framework and then discuss a case involving changes in privacy management systems that may occur in families due to unexpected deathbed disclosures.

Communication Privacy Management Theory

Communication Privacy Management Theory (Petronio, 2002) deals with how people communicatively manage private information with others. The theory defines private information as any content that makes someone feel a degree of vulnerability or sensitivity at the prospect of sharing it with others (Child & Petronio, 2015; Petronio, 2013). Private information is not topically based, since the issues marked as more or less private vary from person to person (Child & Petronio, 2011; Petronio, 2018). For example, some families are uncomfortable talking about sex or religion, whereas other families might freely discuss these topics, yet mark other topics, such as in-depth financial discussions or sexual, political, or occupational identities, as private information (Child, 2015).

Issues of ownership and control are central to Communication Privacy Management Theory (Child & Starcher, 2016; Petronio, 2002). Put simply, people feel they have the right to own who has access to their private information. People control their private information through rules. At the individual level, biological sex and culture exert a core (or more stable and predictable) influence on privacy rule development across time (Petronio, 2013). One prominent example of a cultural-level influence on privacy is the family unit (Child, Duck, Andrews, Butauski, & Petronio, 2015; Petronio, 2010). Families develop unique patterns about how much private information gets shared between members of the unit (the interior family privacy orientation), as well as members outside of it (the exterior family privacy orientation) (Child & Westermann, 2013; Morr Serewicz & Canary, 2008; Petronio, 2010). Motivational, contextual, and risk-benefit ratio calculations are all catalyst-based (or more variable) influences on privacy rule development (Beam, Child, Hutchens, & Hmielowski, 2017; Petronio, 2013). As people age, older adults often exchange privacy needs for healthcare benefits (Petronio & Kovach, 1997). Thus, privacy norms and rules change and vary across a lifespan (Child et al., 2015; Egbert et al., 2017; Petronio, 2002).

When someone discloses or shares private information with others it moves from an individual to a collective expectation and obligation for the future management and control of the co-owned private information (Child, Pearson, & Petronio, 2009). Effective privacy rules at the collective level include specifications about who else can or cannot know the private information (i.e., linkage rules), how much depth and breadth about the co-owned information can and cannot be revealed to others (i.e., permeability rules), and when a co-owner should and should not check back with the original owner of the private information before sharing of it with someone else (i.e., co-ownership rules) (Child & Petronio, 2015; Petronio, 2002). Privacy dilemmas occur when people must choose between honoring a request to keep something private versus determining if it is in the best interest to share the private information in ways not desired by the original owner (Petronio, 2018; Petronio, Jones, & Morr, 2003).

Communication Privacy Management Theory is systems-based because it accounts for a mechanism to correct and readjust privacy in light of breakdowns. Because Communication Privacy Management Theory includes the negotiation of privacy rules between an original owner and co-owners, it places communication and dialogue as central to the theory. When people clearly negotiate and honor expectations for the future management of private information, privacy breakdowns are less likely to occur (Child, Haridakis, & Petronio, 2012). However, sometimes people assume, rather than clearly specify, co-ownership rules and expectations, leading to privacy breakdowns or turbulence (Steuber & McLaren, 2015). Boundary turbulence reflects any necessary readjustments that must occur with privacy rules in order to recalibrate the privacy management system and prevent future breakdowns from occurring (Child, Petronio, Agyeman-Budu, & Westermann, 2011).

Deathbed Disclosure Case Study

The case below highlights how unexpected life changes, like discovering you have an aggressive form of cancer, impacts the sharing of private information within families. Recognizing that a limited amount of time exists in one's life can recalibrate privacy management priorities. Deathbed disclosures impact the entire family system, as members of the unit strive to make sense of new information, how to respond to evolving concerns, and ways to restabilize new privacy norms post-deathbed disclosure. Below, we describe the turning point in a family's disclosure processes, the aftershock to the family after a secret is exposed, and the restabilization process of disclosure and communication practices between family members.

The Turning Point

Chris, a recently retired 64-year-old man, discovered he had an aggressive form of cancer after a minor medical mishap that required a doctor's attention. Peggy, his partner of close to 20 years, was worried not only about her spouse's health and well-being, but about the couple's financial situation. Historically, Chris had not shared any detailed financial information with Peggy and, in fact, actively kept it from her. For example, Chris demanded that Peggy not retrieve mail from the shared mailbox. Additionally, when Peggy inquired about their finances, Chris told her that they were financially secure and not to worry. Despite Chris' assurances, Peggy worried about their finances and repeatedly asked for information. Always, Chris would provide a vague platitude (i.e., "everything is fine") and change the subject. With Chris potentially unable to make financial decisions because of his diagnosis, Peggy's lack of knowledge of their shared financial status caused her great distress and anxiety.

Chris shared his diagnosis with his four children from a previous marriage. Disclosing personal and potentially threating information with family was rare for him. Chris often avoided sharing overly sensitive information with his family, particularly his children. Chris also tended to be emotionally reserved with his family; he associated being vulnerable and sensitive as indictors of weakness. Chris's emotional reservations and reticence to disclose personal information upheld traditional masculine norms; disclosing this information could jeopardize his masculinized identity and his role as father and head of the household in their traditionally paternalistic family unit (Trujillo, 1991).

Up until Chris's revelation, Jordan, Chris's second child, had often been a liaison for information sharing between Chris and the rest of the family. However, while Jordan and Chris had a somewhat close relationship, it did not include frequent conversations marked by in-depth disclosures. Rather, it was marked by occasional phone calls to check in or for Chris to vent about something going on in his life. However, two years prior to Chris' diagnosis, Jordan had changed their interaction style, becoming vulnerable and disclosing to Chris and the family that he identified as gay. Jordan's disclosure was risky because the family held conservative and religious views and were not welcoming to nontraditional identities. Following this disclosure, Jordan and Chris maintained and deepened their mutually respectful and loving relationship.

After Chris revealed his diagnosis, Jordan returned home, recognizing that Chris needed assistance and that their time together was limited. As Chris became less able to walk, he needed more help with his daily routines. Specifically, Jordan started gathering the daily mail, managing the bills, and writing checks to creditors. As Jordan had more access to Chris's bills, he started asking Chris more questions about the nature of his financial state. Chris revealed to Jordan the truth about Chris and Peggy's finances. The situation was much worse than he had told Peggy; their house was double-mortgaged, they were in significant credit card debt, and medical bills were streaming in and not being paid on time.

Jordan was familiar with Chris's masculinized communication style, particularly his tendency to avoid conversations that were potentially emotionally threatening (i.e., financial insecurity) (Guerrero, Jones, & Boburka, 2006). Jordan, on the other hand, could not imagine withholding information about shared finances from a spouse. However, Jordan recognized that discussing personal and potentially threatening information would be a significant shift in his relationship with Peggy. While Jordan and Peggy had traditionally been cordial, they spoke infrequently and rarely, if ever, had emotionally charged conversations about such private issues.

Jordan was managing mixed messages between his father's implied privacy boundaries, a history of a cordial, but distant stepchild/stepparent relationship with Peggy, and his own self-understanding of what appropriate information should be shared between romantic couples (Compton, 2016). Because Chris did not explicitly instruct Jordan to keep this information from Peggy, Jordan chose to rely on his perception of his identity as liaison and his self-perception as a truthful person and revealed everything to Peggy.

The Aftershock

Peggy was surprised and hurt when she learned about her financial situation, particularly when the source was her stepson, rather than her partner. Peggy acknowledged Jordan's liaison status in the family and demanded that he confront Chris about his lack of transparency. Jordan declined, as the violation was between Peggy and Chris and did not involve him. Jordan and Peggy discussed the benefits and risks of her confronting Chris about their finances, given his rapidly deteriorating health. Peggy chose to confront and seek more information about why Chris withheld information, which resulted in Chris denying the problem and ceasing all conversations between them on the topic.

Peggy realized that she was not going to learn anything from Chris, so she turned to Jordan to get more information about their assets and liabilities and engage in sense-making about the newly acquired information. Jordan shared everything that he had learned during his return home. However, Peggy had little experience with managing the family finances and had numerous questions. Jordan had only recently become familiar with the situation and found himself unable to answer most of her questions. Peggy called creditors and financial institutions associated with the debt and discovered that her name did not appear on any of the accounts except the mortgage, effectively blocking her from learning anything else until Chris passed.

The Restabilization

After Chris passed away, Peggy and Jordan needed to address a complex financial situation and a significant amount of debt. Peggy was the beneficiary on Chris's life insurance policies, which awarded her more than enough to repay all of the debt. Because Peggy's name did not appear on most of the debt, Peggy's attorney advised her that she was not financially obligated to repay anything except the mortgage. Jordan told Peggy that even though she was not legally required to repay the debt, she had benefitted from the purchases Chris made (i.e., cars, furniture, clothing, electronics). Peggy was still hurt from Chris's choice to withhold important information from her, which she attributed to Chris not trusting her with important information. Ultimately, Peggy decided to follow her attorney's advice and did not repay anything.

Jordan felt that this decision did not reflect Chris's intent and what Chris had communicated to Jordan when he initially revealed his financial situation. However, Peggy had the authority to make financial decisions without Jordan's input. Over time, Peggy shared less and less with Jordan about financial issues and eventually no longer sought his advice. When Jordan inquired about her financial situation or asked for updates, Peggy responded in a way quite similar to how Chris had responded to her inquiries: "things are fine."

Peggy and Jordan's relationship restabilized into its previously cordial, distant, and superficial interaction style. Because of the turning point of Chris's passing and the turbulence of the management of personal financial information, Jordan was aware that the once-open boundary had been closed firmly by Peggy.

Unpacking the Case Through the Lens of Communication Privacy Management Theory

Privacy boundaries adapt and change over time for a number of reasons and to meet evolving situations, needs, and concerns (Petronio, 2002; 2013). This case presents how one unexpected change, the rapidly declining health of a family member, served as a catalyst-based influence in privacy management adjustments within a family setting (Child et al, 2015; Petronio, 2013; 2010).

Consider how Chris managed private information with his family prior to any health-related concerns. Communication Privacy Management Theory supports the idea that the social construction of biological sex impacts how people engage in opening up, or closing down, individual privacy boundaries (Petronio, 2018). Specifically, ponder the following:

- How are the norms of upholding masculinity inherent in the ways that Chris, in general, managed his identity through disclosure or concealment of private information with others?
- How could Peggy's identity as a woman, a stepparent, and Chris's partner, affect Chris's decisions about disclosure?
- How do we see privacy management norms evolve, and yet also remain consistent, for Chris in the context of revealing sensitive financial information within his family?

Communication Privacy Management Theory contends that risk-benefit ratio calculations factor into the level of comfort (more or less) that individuals feel about opening up their privacy boundaries with others (Child et al., 2009; Child & Petronio, 2015; Petronio, 2010). Again, ponder the following:

- What risks and benefits do you think explain why Chris decided to open up to his son, rather than his partner, about the sensitive financial-based information?
- How did Jordan manage the private information shared with him from his father?

- What might be the risks and benefits of Jordan sharing this information with his siblings?
- What risks and benefits do you perceive impacted his decision to share the private information with his stepparent versus to not talk about it with her?

Communication Privacy Management Theory supports the idea that the most effective way to prevent breakdowns in privacy is to actively negotiate privacy rules with others when sharing sensitive information (Child et al, 2012; Petronio, 2002; 2013). Negotiation allows co-owners to know how to manage private information in desired ways (Child & Petronio, 2015). This case demonstrates that when people do not actively negotiate what information can be shared with whom, people rely on their own disclosure rules. Yet again, please ponder the following:

- Is Jordan to blame for the privacy breakdown between Chris and Peggy?
- Do you think Chris expected Jordan to share the newly acquired private information about his finances with Peggy? If so, why? If not, why not?
- How did both Chris and Peggy rely on Jordan as a third party to work through uncomfortable private disclosures with one another?
- Have you ever been a liaison for dealing with sensitive private information? If so, how?
- What choices would you have made about the management of your parents' private financial information?

Privacy boundaries evolve in light of unexpected situations and circumstances (Petronio, 2013). This case highlights the possible privacy dilemmas that can occur during times of crisis. It also elucidates how a privacy management system may recalibrate in light of deathbed disclosures. For a final time, please ponder the following:

- What about the privacy restabilization process surprised you?
- What recommendations would you give to Jordan if he wanted to reopen a privacy boundary with Peggy?
- What kinds of events in your own family (besides deathbed disclosures) would serve as catalysts to change privacy boundaries in significant ways?
- How do you think the privacy boundaries would restabilize after resolving the unexpected event?

We have considered the questions posed and have some thoughts on how to approach them. You are not limited to our insights and are encouraged to make your own connections. Norms, privacy or otherwise, are established over time.

Sex roles can significantly influence how people understand how they are "supposed" to communicate with each other (think about the division of labor of household tasks). In previous generations, it was men who were generally understood as the head of the house, the decision makers, and in charge of the finances of the household. These "norms" became a part of Chris's identity which in turn affected how he created and maintained privacy boundaries. Something else to think about is how old Chris and Peggy are and the social norms of their generation. Normative roles associated with sex and/or gender identity have significantly shifted over time; all these issues (and other intersectional identities we have not discussed) come into play in understanding the choices that Chris, Peggy, and Jordan make regarding privacy management.

Another interesting component to CPM Theory is the notion of risk-benefit analysis that elucidates privacy management choices. Chris had reinforced the notion that there was no sensitive, problematic, or vulnerable financial information to share with Peggy for their entire marriage. Because their financial situation was so problematic, there was a great deal of risk (with few benefits) for Chris to open up and negate what he had been actively telling Peggy for years. However, because of Chris's imminent death, there was risk to his loved ones if he stayed silent in maintaining his privacy boundaries as he always had. Chris was facing a privacy dilemma. To manage this situation, Chris recognized that admitting financial vulnerability to Jordan was significantly less risky than it would have been to admit anything to Peggy. Peggy, too, likely perceived that Jordan faced less interpersonal risk if he discussed financial issues on her behalf with Chris. Ultimately Chris and Peggy put Jordan in the liaison position and compelled him to co-own sensitive and private information because they did not have established communicative norms for talking about vulnerable topics with each other. Chris was forced to open his privacy boundary in uncharacteristic ways, but to an individual who Chris perceived had less to lose.

While end-of-life processes make people vulnerable, significantly changing family norms related to disclosures makes family communication in this situation an even more intense adjustment (Child et al, 2015; Egbert et al., 2017). This case allows us to see a privacy management trajectory marked by a more closed and protective privacy boundary, the deathbed disclosure significantly altering and opening up the privacy boundary, and then a shift, post breakdown, back to a less open disclosure system. Thus, in this case, we see how privacy boundaries shift and change over time and what circumstances might necessitate such changes.

Discussion Questions

1. What kinds of issues are most commonly marked as private information in your own family and why do you think they are hard to discuss openly?

2. Have you observed any shifts or changes in what you are willing to disclose within your family as you have gotten older? Why do you think some things are easier or harder to discuss in your family?

3. What kinds of end-of-life issues would you like to be able to discuss more openly with your family?

REFERENCES

Beam, M. A., Child, J. T., Hutchens, M. J., & Hmielowski, J.D. (2017). Context collapse and privacy management: Diversity in Facebook friends increases online news reading and sharing. *New Media & Society.* Advance online publication. doi: 10.1177/146144817714790

Child, J. T. (2015). Opening closed doors: Managing identity and privacy with social media. In D.O. Braithwaite & J.T. Wood (Eds.), *Casing interpersonal communication: Case studies in personal and social relationships* (2nd ed., pp 75–80). Dubuque, IA: Kendall Hunt.

Child, J. T., Duck, A. R., Andrews, L. A., Butauski, M., & Petronio, S. (2015). Young adults' management of privacy on Facebook with multiple generations of family members. *Journal of Family Communication, 15,* 349–367. doi:10.1080/1527431.2015.1076425

Child, J. T., Haridakis, P. M., & Petronio, S. (2012). Blogging privacy rule orientations, privacy management, and content deletion practices: The variability of online privacy management activity at different stages of social media use. *Computers in Human Behavior, 28,* 1859–1872. doi: 10.1016/j. chb.2012.05.004

Child, J. T., Pearson, J. C., & Petronio, S. (2009). Blogging, communication, and privacy management: Development of the blogging privacy management measure. *Journal of the American Society for Information Science and Technology, 60,* 2079–2094. doi: 10.1002/asi.21122

Child, J. T., & Petronio, S. (2011). Unpacking the paradoxes of privacy in CMC relationships: The challenges of blogging and relational communication on the internet. In K. B. Wright & L. M. Webb (Eds.), *Computer-mediated communication in personal relationships* (pp. 21–40). New York: Peter Lang.

Child, J. T., & Petronio, S. (2015). Privacy management matters in digital family communication. In C. J. Bruess (Ed.). *Family communication in the age of digital and social media* (pp. 32–54). New York, NY: Peter Lang.

Child, J. T., Petronio, S., Agyeman-Budu, E. A., & Westermann, D. A. (2011). Blog scrubbing: Exploring triggers that change privacy rules. *Computers in Human Behavior, 27,* 2017–2027. doi: 10.1016/j.chb.2011.05.009

Child, J. T., & Staracher, S. C. (2016). Fuzzy Facebook privacy boundaries: Exploring mediated lurking, vague-booking, and Facebook privacy management. *Computers in Human Behavior, 54,* 483–490. doi: 10.1016/j.chb.2015.08.035

Child, J. T., & Westermann, D. A. (2013). Let's be Facebook friends: Exploring parental Facebook friend requests from a Communication Privacy Management (CPM) perspective. *Journal of Family Communication, 13,* 46–59. doi: 10.1080/15267431.2012.742089

Compton, C. A. (2016). Managing mixed messages: Sexual identity management in a changing United States Workplace. *Management Communication Quarterly, 30,* 415–440. doi: 10.1177/0893318916641215

Egbert, N., Child, J. T., Lin, M., Savery, C., & Bosley, T. (2017). How older adults and their families perceive family talk about aging-related EOL issues: A dialectical analysis. *Behavioral Sciences, 7*(2), 1–8. doi: 10.3390/bs7020021

Guerrero, L., Jones, S.m & Boburka, R. (2006). Sex differences in emotional communication. In K. Dindia and D. Canary (Eds.), *Sex differences and similarities in communication* (pp. 242–261). Mahwah, MJ: Erlbaum.

MorrSerewicz, M. C., & Canary, D. J. (2008). Assessments of disclosure from the in-laws: Links among disclosure topics, family privacy orientations, and relational quality. *Journal of Social and Personal Relationships, 25,* 333–357. doi: 10.1077/0265407507087962

Petronio, S. (2002). *Boundaries of privacy: Dialectics of disclosure.* Albany, NY: State University of New York Press.

Petronio, S. (2010). Communication privacy management theory: What do we know about family privacy regulation? *Journal of Family Theory and Review, 2,* 175–196. doi: 10.1111/j.1756-2589.2010.00052.x

Petronio, S. (2013). Brief status report on communication privacy management theory. *Journal of Family Communication, 13,* 6–14. doi: 10.1080/15267431.2013.743426

Petronio, S. (2018). Communication privacy management theory: Understanding families. In D. O. Braithwaite, E. Suter, & K. Floyd (Eds.), *Engaging theories in family communication: Multiple perspectives* (2nd ed., pp. 87–97). Thousand Oaks, CA: Sage.

Petronio, S., Jones, S., & Morr, M. C. (2003). Family privacy dilemmas: Managing communication boundaries within family groups. In L.R. Frey (Ed.), *Group communication in context: Studies of bona fide groups* (pp. 23–55). Mahwah, NJ: Erlbaum.

Petronio, S., & Kovach, S. (1997). Managing privacy boundaries: Health providers' perceptions of resident care in Scottish nursing homes. *Journal of Applied Communication Research, 25,* 115–131. doi: 10.1080/00909889709365470

Steuber, K. R., & McLaren, R. M. (2015). Privacy recalibration in personal relationships: Rule usage before and after an incident of privacy turbulence. *Communication Quarterly, 63,* 345–364. doi: 10.1080/01463373.2015.1039717

Trujillo, N. (1991) Hegemonic masculinity on the mound: Media representations of Nolan Ryan and American sports culture. *Critical Studies in Mass Communication, 8,* 290–308. doi: 10.1080/15295039109366799

Chapter 7

Relational Dialectics Theory: "It is Important for Mom to Be True to Herself"

Diana Breshears, Ph.D., *University of the Free State, South Africa*
Dawn O. Braithwaite, Ph.D., *University of Nebraska-Lincoln*

Communication and Discursive Struggles

When we hear the term "discourse," we often picture some form of interpersonal communication, such as two friends engaging in a conversation. However, discourse also refers to ideologies, worldviews, and points of view (Baxter, 2011). For example, in the United States, many people place a strong value on the discourses of freedom and democracy, while in other cultures, discourses of cooperation and collectivity are more prominent. As we experience everyday life, we are inundated with many different discourses, and these discourses are often in competition with one another. Think about the current social conversation surrounding gun ownership in the United States. As people talk about their views on gun ownership, we recognize that these interactions can become heated very quickly. In these interactions, we can observe discourses that stress constitutional rights and individual freedom to own guns, as well as discourses that reflect the values of public safety and legislation favoring stricter gun control. We can observe how these different discourses play out in talk: in the media, on social media, and in conversations around the dinner table. Opposing discourses are all around us and are a normal part of life.

There are also opposing discourses present in our close relationships. A couple expecting their first child, for example, will negotiate cultural and personal discourses as they discuss whether or not one parent should become a stay-at-home parent, and, if so, who should fill that role. Cultural and personal discourses will also be at play when a family talks about how to best provide care for an older parent while respecting their boundaries and freedom to make their own choices, or when close friends navigate issues of privacy and what to reveal and conceal to others when one of them is experiencing mental health challenges (Suter & Seurer, 2018).

While scholars have been studying cultural discourses and ideologies for many years, the creation of Relational Dialectics Theory gave scholars, and people in close relationships, new and useful ways to understand the discourses that are at play in our interpersonal and family interactions, and how, via the interplay and/or competition of these discourses, we cocreate meaning in our relationships.

Relational Dialectics Theory

Communication scholars Leslie Baxter and Barbara Montgomery started writing about Relational Dialectics Theory (RDT) in their 1996 book, *Relating: Dialogues and Dialectics*. They based their early theorizing on the work of Russian theorist Mikhail Bakhtin. Bakhtin questioned communication based on one voice as central or correct. Rather, he stressed dialogue over monologue. We can understand this perspective in an example from a study by communication scholars Baxter, Braithwaite, Bryant and Wagner (2004). They interviewed young adult stepchildren about communication with their stepparent. As you read what one stepdaughter said, think about the different discourses at play regarding how she wants her stepmother to behave (i.e., what she wants her stepmother to say and do):

> I think that if [my stepmother] would have just said, "You kids need to do this" or "You kids need to come home at a decent time" or "We all need to sit down and discuss this curfew thing," I think that if she would have said that to us, we would have had more respect for her in the long run. We would have respected her for coming to us. At the same time, we would have been mad because we didn't want to come home early.... [Stepparents] need to be involved in [a] child's life. They need to act as if it is their own child but yet give them the space that they need, also. It is a touchy situation, but I think that it is possible to work out.

What we can see in this example is that there are some clear contradictions. For example, the stepdaughter expresses that she wants her stepmother to tell the kids what she wants them to do (for example, what time she wants her stepchildren to be home in the evening). However, the stepdaughter is very clear that if the stepmother does tell them what she wants, that she and her siblings would be angry. The stepdaughter also wants her stepmother to be involved in her life and, at the same time, give her space. At first glance, this seems almost impossible to deal with. As you think about it, you can likely come up with examples from your own experiences that have the same contradictory qualities. For example, you might appreciate it when a partner surprises you with flowers or a home-cooked meal, but if he or she brings you a dozen yellow roses or makes the exact same meal each Friday after work, the gesture might lose its meaning.

We quickly come to realize that what Relational Dialectics Theory scholars labeled "contradictions" or "dialectical tensions" are a common part of everyday interactions in close relationships, such as the example in the stepfamily or during the time a couple might be living and working long distance. For example, Erin Sahlstein (2004) identified a dialectic of being simultaneously together and apart for commuting couples, which both made it possible to function being apart at times and to come together successfully at other times. Dialectical contradictions also frame bigger issues in life as well. For example, communication scholar Paige Toller (2005) interviewed parents whose child had died. One of the things she heard in their talk was that some parents wanted to grieve together with their partner (to share how they were feeling and/or to talk about their child and keep their memory alive). However, talking about the child's death or expressing their feelings of sadness was very difficult for a partner who wanted to grieve alone. The more the one parent wanted to talk, the more likely the other parent would pull away. In another example, Kristen Norwood (2012) studied the experiences of families confronting dialectical contradictions when they have a transgender member, experiencing the relationship as both similar to the past, before the person transitioned, and different at the same time, with feelings of grief commonly experienced by the transgendered person and members of their family.

There have been two main versions of Relational Dialectics Theory. In the first version of the theory that we have been describing so far, scholars focused on identifying and understanding the dialectical tensions or contradictions present in close relationships around a number of dialectical pairs, such as (a) the need for autonomy and the need for connectedness, (b) the need for predictability and the need for spontaneity, and/or (c) the need for revealing and the need for privacy (Baxter & Montgomery, 1996). You might notice in this list we are not talking about these dialectical tensions in terms of "versus" (autonomy *versus* connection), but rather "and," as they both exist at the same time and are a tension without necessarily being oppositional. In reality, we cannot have one without the other. For example, being open does not exist without the possibility of being closed, so we phrase them to help us realize that we have a need for both stability *and* change in our relationships.

You can likely think of examples where you have faced challenges over each of these dialectical tensions. For example, one newlywed couple experienced challenges of different ways of handling revealing or concealing information. The wife, who was raised in a family that valued privacy and stressed keeping information about the family within the family, married a man whose family was very open and discussed topics that the wife deemed private. The young wife was embarrassed when, at a family dinner, her husband described a fight they had to his family and asked their advice (Petronio, 2015). From the perspective of Relational Dialectics Theory, it is important to understand that dialectical contradictions are not bad and that we really cannot avoid them. These tensions are part of life in close relationships (Baxter & Braithwaite, 2010). For example, parents who adopted children who did not look like them, expressed both how their adoptive family was similar to all other families and, at the same time, how their adoptive family was different and unique (Harrigan & Braithwaite, 2010).

Using Relational Dialectics Theory to understand communication in our close relationships helps us identify tensions/contradictions in different relationship types and contexts and to develop different ways to better understand or manage contradictions. Understanding Relational Dialectics Theory can help romantic partners, family members, and friends communicate and negotiate how to best handle dialectical contradictions. For example, going back to the experiences of the stepmother and stepdaughter above, while the stepmother probably cannot solve, or even avoid, some of the landmines of dialectical tensions with her stepdaughter, it will likely help her to understand that her stepdaughter both wants and does not want her to act like a mother to her. The stepmother can think this through and identify times when she wants to make her preferences known and other times it would be best to keep her desires to herself. She might even raise these contradictions with her daughter in a calm moment and they might try to problem-solve these contradictions together. If nothing else, understanding that dialectical tensions exist helps us understand the complexities of relational life and make choices about what we want to do and say.

The major challenge with the earlier version of Relational Dialectics Theory, however, was that the theory helped scholars identify the presence of these tensions in relationships without exploring how the tensions function together, or interplay, to create meaning. Thus, in 2011, Baxter updated the theory to what she called Relational Dialectics Theory 2.0, in her book, *Voicing relationships: A dialogic perspective*. In this new rendition of Relational Dialectics Theory, she placed greater emphasis on understanding how discourses are related to struggles and power. Baxter and scholars working with Relational Dialectics Theory 2.0 highlighted how some discourses are centered and given credibility or influence, and others are pushed to the margins (Baxter, 2011; Suter & Seurer, 2018). For example, you were likely raised with certain religious beliefs reflected in the values you hold and the holidays you celebrate. Think about the experience of a person who celebrates the Jewish remembrances of Passover and Hanukkah and who marries into a family that does not celebrate these holidays, but rather observes the Christian holidays of Christmas and Easter. This person might feel pressured to adopt the beliefs and rituals of their new family, giving up the beliefs and practices of their family of origin. Or perhaps the marital partners are able to come to an agreement that they are going to adopt some of the practices of both families in their own home. In Relational Dialectics Theory 2.0, Baxter focused on what she labeled "discursive struggles," focusing on how discourses interact to create meaning within interpersonal and family relationships. Relational Dialectics Theory 2.0 represents a critical framework because it focuses on issues of power, legitimacy, and marginalization. For instance, communication scholar Diana Breshears interviewed children who were raised knowing their parents as heterosexual and had one parent come out as lesbian, gay, or bisexual. Breshears learned how these children manage the discursive struggles of loving and accepting their parent, while other family members, perhaps their other parent or a respected grandparent, are declaring that homosexuality is unacceptable or immoral (Breshears & Braithwaite, 2014). Relational Dialectics Theory 2.0 helps us focus on the power struggles of competing discourses and to understand what happens when some discourses are marginalized or rejected (Baxter & Norwood, 2015; Suter & Seurer, 2018). To follow, we highlight two important concepts that Baxter contributed in Relational Dialectics Theory 2.0: the utterance chain and discursive interplay.

The utterance chain. When we communicate in close relationships, no single utterance happens in isolation. Everything we say is linked to past discourses and interactions and to the responses we anticipate will follow. It is this link of past, present, and anticipated/future discourse that is referred to as the "utterance chain." There are four types of utterances that occur in the utterance chain organized around distal discourses originating in the culture and proximal discourses originating in the relationship. First, the *Distal Already-Spoken* utterance refers to cultural discourses or ideologies we bring to our current relationships. For example, when a romantic couple discusses their sexual boundaries and expectations, the cultural discourses at play in that conversation may reflect different ideologies they bring to the relationship. For one partner, this might be a belief in waiting to have sex until marriage, while the other partner may subscribe to an alternative cultural discourse reflecting an expectation for physical intimacy once the couple has committed to becoming exclusive. Second, the *Proximal Already-Spoken* discourse refers to past meanings that have been established in the relationship that are brought into the present. That is, our present relational interactions are influenced by our relational history and past interactions. For example, our dating couple's present conversation about physical intimacy will be influenced by past communication and understandings within their relationship. If they have discussed and agreed that both partners' feelings will be honored and no one will be pressured into anything she or he is not ready for, they will bring that to bear in current and future discussions about sex. Third, the *Distal Not-Yet-Spoken* utterance refers to the anticipated response we would expect to receive from a generalizable "other" in society. For example, the first time a young woman tells her boyfriend that she is not ready to have sex, his response to her utterance will be influenced by how he believes most men would respond to this message from their girlfriends. Finally, the *Proximal Not-Yet-Spoken* utterance refers to the anticipated response from our relational partner based on our past communication with him or her. If, for example, the woman in the romantic couple believes that her boyfriend will respect her wish to wait to have sex (based on a *Proximal Already-Spoken* discourse), she will likely anticipate a supportive response when the topic comes up the next time.

Of course, we know that relationships are complex and ever-changing, and that fact is reflected in a number of interrelated, and sometimes contradictory, discourses we experience. For example, for this couple, both partners are influenced by what it means to be a "good boyfriend" or "good girlfriend" to one another. At the same time, one or both of the partners might be concerned about being teased by others if they found out that the couple is abstaining from sex or perhaps judged negatively for talking about sex from family or church members. When we communicate in our relationships, all four of these utterance types are interacting to create meaning within the relationship.

Interplay of discourses. While some discourses can coexist without conflict (for example the discourse of good boyfriends supporting the wishes of their girlfriends and the discourse of waiting until marriage to have sex), the reality is that many discourses do conflict and are in competition with one another to be the accepted discourse, resulting in discursive struggles (Baxter, 2011). When conflicting discourses are present in our talk, one discourse is dominant over the more marginalized discourses. Discourses become dominant either by becoming the only accepted discourse or by being the most acceptable discourse. For example, children with a gay father may struggle with supporting their parent and his new partner, while understanding and supporting their mother who is hurt at the loss of her marriage and expresses her strong belief that the father has made an immoral choice. Dominant discourses are those that are deemed "normal," "typical," or "natural," while marginalized discourses (those with less power) are deemed "nonnormative," "unnatural," or "deviant" (Suter & Seurer, 2018).

It is through the power struggle, the interplay of different discourses, that meaning is coconstructed in close relationships. Thinking back again to our dating couple, as they grow closer and negotiate sexual expectations and boundaries, they must navigate interrelated relational discourses (i.e., trust, support, respect, desire) and cultural discourses (i.e., waiting until marriage, expectations of romantic love and sex, societal judgment). Complicating things, all of these discourses are present, conflicting, competing, and changing over time. Individually and together, the couple communicates, and gives credence to, certain discourses and marginalizes others in their talk as they cocreate meanings. Over time and in interaction, Relational Dialectics Theory helps us understand how new meanings and understanding can emerge or how relational parties can become stuck in ongoing negotiations or discursive struggles on an ongoing basis. In the best of circumstances, communication becomes a view of "communication as creation" of selves and relationships (Baxter, 2006, p. 105), as partners communicate and cocreate new meanings from competing discourses (Suter & Seurer, 2018).

The Case Study

Emma is having the strangest day of her life. After taking the last final exam of the semester, she leaves the university feeling a sense of relief and excitement to finally spend her time relaxing, spending time with friends, and binge-watching TV shows. She is looking forward to a late lunch with her mother, Erica, and her younger brother, David. She hasn't caught up with them in weeks, as her nose has been shoved into textbooks, studying. Emma swings by the high school to pick David up, and they drive together to a restaurant where their family often goes.

As they arrive at the restaurant, Emma finds her mom sitting in a booth, staring out the window. Erica does not even notice that her children have arrived until they are standing in front of her at the table. Her mom looks nervous, or worried, or…something. It isn't long until Emma learns why her mom is acting so strangely. After their food arrives, Erica says she has an announcement to make. After a silence that seems to last forever, Erica takes a deep breath and tells Emma and David that she is gay.

The rest of the conversation is a blur for Emma. It is a bizarre feeling: listening to the words coming out of her mother's mouth, but also being lost in her own thoughts and emotions. David looks frozen, saying nothing as their mother explains the changes in her life. For Emma, it is almost as if her consciousness is split into two. She hears her mom explain that she always knew that she was different, but that she could never quite figure out why. That she married and had children because that's what was expected of her, but that she was never happy in her marriage, explaining that perhaps that is why she divorced their dad six years ago. The words pour out of Erica, explaining that she doesn't regret anything that has happened, especially because she has two amazing children that she wouldn't give up for anything, but that she feels like she needs to be true to herself now. Erica goes on to explain that she has met someone and they've been dating for months now. She's wanted to tell them for so long, but was worried about hurting her kids and afraid about what they would think and worried they would reject her. Erica stresses that her kids are more important to her than anything in the world, and she never wants to do anything to hurt them. She will never stop loving them and hopes that they will still love her.

Emma is crying by the end of Erica's announcement, feeling so overwhelmed. Her mind is going in a hundred different directions. There are so many things she wants to say, so many questions that she wants to ask, but she is speechless. She looks over at David, who has gone completely pale, and is just staring, open-mouthed, at his mother. Emma can see her mom staring at her with tears running down her cheeks by now. She looks terrified. Emma slides across the booth and sits next to her mom, placing her arm around her, and says, "Mom, we love you. That's not going to change."

The three of them sit in silence for a while and then ask for the bill. Erica has to get back to work, so they decide to meet at home later that evening to continue their conversation. Before they leave, they have a big group hug in the parking lot. David and Emma reassure their mother that they love her and that they will never stop loving her. Then Emma and David climb into her car and just sit in silence for what feels like ages. Finally, Emma breaks the silence.

Emma: What just happened?

David: I have no freaking idea! I mean, Mom is a—a lesbian now?

Emma: I guess so. Wow! Are you ok?

David: Yeah, I guess. I just feel like I'm in an episode of the Twilight Zone or something. Is this really happening? I mean, it's MOM. Mom can't be gay... she's Mom.

Emma: I need some time to wrap my head around this.

The two siblings go silent again. Emma considers starting the car and driving home, but she's not sure she can drive at the moment. Her head is swimming with thoughts. After a few minutes she starts talking again.

Emma: Did you have any idea? I mean, I spend most of the year at the dorm. You spend more time with her than I do. Weren't there signs?

David: I don't spend *that* much more time with her. You've only been out of the house for a year and a half. You should have picked up on stuff, too... Unless... you know, there has been a friend that Mom keeps talking about. Mindy. She hangs out with Mindy sometimes. Do you think that's her girlfriend?

Emma: Maybe. She's mentioned Mindy to me, too, but I thought they were just close friends. This is all so...unreal.

Emma thinks back to her childhood. Her mom was never like the other moms. She never wore a lot of makeup and always dressed very outdoorsy. She liked to camp and she liked to fix things. She had more tools than their dad did. But these shouldn't be signs of her being a lesbian, right? It would be stereotypical to say that women who are less feminine are automatically gay. But she *is* gay, so what does that mean? As Emma continues to think about her childhood (the family vacations, the holidays, dinners around the table), an overwhelming sadness comes over her. She begins to cry.

David: What's wrong?

Emma: I just feel like our whole childhood was a lie. Like, here I thought we had a normal family, like everyone else. We did normal family things. Mom was just a mom, and Dad was just a dad. They went to work, we went to school, we came home for dinner…we were normal. Even the divorce felt normal, in a way, since so many of my friends' parents were already divorced. But was all of that just a show? Did she even love Dad? Was Mom just faking it all those years?

David: I don't think so. I don't think you can fake something like that for so long. I'm not sure it's fair to say that our childhood was a lie. I think she probably just didn't know. Being gay wasn't accepted back then as it is now. You didn't see gay people on TV, and it wasn't talked about in schools like it is now. It was probably just harder to figure out who she was back then.

Emma: How can you stay so calm?

David: I'm not calm. I'm freaking out here. What are people at school going to say? What are my friends going to say?

Emma: But you JUST said that it's socially acceptable now and talked about at school. Why are you worried about what your friends will say?

David: It is. It's just—I don't know. Like, it seems fine for other people to be gay. I have gay friends, and it's never bothered me before. I always thought people should be proud of who they are. It just feels different when it's someone in your family who comes out. Especially your own mother! What if people think that I'm gay now too?

Emma: That's ridiculous, David. Who would think that?

David: I had a friend in junior high school who had two dads and the other kids always teased him and said that he was going to be gay because he was being raised by gay men. And there are the super religious kids at school who always speak out against anything the GLBT club tries to do. I don't think I can handle people telling me that Mom is going to hell because she's a lesbian.

Emma: Some people are just ignorant. They're afraid of anyone who is different from them. They act like being gay is a choice, but it's no different than any other identity you were born with. You can't choose what sex you are born with, how tall you're going to be, or what race you are. Discriminating against gay people is no different than being racist.

David: Yeah, I know all of that. But that's not going to make it any easier to deal with. I guess we'll have time to get used to the idea before people start finding out.

There is silence in the car again. Both siblings are lost in their own thoughts. Then something occurs to Emma.

Emma: I wonder if Dad knows about Mom.

David: He probably doesn't. I don't think she would tell him before she told us.

Emma: How do you think he's going to react?

David: I don't think he'll react badly. He always told us that gay people are no different than us and that we shouldn't judge them.

Emma: Maybe he'll be relieved. Like, maybe Mom asking for a divorce wasn't because of who he is, but because Mom is gay.

David: Or he'll be worried that he turned her gay.

Emma: Oh, come on, David. People don't actually believe that. They just say it as a joke.

David: I'm not really worried about Dad. I think he'll be cool about it. It's Grandma who is going to lose it.

Emma: Oh, my god, yes! She is totally going to freak out! She's always bragging about Mom's accomplishments to her church friends. She's going to disown her now.

David: Poor Mom. She's probably scared. I can't imagine having to come out to everyone I know.

Emma: *If* she comes out. Maybe she isn't going to tell anyone else besides us.

David: We should ask her so we know if we're supposed to keep it a secret. I hope she doesn't hide it, though. She's kept the secret for so long as is. I think it's more important for her to be true to herself and be proud of who she is, even if that means we aren't as normal as we thought we were.

Emma: Yeah. Keeping it a secret would be like being ashamed of who you are. Being gay isn't something to be ashamed of. Who cares who she falls in love with? Love is love. That is what matters above all else.

David: Are you feeling better?

Emma: Yeah, I think I am over the initial shock. I just have a lot of questions now. Like, when did she know? Was this why she divorced Dad? Who is this person she's dating? Who can we tell? There are so many questions.

David: Yeah, me too. We can start asking her questions tonight.

Emma: Let's not bombard her, though. I don't want her to feel like we're interrogating her. And she needs to know that we love her no matter what.

David: Ok. Em, this is so weird.

Emma: Totally.

Understanding the Case Study

Baxter (2011) helped us understand that Relational Dialectics Theory is appropriately applied to situations where there is a change, a challenge, or a rupture in a close relationship, because the interplay of competing discourses is likely salient during those times. In the case study, Emma and David are trying to make sense of their mother's coming out, which is a clear change that is occurring in their family relationship. There are many discourses at play as the two siblings discuss their mother's disclosure and the consequences of their new family identity. Thinking about the utterance chain, we can identify examples of the four types of utterances in the sibling's dialogue. Remember that *Distal Already-Spoken* utterances are cultural discourses or ideologies that are brought into play in our current talk. Examples of this type of utterance present in the case study include the viewpoints of homosexuality as a sin, of the importance of staying true to yourself, and of the ideas of what a "normal" family looks like.

Distal Not-Yet-Spoken utterances are the anticipated responses we would get from a generalized "other." In the case study, we saw this type of utterance when David was voicing his concern about what people at school would say when they found out that his mother is a lesbian. He was concerned that people may think he is also gay or that he would face judgment from religious individuals.

Proximal Already-Spoken utterances are those messages and meanings that have already been established in relationships and *Proximal Not-Yet-Spoken* utterances are anticipated discourses that we will receive from our relational partners. In the case study, the siblings discuss how their father might react to their mother coming out as gay. David concludes that his father will not react badly (a *Proximal Not-Yet-Spoken* discourse) because his father has always told them that gay people should not be judged (a *Proximal Already-Spoken discourse*). Similarly, the siblings anticipate a negative reaction from their grandmother based on their relational history with her. There are many other discourses at play in the sibling's dialogue, but, by now, you have a sense of how discourses (at various points on the utterance chain) are present in our relational communication.

Not only is it important to be able to identify the discourses at play in the dialogue above, but also how these discourses interact and/or compete with one another. If all of the discourses in the sibling's conversation were supportive of their mother coming out, and of homosexuality in general, there would not be any competition among the discourses. However, as Emma and David explore the reactions that people may have (both supportive and judgmental) and discuss the various cultural discourses (both condemning homosexuality and asserting the importance of being true to oneself), we see clear contradictions between positive and negative discourses surrounding sexual orientation.

We also see how the siblings organize the discourses as they talk through the issue, privileging some and marginalizing others. Consider the following excerpt from their conversation:

> **David:** I had a friend in junior high school who had two dads and the other kids always teased him and said that he was going to be gay because he was being raised by gay men. And there are the super religious kids at school who always speak out against anything the GLBT club tries to do. I don't think I can handle people telling me that Mom is going to hell because she's a lesbian.
>
> **Emma:** Some people are just ignorant. They're afraid of anyone who is different from them. They act like being gay is a choice, but it's no different than any other identity you were born with. You can't choose what sex you are born with, how tall you're going to be, or what race you are.

In this example, we see Emma marginalizing the cultural discourses that condemn homosexuality by dismissing them as ignorant. Instead, she gives privilege to the discourse of homosexuality as acceptable by claiming that homosexuality is something that one is born with and that is as innate as one's height. We can see that at the beginning of their conversation, Emma and David are in shock and are not sure what to think about their mother coming out. By the end of the conversation, however, it is clear that they are on the path to accepting their mother and expressing support for her. At this point in the conversation Emma and David overwhelmingly reject negative discourses and give power to discourses of acceptance.

In this case, the interplay of the competing discourses creates meaning in their familial relationship and identity, and we can see how the interplay of discourses can function in our own communication and relationships. The positioning of the discourses in the talk of this brother and sister (favoring of a supportive discourse and marginalizing the negative discourse about their mother) provides them with a favorable view of their mother and of their new, nontraditional family identity. Had the discourses been positioned differently (i.e., if the discursive struggle ended with different results), the siblings could have left with completely different meanings. For example, had the discourses of shame, embarrassment, and "homosexuality as sin" been given the dominant position in their talk, they could have left the conversation feeling angry at their mother, feeling ashamed of their family, deciding to keep the information secret, or even rejecting their mother completely. Indeed, many conversations such as the one between Emma and David take place every day and different people have different reactions to their parents' coming out as gay. The meaning of having a lesbian/gay parent emerges from relational communication such as the one above.

Discussion Questions

1. Explain the differences between the four types of utterances on the utterance chain.

2. What other discourses can you identify in the sibling's conversation about their mother coming out? Where do these discourses fall on the utterance chain?

3. Choose a hotly debated topic and come up with examples of the four types of utterances that may appear when a man and his father discuss the topic.

4. Think of ways that discourses are given power and are marginalized in relational communication.

5. Think of different scenarios of how the sibling's conversation could have ended. What discourses would have been given power to reach these various endings?

6. How can Relational Dialectics Theory inform different issues in your own close relationships? Think of examples where competing discourses make meaning in your own life.

REFERENCES

Baxter, L. A. (2011). *Voicing relationships: A dialogic perspective.* Thousand Oaks, CA: Sage.

Baxter, L. A., & Braithwaite, D. O. (2010). Relational dialectics theory, applied. In S. W. Smith & S. R. Wilson (Eds.), *New directions in interpersonal communication* (pp. 48–66). Thousand Oaks, CA. Sage.

Baxter, L. A., Braithwaite, D. O., Bryant, L., & Wagner, A. (2004). Stepchildren's perceptions of the contradictions in communication with stepparents. *Journal of Social & Personal Relationships, 21,* 447–467.

Baxter, L. A., & Montgomery, B. M. (1996). *Relating: Dialogues and dialectics.* New York, NY: Guilford Press.

Baxter, L. A., & Norwood, K. M. (2015). Relational dialectics theory: Navigating meaning from competing discourses. In D. O. Braithwaite & P. Schrodt (Eds.), *Engaging theories in interpersonal communication: Multiple perspectives* (2nd ed., pp. 279–292). Thousand Oaks, CA: Sage.

Breshears, D., & Braithwaite, D. O. (2014). Discursive struggles animating individuals' talk about their parents' coming out as lesbian or gay. *Journal of Family Communication, 14,* 189–207.

Harrigan, M., & Braithwaite, D. O. (2010). Discursive struggles in families formed through visible adoption: An exploration of dialectical unity. *Journal of Applied Communication Research, 38,* 127–144.

Norwood, K. (2012). Transitioning meanings? Family members' communicative struggles surrounding transgender identity. *Journal of Family Communication, 12,* 75–92.

Petronio, S. (2015). Embarrassment of disclosing private information in public: Newly married couples. In D. Braithwaite & J. Wood (Eds.). *Casing Interpersonal Communication: Case Studies in Personal and Social Relationships.* Dubuque, IA: Kendall Hunt Publishing.

Sahlstein, E. M. (2004). Relating at a distance: Negotiating being together and being apart in long-distance relationships. *Journal of Social and Personal Relationships, 5,* 689–710.

Suter, E.S., & Seurer, L. M. (2018). Relational dialectics theory: Realizing the dialogic potential of family communication. In Braithwaite, D. O., Suter, E. A., & Floyd, K. (Eds.). *Engaging theories in family communication.* (2nd ed., pp. 244–254). New York, NY: Routledge.

Toller, P. W. (2005). Negotiation of dialectical contradictions by parents who have experienced the death of a child. *Journal of Applied Communication Research, 33,* 46–66.

Chapter 8

Integrative Communication Theory of Cross-Cultural Adaptation

Young Yun Kim, Ph.D., *University of Oklahoma*

On any given day, countless people around the world cross cultural boundaries. Immigrants and refugees change homes seeking a new life, and temporary sojourners relocate in a foreign land for a variety of professional and personal reasons. Domestic ethnic minorities leave their familiar surroundings to resettle in a significantly different cultural environment. While unique in individual circumstances and varied in scope, intensity, and duration, everyone entering a new and unfamiliar cultural environment embarks on the common project called *cross-cultural adaptation.* Even short-term sojourners are at least minimally concerned with building a level of proficiency in carrying out the activities of daily living. Given sufficient time, they will find themselves having been changed in some way by the new experience.

This ongoing reality is illuminated in the integrative communication theory of cross-cultural adaptation (Kim, 1988, 2001, 2005, 2009, 2012, 2018). Bringing together a wide range of salient research concepts and theories across social science disciplines into a single frame, this theory provides a "big picture" of the cross-cultural adaptation phenomenon, a broadly based interdisciplinary insight into how and why, over time, newcomers in an unfamiliar cultural environment are able to achieve a relatively stable functional and psychological relationship with the new sociocultural system.

The initial groundwork for the development of this theory was laid in the author's dissertation study (Kim, 1976) among Korean immigrants in the Chicago area. A book-length presentation of the theory was first presented in *Communication and Cross-Cultural Adaptation: An Integrative Theory* (Kim, 1988), and was further elaborated in *Becoming Intercultural: An Integrative Theory of Communication and Cross-Cultural Adaptation* (Kim, 2001). Over the past three decades, this theory has been extensively utilized in studies conducted across social science disciplines, including intercultural communication, mass communication, cross-cultural and social psychology, migration studies, education, social work, and business management.

Foundational Ideas

The theory is built on the basic conception of adaptation as a fundamental human condition, just as it is to all other forms of life. As explained in the General Systems Theory (Bertalanffy, 1968; Ruben & Kim, 1972), adaptation manifests a natural instinct inherent in all "open systems" that exist in, and coevolve with, the environment through continuous interactions. Cross-cultural adaptation, then, is simply a special case of the life-sustaining and life-enhancing activities people in a new cultural environment naturally undertake. Thanks to the built-in human plasticity and self-organizing capacity, each person is capable of acquiring new cultural habits and, in so doing, achieve a degree of "fitness" in a new environment.

Cross-cultural adaptation takes place in, and through, the process of communication interfacing between the person and the environment. From passive observations to direct one-on-one encounters with members of the host community to utilization of various local and national mass media, communication is the vehicle through which individuals adapt to the host environment. Highlighting the vital function of communication, Kim (2001) defines cross-cultural adaptation as: *"the entirety of the dynamic process by which individuals who, through direct and indirect contact and communication with a new, changing, or changed environment, strive to establish (or reestablish) and maintain a relatively stable, reciprocal, and functional relationship with the environment"* (p. 31).

The theory employs the concept of "stranger." Initially coined by Simmel (1908/1950), and subsequently applied to the context of intercultural communication (Gudykunst & Kim, 2003), this concept serves as a heuristic concept for analyzing the social processes involving individuals who find themselves as "outsiders" in an unfamiliar social milieu. In the present theory, this broad term includes all individuals moving to, and resettling in, a new cultural environment, including immigrants, refugees, and temporary sojourners who resettle for various lengths of time, as well as those who cross domestic subcultural boundaries and undergo the process of adapting to their new environment.

Based on these foundational ideas, the theory addresses two key questions: *how does the cross-cultural adaptation process unfold over time, and, given the same length of time, why do some strangers attain a higher (or lower) level of cross-cultural adaptation than others?*

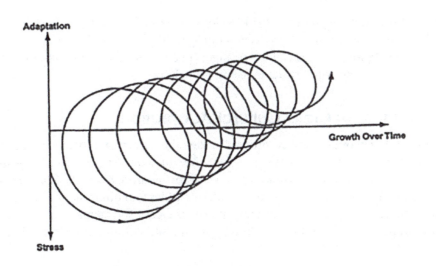

Adaptation

Growth Over Time

Stress

Figure 1. The Process Model: The Stress-Adaptation-Growth Dynamic.

The Process of Cross-Cultural Adaptation

The theory addresses the first question by offering a three-pronged process model, the *stress-adaptation-growth dynamic* depicted in *Figure 1*. This process model identifies the *stress* experienced by all strangers, a natural response to the uncertainties confronting a stranger, particularly during the initial phase of resettlement, as has been documented in many "culture shock" studies. Stress is a natural and inevitable state of disequilibrium prompted by the inner conflict between the desire to retain the habitual mind on the one hand, and the necessity to seek congruence with the new environment on the other.

The direct response to the heightened self-awareness in the state of stress is *adaptation*, the psychological drive propelling the stranger to mobilize inner resources to overcome the unsettling experience of stress. Each stress experience, and the subsequent adaptive move, presents a stranger with an opportunity to recreate oneself. What follows a successful and cumulative management of the stress-adaptation experience is a subtle, and often imperceptible, psychological *growth*, a form of internal transformation accompanying a higher level of perceptual and cognitive complexity with which to respond to environmental challenges.

The stress-adaptation-growth dynamic does not happen in a smooth, arrow-like, linear progression, but in a cyclic and fluctuating "draw-back-to-leap" pattern, with an overall forward-and-upward movement in the direction of increasing chances of success in meeting the demands of the host environment. Intense experiences of stress, and large and sudden adaptive adjustments, are most likely to occur during the initial phase of exposure to a new culture. Over time, the fluctuations of stress and adaptation subside to lower levels of intensity, rendering the overall calming trend of the stress-adaptation-growth dynamic. The diminishing severity of fluctuation, in turn, allows strangers to carry out their daily activities in the new environment with greater ease and proficiency.

The Structure of Cross-Cultural Adaptation

Building on the above-described process model, the theory presents a structural model addressing the second basic question: *given the same length of time, why do some strangers attain a higher (or lower) level of cross-cultural adaptation than others?* As shown in *Figure 2*, this structural model identifies four dimensions of factors, working together, interactively, to facilitate (or impede) the adaptation process: communication, predisposition, environment, and intercultural transformation.

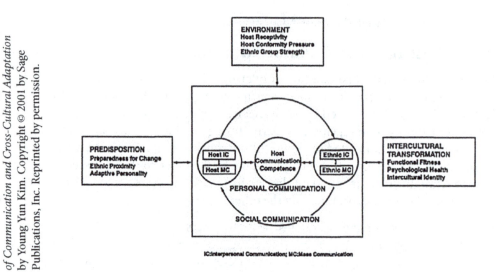

From *Becoming Intercultural: An Integrative Theory of Communication and Cross-Cultural Adaptation* by Young Yun Kim. Copyright © 2001 by Sage Publications, Inc. Reprinted by permission.

Figure 2. The Structural Model: Factors Influencing the Process of Cross-Cultural Adaptation

Communication at the Core

Placed at the center of the structural model, strangers' communication activities are grouped in two interdependent categories: *(intra)personal communication*, or the mental activities that occur within individual strangers, disposing and preparing them to act and react in certain ways in actual social situations, and *social communication*, which takes place whenever they participate in face-to-face or mediated forms of interactions with other people.

The (intra)personal communication factor is explained as the stranger's *host communication competence*. That is, the capacity to appropriately and effectively receive and process information and to design and execute mental plans in initiating or responding to messages from the host environment. Host communication directly influences, and is influenced by, the stranger's participation in *host interpersonal communication* activities, including those via social media, which help strangers to obtain vital information and insight into the mindsets and behaviors of the local people. Likewise, the stranger's use of various forms of *host mass communication* (including radio and television programs, magazine and newspaper articles, movies, museum exhibits, and theater performances) exposes him to the larger social environment and, thereby, facilitates, and is facilitated by, the stranger's host communication competence.

In many communities in contemporary societies, strangers' social communication activities include *ethnic interpersonal communication* involving fellow coethnics or conationals. Also, with the advent of Internet websites and direct satellite (and cable) broadcasts, they have access to various sources of *ethnic mass communication*. During the initial phases of relocation, when strangers lack host communication competence, ethnic communication activities provide a relatively stress-free cultural refuge and emotional support. The theory explains, however, that exclusive and prolonged reliance on ethnic social communication activities help maintain strangers' original cultural habits, while discouraging their active participation in host interpersonal and mass communication processes.

Environmental Conditions

A stranger's (intra)personal communication (host communication competence) and social (interpersonal, mass) communication are closely linked to the conditions of the new environment. The theory identifies three key environmental factors: *host receptivity*, *host conformity pressure*, and *ethnic group strength*.

Host receptivity refers to the degree to which the environment is open to welcoming and accepting strangers into its social processes. A given host environment can be more receptive toward certain groups of nonnatives, while unwelcoming toward certain others. Such differences are attributable to the favorable or unfavorable attitudes held among the local population against certain groups of nonnatives for various reasons, including the cultural, religious, and political differences and conflicts between the two cultures. The stranger's host communication competence and communicative engagement in host social processes are also influenced by *host conformity pressure*. Ethnically diverse communities in large metropolitan areas in the United States tend to hold greater accommodation of different languages and cultures, thereby exerting less pressure on nonnatives to adopt the normative language and communication practices of the host culture. The third environmental factor, *ethnic group strength*, is associated with the overall size and status associated with the stranger's ethnic group and the material and social support it provides for newly arrived members. In the long run, heavy and prolonged reliance on such ethnic community resources tends to help maintain the ethnic culture and language while discouraging active participations in the host social communication processes.

Individual Predisposition

A stranger's host communication competence and host social communication activities are further influenced by three key aspects of his or her predisposition: *preparedness for change*, *adaptive personality*, and *ethnic proximity/distance*. These background characteristics serve as the baseline on which each stranger embarks on the cross-cultural adaptation process.

Strangers move to the host culture with differing levels of *preparedness for change*, or the preexisting cognitive, affective, and operational capacity to undertake the challenges of adapting to a new culture. Among the various ways of being prepared are the knowledge of the host language and culture, the psychological readiness to embrace the challenges they are likely to face in the host environment, and the desire to succeed in the new environment. Also playing a role in the cross-cultural adaptation process is the *ethnic proximity/distance*, or the overall degree of similarity/difference and compatibility/incompatibility, of a given stranger with respect to the dominant ethnicity in the host environment. It does so by affecting the level of ease or difficulty each stranger is likely to experience in developing host communication competence and participating in host social communication activities.

In addition, each stranger faces the challenges of the new environment within the context of his or her *adaptive personality*: the overall internal resource that would help them endure and persist in his or her adaptive efforts. *Openness* is such a personality resource. As a psychological posture that is receptive to new information, openness enables strangers to minimize their resistance and maximize their willingness to attend to the new and changed circumstances. The *strength* of one's personality represents a range of interrelated personality attributes such as resilience, risk-taking, hardiness, persistence, patience, elasticity, and resourcefulness (the inner quality that absorbs shocks from the environment and bounces back without being seriously damaged by them). The *positivity*, an affirmative and optimistic outlook of mind, further helps strangers to embrace and endure many stressful encounters with a belief that things will turn out as they should in the end.

Intercultural Transformation

The structural model identifies three key facets of internal change taking place in strangers as they undertake the process of cross-cultural adaptation through intrapersonal and social communication activities: greater *functional fitness* in carrying out daily transactions, improved *psychological health* in dealing with the environment, and an increasingly *intercultural identity* orientation.

Functional fitness of strangers increases as they conduct continuous experiments in the host environment as they strive to "know their way around." Through repeated activities resulting in new learning and mental reorganizing, they achieve some level of appropriate and effective ways to communicate and relate to the host environment. Accompanying increased *functional fitness* is greater *psychological health* with respect to the host environment. In the early stages of cross-cultural adaptation, strangers experience frustration and anxiety about their lack of host communication competence necessary to carry out their daily life activities with proficiency. As their host communication competence improves, they are better able to meet their personal needs with a greater sense of confidence and efficacy.

Long-term adaptive change further includes the emergence of an *intercultural identity*: a self-other orientation that transcends the boundaries of a single culture. While rooted in the original cultural identity, individuals with a highly developed intercultural identity are better able to see themselves and others more on the basis of unique personal qualities (individuation) and the shared humanity beyond conventional cultural group categories (universalization).

Theorems

Altogether, the linkages identified in this structural model signify mutual stimulations between and among the four dimensions of factors: communication, environment, predisposition, and intercultural transformation. Like a locomotive engine, the workings of each unit operating in this process affect, and are affected by, the workings of all other units, moving together in the direction of an increasing level of functional and psychological fitness in the host environment and the emergence of an intercultural identity.

The interlocking relationships identified in the structural model are formally specified in a total of 21 theorems (see Kim, 2001, pp. 91–92). The nature of each theoretical linkage in the model is specified as a theorem: a generalizable and predictive statement of a functional relationship, such as *the greater the host communication competence, the greater the participation in host interpersonal and mass communication* (Theorem 1); *the greater the host interpersonal and mass communication, the greater the intercultural transformation (functional fitness, psychological health, and intercultural identity)* (Theorem 5); and *the greater the adaptive personality, the greater the host interpersonal and mass communication* (Theorem 20).

From Theory to Reality

The viability of a given theory rests on the reality to which it is directed. To the present theory, the reality is the adaptive changes commonly experienced by people who, at this very moment and at all corners of the world, are striving to forge a new life away from their familiar grounds.

In the process model, the theory captures the dynamic interplay of stress, adaptation, and growth experiences as the common denominator in all strangers' experiences, through which they become increasingly "fit" in the host environment, both functionally and psychologically, as they undergo a subtle and largely unconscious transformation from a monocultural identity to an increasingly individuated and universalized intercultural identity. In the structural model, the theory emphasizes the centrality of individual strangers' host communication competence and their active engagement in the host interpersonal and mass communication activities of the host environment as the main force driving their adaptation process. Also explained are the influences of their personal background (*ethnicity, personality, preparedness for change*) and the host environment (*host receptivity, host conformity pressure, ethnic group strength*) on the extent of their capacity to communicate with (*host communication competence*), and participate in, the host social communication processes (*host interpersonal communication* and *host mass communication*).

While individual backgrounds and the conditions of the environment play an important role in the adaptation process, the theory also points to strangers' willingness to make personal efforts to take part in the host social communication processes as being essential in achieving the adaptive changes necessary to attain the level of functional proficiency and psychological well-being they seek. Strong adaptive efforts are made by those strangers highly motivated to facilitate their own cross-cultural adaptation, even when their ethnic backgrounds are severely different from that of the mainstream ethnicity of the local community, and even when they have easy access to a well-established ethnic community support system of their own.

Such was the case of a former Peace Corps volunteer, Vicki Holmsten. Upon completion of her training, she was assigned to a small town called Foequellie, Liberia, where she taught language arts and some math to elementary and junior high school students. During her two-year stay, she kept a diary reflecting on her cross-cultural experiences, excerpts of which were published in *The Chicago Tribune* (May 27, 1978, Sec. 1, p. 10). Here is a condensed version of the published excerpts, highlighting only some of her experiences of cross-cultural adaptation over the course of her two-year sojourn.

> **December 12, 1975:** I am … in the bush!
>
> **February 19, 1976:** Rice, rice, rice. If I see another bowl of rice …
>
> **April 6, 1976:** The students are trying hard … On good days it is challenging, on bad days it is impossible.
>
> **October 17, 1976:** I am only just now coming to terms with Africa.
>
> **January 16, 1977:** Eleven months to go. I'm sure now that I can do it.
>
> **March 25, 1977:** Today I ate roasted termites. Not bad.
>
> **September 10, 1977:** I finally belong … It's almost time for me to leave.
>
> **December 6, 1977:** I'm sad to be going home.

The Gift of Human Resilience

No matter how willing and prepared we are, the cross-cultural journey is seldom smooth. Life in an unfamiliar environment entails some of the most stressful experiences we may ever face. Acute stress necessarily occurs to the extent that we are challenged to live and work in accordance with the norms and practices of the new culture. We are bound to encounter moments of self-doubt that grow out of the restless inner spirit that seeks the familiar and the constant when familiar relationships and routines are broken.

Yet, as explained in the process model of the present theory, those moments are the very force that brings about the unfolding of the *stress-adaptation-growth dynamic* underpinning the process of cross-cultural adaptation. We can see glimpses of this internal dynamic from Vicki Holmsten's diary. During the initial months of her two-year sojourn, Holmsten wrote about the frustrations she was experiencing in a culture vastly different from her own (*stress*). These entries were juxtaposed with reflections on her new learning and acceptance of the local African cultural practices (*adaptation*), along with indications of her own personal development in the form of the deepening of her insights into, and appreciation of, the local people (*growth*). We can also glean from her writings that, through the experiences of stress, adaptation, and growth, Holmsten was able to gain in the three key facets of *intercultural transformation* identified in the structural model: the heightened sense of confidence in her work as a Peace Corps teacher (*functional fitness*), a stronger sense of belonging and enjoyment of life in her home away from home (*psychological health*), and the incorporation and internalization of the new cultural experiences as a part of her own personhood (*intercultural identity*).

We can also infer that the most immediate and direct sources of intense stress Holmsten was experiencing during the initial months was the profound lack of similarity (*ethnic proximity*) between her own American cultural upbringing and that of the local people in the small Liberian town of Foequellie, coupled with the challenges of having to live and work almost entirely according to the local culture and language (*host conformity pressure*). As is the case for most Peace Corps operations around the world, she was, by design, compelled to implement her work as a Peace Corps volunteer fully immersed in the local community, and largely on her own with limited contacts with fellow Americans and American mass media (low-levels of *ethnic group strength, ethnic interpersonal communication,* and *ethnic mass communication*).

Yet, we can further surmise that Holmsten was able to cope with, and overcome, these challenges through her own personal openness, inner strength, and positive outlook on life (*adaptive personality*). Assisting her in her adaptive endeavor was the extensive presojourn language and cultural training provided by the Peace Corps (*preparedness for change*), as well as the welcoming attitudes that were most likely to have been extended to her by the local people (*host receptivity*). These predispositional and environmental conditions undoubtedly supported her in her effort to dedicate herself to her daily face-to-face interactions with the local people (*host interpersonal communication*) and through various public communication activities such as festivals, markets, and other local community events (*host mass communication*). Such active engagements in the host social communication processes, in turn, further strengthened her cognitive, affective, and operational capacity (*host communication competence*) to relate to the local people more deeply and to experience greater efficacy in carrying out her mission as a Peace Corps volunteer.

Holmsten's journey of cross-cultural adaptation and intercultural transformation is not unique to her, or only to other Peace Corps volunteers. Indeed, they are shared by numerous others who have engaged themselves in the social and cultural milieu of their new life earnestly and meaningfully. In some deep place in their consciousness, these individuals know that the process of crossing cultural boundaries challenges the very basis of who they are as cultural beings, and yet, in the most unsettling moments, a new formulation of life arises. Their successful undertaking is a testament to the ever-present gift of resilience—the basic human condition that gives the project of cross-cultural adaptation its ultimate meaning. In the words of Charles Austin Beard, an early 20th-century American historian, "when the skies grow dark, the stars begin to shine."

Discussion Questions

1. The author describes cross-cultural adaptation as "a special case of the life-sustaining and life-enhancing activity people in a new cultural environment naturally undertake." What are the various cross-cultural situations that require at least some level of adaptation?

2. The stress-adaptation-growth dynamic explains how strangers undergo the process of intercultural transformation through prolonged communicative engagements with the host environment. Thinking more broadly beyond cross-cultural situations, how can this theoretical model be applied to understanding the personal growth we are able to achieve when we make significant adaptive efforts to meet some of the important challenges in our own lives?

3. Cross-cultural adaptation takes place "in, and through, the process of communication interfacing the person and the environment." Accordingly, host communication competence and active participation in the host interpersonal and mass communication activities serve as the very engine driving the cross-cultural adaptation process. What deliberate efforts can strangers make to facilitate their communicative engagement with the new environment?

4. There are immigrants or sojourners whose daily interactions take place almost exclusively within their own ethnic communities. How is their lack of contact and communicative engagement with native members of the host society likely to affect their long-term adaptation to the larger society?

5. Openness, strength, and positivity are the three key personality factors identified in the theory as facilitating individual strangers' cross-cultural adaptation. How is each of these factors likely to influence individual strangers' communication behavior and adaptation? Can these personal qualities be cultivated and strengthened through deliberate efforts?

REFERENCES

Bertalanffy, L. (1968). *General system theory.* New York, NY: Braziller.

Gudykunst, W. B., & Kim, Y. Y. (2003). *Communicating with strangers: An approach to intercultural communication* (4th ed.). New York, NY: McGraw-Hill.

Kim, Y. Y. (1976). *Communication patterns of foreign immigrants in the process of acculturation: A survey among the Korean population in Chicago.* Unpublished doctoral dissertation, Northwestern University, Evanston, IL.

Kim, Y. Y. (1988). *Communication and cross-cultural adaptation: An integrative theory.* Clevedon, UK: Multilingual Matters.

Kim, Y. Y. (2001). *Becoming intercultural: An integrative theory of communication and cross-cultural adaptation.* Thousand Oaks, CA: Sage.

Kim, Y. Y. (2005). Adapting to a new culture: An integrative communication theory. In W. Gudykunst (Ed.), *Theorizing about intercultural communication* (pp. 375–400). Thousand Oaks, CA: Sage.

Kim, Y. Y. (2009). Cross-cultural adaptation theory. In S. Littlejohn & K. Foss (Eds.), *Encyclopedia of communication theory* (pp. 243–247). Thousand Oaks, CA: Sage.

Kim, Y. Y. (2012). Cross-cultural adaptation. In V. S. Ramachandran (Ed.), *Encyclopedia of human behavior* (Vol. 1, pp. 623–630). Burlington, MA: Academic Press.

Kim, Y. Y. (2018). Integrative communication theory of cross-cultural adaptation. In Y. Y. Kim (Ed.), *The international encyclopedia of intercultural communication* (Vol. 2, pp. 929–941). Hoboken, NJ: Wiley & Sons. doi:10.1002/9781118783665.ieicc0041

Ruben, B. D., & Kim, J. Y. (Eds.). (1972). *General systems theory and human communication* (pp. 120–144). Rochelle Park, NJ: Hayden.

Simmel, G. (1908/1950). The stranger. In K. Wolff (Ed. and trans.), *The sociology of Georg Simmel.* New York, NY: Free Press.

Chapter 9

Co-Cultural Theory: Performing Emotional Labor from a Position of Exclusion

Robert Razzante, M.Ed. | Sarah Tracy, Ph.D.

Earlier this week we met with the board of trustees, and I was the only African American woman in the room. There was an Ethiopian–African man in the room who was of color, but I was the only African American female. In the room was a White male here and another White male there. Basically, there were three little brown specks in a room of like 30. It is one of those things that I don't let bother me as much. Sometimes you feel like (audible sigh), but you just shake it off.

–Michelle

The quote above comes from an interview with Michelle, an academic administrator in a predominately White, private institution in Philadelphia. Michelle is a Black female who works with mostly White men. As demonstrated by her quote, Michelle sometimes suppresses her upset emotions at work due to being one of the only women of color in her work meetings and, instead, works to project a positive, unaffected demeanor. Co-Cultural Theory (Orbe, 1998) becomes a useful lens when seeking to understand the experiences of historically marginalized employees in a workplace. As demonstrated by Michelle's quote above, being a Black female in a predominantly White, male workplace may cause lots of distress. To deal with such distress, Michelle, and other co-cultural group members, may find themselves practicing emotional labor. In this chapter, we explore emotional labor literature as a foreground for describing ways that historically marginalized groups manage their communication while at work. More specifically, we explore how marginalized people manage their emotions in workplaces that seek to intentionally or unintentionally create division between those who have power and those who do not. In this chapter we use Co-Cultural Theory and emotional labor to explore how and why marginalized people communicate in similar ways as Michelle in the excerpt above.

Emotional Labor

Anyone who has ever pretended to adore a gift that they did not want, or who has suppressed their giggles when sternly reprimanding a pet for bad behavior, has engaged in *emotion management*. The experience of performing or suppressing emotions as part of a paid job for organizational benefit is called *emotional labor*. Sociologist Arlie Hochschild first coined the term "emotional labor" through her research on the ways that airline flight attendants were expected to put on a happy face and how bill collectors were taught to be angry and intimidating with delinquent clients (1983). Specifically, emotional labor refers to "the management of feeling to create a publicly observable facial and bodily display" for commerce (Hochschild, 1983, p. 7). It is easy to see how this type of work is integral to many different types of jobs, including those in service, teaching, and human interaction. Firefighters act tough (Scott & Meyers, 2005), cruise ship employees smile (Tracy, 2000), nurses show compassion (Way & Tracy, 2012), judges suppress their amusement (Scarduzio, 2011), TSA agents absorb passenger irritation (Malvini Redden, 2013), 911 call-takers calm frightened citizens (Tracy & Tracy, 1998), and border patrol agents navigate the tensions of upholding the law while being kind to suffering border crossers (Rivera, 2015). Although some jobs require very specific types of emotional labor, typical emotional labor expectations mark almost all organizational settings, such as the norms that subordinates act respectful toward bosses and that frontline employees absorb irritation from customers without complaint.

Employees engage in emotional labor through suppressing, amplifying, and/or masking their emotions, or a combination thereof (Tracy, 2005). As Michelle explains in the excerpt at the beginning of this chapter, internally, she feels upset. However, she suppresses her distress, and does not voice the difficulty and sadness of feeling like a token Black woman in the sea of White faces. She, instead, "shakes it off," presumably through various bodily and facial displays. She may mask her distress by smiling at the other employees or by pretending to be engrossed in the meeting agenda.

Employees manipulate their emotions in two main ways. *Surface acting* is when employees transform (or fake) their outward emotional displays to fit the organizational expectation, while not authentically feeling what the organization expects (Hochschild, 1983). In this particular case, Michelle is surface acting because she is still clearly upset, but she is pretending not to be. However, faking emotion can go one step further to *deep acting*, which is when employees convince themselves to deeply and internally feel the expected organizational emotion. In such cases, employees no longer need to "fake" the expected emotional display because they have changed their real feelings, and the emotional expression follows suit

(Hochschild, 1983). Deep acting, in Michelle's case, could mean that she reframes her minority status so she can see it as normal, natural, or even evidence that, as a Black woman, she must be very lucky to be there. If Michelle convinced herself of this framing, she would be deep acting, and taking as her own the organizational expectations for not making a fuss about being among the only people of color in her organization's leadership.

Emotional labor is fundamental to organizational productivity, profitability, and easing employee interactions. However, engaging in emotional labor can be problematic for employees. This is intuitive for some employees, such as correctional officers, who are encouraged to amplify angry or jerk-like behaviors (Tracy, 2005), as these types of excessive, negative emotional expressions release harmful hormones and reduce immune functioning (Conrad & Witte, 1994). However, negative outcomes are also linked to *suppressing* negative emotion and faking positive emotion. Whenever there is a discrepancy between the performed and felt emotion, this creates *emotional dissonance*, or a clash between authentic feeling and expressed emotion (Ashforth & Humphrey, 1993). Emotive dissonance is especially painful when employees feel required to perform emotions that they do not agree they should have to perform, called *faking in bad faith* (Rafaeli & Sutton, 1987). The pain of emotional labor is also exacerbated when employees must perform emotions that mark them as a low status employee; for example, they have to act submissive or respectful (Tracy, 2005). Meanwhile, emotive dissonance is not nearly as difficult when employees believe that the emotional performance is useful and important, called *faking in good faith* (Rafaeli & Sutton, 1987), or when the performance aligns with their preferred identity and higher status (Tracy, 2005). Furthermore, when employees engage in deep acting and actually transform their internal feelings to align with organizational expectations, they can become alienated from the signals that emotions are designed to provide. Evolutionarily, emotions help human beings to survive. Fear triggers retreat. Love triggers connection. When people force themselves not to feel certain emotions due to organizational norms (i.e., firefighters are expected to be tough and mask their fear), employees may overlook emotion signals that provide important and lifesaving information (i.e., fear could be telling firefighters that a fire is so dangerous that they should retreat) (Tracy & Scott, 2006).

Michelle's comment at the opening of this chapter does not explicitly indicate whether or not she feels like she should be required to suppress her distress. However, as indicated by her deep sigh, she likely feels resigned and sad to be just one of the "brown specks" in the meeting. Resignation is different than endorsement and, therefore, indicates that Michelle does not fully buy into the idea that her emotional labor is justifiable. Furthermore, one could argue that by suppressing distress, this indicates a lower status identity and unpreferred identity. Unlike some people, Michelle may feel as though she is not allowed to make a fuss or speak up. As such, the research on emotional labor would suggest that if Michelle continues to fake her emotions in bad faith, this will lead to burnout. Indeed, emotional dissonance can "lead to personal and work-related maladjustment, such as poor self-esteem, depression, cynicism, and alienation from work" (Ashforth & Humphrey, 1993, pp. 96–97). And, what if Michelle actually changes her viewpoint, deep acts, and convinces herself not to feel upset? This would be faking in good faith. However, faking in good faith might completely alienate Michelle from emotions of distress that usefully signal the fact that something problematic (like systematic racism) is going on here. By turning off these emotions, she turns off an important way of knowing, and potentially transforming, the world. A primary question to ask, too, is how her emotional labor is associated with her being a woman of color, a "co-cultural member," and, with that, we turn to a discussion of Co-Cultural Theory.

Communicating from Marginalization

Co-Cultural Theory attempts to understand and describe how historically marginalized groups of individuals communicate when interacting with dominant group members (Orbe, 1998). As seen below, historical marginalization and dominant group membership are characterized through the understanding that, in US society, there are some groups of people who have power and privilege, and others who do not. As such, Co-Cultural Theory sheds light on Michelle's communication patterns through exploring her positionality as a female administrator of color in a predominantly White institution. It is first valuable to understand the theoretical foundations on which Co-Cultural Theory was built.

Standpoint Theory

Standpoint Theory (Smith, 1987) works under the assumption that certain groups live life in the center, whiles other live on the margins. For example, in Michelle's example above, she works from a standpoint that lies on the margins in terms of being Black in a predominantly White institution. She is reminded about her marginality when interacting in an environment where her body is marked as an "other." Meanwhile, her White colleagues live life in the center, where they can choose to ignore the lack of diversity at work. Standpoint Theory offers a unique way of understanding how we may be in the center in terms of some identities (i.e., Michelle being an administrator), while on the margins in another (i.e., Black and female).

Muted Group Theory

Muted Group Theory (Kramarae, 1981) embraces the same critical lens as Standpoint Theory, but specifically focuses on gender dynamics at work. That is, the theory offers a framework for understanding how women in particular experience silence at work. The theory works under the assumption that, in a predominantly or historically male working environment, women may become silenced or their viewpoints will not hold as much power. In the case of Michelle, she recognized her positionality as not only African American, but an African American *female*. Muted Group Theory offers a lens to understand how Michelle might experience marginality not only due to her race, but also due to her gender.

Co-Cultural Theory

Taking into consideration Standpoint Theory and Muted Group Theory, Co-Cultural Theory attempts to localize discourses of marginalization within the field of intercultural communication. maintains the assumption that certain groups experience privilege based on race (Whites), class (upper- and middle-class), gender (cis-men), etc., whereas other groups experience marginalization (people of color, working-class, women and trans-folks). When communicating from a position of exclusion, marginalized groups (referred to as co-cultural groups) adapt their communication to fit the norms established by those with power and privilege. Working from this assumption, Orbe (1998) conducted a phenomenological study of stories from people who experienced marginalization in one way or another. He was interested in how marginalized group members (referred to as co-cultural group members) communicated across the power imbalance with dominant group members (those in the center, privileged group). Through the stories, Orbe identified 26 key communicative practices, and six influential factors, that informed the way co-cultural members communicated with dominant group members.

Co-cultural group members consciously choose communicative practices based on the following six factors: *preferred outcome, communication approach, field of experience, abilities, situational context,* and *perceived costs and rewards.* Of the six factors, preferred outcome and communication approach emerged as the two most influential factors that determined one's selection. As seen in Table 1, all 26 practices are listed within a grid between the two influential factors. While the other four factors are not explicitly present, they remain integral components to one's selection. In other words, a co-cultural member's use of a particular communication practice is influenced by his/her abilities, field of experience, situational context, and perceived costs/rewards. What follows is the in-depth exploration

Communication Approach	Preferred Outcome	Communication Practices
Nonassertive	Separation	Avoiding Maintaining Interpersonal Barriers
Nonassertive	Accommodation	Visibility Dispelling Stereotypes
Nonassertive	Assimilation	Emphasizing Commonalities Developing Positive Face Censoring Self Averting Controversy
Assertive	Separation	Communicating Self Intragroup Networking Exemplifying Strengths Embracing Stereotypes
Assertive	Accommodation	Communicating Self Intragroup Networking Utilizing Liaisons Educating Others
Assertive	Assimilation	Extensive Preparation Overcompensating Manipulating Stereotypes Bargaining
Aggressive	Separation	Attacking Sabotaging Others
Aggressive	Accommodation	Confronting Gaining Advantage
Aggressive	Assimilation	Dissociating Mirroring Strategic Distancing Ridiculing Self

Table 1. Co-Cultural Communication Orientations and Practices (Adapted from Orbe, 1998)

of *preferred outcome* and *communication approach*, specifically. We recommend having a copy of Table 1 easily accessible when reading through the subsequent paragraphs to help visualize how preferred outcome and communication approach relate to one another.

Preferred outcome articulates a co-cultural group member's aspired outcome of an interaction with a dominant group member. Preferred outcome, as demonstrated in Table 1, can be viewed as a continuum from assimilation to separation. *Assimilation* becomes a preferred outcome when the co-cultural group member wishes to reduce differences in order to lessen the power distance with dominant group members (i.e., censoring self, mirroring, ridiculing self) (Orbe, 1998).

Contrary to assimilation lies separation. Instead of reducing power distances, *separation* seeks to uphold such distance (i.e., avoiding, embracing stereotypes, attacking). Within the tension between assimilation and separation lies accommodation. *Accommodation* exhibits the desire to negotiate power distances between co-cultural group members and dominant group members (i.e., dispelling stereotypes, communicating self, confronting).

As explored through Co-Cultural Theory, depending on one's goals, a marginalized group member in a working environment may enact one of the practices listed under those headings. That is, using assimilation, accommodation, or separation becomes a strategic move among co-cultural group members seeking to navigate structures that privilege dominant group members and suppress co-cultural members. Depending on the context, one's abilities, their perceived costs and rewards, field of experience, and situational context, a co-cultural group member may choose one approach over the other. The effects of a particular approach depend on the situational context in which the communication approach occurs. There is no right or wrong way for a co-cultural group member to act. Rather, like all communication, decisions become contextually based. In addition to envisioning a preferred outcome, co-cultural group members may employ specific approaches to achieve their desired goal. What follows is an exploration of three communication approaches co-cultural group members might employ as a means to achieve their preferred outcome. When in a working environment, it becomes necessary to develop such communication skills to be able to advocate for oneself. As such, Co-Cultural Theory generally, and *communication approaches* specifically, provide a lens to understand how a co-cultural group member might be able to communicate to achieve his/her intended goal.

Employees can achieve their preferred outcome via a variety of communication approaches, which can range from nonassertive to aggressive. A *nonassertive* communication approach transpires when a co-cultural group member elevates the needs of the dominant group member before his/her own (Orbe, 1998). Contrarily, an *aggressive* communication approach occurs where co-cultural group members emphasize their own needs/desires while disregarding the needs/desires of dominant group member (Orbe, 1998). In between nonassertive and aggressive communication lies an *assertive* communication approach. An assertive approach manifests when the needs/desires of both co-cultural and dominant group members are considered when attempting to achieve a preferred outcome. Assertive communication approaches demonstrate one's ability to think about both him/herself in relation to another person. Such an approach demonstrates self-awareness, and awareness for others, in an interaction.

As previously mentioned, co-cultural members also consider four additional factors when choosing how to communicate with dominant members (Orbe, 1998). First, they consider their *field of experience*, which accounts for one's worldview based on their lived experiences. If they have had experiences where speaking out is rewarded, for example, they may be more likely to speak out. *Abilities* speak to one's ability to respond to a dominant group member in a particular situation. *Situational context* refers to the environment in which the conversation takes place (i.e., at work, in a coffee shop, at a sporting event); someone might feel more emboldened to speak in one context versus another. Finally, *perceived costs and rewards* are taken into consideration based on one's past experiences when employing a particular communicative behavior in effort to achieve his/her intended goal. When taken together, all six influential factors (abilities, field of experience, situational context, perceived costs and rewards, communication approach, and preferred outcome) help to inform why and how a marginalized individual speaks out to dominant group members. To better understand how Co-Cultural Theory can be applied, we turn to the previous example of Michelle.

Michelle Revisited

Together, Co-Cultural Theory and emotional labor offer lenses to understand the difficulties co-cultural members might face at work as they routinely manage their emotional displays and suppress upset feelings. Let us return to Michelle's reflection on being one of the few women of color in her predominantly White institution. While we cannot speak on behalf of Michelle, we can try to understand the emotional labor Michelle performs as a result of being one of few women of color in a predominantly White male work-environment. In reviewing Michelle's response, we use the six factors of Co-Cultural Theory to understand what might have been going through Michelle's mind while choosing to "just shake it off." Doing so may provide a heuristic device that highlights how emotional labor and Co-Cultural Theory manifest in daily practice.

We begin by reviewing Michelle's *field of experience*. Earlier in the interview with Michelle, she described her previous job at a predominantly White university in rural Appalachia. She spoke about the difficulties of living in the community as a Black female. For example, if she wanted to get her hair cut, braided, or styled, she would need to travel an hour and a half to the nearest city to do so. As such, the resources for a comfortable style of living were scarce. In moving to Philadelphia, she found the increase in diversity that she had been looking for. However, her work environment had not changed. Like her previous institution, her new workplace was also predominantly White and male. As such, the accumulative experience of sitting on the margins added up for Michelle. As such, her communicative practices are heavily informed by being an outsider within.

As seen in Table 1, it appears Michelle had many practices to choose from when communicating with her colleagues. However, Michelle's *abilities* were hindered by organizational norms. As a new administrator, Michelle felt that she needed to listen more than speak. Whether or not she would have been allowed, by others, to speak up, Michelle had internalized the notion that she had to remain silent. As such, her abilities were influenced by the environment in which she worked. As seen here, *situational context* highly informs one's perceived abilities to employ a communicative practice in order to achieve a preferred outcome. If she was with her colleagues after work at happy hour, Michelle may have felt more comfortable speaking up and showing her distress. However the *perceived costs* of speaking up to her colleagues in that setting outweighed the *perceived rewards* of suppressing her feelings.

To reemphasize, Michelle's situational context, abilities, perceived costs/rewards, and field of experience inform the enactment of a particular communicative practice. To revisit, a *nonassertive* communication approach is one where co-cultural group members downgrade their own needs in order to focus on the needs/desires of the dominant group members. *Assimilation* occurs when the goal of the interaction is to reduce power differences between the dominant group members and oneself. In this case, Michelle chose nonassertive assimilation via emotional suppression and masking as a means to "fit in" and "play nice" with her White, male colleagues. By "shaking it off," Michelle reproduced the status quo while biting her tongue.

To review, emotional labor occurs when someone performs a façade that misaligns with his/her authentic feelings. Although Michelle may have desired to speak up, she chose to keep quiet instead. More specifically, Michelle engaged in *developing positive face, self-censorship*, and *averting controversy*. In doing so, Michelle averted controversy by censoring her emotional state as a means to save face for both herself and her colleagues. If she had refused to engage in this emotional labor, her meeting might have unfolded in a much different manner. For example, she may have decided to engage in aggressive accommodation to confront her colleagues and the unwelcoming environment they create. It is tough to speculate what would have happened had Michelle used this approach. However, her past experiences may have told her that this was not a good idea. Ideally, workplaces would exist where individuals can express their concerns without having to think about the threat of being looked down upon by their peers. Taking all of these theoretical applications into mind, we end this chapter with implications for practice.

Implications for Practice

Co-Cultural Theory provides a framework for understanding and describing why co-cultural group members communicate the way they do. When considered within the framework of organizational literature generally, and emotional labor specifically, Co-Cultural Theory provides a critical-cultural lens for understanding the challenges faced by marginalized employees, and the power dynamics at play when they interact with dominant members at work. Considering the many influential factors at play, there exist practical implications for both co-cultural group members and dominant group members.

First, many people who are marginalized at work feel alone and wonder, "is it just me who feels these challenges?" Simply having the language provided by emotional labor and Co-Cultural Theory provides a framework to map onto their lived experiences (Barge, 2001). That is, the theories become useful resources in order to understand the factors behind workplace challenges and provide a vocabulary for different communication options. In understanding these factors, one can critically reflect on challenging workplace situations in different ways as a means to take control of one's communication. When used this way, Co-Cultural Theory can become used as a means for liberatory praxis (hooks, 1994). That is, one can use theory and practice as a means to understand how larger discourses influence one's daily communicative practices. In understanding these larger discourses, one can then reclaim a lost sense of perceived agency.

Second, these theories are also important for dominant group members to understand, as they highlight the specific challenges faced by their co-cultural colleagues, and how, as dominant members, they might intervene or communicate to transform these challenges. Dominant group members have a significant role to play in disrupting or reinforcing structures that allow for privilege and marginalization in the first place (Razzante & Orbe, 2018; Razzante, Tracy, Orbe, In Press). Through their talk and interaction, dominant group members communicatively coconstitute organizational norms open to the challenging abuses of power and privilege. For example, in Michelle's case above, White colleagues could affirm Michelle's concern that the workplace is unwelcoming to herself and her colleagues of color. Furthermore, Michelle's White colleagues could even move themselves to create the space where racial minorities feel free to talk honestly without being labeled as "angry people of color." With roots in Co-Cultural Theory, Dominant Group Theory (Razzante & Orbe, 2018) becomes a useful theory to understand communicative practices of those who maintain positions of power and privilege. When considered together, Co-Cultural Theory and Dominant Group Theory provide a useful framework for understanding how interpersonal/intercultural interactions inform organizational culture around difference in social identities.

Third, this analysis suggests that employees consider the variety of intersectional ways that employees might feel marginalized or the factors that contribute to the mal-effects of performing emotional labor. That is, rather than essentializing someone as only a co-cultural group member or a dominant group member, we recommend considering how a single individual may be both a co-cultural member and a dominant group member. For example, although Michelle is a co-cultural group member in terms of race and gender, she is a dominant group member in terms of class, educational level, and ability. As seen in Dominant Group Theory, most dominant group members, especially if they live long enough to be considered "old" (itself a marginalized identity category), will eventually become a co-cultural group member (Razzante & Orbe, 2018). In taking an intersectional approach, readers can develop a more nuanced and holistic understanding of privilege and marginalization as it manifests in the workplace.

Finally, while this chapter provides a conceptual overview of Co-Cultural Theory and emotional labor, we recommend using this knowledge to transform one's life as lived. That is, we encourage readers to take this knowledge to engage in critical self-reflexivity to challenge one's own assumptions about him/herself and others (Cunliffe, 2004). Questions to ask oneself include the following:

1. How am I a dominant or marginalized group member at work?

2. In what ways might I be intentionally or unintentionally be making it difficult for marginalized people to speak up?

3. How might I consider issues like organizational context or experience so as to provide an environment where all organizational members have the opportunity to be self-expressed?

Indeed, critically questioning the factors behind one's own, and others', communication can lead to more competent and effective dialogue and interaction at work. Moreover, readers are left to imagine and create workplaces that thrive through difference by embodying Co-Cultural Theory, Dominant Group Theory, and emotional labor literature through their everyday interactions. When this happens, Michelle and others like her may be released from an unjust burden of emotional labor.

Discussion Questions

1. What previous jobs of yours required you to perform surface level and/or deep level acting?

2. What ways can workplaces come to create a workplace environment where emotional labor ceases to exist?

3. Think back to a time when you performed emotional labor. Did you suppress, amplify, or mask emotion? Did you agree with performing it? Did you find the performance easy or difficult, and why?

4. In what ways do you identify as a co-cultural group member? Identify a time when you performed emotional labor as a result of your co-cultural group membership.

5. How might you interact at work so as to encourage an environment where co-cultural group members are as likely to speak up as dominant group members?

6. How might you personally use what you now know about emotional labor and co-cultural theory to inform your communication at work?

7. What are some of co-cultural theory's limitations? How might the theory be extended?

REFERENCES

Ashforth, B. E., & Humphrey, R. H. (1993). Emotional labor in service roles: The influence of identity. *Academy of Management Review 18(1)*, 88–115. doi:10.5465/AMR.1993.3997508

Barge, J. K. (2001). Practical theory as mapping, engaged reflection, and transformative practice. *Communication Theory, 11(1)*, 5–13.

Conrad, C. & Witte, K. (1994). Is emotional expression repression oppression? Myths of organizational affective regulation. *Annals of the International Communication Association 17(1)*, 417–428. doi:10.1080/23808985.1994.11678895

Cunliffe, A. L. (2004). On becoming a critically reflexive practitioner. *Journal of Management Education, 28(4)*, 407–426.

Kramarae, C. (1981). *Women and men speaking.* Rowley, MA: Newbury House. doi: 10.2307/413973

Malvini Redden, S. (2013). How lines organize compulsory interaction, emotion management, and "emotional taxes": The implications of passenger emotion and expression in airport security lines. *Management Communication Quarterly 27(1)*, 121–149. doi:10.1177/0893318912458213

Martin, J. N., & Nakayama, T. K. (2017). *Intercultural Communication in Contexts.* 7th ed. Boston, MA: McGraw-Hill.

Orbe, M. P. (1998). *Constructing co-cultural theory: An explication of culture, power, and communication.* Thousand Oaks, CA: Sage.

Rafaeli, A, & Sutton, R. (1987). Expression of emotion as part of the work role. *Academy of Management Review 12(1)*, 23–37. doi:10.5465/AMR.1987.4306444

Razzante, R., Tracy, S., Orbe, M. (2018). How dominant group members can transform workplace bullying. In R. West & C. Beck (Eds.), *The Routledge handbook of communication and bullying* (pp. 46–56). New York, NY: Routledge.

Rivera, K. D. (2015). Emotional taint: Making sense of emotional dirty work at the US Border Patrol. *Management Communication Quarterly 29(2)*, 198–228. doi:10.1177/0893318914554090

Scarduzio, J. A. (2011). Maintaining order through deviance? The emotional deviance, power, and professional work of municipal court judges. *Management Communication Quarterly 25(2)*, 283–310. doi:10.1177/0893318910386446

Scott, C. & Myers, K. (2005). The socialization of emotion: Learning emotion management at the fire station. *Journal of Applied Communication Research 33*(1), 67–92. doi:10.1080/00909880042000318521

Smith, D. E. (1987). *The everyday world as problematic: A feminist sociology of knowledge.* Boston, MA: Northeastern University Press.

Tracy, S. J. (2000). Becoming a character for commerce: Emotion labor, self-subordination, and discursive construction of identity in a total institution. *Management Communication Quarterly 14(1)*, 90–128. doi:10.1177/0893318900141004

Tracy, S. J. (2005). Locking up emotion: Moving beyond dissonance for understanding emotion labor discomfort. *Communication Monographs 72(3)*, 261–283. doi:10.1080/03637750500206474

Tracy, S. J., & Tracy, K. (1998). Emotion labor at 911: A case study and theoretical critique. *Journal of Applied Communication Research 26(4)*, 390–411. doi:10.1080/00909889809365516

Tracy, S. J. & Scott, C. (2006). Sexuality, masculinity and taint management among firefighters and correctional officers: Getting down and dirty with "America's heroes" and the "scum of law enforcement." *Management Communication Quarterly, 20*, 6–38.

Way, D., & Tracy, S. J. (2012). Conceptualizing compassion as recognizing, relating and (re)acting: An ethnographic study of compassionate communication at hospice. *Communication Monographs, 79(1)*, 292–315.

Chapter 10
Violence and Cultivation Theory: A Case Study

Michael Morgan, Ph.D. *University of Massachusetts/Amherst*
James Shanahan, Ph.D. *Indiana University*
Nancy Signorielli, Ph.D. *University of Delaware*

Since the 1950s, television has been not only the most prominent of all mass media, but also a defining element of modern life. Television's institutional structure and technology, as well as its programming, have seen immense changes, yet it remains the source of our most widely shared cultural stories, images, and lessons. Its importance and centrality in our lives are enhanced by new technologies (such as on-demand, online streaming, and mobile devices) that make television easier to watch whenever and wherever we want. Nevertheless, as a society, we continue to have concerns about the effects of its portrayals of violence, sex, gender and racial/ethnic stereotypes, the family, medicine, politics, health, nutrition and weight, drugs and alcohol, mental illness, and much more (Bryant, Thompson, & Finklea, 2012; Singer & Singer, 2012). Violence, in particular, has been a focus of concern since television entered our lives (Ferguson & Faye, 2018; Friedrich-Cofer & Huston, 1986; Gentile, 1983; Strasburger, 2014); thousands of studies have been conducted and Congress has held more than two dozen hearings on the topic.

This chapter discusses the question of television violence from the perspective of cultivation analysis, which was developed by George Gerbner (1919–2005) as a new way to explore the effects of television. Growing up in prewar Hungary, Gerbner was struck by the way the folk stories and songs of peasants in the rural Hungarian villages both reflected and recreated their particular ways of seeing the world. Later, as a young scholar in mid-20th century America, he was similarly struck by the fact that the cultural process of storytelling had undergone a profound transformation. No longer handcrafted and passed on face-to-face, folktales were now being mass-produced by commercial conglomerates and mass-consumed to an historically unprecedented degree. Gerbner devoted his career to investigating how these manufactured stories both reflected and shaped the culture that produced them (Morgan, 2012).

Gerbner's goal was to understand the consequences of growing up in a cultural environment dominated by mediated, profit-driven, mass communication (Gerbner, 1973). He devised a three-pronged approach, called Cultural Indicators, to investigate (1) the processes underlying the selection and production of media content ("institutional process analysis"), (2) the most prevalent, aggregate images in that content ("message system analysis"), and (3) the contribution of that content to audience beliefs and behaviors ("cultivation analysis"). While this model, its conceptual assumptions, and its methodological procedures can be applied to any dominant medium of communication (or any system of storytelling), cultivation analysis has mostly focused on television, since no other medium exceeds its hold on our time and attention. In its simplest form, cultivation analysis asks if those who watch more television ("heavy viewers") have conceptions of social reality that are more reflective of what they see on television as compared to people who have similar demographic characteristics but who watch less television. Cultivation analysis, then, examines how the stories we—as a culture—watch on television contribute to our beliefs and attitudes about the "real" world.

Cultivation was conceived as a critical alternative to traditional approaches to the study of media "effects," which typically examined whether exposure to some specific media message produced a change in attitude or behavior. Gerbner was not interested in such "immediate" or short-term shifts; those were questions for persuasion and marketing research. Rather, he wanted to explore what shared cultural outlooks and assumptions might be nurtured, maintained, and reinforced by television's aggregate messages in large communities over long periods of time (Gerbner 1973, 1999). All communication, he argued, reciprocally cultivates the assumptions, points of view, and relationships on which it is premised. With mass communication, what is cultivated is standardized and more widely shared than was ever before possible. The common, symbolic environment in which we grow up and live gives shape and meaning to all that we do; the more we "live" in that synthetic, but coherent, world, the more it cultivates our conceptions of social reality.

To some, this was a common-sense idea. However, it raised the hackles of many social scientists who saw a too simplistic criticism of television or even a misuse of social science research methods. As a result, it provided an opportunity for innumerable colloquies, critiques, revisions, and reappraisals (see Shanahan & Morgan, 1999, for a review). But despite, or perhaps because of, the enormous amount of criticism that has been leveled at cultivation, it is one of the most frequently cited theories of mass communication. Various studies of the literature regularly place cultivation, along with agenda setting and uses and gratifications, as one of the three most cited theories of media effects (Bryant & Miron, 2004). One analysis found that cultivation was *the* most cited theory in media effects research articles published between 1993 and 2005 (Potter & Riddle, 2007). By 2018, more than 900 relevant studies had been published (two-thirds of which are extensions, replications, reviews, and critiques conducted by independent researchers not associated with Gerbner and the original research team).[1] Cultivation studies have been carried out in Argentina, Australia, Belgium, Brazil, China, England, Germany, Hungary, Israel, Japan, Mexico, Russia, South Korea, Sweden, Thailand, and elsewhere. Clearly, such a large body of work—and all the complex issues and implications it raises—cannot be exhaustively treated here; this chapter attempts to provide only a general introduction to this area of research focusing particularly on the example of violence. (For more extensive examinations of the cultivation literature, see Morgan, Shanahan, & Signorielli, 2009, 2012; Shanahan & Morgan, 1999).

Cultivation Analysis Methods

Cultivation analysis begins by identifying the most common and stable patterns in television content, emphasizing the consistent images, portrayals, and values that cut across program genres. This is accomplished either by conducting a message system (content) analysis or by examining existing content studies. Once those patterns are identified, the goal is to ascertain if those who spend more time watching television are more likely to perceive the real world in ways that reflect those particular messages and lessons.

In relation to violence, content patterns consistently reveal high levels of violence in prime-time TV programs. During the past 50 years, violence has appeared in 70% of primetime programs, at a rate of 5.3 violent actions per hour, with more than 40% of characters involved in violence as either a victim of violence, someone who commits violence, or both (Signorielli, Morgan, & Shanahan, 2019). Based on this, one task for cultivation analysis is to determine if heavy viewers (having been extensively and deeply immersed in the violent world of television) are more likely to see the world as a violent place. (It should be stressed that this approach is in sharp contrast to most research and debate on television violence, where the concern is that exposure to violent content will result in imitation or violent behavior.)

---

[1]A complete bibliography of Cultural Indicators work is located at: http://people.umass.edu/mmorgan/CulturalIndicatorsBibliography.pdf.

Cultivation hypotheses, such as this one, are most often tested using survey procedures to examine relationships between amount of television viewing and conceptions of social reality among large groups of people. Several different types of questions are asked. Some juxtapose answers reflecting the statistical "facts" of the television world with those more in line with reality (often referred to as "first-order" cultivation measures). As an example, compared to light viewers, heavy viewers are more likely to think that there are more law enforcement professionals in the workforce (Gerbner & Gross, 1976). Other questions examine symbolic transformations and more general implications of the message system data (often referred to as "second-order" cultivation measures). For example, considerable research has focused on the "Mean World Syndrome," which refers to the role of television viewing in cultivating mistrust, anxiety, fear of crime, perceptions of victimization, and the like.

Studies use different types of samples (national probability, regional, convenience) of children, adolescents, or adults, and assess the amount of viewing by asking how much time the respondent spends watching on an "average day" (although investigators have measured amount of viewing in many different ways). These data may be used in their original form (a ratio scale) or may be grouped by level of exposure ("light," "medium," and "heavy" viewing), on a sample-by-sample basis.

As with many media effects studies, cultivation analyses typically generate small to moderate effect sizes. Even those who watch relatively little television may watch seven to 10 hours a week—and these viewers certainly interact with those who watch more. Thus, the cards can be statistically stacked against finding evidence of cultivation, because everyone is exposed to its messages to some degree. Nevertheless, even small differences between light and heavy viewers may indicate far-reaching consequences. With very large audiences, a difference of a fraction of a percentage point in ratings can indicate the success or failure of a program (and be worth millions of advertising dollars), and a difference of a few percentage points (or less) in an election will determine who wins or who loses. Similarly, small relationships across large populations of heavy and light viewers may indicate profound social effects, especially as they cumulate over time.

Critiques and Refinements

Few theories of media effects (and perhaps few areas of social research in general) have been critiqued as heavily and fiercely as cultivation. (For some examples, see Doob & McDonald, 1979; Hirsch, 1980; Hughes, 1980; Potter, 1993, 1994, 2014; Wober, 1978; see also Shanahan & Morgan, 1999.) These critiques have focused on many issues, including cultivation's emphasis on overall amount of television exposure (as opposed to specific types of programs), the way television viewing is measured and divided into relative levels of exposure, justifications for interpreting television-world answers, the linearity of cultivation associations, and much more.

Some of the most heated issues of contention have revolved around questions of spuriousness and the proper use of statistical controls. Early analyses typically applied a single control variable at a time. For example, to control for education, the association between television viewing and some belief is examined separately for those with more education and those with less, or the patterns are examined separately... and so on. This helps insure that relationships between amount of viewing and beliefs are not actually due to some other variable. But various critics—sometimes reanalyzing the same data—argued that when *multiple* controls were applied at the *same* time, the relationships between television viewing and attitudes mostly disappeared. This led them to conclude that there was essentially no evidence to support the cultivation hypothesis.

Gerbner and his colleagues countered that even if a relationship disappears under multiple controls, significant patterns may still exist *within* specific subgroups, often reflecting a pattern they called "mainstreaming" (Gerbner, Gross, Morgan, & Signorielli, 1980). Among light viewers, people who differ in terms of background factors, such as age, sex, education, social class, political orientations, and region of residence, tend to have sharply different conceptions of social reality regarding violence, interpersonal mistrust, gender-role stereotypes, and a broad range of political and social outlooks. Yet, among heavy viewers across those same groups, those differences tend to be much smaller or even to disappear entirely.

For example, Gerbner et al. (1980) found that low-income respondents were more likely than those with higher incomes to say that "fear of crime is a very serious personal problem" (p. 16). Among low-income respondents, the amount of television viewing was not related at all to perceptions of crime. In contrast, although higher-income respondents, as a group, were less likely to think of crime as a serious personal problem, the heavy viewers with higher incomes were much more likely than the light viewers to be especially worried about crime. Heavy viewers with higher incomes had the same perception as those with lower incomes; among heavy viewers, the difference stemming from income was sharply diminished.

A second process also emerged to explain and predict how viewing may impact different viewers. Specifically, direct experience may be important for some viewers. The phenomenon called *resonance* was proposed to illustrate how a person's everyday reality, and patterns of television viewing, may provide a double dose of messages that "resonate" and amplify cultivation. For example, those who live in high crime urban areas often show stronger relationships between the amount of viewing and self-reported fear of crime (Doob & Macdonald, 1979). The idea here is that both the "TV world" and the real world reinforce the impression that violence is widespread.

Shanahan and Morgan (1999) reviewed over 20 years' worth of cultivation studies in a meta-analysis. This analysis found that the body of cultivation research, as a whole, exhibited a small, but persistent, relationship between television exposure and beliefs about the world. The number of cultivation studies has grown substantially since then. At this point, we can say that hundreds of studies conducted over the past five decades have (mostly) found that there are consistent and meaningful relationships between how much time people spend watching television and how they think about the world.

Recent Extensions of Cultivation

One of the most fruitful and active areas of development in recent cultivation research has illuminated the cognitive mechanisms that account for the cultivation process. In an extensive series of studies, Shrum (see Shrum & Lee, 2012 for a comprehensive summary) has examined television's role in how people make first-order judgments (estimates of frequency in the real world) and second-order judgments (attitudes, opinions, and feelings). Shrum and Lee (2012) posit that very different cognitive processes are at work when making these different types of judgments. First-order cultivation judgments are memory-based and formed through heuristic processes. Television images influence these judgments when someone recalls relevant information often seen in television programs. It occurs because people take cognitive shortcuts when forming a judgment. For heavy viewers, television-based information is more accessible, available, recent, and vivid, and these factors lead the images to be more available to heavy viewers taking the shortcut (Shrum, 1996).

On the other hand, second-order cultivation judgments are formed in an "online" process, in which "the influence of television on judgment occurs during viewing, as information is processed" (Shrum & Lee, 2012, p. 162). Although "active" processing can sometimes counteract first-order cultivation (by making people aware of television as the source of their images), deep involvement or "transportation" in a story can enhance second-order cultivation.

Another issue in more recent cultivation research is whether the "realism" of TV content matters for cultivation. Many scholars have examined the notion of realism, particularly "perceived realism," as a critical component in understanding cultivation. While many researchers have assumed that only programs perceived as realistic would influence beliefs about the world, recent research shows that the situation is not that simple. For example, the research of Busselle and Bilandzic (2012) suggests that perceived realism is a default condition during viewing, and that most content, even that recognized as fantasy, can contribute to viewers' understanding of the real world.

Another issue is genre. "Classic" cultivation has always been concerned with the long-term effects of living with television in general. As Shanahan and Morgan (1999) note, it "is the pattern of settings, casting, social typing, action and related outcomes that cuts across program types and viewing modes and defines the world of television" (p. 30). Consequently, "orthodox" cultivation studies predict that those who watch more *in general*, television's "heavy viewers," see more of these images and messages on a regular basis and that their views of social reality are influenced by the messages and images they see day in and day out, regardless of their individual selections or favorite programs.

Nevertheless, many researchers see genre as an important element in cultivation research. Some scholars, for example, believe that cultivation research should focus on different genres of programs because they assume that viewers watch more selectively than ritualistically (especially now, with many more channels and many more options), and that different types of programs present diverse and distinct views of the world and social reality (Bilandzic & Rössler, 2004). Cohen and Weimann (2000) note that different genres are driven by their own specific formulas and present viewers with diverse and distinct views about the world. Crime dramas or action adventure programs, for example, focus on public life and the social order, while situation comedies, family dramas, and soap operas focus on domestic issues, family relationships, and friendships. Grabe and Drew (2007) also point out that content analyses show variation in portrayals among genres. For example, situation and romantic comedies typically present considerably less violence than do crime drama and action adventure programs. In addition, Bilandzic and Busselle (2012) argue that genre's status, as an important component of narrative, implies that it is useful to look at cultivation within genres (such as crime programs).

Some researchers postulate that viewers' conceptions about fear and violence are specifically the result of viewing crime-related programming (as opposed to overall amount of viewing), and several studies do show relationships between conceptions about crime and the viewing of crime programs. For example, Holbert, Shah, and Kwak (2004) found that viewing television news and police reality programs was related to fear of crime, but that viewing crime dramas was not. This analysis also found that nonfiction viewing (such as police reality programs) tended to be more strongly related to conceptions of social reality than the viewing of fictional crime dramas. They attributed this difference to the greater perceived realism of the police reality programs. Many other genre-based studies have produced a wide variety of genre-related findings (e.g., Bilandzic & Bosselle, 2008; Egbert & Belcher, 2012; Kahlor & Eastin, 2011; Segrin & Nabi, 2002).

It may not be surprising that there are many instances in which exposure to very specific media, particularly specific genres of television programs, is related to having very specific views about the world and social reality. The cultivation perspective, however, focuses more on people's general viewing habits and their cumulative exposure to the broad spectrum of television programs. Even in today's fragmented viewing world, viewing more television tends to mean greater exposure to what Gerbner conceived as the message "system," not just a collection of disparate and idiosyncratic viewing experiences. Patterns and similarities across all viewing genres are what matter most for the idea of cultivation. Even if people state that they prefer watching a specific genre (as we all do), overall media use normally encompasses viewing many different types of programs (as well as using other media, such as magazines and newspapers and websites). Although someone may profess to have a television diet consisting primarily of viewing crime programs, such as the *Law and Order* or *CSI* series, the images to which they are exposed may go far beyond just crime and violence. For example, while *Law and Order* and *CSI* are based primarily on the investigation of crime, these programs also offer images of interpersonal and family relationships, as well as other thematic elements showing how the world works. Consequently, heavy viewers of these programs will not only learn about crime and violence, they will also learn important life lessons about how people interact with each other.

Case Study: School Shootings

The problem of school shootings illustrates how the cultivation perspective can take us beyond conventional wisdom when trying to understand a complex social issue. Because cultivation occurs over a lifetime of viewing—of "living with television" (Gerbner & Gross, 1976)—there may be no exact event or point in time that exemplifies when it "happens." Indeed, very few cultivation studies have claimed to be able to illuminate a moment of causal clarity that shows us the presumed "effect." And, as we have seen, the point of cultivation is that we are *not* looking for a change that will delineate "before and after" television viewing. Rather, we are examining stable relationships that develop and deepen over time.

However, there are ways we can look at real-world situations to see how people talk about media effects, and to see how cultivation provides a different viewpoint. One powerful example is the case of school shootings (or other mass shootings) that have occurred with unfortunate frequency in the US. In these cases, with Columbine as the archetype, and Newtown, Parkland, and others as more recent examples, there is a natural human tendency to point fingers. A common explanation that goes back to television's early days is that media violence produces real violence in the social world, that these cases are tips of a very violent iceberg whose cause is in the media, in the images that we see on a daily basis.

In the wake of the Parkland shooting, President Donald Trump was quick to suggest that the real culprit might be video games:

> "I'm hearing more and more people say the level of violence on video games is really shaping young people's thoughts," the president said during a meeting with state and local officials on school safety a little more than a week after the Parkland shooting... "It's hard to believe that, at least for a percentage—and maybe it's a small percentage of children—this doesn't have a negative impact on their thought process. But these things are really violent," he continued. (Phelps, 2018)

Following the Las Vegas shootings, and appearing on CBS' "Face the Nation," NRA then-President Wayne LaPierre commented on who builds support for gun violence:

> You want to talk about irresponsible use of firearms? The number one person teaching irresponsible use of firearms is all these elites' employer, the Hollywood, television, gaming industry. We spend millions teaching responsible use of firearms. They make billions every single day ... teaching irresponsible use of firearms. They're so hypocritical it's unbelievable. (Rubin, 2017)

NRA President Oliver North picked up on the argument, that violent media—not guns—need to be controlled. "The problem that we've got is we're trying like the dickens to treat the symptom without treating the disease... And the disease in this case isn't the Second Amendment. The disease is youngsters who are steeped in a culture of violence" (Mele & Caron, 2018).

There is, however, little direct evidence that fictional gun violence can be directly tied in any way to real-world violence. The NRA and others use this specious argument for their own purposes. At the same time, as tragic as they are, perceptions of an "epidemic" of school shootings are blown out of proportion in relation to the facts (Levitz, 2018; Unsworth, 2018); moreover, violent crime has actually been decreasing in recent decades, even as levels of fear continue to rise (Gramlich, 2018).

From the perspective of cultivation, then, the question is whether television and other media play a role in cultivating the belief that we need more guns, that guns are glamorous, or any number of similar attitudes that might be held about gun ownership. America has a gun culture, and our media are an integral part of that culture. And if media play a role in stoking demand for guns by glamorizing them, the NRA assures the demand for them through hysterical defense of exaggerated Second Amendment claims.

Again, cultivation offers critical insights, based on the finding that exposure to violence in the media results not in imitation but in the cultivation of fear. Portrayals of school shootings and crime in our cities provide a perfect opportunity to argue for increased police control, for greater fear of "others" (such as immigrants or minorities), for more guns, and for greater authoritarian civil measures of "protection" as well. Morgan and Shanahan (2017) highlighted this finding in looking at American support for authoritarian stances. Heavy television viewing is linked to greater support for authoritarian values, and is even linked to the election of Donald Trump, a self-professed authoritarian. Scare tactics based on school shootings have worked well—to the point that some are suggesting we arm schoolteachers—and it is only a little ironic that the NRA itself takes the opportunity of mass shootings to argue that we need more, not fewer guns.

All of this is quite consistent with the cultivation perspective. Cultivation research never bothered to examine whether media cause direct imitation of violence, because it is self-evident that they do not. We see many murders on TV; very few of us are murderers. But how do we explain greater fear in an era when crime and violence are actually decreasing? Cultivation tells us to look first for the *lessons* of media violence, not for potential imitation. A lesson from most school shootings is that they are random and probably the result of mental illness, as well as of greater and easier access to guns, particularly assault rifles. Apart from the fear that this generates, the perceived need to arm oneself is an outcome that Gerbner would have foreseen.

Theoretical Implications of the Case Study

Applying some of the concepts we have looked at, we can see that there could be both first-order and second-order phenomena going on. In terms of understanding how many people own guns, the heavy viewer is likely to construct an estimate based on the raw frequency with which guns are portrayed on TV (very commonly) and also perhaps to rely on other heuristics (such as the vividness with which they are seen as problem-solving mechanisms in programming). As we have seen, such heuristics when relied upon will mean that the heavy viewer is more likely to overestimate the frequency of gun ownership.

In terms of attitude, Shrum's model would indicate that heavy viewers are building attitudes about guns as they watch programs. The frequency of school shootings is one factor, with viewers likely concluding that gun violence is an inevitable fact of life, and that strong measures should be taken. But more importantly, such message effects come against a massive background of dramatic violent entertainment that has normalized and taken for granted the presence of guns in our lives. Our long-term exposure to the fictional world of guns is highly relevant for our experience of them in reality, with both potentially contributing similar conclusions.

In broader terms, cultivation's "case study" is the culture itself. Media impacts upon culture are complex, changing, and subject to many contingent factors that social science cannot always easily explain. Nevertheless, the complexity of the issue should not hide the reality that we are all as individuals inscribed to some degree within this culture. Even for the nonviewer of television, the messages and lessons of the storyteller cannot escape unnoticed. In today's media saturated environment, is it even possible to not be exposed, either directly or indirectly, to television's messages?

While fear of imitative violence is understandable, our concern should not be with this alone. If violent imitation were as frequent as we sometimes worry about— with the high levels of violence on television and the large number of violent actions we see on a day-to-day basis—none of us could step out of our homes; we all would be hiding under our beds. The more important implication for cultivation is that watching makes us fearful and may make us less willing to think for ourselves. Parents, thus, might be more concerned with limiting how much television their children watch and more willing to talk to their children about the images they see. For example, how do these images lead to bullying? How can we use these images to help prevent bullying?

Cultivation continues to be a theory that is frequently tested, cited, and scrutinized, as it continues to evolve (see, for example, Morgan et al., 2012). New studies are already beginning to extend cultivation theory to social media (Intravia, et al., 2017; Roche, et al. 2016). We believe that cultivation's stature as one of the most well-known and well-used theoretical approaches in communication is well-justified, and we hope that this chapter provides a useful view of the research and how it can be applied to many social issues. We look forward to seeing where research on cultivation will lead us in the years ahead.

Discussion Questions

1. Think about what sorts of people are featured in most TV programs. In terms of age, race/ethnicity, gender, social class, and other categories, who do we see the most? Who do we not see very often?

2. Most of us have not spent much, if any, time in places like courtrooms and hospitals and prisons, but we "know" what they are like based on what we have seen countless times in fictional television programs. Can you think of other images you've learned, not from direct experience, but from dramatic representations?

3. Keep a media log for a few days. Can you differentiate between your viewing of mainstream TV and streaming video? Which is more important to you and why?

4. What role does social media play in your life? Are the lessons from social media similar to or different from those of the media?

5. Do you think cultivation theory can be expanded to include today's immersion in social media?

6. Do you believe that today's immersion in media is related to people's likelihood to express hatred for those who are "different" from them? If so, how and why?

7. How might cultivation theory explain the greater expression of hatred in today' society?

REFERENCES

Bilandzic, H., & Busselle, R. (2008). Transportation and transportability in the cultivation of genre-consistent attitudes and estimates. *Journal of Communication, 58*(3), 508–529.

Bilandzic, H., & Busselle, R. (2012). A narrative perspective on genre-specific cultivation. In M. Morgan, J. Shanahan, & N. Signorielli (Eds.), *Living with television now: Advances in cultivation theory and research* (pp. 261–285). New York, NY: Peter Lang.

Bilandzic, H., & Rössler, P. (2004). Life according to television. Implications of genre-specific cultivation effects: The Gratification/Cultivation model. *Communications: The European Journal of Communication Research, 29*(3), 295–326.

Bryant, J., & Miron, D. (2004). Theory and research in mass communication. *Journal of Communication, 54,* 662–704.

Bryant, J., Thompson, S., & Finklea, B. W. (2012). *Fundamentals of media effects* (2nd ed.). Long Grove, IL: Waveland Press.

Busselle, R., & Bilandzic, H. (2012). Cultivation and the perceived realism of stories. In M. Morgan, J. Shanahan, & N. Signorielli (Eds.), *Living with television now: Advances in cultivation theory and research* (pp. 168–186). New York, NY: Peter Lang.

Cohen, J., & Weimann, G. (2000). Cultivation revisited: Some genres have some effects on some viewers. *Communication Reports, 13*(2), 99–114.

Doob, A., & Macdonald, G. (1979). Television viewing and fear of victimization: Is the relationship causal? *Journal of Personality and Social Psychology, 37*(2), 170–179.

Egbert, N., & Belcher, J. D. (2012). Reality bites: An investigation of the genre of reality television and its relationship to viewers' body image. *Mass Communication & Society, 15*(3), 407–431.

Ferguson, C. J., & Faye, C. (2018, 1 Jan.). A history of panic over entertainment technology. *Behavioral Scientist.* Retrieved from http://behavioralscientist. org/history-panic-entertainment-technology/

Friedrich-Cofer, L., & Huston, A. C. (1986). Television violence and aggression: the debate continues. *Psychological Bulletin, 100*(3), 364–371.

Gentile, D. A. (Ed.). (2003). *Media violence and children: A complete guide for parents and professionals.* Westport, CT: Praeger.

Gerbner, G. (1973.). Cultural Indicators: The third voice. In G. Gerbner, L. Gross, & W. Melody (Eds.), *Communications technology and social policy* (pp. 555–573). New York: John Wiley & Sons.

Gerbner, G. (1999). Foreword: What do we know? In J. Shanahan & M. Morgan, *Television and its viewers: Cultivation theory and research* (pp. ix–xiii). Cambridge: Cambridge University Press.

Gerbner, G., & Gross, L. (1976). Living with television: The violence profile. *Journal of Communication, 26*(2), 173–199.

Gerbner, G., Gross, L., Morgan, M., & Signorielli, N. (1980). The 'mainstreaming' of America: Violence profile No. 11. *Journal of Communication, 30*(3), 10–29.

Grabe, M. E., & Drew. D. (2007). Crime cultivation: Comparisons across media genres and channels. *Journal of Broadcasting & Electronic Media,* 51(1), 147–171.

Gramlich, J. (2018, January 30). 5 facts about crime in the U.S. Retrieved from http://www.pewresearch.org/ fact-tank/2018/01/30/5-facts-about-crime-in-the-u-s/

Hirsch, P. (1980). The "scary world" of the nonviewer and other anomalies: A reanalysis of Gerbner et al.'s findings of cultivation analysis, Part I. *Communication Research, 7*(4), 403–456.

Holbert, R. L., Shah, D. V., & Kwak, N. (2004). Fear, authority, and justice: crime-related TV viewing and endorsements of capital punishment and gun ownership. *Journalism & Mass Communication Quarterly, 81*(2), 343–363.

Hughes, M. (1980). The fruits of cultivation analysis: A re-examination of the effects of television watching on fear of victimization, alienation, and the approval of violence. *Public Opinion Quarterly, 44*(3), 287–302

Intravia, J., Wolff, K. T., Paez, R., & Gibbs, B. R. (2017). Investigating the relationship between social media consumption and fear of crime: A partial analysis of mostly young adults. *Computers in Human Behavior, 77*, 158–168.

Kahlor, L., & Eastin, M. S. (2011). Television's role in the culture of violence toward women: A study of television viewing and the cultivation of rape myth acceptance in the United States. *Journal of Broadcasting & Electronic Media, 55*(2), 215–231.

Levitz, E. (2018, March 1). There is no "epidemic of mass school shootings". Daily Intelligencer. Retrieved from http://nymag.com/daily/intelligencer/2018/03/there-is-no-epidemic-of-mass-school-shootings.html

Mele, C., & Caron. C. (2018, May 21). Oliver North blames 'culture of violence' for mass shootings. *The New York Times.* Retrieved from https://www.nytimes.com/2018/05/21/us/nra-oliver-north.html

Morgan, M. (2012). *George Gerbner: A critical introduction to media and communication theory.* New York: Peter Lang.

Morgan, M., Shanahan, J., & Signorielli, N. (2009). Growing up with television: Cultivation processes. In J. Bryant & M. Oliver (Eds.), *Media effects: Advances in theory and research,* (3rd ed., pp. 34–49). Hillsdale, NJ: Erlbaum.

Morgan, M., Shanahan, J., & Signorielli, N. (2012). (Eds.) *Living with television now: Advances in cultivation theory and research.* New York: Peter Lang.

Morgan, M., & Shanahan, J. (2017). Television and the cultivation of authoritarianism: A return visit from an unexpected friend. *Journal of Communication, 67*(3), 424–444.

Phelps, J. (2018, March 8). Trump turns spotlight on violent video games in wake of Parkland shootings. [ABC News report.] Retrieved from https://abcnews.go.com/Politics/trump-turns-spotlight-violent-video-games-wake-parkland/story?id=53593714

Potter, W. J. (1993). Cultivation theory and research: A conceptual critique. *Human Communication Research, 19*, 564–601.

Potter, W. J. (1994). Cultivation theory and research: A methodological critique. *Journalism Monographs, 147*, 1–35.

Potter, W. J. (2014). A critical analysis of cultivation theory. *Journal of Communication, 64*(6), 1015–1036.

Potter, W. J., & Riddle, K. (2007). A content analysis of the media effects literature. *Journalism & Mass Communication Quarterly, 84*(1), 90–104.

Roche, S. P., Pickett, J. T., & Gertz, M. (2016). The scary world of online news? Internet news exposure and public attitudes toward crime and justice. *Journal of Quantitative Criminology, 32*(2), 215–236.

Segrin, C., & Nabi, R. L. (2002). Does television viewing cultivate unrealistic expectations about marriage? *Journal of Communication, 52*(2), 247–263.

Shanahan, J., & Morgan, M. (1999). *Television and its viewers: Cultivation theory and research.* Cambridge: Cambridge University Press.

Shrum, L. J. (1996). Psychological processes underlying cultivation effects: further tests of construct accessibility. *Human Communication Research, 22*(4), 482–509.

Shrum, L. J. (2004). The cognitive processes underlying cultivation effects are a function of whether the judgments are on-line or memory-based. *Communications, 29*, 327–344.

Shrum, L. J., & Lee, J. (2012). Multiple processes underlying cultivation effects: How cultivation works depends on the types of beliefs being cultivated. In M. Morgan, J. Shanahan & N. Signorielli (Eds.). *Living with television now: Advances in cultivation theory and research* (pp. 147–167). NY: Lang.

Signorielli, N., Morgan, M., & Shanahan (2018). The violence profile: Five decades of cultural indicators research. Mass Communication & Society, 22(1), 1-28. doi:10.1080/15205436.2018.1475011

Singer, D. G., & Singer, J. L. (2012). *Handbook of children and the media* (2nd ed.). Thousand Oaks, CA: Sage.

Strasburger, V. C. (2014). Twenty questions about media violence and its effect on adolescents. *Adolescecnt Medicine, 25,* 473–488.

Unsworth, D. (2018, March 27). Data on mass shootings at school don't live up to the hysteria. Washington Examiner. Retrieved from https://www.washingtonexaminer.com/opinion/op-eds/ data-on-mass-shootings-at-school-dont-live-up-to-the-hysteria.

Wober, J. M. (1978). Televised violence and paranoid perception: The view from Great Britain. *Public Opinion Quarterly, 42*(3), 315–321.

Chapter 11

Social Information Processing Theory and a Case Study of Idealized Perceptions and Misrepresentation Within an Online Community for Alcohol Addiction

Kevin B. Wright, Ph.D., *George Mason University*

Consumer use of online, health-related communities/resources has been the focus of considerable attention in recent years, as the number of people relying on online health information has steadily increased (Wright et al., 2011). The number of health-related, online communities has flourished as more individuals seek to access alternate sources of health information or to connect with other people with the same or a similar disease. Health problems affect not only physical health, but also psychological health and an individual's relationships (Cohen, 1988; Van Ingen, Utz, & Toepoel, 2016). For example, concerns for the future or thoughts about mortality (in cases of life-threatening illness), as well as the need to navigate a potentially complicated medial system, can be significant sources of stress, which can tax one's psychological well-being. Socially, the demands that one's health condition places on friends and family who serve as caregivers can strain one's most important relationships. Despite their best intentions, friends and family may have difficulty fully understanding the nuances or magnitude of a person's health circumstances, or they may stigmatize (e.g., act negatively toward) the person if they perceive the health behavior is looked down upon (such as alcohol or drug addiction) or seen as controllable by the person experiencing the problem. In some cases, social network members may even withdraw or otherwise become distant. Health problems can also make it challenging for people to maintain contact with others, reduce one's contact with others, or leave people detached from their social network, especially with health problems that lead to loss of time at work or other social settings (Cohen, 1988; Van Ingen et al., 2016).

Despite the potential wealth of information offered by such online communities, people who go online to seek information and connect with others regarding their health sometimes face challenges in this environment, such as making decisions about the credibility of information and the true identity of other community members. These communities often lack professional gatekeepers, who filter information in ways that differ radically from older forms of media. Web 2.0 technology allows almost anyone with access to the Internet to potentially contribute medical information on wikis, blogs, Facebook, Twitter, or message boards. Additionally, the Internet is marked by the blending of advertising and informational content, such as sponsored content (Flanagin & Metzger, 2013). Some pharmaceutical websites, for example, offer extensive medical information and simultaneously make consumers aware of their products via sponsored content "stories" about a wide range of health issues that are often posted within online health-related communities. Such features of new media can present challenges for some individuals to assess the credibility of health information (Flanagin & Metzger, 2013; Rains & Karmikel, 2009).

Moreover, different comfort levels of using social media, health literacy, numeracy, and other issues tied to level of education and experience may influence the degree to which individuals are able to access and understand (often complex) health information online (Basu & Dutta, 2008; Lustria, Smith, & Hinnant, 2011). The Internet offers a wide range of medical information and advice via online communities that may vary widely in terms of quality. For example, Eysenbach et al. (2002) conducted a meta-analysis of 79 studies that examined over 5,900 health-related websites and communities, reporting that consumers struggle with locating accurate, complete, and quality online health information. The vast range of health communities that are currently available via social media is daunting. They include forums on popular websites like WebMD, hospital/medical center-affiliated websites, health wikis, online support communities, pharmaceutical product websites, and medical tourism websites. In addition to illness, a growing number of health-related online communities are focused on prevention of health problems. These include virtual/real world community games designed to increase physical activity, locally based Facebook sites for runners, vegetarians, vegans, and a host of other health-inspired groups.

Our understanding of health-related online communities can be aided by the use of theories that have been developed by scholars who study social media, computer-mediated communication, online relationships, and the like. Social Information Processing Theory has emerged as an important theory for understanding the new media environment, including the study of online support communities. Specifically, Social Information Processing Theory has been helpful in terms of shedding light on online communication processes and our perceptions of others who we meet in cyberspace.

The following sections of this chapter provide more detailed information on key concepts from Social Information Processing Theory and how they apply to our perceptions of people with whom we interact via email, chat rooms, blogs, Facebook, Twitter, Instagram, and a growing list of other social media platforms. This is followed by a case study of communication within an online, health-related support community for individuals living with alcohol addiction. Specifically, the case study focuses on problems that occurred within the group due to misperceptions of other online community participants and how Social Information Processing Theory can be used to understand both the communication between participants and their perceptions of others.

Social Information Processing Theory

As stated earlier, Social Information Processing Theory (Walther, 1992; 2007) is an important framework for understanding the effects of computer-mediated channels on the communication and perceptions of individuals, including within health-related online communities (Walther & Boyd, 2002; Wright & Bell, 2003). The following sections provide a brief overview of some of the key concepts from Social Information Processing Theory and how they help us to understand communication and perceptions within online communities.

Optimal Self-Presentation and Idealized Perceptions

Walther (1992; 2007) asserts that computer-mediated communication (CMC), such as interacting with others via social media or the Internet, is fundamentally different than face-to-face interaction. The nature of computer-mediated communication often leads people to engage in optimal self-presentation (revealing only certain [usually positive] aspects of themselves and their personalities) in online settings, which can contribute to the formation of idealized perceptions of the self on the part of receivers. For example, message senders tend to portray themselves in a socially favorable manner to draw the attention of message receivers and foster anticipation of future interaction. This typically involves being highly selective in terms of self-disclosures when communicating with other members of the community. In the face-to-face world, most of our perceptions of others tend to be heavily influenced by nonverbal cues (dress, appearance, body language, voice qualities, etc.). Many of these cues are absent or reduced in computer-mediated communication, especially more text-based communication (e.g., texting, email, posting messages to Facebook, tweets, etc.) due to the limitations of the medium. Even Skype and other synchronous and richer online communication channels can influence perceptions of others in a biased way due to more limited information compared to face-to-face interaction.

According to Walther (1996), the reduced number of available nonverbal cues in CMC increases message-editing capabilities, and the temporal features of CMC allow communicators to be more selective and strategic in their self-presentation, form idealized impressions of their partners, and, consequently, engage in more intimate exchanges than people in face-to-face situations. These features of computer-mediated communication appear to offer people more interactional control over face-to-face communication, and they appear to influence perceptions of the attractiveness of online relational partners. For instance, Walther, Slovacek, and Tidwell (2001) found that individuals rated online interaction partners as more socially attractive and affectionate when a photo was not present compared to those who did view a photo of the interaction partner. In addition, dyads in computer-mediated settings also appear to self-disclose more than face-to-face dyads (Tidwell & Walther, 2002).

Idealized perceptions of others in online communities often develop when message receivers have limited information about others in the community due to the lack or reduction of nonverbal cues. There is also a tendency for people to overvalue minimal, text-based cues during online interaction. In other words, people tend to pay attention to, and focus on, verbal messages from the sender since there may be few or no nonverbal cues in an online community (such as physical appearance) that would normally shift a receiver's attention away from verbal messages. For example, in the face-to-face world, the way a person dresses, how they talk, their body language, etc., tends to override what he/she actually communicates, verbally. In the online world, we may never see or hear these important social cues, which leads us to rely more heavily on verbal information. Additionally, given the absence of information, Walther (1992) contends that receivers "fill in the blanks" by imposing their own (often skewed) perceptions of what a person might look like, sound like, behave, etc. based solely on verbal messages. These processes are thought to explain why people develop idealized perceptions of others online.

Idealized perceptions and optimal self-presentation in the computer-mediated communication process tend to intensify in the feedback loop, and this can lead to what Walther (1996) labeled "hyperpersonal interaction," or a more intimate and socially desirable exchange than in face-to-face interactions.

Hyperpersonal interaction is enhanced when no face-to-face relationship exists, so that users construct impressions and present themselves "without the interference of environmental reality" (Walther, 1996, p. 33), and it appears to skew perceptions of relational partners in positive ways and, in some cases, online relationships may exceed face-to-face interactions in terms of intensity (King & Moreggi, 1998; Walther, 1996; Wright, 2000). Despite the fact that individuals often disclose negative aspects of their health concerns in online communities, these studies have used hyperpersonal interaction to explain online community communication and relationships. For example, Wright (2000) found that online support group participants perceived others in the group to be more interpersonally competent and able to provide higher quality support than members of their face-to-face network.

Finally, people seeking to form impressions of their communication partners online must assess not only the content of the identity claims made by others, but also the veracity of these claims. In other words, in order for a message to have its intended effect, the receiver must both understand and believe it. Although deception in offline environments is common, the ability to selectively self-present online means that some kinds of misrepresentation are more easily accomplished via CMC. Users in online environments rely on a variety of cues to make determinations about one another; however, all of these cues are not deemed equally credible. For instance, identity cues can be intentionally given or unintentionally given off and we are more likely to privilege those cues that are perceived to be unintentional as opposed to strategically constructed. This ability to engage in deceptive self-presentation online is compounded when interactants do not share a social network in the face-to-face world and, therefore, have less access to "information triangles," such as mutual friends who might confirm or deny information.

Application of Social Information Processing Theory to Health-Related Online Communities

In terms of health-related online communities, Wright (2000) found that older adults using *Seniornet* reported disclosing information about their health to anonymous members of the online community that they were reluctant to discuss with family members and friends in face-to-face settings because the features of community message boards did allow people to see or track the location of others. This led seniors using the community to feel safer disclosing health information within the group. Walther and Boyd (2002) found that hyperpersonal interaction within online communities enhanced the attractiveness of seeking support within this context, particularly in terms of perceived social distance from other participants, which facilitated perceptions of reduced risk in terms of disclosing sensitize or stigmatized issues (including health concerns). Eysenbach (2003) drew upon Social Information Processing Theory, and he found that anonymity of virtual support communities was particularly helpful in terms of facilitating the participation of men living with health concerns to interact with others within these groups. Eysenbach (2003) argued that the reduced cues in this environment were particularly helpful for men to obtain online support for health concerns since they tend to be culturally and socially conditioned not to ask for help and support. The majority of social interactions that currently occur within online, health-related communities still consist of on-screen text (e.g., bulletin board postings) and therefore a large amount of visual information typical of traditional face-to-face interactions is concealed during online communication.

These, and other features of online communities, have been found to increase relational development by creating a more comfortable social situation for socially anxious individuals, or individuals who are often stigmatized by others due to their health issues in offline interactions. Walther & Boyd (2002) argue that the online environment has several characteristics, such as nonsynchronicity, that facilitate disclosure of an idealized self and that help individuals gain intimacy with others through online self-disclosure (Walther & Boyd, 2002). But online communities provide more affordances for individuals coping with health issues, such as increased controllability of online presentation (Green-Hamman & Sherblom, 2014; Wright & Bell, 2003). These features make online community use a less risky and more controllable environment in which people with health problems can communicate with greater confidence compared to offline contexts. Studies have confirmed this by indicating that individuals with poor offline self-presentation and lower communication skills may prefer online communication tools to interact with others (Morahan-Martin & Schumaker, 2003).

Case Study: Idealized Perceptions and Misrepresentation within an Online Community for Alcohol Addiction on Facebook ("New Beginnings in Alcohol Recovery")

Case Study Background

The case study for this chapter is one the author encountered approximately five years ago when conducting research on health-related online support communities for people who were struggling with alcohol addiction. The community, which I will call "New Beginnings in Alcohol Recovery," in an effort to preserve the anonymity of the participants, was a Facebook community. While it was a closed community for people coping with alcohol addiction, anyone who was interested in joining the community could do so by sending a message to one of the community moderators. As a researcher, I was granted access to the community to conduct a content analysis of supportive messages exchanged by participants in the community, as well as to distribute an online survey to participants for the purposes of understanding how similar online communities might benefit other individuals recovering from alcohol addiction. The study was conducted over a three-month time period, and I will only present an overview of the key issues that relate to Social Information Processing Theory in the study, as opposed to detailed findings (which are published elsewhere).

Online Community Participant Characteristics. According to the survey data from the study of "New Beginnings in Alcohol Recovery," the participants were mixed in terms of how long they had been in recovery from alcohol addiction. Most of the people in the online community were what are referred to as "newcomers" in the recovery world (i.e., people who have been sober for less than 30 days), although there were numerous individuals who had achieved longer periods of sobriety in the community (e.g., five years or more without consuming alcohol). Participants were from small towns or rural areas, as well as larger urban areas. There was about an equal mix of men and women in the community, and the respondents indicated, on the survey, a broad range of educational levels, age groups, and socioeconomic backgrounds. Individuals reported feeling stigmatized by members of their traditional, face-to-face, support network members (i.e., family and friends) or living in a small community where they did not know others who struggled with alcohol addiction, as key motivations for joining the online community. Many of the participants reported feeling confused by information about alcohol addiction and recovery they found using standard websites, such as those from the Center for Disease Control or the National Institutes of Health. While they wanted more information about alcohol addiction from physicians and medical researchers, they also felt the need to obtain experienced-based information and emotional support from other people struggling (or who have struggled in the past) with alcohol addiction.

Idealized Perceptions and Misrepresentation with the Online Community

One of the most striking communication patterns that was uncovered in the content analysis of messages exchanged by the members of the "New Beginnings in Alcohol Recovery" online community was a high number of messages exchanged by participants that contained idealized perceptions of others. For example, members of the community frequently mentioned, in their posts to others in the community, that they felt much more comfortable discussing their struggles with alcohol addiction with other community members compared to closer, face-to-face relationships. Members discussed problems they faced in terms of their loved ones not understanding how powerful alcohol addiction can be, being blamed for drinking episodes by loved ones who don't understand how easy it is to overdrink once one alcoholic beverage is consumed. Researchers have found support for the disease model of alcoholism, which posits that people suffering from alcohol addiction disorder tend to process alcohol differently than other people at the biological level (Manzo-Avalos & Saavedra-Molina, 2010). For example, studies have found that the mitochondria in the cells of alcoholic individuals process alcohol differently than nonalcoholics (Manzo-Avalos & Saavedra-Molina, 2010). Physical dependence and craving for alcohol are experienced much differently by people with this disorder than people without it, and consumption of only a small amount of alcohol can trigger subsequent heavy drinking behavior. Since most people are not alcoholics and have more control over the amount of alcohol they consume, they typically don't understand the behavior of someone suffering from alcohol addiction (even if he or she is a loved one). Since one drink (even after months or years of remaining sober) can trigger heavy drinking and alcohol dependency among people who suffer from alcohol addiction disorder, it is important for recovering alcoholics to maintain a strong social support network of individuals who can help them manage the stress of sobriety over a long period of time.

In the survey of the community, participants mentioned that most of the people they communicated with in the community were individuals they had only communicated with online and had never met in the face-to-face world. Although these individuals were relative strangers, participants reported feeling more interpersonally close and connected with other community members compared to their traditional face-to-face relationships. They were less embarrassed to discuss mistakes made while drinking, feelings about stress and relationships, and they reported feeling less judged or stigmatized by other group members. One of the reasons they felt a connection with others was due to the similarity of experiences, feelings, and behaviors related to alcohol abuse and recovery. In other words, the online community members were drawn to the stories revealed by other community members since they reflected similar experiences with alcohol addiction. Participants reported feeling very satisfied with the support they received from other community members and the opportunities to not only learn from members who had achieved longer periods of sobriety, but also with the opportunity to help newer members with their own experiences.

While these aspects of "New Beginnings in Alcohol Recovery" appear to be beneficial to the members of this online community (and, in many cases, they likely were beneficial), other data from the content analysis and the online survey of the community revealed that some of the perceptions of others were likely idealized, and problems with participant misrepresentation were revealed.

Social Information Processing Theory helps to explain both problems. For example, when a person focuses on verbal messages of others (while simultaneously not paying attention to nonverbal communication cues that would typically provide additional information about people), they may develop idealized perceptions of others that are not necessarily beneficial to them. For example, one male respondent to the survey of the online community mentioned that "the people I talk to in this community are more sensitive and care about me more than my own family members," and a female participant said, "…there is nothing I would not share with people in this community about my life and my struggles with alcohol." While these comments appear to reflect the idea that the online support community was perceived by these and other participants as a safe haven, where they could safely reveal things about their life and receive much more care and understanding from others than their traditional support network, it is also likely that these perceptions of others recovering from alcohol addiction were idealized due to the processes explained by Social Information Processing Theory. The average time of being a member of the community was just under two months. While relational development can certainly occur in this amount of time, it seems unlikely that such new relationships would always be qualitatively better than relationships with people that an alcoholic has known for many years (e.g., close friends and family members). As a result, it is hard to know if the relationships formed within "New Beginnings in Alcohol Recovery" would be perceived as superior to other relationships if these individuals were to interact with each other in the face-to-face world.

Deception and misrepresentation within "New Beginnings in Alcohol Recovery" was another issue that was revealed through the online survey of members. A relatively small, but more nefarious, finding was that some respondents revealed that they actually had been actively drinking, but they still gave advice and support to others about ways they could cope with alcohol addiction. A few survey respondents mentioned that they were actually in pharmaceutical sales and used the community to promote the benefits of products like Antibuse and other medications for alcohol addiction (that reportedly reduce cravings), as opposed to the traditional recovery method of abstinence from alcohol coupled with social support. In addition, a number of respondents to the survey mentioned that they often disagreed with things that other members said about the nature of alcohol addiction or advice that was given, but they decided to remain lurkers within the community, as opposed to actively posting comments and challenging these suggestions. Other participants discussed using the community to appease someone in their family who wanted them to do something about problem drinking behaviors (e.g., showing a loved one that you have posted on the community while continuing to drink). Finally, the content analysis revealed links to information about alcohol addiction recovery that is not supported by scientific studies or is very controversial.

Implications for the Study of Health-Related Online Support Communities from a Social Information Processing Theory Perspective

In short, despite the large number of comments, both within the community and on the survey questionnaire, about the positive merits of other members of "New Beginnings in Alcohol Recovery," other information from the study revealed that some of these perceptions may be idealized perceptions that can be explained by the computer-mediated communication processes from Social Information Processing Theory. The misrepresentations of self within the community that were identified/reported in the study of the community certainly suggest that some of the participants were not necessarily honest or trustworthy (despite being perceived as such) in their interactions with others in the community. In a world where information about others is garnered through mostly verbal (textual) information and perceptions are formed from this information, the risk of idealizing perceptions has been found to be greater in a variety of field and experimental studies. This leads to larger questions regarding the credibility of information and (in particular) the sources of information that people receive regarding health issues in online communities like "New Beginnings in Alcohol Recovery." While there is certainly evidence that suggests that similar online communities may be beneficial to members in terms of informational and emotional support, more research is needed to understand the potential problems associated with idealized perceptions of others and misrepresentation of self in this context. Social Information Processing Theory posits that positive interpersonal relationships can develop in online communities over time (albeit often with skewed perceptions of others). Less is known about the effects that misrepresentation, outright deception, lurker vs. active members, and skewed perceptions of others may have and how these may ultimately lead to potentially damaging effects. For example, if a participant within this type of online community discovers negative information about a person with whom he or she has revealed guarded health information in community interactions, it would likely lead to a violation of trust or undermine the credibility of the information about alcohol addiction that a person receives. This could lead to a number of issues, including negative perceptions of the community, withdrawal from the community, or negative behaviors such as drinking and relapse. Future research needs to explore the darker side of health-related, online communities based on cases like the one presented here, as well as similar communities.

Conclusion

With more and more people turning to the Internet and social media for health information and support, it is important to have an understanding of how communication processes and perceptions within this context may enhance or undermine physical, psychological, and social outcomes for people who use health-related online communities. Much of the research in this area had identified a number of promising outcomes of using such communities, while a growing amount of research has begun to uncover potential negative outcomes of participation. Social Information Processing Theory offers an important theoretical perspective and explanation of communication behaviors and perceptions in computer-mediated environments. Future research should continue to explore the promises and pitfalls of these types of online communities and the health effects for participants.

Discussion Questions

1. What other perceptions of online support community members might be influenced by the lack of nonverbal communication cues based on Social Information Processing Theory?

2. How can individuals verify the credibility of health information that they obtain online from other individuals within online support communities or social networking sites?

3. Provide an example of hyperpersonal interaction in an online community or a social networking site. What experiences have you had in terms of optimal self-presentation and idealized perceptions of others within these contexts?

4. How might Social Information Processing Theory be used to better understand other health issues that are discussed between people within online communities or social media?

REFERENCES

Basu, A., & Dutta, M. J. (2008). The relationship between health information seeking and community participation: The roles of health information orientation and efficacy. *Health communication, 23*(1), 70–79.

Cohen, S. (1988). Psychosocial models of the role of social support in the etiology of physical disease. *Health Psychology, 7*(3), 269.

Eysenbach, G., Powell, J., Kuss, O., & Sa, E. R. (2002). Empirical studies assessing the quality of health information for consumers on the world wide web: a systematic review. *JAMA, 287*(20), 2691–2700.

Eysenbach, G. (2003). The impact of the Internet on cancer outcomes. *CA: a cancer journal for clinicians, 53*(6), 356–371.

Flanagin, A. J., & Metzger, M. J. (2013). Trusting expert-versus user-generated ratings online: The role of information volume, valence, and consumer characteristics. *Computers in Human Behavior, 29*(4), 1626–1634.

Green-Hamann, S., & Sherblom, J. C. (2014). The influences of optimal matching and social capital on communicating support. *Journal of Health Communication*, Available: doi: 10.1080/10810730.2013.864734

King, S. A., & Moreggi, D. (1998). Internet therapy and self-help groups: The pros and cons. In J. Gakenbach (Ed.), *Psychology of the Internet: Intrapersonal, interpersonal, and transpersonal implications* (pp. 77–109). San Diego, CA: Academic Press.

Lustria, M. L. A., Smith, S. A., & Hinnant, C. C. (2011). Exploring digital divides: an examination of eHealth technology use in health information seeking, communication and personal health information management in the USA. *Health Informatics Journal, 17*(3), 224–243.

Manzo-Avalos, S., & Saavedra-Molina, A. (2010). Cellular and mitochondrial effects of alcohol consumption. *International Journal of Environmental Research and Public Health, 7*(12), 4281–4304.

Morahan-Martin, J., & Schumacher, P. (2003). Loneliness and social uses of the Internet. *Computers in Human Behavior, 19*(6), 659–671.

Rains, S. A., & Karmikel, C. D. (2009). Health information-seeking and perceptions of website credibility: Examining Web-use orientation, message characteristics, and structural features of websites. *Computers in Human Behavior, 25*(2), 544–553.

Tidwell, L. C., & Walther, J. B. (2002). Computer-mediated communication effects on disclosure, impression, and interpersonal evaluations: Getting to know one another a bit at a time. *Human Communication Research, 28,* 317–348.

Van Ingen, E., Utz, S., & Toepoel, V. (2016). Online coping after negative life events: Measurement, prevalence, and relation with Internet activities and well-being. *Social Science Computer Review, 34*(5), 511e529. http://dx.doi.org/10.1177/ 0894439315600322.

Walther, J. B. (1996). Computer-mediated communication: Impersonal, interpersonal, and hyperpersonal interaction. *Communication Research, 23,* 3–43.

Walther, J. B. (2007). Selective self-presentation in computer-mediated communication: Hyperpersonal dimensions of technology, language, and cognition. *Computers in Human Behavior, 23,* 2538–2557.

Walther, J. B., & Boyd, S. (2002). Attraction to computer-mediated social support. In C. A. Lin & D. Atkin (Eds.), *Communication technology and society: Audience adoption and uses* (pp. 153–188). Cresskill, NJ: Hampton Press.

Walther, J. B., Slovacek, C. L., & Tidwell, L. C. (2001). Is a picture worth a thousand words? Photographic images in long-term and short-term computer-mediated communication. *Communication Research, 28*(1), 105–134.

Wright, K. B. (2000). Perceptions of online support providers: An examination of perceived homophily, source credibility, communication and social support within online support groups. *Communication Quarterly, 48,* 44–59.

Wright, K. B., & Bell, S. B. (2003). Health-related support groups on the Internet: Linking empirical findings to social support and computer-mediated communication theory. *Journal of Health Psychology, 8,* 37–52.

Wright, K. B., Johnson, A. J., Bernard, D. R., & Averbeck, J. (2011). Computer-mediated social support: Promises and pitfalls for individuals coping with health concerns. In T. L. Thompson, R. Parrott, & J. F. Nussbaum (Eds.), *The Routledge handbook of health communication, 2nd ed.* (pp. 349–362). New York: Routledge.

Chapter 12

Advice Response Theory: Understanding Responses to Health Advice

Erina MacGeorge, Ph.D., *Pennsylvania State University*

Kasey A. Foley, M.A., *Pennsylvania State University*

No matter how good your life is, there are always hassles, stresses, and problems that arise…and decisions to be made about how to address them. For example, as a semester comes to an end, you might need to make plans for holiday travel, choose a place to live for the next semester or school year, find a job or internship, or decide whether to maintain a romantic relationship that will become long-distance. Although people can and do handle some of their problems and decisions independently, many also obtain advice on what to do from friends, family, and others in their social and professional networks.

Advice, defined as recommendations about what to do, think, or feel in response to a situation (MacGeorge, Feng, & Thompson, 2008), is both a form of social support and a form of interpersonal influence. Advice is distinguished from other forms of support by its focus on future action to be taken by the support recipient, and from other forms of influence by the intention to be helpful in response to the recipient's situation (though advisors can easily have self-interested motives, too) (MacGeorge & Van Swol, 2018a). Advice is also characterized by a disparity between the advisor's expertise and the recipient's expertise, though the advisor's claim to expertise may be very slight or temporary (e.g., your friend has seen a movie and you haven't) or disputed by the recipient (e.g., your uncle thinks he knows a lot about job interviewing, but you disagree). In addition, although it is possible for advice to be designed by committee, or directed at mass audiences (e.g., advice columns, self-help books), advice is more typically an interpersonal phenomenon: communication designed by one advisor for one recipient.

Advice can do a lot of good. It can help recipients make better decisions and cope more effectively with problems that range from everyday hassles (MacGeorge, Guntzviller, Hanasono, & Feng, 2016) to personal relationships (MacGeorge & Hall, 2014) to academic challenges (Waring & Song, 2018) to getting things accomplished at work (Bonaccio & Paik, 2018). However, advice is also associated with a host of less positive outcomes. For example, recipients may perceive advice as intrusive or demeaning rather than supportive (Goldsmith & Fitch, 1997). They may prefer other forms of support, perhaps especially when problems are highly distressing and have no clear resolution (Servaty-Seib & Burleson, 2007). Research indicates that those to whom advice is provided tend to underutilize it, even when it comes from advisors with clear expertise and the advice would result in better decisions (Yaniv, 2004; Yaniv & Kleinberger, 2000).

Given this potential for advice to go wrong, many people, including communication scholars, have wondered what advisors can do to give "better" advice and how recipients can make the best use of it (MacGeorge & Van Swol, 2018b). Advice Response Theory (ART) synthesizes key insights about the exchange of advice, with a focus on when and why advice evokes more or less positive responses (MacGeorge et al., 2016). Consequently, it also speaks to ways that advisors can generate advice that will be valued and implemented (MacGeorge et al., 2008).

Advice on any topic can matter intensely to its recipient, but because health is so important to one's quality of life, advice on health-related topics tends to be especially important to many people. People of all ages seek advice on mental and physical health from their health care providers (D'Angelo & D'Angelo, 2018), their friends and families (Perry & Pescosolido, 2015), and increasingly, from online sources (Feng, Zhu, & Malloch, 2018). Health advice can be a powerful force for good (i.e., reducing stress, motivating healthy behavior, and improving long-term health outcomes (D'Angelo & D'Angelo, 2018), but it can also be problematic (i.e., making patients feel worse about their health problems (Rose, Poynter, Anderson, Noar, & Conigliaro, 2013). The following sections provide an overview of Advice Response Theory's primary claims, along with some recent extensions of the theory, an extended case study focused on health, and an analysis of the case informed by the theory.

Advice Response Theory: The Basics

According to Advice Response Theory, the way people respond to advice is influenced by a set of factors that include (a) the features of the message content (i.e., what is advised), (b) the characteristics of the advisor, (c) the elements of the situation, and (d) the traits of the recipient (MacGeorge et al., 2008; Mac-

George et al., in press). The theory further proposes that these factors work with each other in some specific ways. As is often the case with newer theories, recent work points to some ways that the theory may need revision or expansion to address more of the complexity of advising across different relationships and contexts. These topics are all addressed below.

Message Features

Advice Response Theory identifies the content features of the advice message as the primary influence on how recipients respond to advice. In other words, first and foremost, people pay attention to what they are being advised to do. More specifically, they evaluate the *efficacy* or effectiveness of the advised action (will it work?), its *feasibility* (can I do it?), and its *limitations* (does this action have drawbacks?) (Feng & Burleson, 2008; MacGeorge et al., 2004). The higher the perceived efficacy and feasibility, and the lower the perceived limitations, the more likely that advice will have positive outcomes. Advice Response Theory distinguishes among three types of outcomes: perceived *advice quality* (is the advice good?), *facilitation of coping* (does the advice help the person deal with the problem?), and *implementation intention* (will the person follow the advice?). Thus, if you have a bad cold, and your classmate advises going to the student health center, Advice Response Theory says you are more likely to value and implement the advice if you think that going to the center will help you get better (efficacy) and it is convenient and affordable for you (feasibility). Further, you will be more likely to go if you do not have significant concerns about going there (limitations; e.g., quality of care provided, exposure to other students' illnesses). According to Advice Response Theory, advice recipients are also influenced by whether the advice is a *confirmation* of something they already planned on doing (Feng & MacGeorge, 2010; MacGeorge, Guntzviller, Hanasono, & Feng, 2016); advice that is more confirming elicits more positive responses. This egocentric bias (Yaniv, 2004; Yaniv & Kleinberger, 2000) toward confirming advice probably occurs because we have the most familiarity with, and confidence in, our own ideas, but, unfortunately, it can cause people to ignore or underutilize advice that could help them. Thus, if you haven't already thought of going to the student health center, you may be less likely to follow your friend's advice.

According to Advice Response Theory, advice recipients are also influenced by the linguistic style of the advice message and respond more positively to advice given with greater *politeness*, or concern for the recipient's public "face." Politeness has several dimensions, including solidarity (showing connection between advisor and recipient), approbation (conveying that the recipient is competent), and tact (displaying respect for the recipient's autonomy) (Lim & Bowers, 1991).

Advice can feel bossy or critical, but delivering it with polite language helps to reduce that feeling. For example, when advising about the health center, your friend might show solidarity by saying "I've been sick like you are," approbation by saying "I know you try to take care of yourself," and tact by saying "If you decide it's a good idea…"

In support of Advice Response Theory, research indicates that when advice recipients perceive the advised action as good (i.e., efficacious, feasible, not having too many limitations) and the message style as polite, they are more likely to perceive advice as high quality, feel that it helps them cope, and be persuaded to implement the advice (Feng & MacGeorge, 2010; MacGeorge et al., 2004; MacGeorge et al., 2016). However, the theory also asserts that content and style affect these outcomes somewhat differently. Recent research (MacGeorge et al., 2016) indicates that the politeness of the advice message is important for making recipients like the advice and feel able to cope with their problems, but the content of the message is more important for determining whether the recipients actually implement the advised actions. Thus being polite will make people like your advice and feel more confident about resolving their problems, but if you want your advice to affect what they do, you will have to come up with actions that are well chosen from their perspective.

Recently, researchers studying advice have begun shifting some of their focus away from the qualities of advice messages themselves, and toward the qualities of the interactions in which advice is given. For example, some research indicates that when advisors give higher quality emotional support (MacGeorge, Guntzviller, et al., 2017), and do so before giving advice (Feng, 2009), their advice gets a better reception. This work has yet to be formally incorporated within Advice Response Theory, but is one direction for theoretical expansion and improvement.

Advisor Characteristics

While emphasizing the impact of advice messages, Advice Response Theory also explains the role played by the source of these messages: the advisor. Specifically, Advice Response Theory asserts that characteristics of the advisor influence responses to advice by "biasing" how advice messages are perceived (Feng & MacGeorge, 2010; MacGeorge et al., 2013). Influential characteristics of the advisor include *expertise, trustworthiness, likeability,* and *similarity* to the recipient (Bonaccio & Dalal, 2006; Feng & MacGeorge, 2010). Recent research indicates that the advisor's past provision of support also affects the evaluation of advice (Guntzviller, MacGeorge, & Brinker, 2017). Rather than directly determining responses to advice, Advice Response Theory argues that these advisor characteristics influence how advice messages are evaluated, which, in turn, influence responses to advice. Consider advisor trustworthiness as an example. Advice Response Theory says that, in general, the advisor's level of trustworthiness does *not* directly determine whether recipients like or follow advice (e.g., "you are trustworthy, so I will do what you say"). Instead, the advisor's level of expertise sways the recipient to evaluate the advice message more positively (e.g., you are highly trustworthy, so I perceive your advised action as more efficacious than I would if you were less so"). If you got advice to visit the health center from someone who had never been there, or whom you didn't trust or like very much, you would tend to see getting an appointment as less valuable advice than if you got the same recommendation from a trusted, liked friend who was doing an internship there.

Recipient Traits and Situational Elements

As noted above, Advice Response Theory asserts that recipient traits and situational elements also influence responses to advice. In particular, the theory suggests that these factors influence responses to advice by moderating (increasing or decreasing) the attention recipients pay to message features and advisor characteristics (MacGeorge et al., 2016). Recipient traits are enduring characteristics of the recipient, such as gender, culture, and personality. Situational elements include aspects of the problem or decision, such as the seriousness of the problem (Feng & MacGeorge, 2010) or the type of decision being made (Van Swol, 2011). They also include characteristics of the recipient that are specific to that situation, such as the recipient's emotional state (MacGeorge, Smith, Caldes, & Hackman, 2017).

To date, there are not many studies testing how recipient traits or situational elements influence advice evaluation. There is evidence consistent with the theory showing that culture (a recipient trait) moderates how advisor characteristics influence advice outcomes. Specifically, Chinese students' responses to advice were somewhat more strongly affected by advisor expertise, trustworthiness, and so forth than were the responses of American students (Feng & Feng, 2012). This finding is consistent with a greater emphasis placed in collectivist cultures (such as that in China) on interdependence and harmony in close relationships. Another study (Feng & MacGeorge, 2010) found that when advice recipients' problems are more serious (a situational element), their responses to advice are more strongly influenced by how they evaluate the message content (Feng & MacGeorge, 2010).

However, there is also reason to believe that Advice Response Theory's claims about the role of situational elements may need to be revised as further research accumulates. A recent study suggests that problem seriousness may not affect recipients' immediate responses to advice, but, instead, affects how they respond after a period of time in which to contemplate the advice (MacGeorge et al., 2016). Other studies focused on health advice (MacGeorge, Smith, et al., 2017) indicate that some kinds of situational elements (i.e., negative emotions) may act directly to motivate a positive or negative response to advice rather than affecting how the advice content is evaluated.

Stress Management Advice for Jane

Advice Response Theory helps to explain how people evaluate and respond to the advice they receive. The following case was written to illustrate how one person might receive advice from multiple advisors over a few days' time. Some of the advice included in this case was adapted from conversations recorded in the authors' research on doctor-patient interactions. As you read the case, consider the advice messages and advisors, along with the situation and what you learn about Jane, the recipient. How does Advice Response Theory suggest Jane will respond to the advice she receives?

Jane is a nursing major in her second year at State University. She is taking 18 credits-worth of coursework, including organic chemistry, human physiology, nutrition, public speaking, calculus, and art history. She works part-time at the student mail center, volunteers for a local pet shelter, and is actively involved in several clubs on campus. Final exams are approaching and Jane has been working late every night, trying to balance school, work, and extracurricular activities. A few days before her first final, Jane wakes up with a sore throat. Given her schedule over the next week, she does not have the time to be sick! In addition to final exams approaching, Jane will be running in a marathon with some of her friends this weekend. Jane is not typically a runner, but the proceeds from the marathon go to her favorite animal charity, so she wanted to be involved and has been training all year to get in shape for it. On top of all that, Jane is aware that she needs to maintain a grade of C+ or higher in all of her classes in order to continue in the program, and this has been a struggle in both her organic chemistry and calculus courses.

Stressed about how to balance all of her commitments and still do well on finals, Jane turns to her roommate, Natalie. Natalie is a first-year mathematics major who Jane often goes to for advice on school and relationships. Natalie is usually on top of her school work, but often stays up later than Jane and only sleeps a few hours per night. Jane explains that she doesn't want to miss her marathon, but still wants to do well on her exams, and thinks she is starting to get sick.

> **Natalie:** Aw, man, yeah I get it. This is a super stressful time of the semester, and calculus is kicking my butt, too. Have you tried caffeine pills?
>
> **Jane:** Um…no. Aren't they really bad for you?

Natalie: Well, I mean, they're not super healthy, but I took them with a few energy drinks last finals week when I was freaking out and they gave me lots of energy—kept me focused when I was studying. You crash hard after, but you can get up earlier and get stuff done.

Jane: I don't know…

Uncertain about whether Natalie's idea is safe or not, Jane suggests grabbing a bite to eat at the dining hall before their class. Natalie agrees and they head out.

A few hours later, Jane is in her organic chemistry class, and the professor asks if anyone has questions about the final exam. Garret, a second year chemistry student in Jane's class, raises his hand. "Which chapters are we going to have to know again?" he asks. Jane had never spoken to Garret before. From the urgency in his voice and the sleepiness of his appearance, Garret also seemed stressed about the upcoming exam, but not particularly well prepared. Following class, Jane runs into Garrett and, as a courtesy, asks him how his studying is going.

Garret: I haven't really started. I think it'll be an easy test. I'll just cram during the two days leading up to it and see how I do. What about you?

Jane: I've studied some. I won't have much time this weekend since my friends and I are running a marathon on Saturday, but I really need to do well on this test.

Garret: You know what you should do? Talk to the professor about getting a few extra days to study for the exam. Maybe she'll even push it back for the rest of us.

Jane: Yeah… maybe.

Jane doesn't really want Garret's advice on the weekend and is irritated that he offered it. She certainly does not think that her professor will allow her to postpone her final with only a few days' notice. Jane wishes Garrett luck on studying, and the two part ways.

Later that afternoon, Jane walks to the student health center for a same-day doctor's appointment she had scheduled for her sore throat. She is seeing Sue, a nurse practitioner who she has seen a few times before and likes.

Sue: Your throat does seem red and irritated. It's difficult to tell what's causing it this early on. It could be anything from the start of a viral or bacterial infection to dry air in your dorm room while you're sleeping. I recommend getting some rest, taking Tylenol for the pain, drinking lots of fluids, and using a humidifier if you have one for your room. If it's still hurting next week, call us and we'll get you in for another appointment.

Jane: Okay. I just have a marathon this weekend, and I need to do well on two of my finals next week so I can stay in my program. I'm trying to avoid getting sicker if I can help it.

Sue: Would you like my advice on that?

Jane: Yes, that would be great.

Sue: I would suggest getting some rest before you go into a stressful week of exam-taking. I know you don't want to let your friends down, but maybe staying home from your marathon would give you some time to study and sleep. School is the reason you're here and it may not be worth your health or your grades to compete this weekend.

Jane: Yeah…

Sue: When I was in nursing school, I had to miss a dance marathon so I could study for my licensing exam. It wasn't any fun, but it paid off in the long run.

Jane: Thanks, yeah, my roommate said she took caffeine pills during her last exams to stay on top of things.

Sue: Please don't take caffeine pills. In addition to nervousness and restlessness, they can cause stomach irritation, nausea, vomiting, and a whole heap of other issues—which could not only make you feel terrible for your meet and exams, but can also lead to long-term sleep issues.

Jane: Okay, yeah, I wasn't sure. I didn't think they were safe.

Sue and Jane finish up their visit, and Sue points Jane in the direction of front desk for check out.

That night, Jane calls her grandma for their weekly phone call. Her grandma talks for a while about her week, and then asks Jane how she is doing. Jane describes the stress she was feeling about finals, getting sick, and her upcoming marathon.

Grandma: Oh, darling, you have so much going on. You're running yourself ragged!

Jane: Yeah, I just want to do well on my tests, but I've been looking forward to this marathon all semester.

Grandma: You've very smart. You'll figure something out. Anything you decide to do, you will do well. I'm just worried about you taking care of yourself. Are you getting enough sleep?

Jane: Yeah, most of the time.

Grandma: Okay, good. You know I'm always worried about you. I can't wait for you to come home this summer! Your grandfather and I were just talking about how much we were looking forward to having you around again.

Jane: Aww, thanks, grandma. I love you.

Grandma: Love you too, honey.

Shortly thereafter, Jane receives a call from her brother, Matt. Matt is a chemical engineer who graduated from a competitive engineering program a few years ago. Jane and Matt don't get the chance to talk often, so Jane is excited to hear from him. After catching up, Jane tells Matt about her situation.

Matt: Are there any other marathons happening in the near future? I know you like the charity the proceeds from this marathon are going toward, but you already paid your registration fee. You could go for part of the time to cheer your friends on and then sign up for a different one to run this summer.

Jane: Yeah, I think there might be one next month…

Matt: Great, there you go! That way, you will have more time to sleep and study, but you don't have to lose all the hard work you put into training.

Jane: Yeah, thanks.

Matt: Anytime, sis. When are you coming home next? I miss seeing you!

Jane: Probably next weekend. Once I get through this rough week…

Matt: You've got this. You have always been the smart one! Good luck!

At this point, it is late, Jane is tired, and she decides to sleep on it.

Case Analysis

Whose advice do you think Jane will follow? According to Advice Response Theory, Jane's responses to the advice she received will be determined by her perceptions of the message features and advisor characteristics, as well as situational elements and personal traits. Jane clearly feels that balancing her work, health, and friends' expectations is a serious problem, which Advice Response Theory predicts will cause her to be especially influenced by the message features. The case also indicates that Jane has a tendency to take decision-making seriously, a recipient trait that might cause her to think more carefully about the situation and the advice she receives than someone like her classmate, Garret (see Feng & Lee, 2010). Keeping these potential influences in mind, you can examine the details of the message features and advisor characteristics and use Advice Response Theory as a framework for predicting how Jane might respond.

Advice Response Theory indicates that message features (content and politeness) will be a dominant influence on Jane's responses. Comparing the advice given by Natalie with that given by Jane's brother helps to illustrate how these features may affect Jane. Consider Natalie's advice to get up earlier each day and take caffeine pills or drink energy drinks. While this advice is *feasible*, in that Jane likely has access to both caffeine pills and energy drinks, it lacks *efficacy* for actually solving Jane's issue. If she gets up earlier, drinks sugary drinks, and consumes too much caffeine, she runs the risk of further compromising her immune system and becoming even sicker by the time she takes her final exams, which will not only not solve her problem, but make it worse. Additionally, as we learned from Sue during Jane's medical visit, taking caffeine pills can lead to several adverse outcomes (i.e., upset stomach, nausea, and vomiting) and can contribute to long-term sleep issues, so there are major *limitations*, or drawbacks, to this plan. The advice may also lack *confirmation*. Consuming caffeine pills clearly does not align with Jane's plans for resolving her problem, as evident from her concern about the safety of consuming caffeine pills during both her conversation with Natalie and Sue. Assuming that Jane perceives Natalie's advice as lacking in efficacy, confirmation, and having limitations, Advice Response Theory predicts that she will not implement the advice.

Compared to the advice from Natalie, the advice from Jane's brother, Matt, appears to have superior features. Matt's advice to go to part of the marathon so she can cheer on her friends and sign up for a different race in the near future appears to be *feasible* for Jane. In addition, the advice to still go to part of the marathon this weekend basically *confirms* what she is already planning on doing, but allows for more time for studying…and signing up for a future race means she does not have to be worried about losing all the hard work she has put into training. Both actions seem directed at resolving the problem, which could result in positive perceptions of *efficacy*. Matt conveys that he has confidence in Jane and thinks well of her (*approbation*), which could contribute to Jane perceiving the advice as more polite than Natalie's. Assuming that Jane perceives her brother's advice as efficacious, feasible, confirming, not having too many limitations, and polite, Advice Response Theory predicts that she is likely to appreciate and implement the advice.

Advice Response Theory also indicates that Jane's responses to advice will be influenced by characteristics of her advisors. Here, a comparison of the advice provided by Garret and Sue is useful for understanding Advice Response Theory's predictions. Garret's experience taking the organic chemistry class and completing his first year of a STEM program (i.e., chemistry) does give him some *expertise* that may motivate Jane to take his advice, but it is clear from the question he asked in class, and his nonchalance about the exam, that he is not as committed to his schoolwork as Jane is, indicating a lack of *similarity*. Garret and Jane are also dissimilar in gender and major. In addition, since he and Jane do not know each other well, there probably isn't a lot of *trust* or *liking* to improve how Jane views his advice. The case suggests that Jane is already in the process of dismissing Garret's advice as she leaves the conversation, which is consistent with Advice Response Theory's prediction that a lack of similarity, trust, and/or liking will lead to negative evaluations of the advice message.

In contrast, Sue, Jane's nurse practitioner, does not have Garret's experience in taking that particular organic chemistry course or knowing the professor, but her *expertise* in medicine motivated Jane to seek health advice from her. Sue is also a nurse practitioner who successfully graduated from her own nursing program, indicating a level of both *expertise* and *similarity*. Sue and Jane are also similar in gender. Additionally, Jane has seen Sue before for other medical concerns and seems to have established both a sense of *trust* and *liking*. Overall, Advice Response Theory suggests that Jane's view of Sue as an advisor will be positive and this, in turn, will cause her to evaluate Sue's advice more positively. Now, consider how Garret and Sue compare as advisors to Natalie and Jane's brother. Which of them do you think has the best advisor "profile" for influencing Jane?

Finally, recent research also indicates that advice is evaluated more positively when advisors first offer emotional support (i.e., expressions of sympathy and caring) and discuss the problem with the recipient. Compared to the conversations Jane had with Matt, Sue, and Garret, Jane's grandmother, by far, provided Jane with the most emotional support. In addition to being polite, by communicating that she loves Jane (*solidarity*), thinks well of her (*approbation*), and respects her choices (*tact*), which could lead Jane to see any advice she provided more positively than advice given by the others, Jane's grandmother conveys that she is concerned about Jane, expressing empathy for everything Jane has on her plate. However, Jane's grandma did not provide any specific guidance toward resolving her problem, other than ensuring she gets enough sleep. Therefore, while the conversation with her grandmother may have been enjoyable, it likely will not help improve Jane's situation. In addition, Natalie offers Jane emotional support before providing advice when she acknowledges the stressfulness of her situation and the difficulty of their calculus class. Research on advice would suggest that if Jane perceived Natalie as providing emotional support, she would evaluate Natalie's advice more positively.

As this case illustrates, Advice Response Theory provides a framework for analyzing and understanding how advice recipients evaluate and make use of advice, and therefore the kinds of things advisors need to consider in order to give advice that will be better appreciated by recipients. Like any social scientific theory, it is designed to explain generalities in human behavior, and is therefore unlikely to capture all of the factors that influence how you as a unique individual respond to specific instances of advising in your life. Further, as previously noted, there are ways in which the theory itself will likely require expansion or even correction as researchers continue to test its accuracy and scope. Nonetheless, it should provide a useful foundation for understanding your experiences and guiding your behavior as both a consumer and producer of advice, whether that advice be about health or other matters.

Discussion Questions

1. Having considered ART, Jane's situation, and the other advice she's received, what advice would you give her? How would you increase the likelihood that your advice would be implemented?

2. ART indicates that people evaluate advised actions on the basis of their efficacy, feasibility, and limitations, and with reference to actions they've already planned. Can you think of other features of messages that might influence responses? Do you ever go looking for advice specifically to confirm your plans?

3. Have you ever been given advice in a way that you felt was impolite? Did you feel that the message lacked solidarity, approbation, or tact—or something else?

4. What do you think about ART's claim that some situational elements and recipient traits cause people to evaluate advice more or less critically? Can you identify situational elements or personal traits that affect how much attention you pay to the details of advice or the characteristics of advisors?

5. Recent research indicates that advice is evaluated more positively when advisors first offer emotional support and discuss the problem with the recipient. What explanation(s) would you give for this finding?

6. When advice is given in close relationships, there can be "ripple effects." How do you think Jane's roommate or brother or will respond if Jane ignores their advice?

REFERENCES

Bonaccio, S., & Paik, J. E. (2018). Advice in the workplace. In E. L. MacGeorge & L. M. V. Swol (Eds.), *The Oxford Handbook of Advice* (pp. 255–276). Oxford, UK: Oxford University Press.

D'Angelo, J., & D'Angelo, A. (2018). Advice from healthcare professionals. In E. L. MacGeorge & L. M. V. Swol (Eds.), *The Oxford Handbook of Advice* (pp. 197–216). Oxford, UK: Oxford University Press.

Feng, B. (2009). Testing an integrated model of advice-giving in supportive interactions. *Human Communication Research, 35*, 115–129. doi: 10.1111/j.1468-2958.2008.01340.x

Feng, B., & MacGeorge, E. L. (2010). The influences of message and source factors on advice outcomes. *Communication Research, 37*, 576–598. doi: 10.1177/0093650210368258

Feng, B., Zhu, X., & Malloch, Y. Z. (2018). Advice communication in cyberspace. In E. L. MacGeorge & L. M. V. Swol (Eds.), *The Oxford Handbook of Advice* (pp. 363–380). Oxford, UK: Oxford University Press.

Goldsmith, D. J., & Fitch, K. (1997). The normative context of advice as social support. *Human Communication Research, 23*, 454–476. doi: 10.1111/j.1468-2958.1997.tb00406.x

Guntzviller, L. M., MacGeorge, E. L., & Brinker, D. L. (2017). Dyadic perspectives on advice between friends: Relational influence, advice quality, and conversation satisfaction. *Communication Monographs, 84*, 488–509. doi: 10.1080/03637751.2017.1352099

MacGeorge, E. L., Feng, B., & Thompson, E. R. (2008). "Good" and "bad" advice: How to advise more effectively. In M. T. Motley (Ed.), *Studies in Applied Interpersonal Communication* (pp. 145–164). Thousand Oaks, CA: Sage.

MacGeorge, E. L., Guntzviller, L. M., Brisini, K. S., Bailey, L. C., Salmon, S. K., Severen, K., … Cummings, R. D. (2017). The influence of emotional support quality on advice evaluation and outcomes. *Communication Quarterly, 65*, 80–96. doi: 10.1080/01463373.2016.1176945

MacGeorge, E. L., Guntzviller, L. M., Hanasono, L. K., & Feng, B. (2016). Testing advice response theory in interactions with friends. *Communication Research, 43*, 211–231. doi: 10.1177/0093650213510938

MacGeorge, E. L., & Hall, E. D. (2014). Relationship advice. In C. Agnew (Ed.), *Social influences on close relationships: Beyond the dyad* (pp. 188–208). Cambridge, UK: Cambridge University Press.

MacGeorge, E. L., Smith, R. A., Caldes, E., & Hackman, N. (2017). Toward reduction in antibiotic use for pediatric otitis media: Predicting parental compliance with "watchful waiting" advice. *Journal of Health Communication, 22*, 867–875.

MacGeorge, E. L., & Van Swol, L. M. (2018a). Advice across disciplines and contexts. In E. L. MacGeorge & L. M. V. Swol (Eds.), *The Oxford Handbook of Advice* (pp. 3–20). Oxford, UK: Oxford University Press.

MacGeorge, E. L., & Van Swol, L. M. (Eds.). (2018b). *The Oxford Handbook of Advice.* New York, NY: Oxford.

Perry, B. L., & Pescosolido, B. A. (2015). Social network activation: the role of health discussion partners in recovery from mental illness. *Social Science & Medicine, 125*, 116–128.

Rose, S. A., Poynter, P. S., Anderson, J. W., Noar, S. M., & Conigliaro, J. (2013). Physician weight loss advice and patient weight loss behavior change: a literature review and meta-analysis of survey data. *International Journal of Obesity, 37*, 118–128.

Servaty-Seib, H. L., & Burleson, B. R. (2007). Bereaved adolescents' evaluations of the helpfulness of support-intended statements: Associations with person centeredness and demographic, personality, and contextual factors. *Journal of Social and Personal Relationships, 24*, 207–223. doi: 10.1177/0265407507075411

Waring, H. Z., & Song, G. (2018). Advice in education. In E. L. MacGeorge & L. M. V. Swol (Eds.), *The Oxford Handbook of Advice* (pp. 217–236). Oxford, UK: Oxford University Press.

Yaniv, I. (2004). Receiving other people's advice: Influence and benefit. *Organizational Behavior and Human Decision Processes, 93*, 1–13. doi: 10.1016/j.obhdp.2003.08.002

Yaniv, I., & Kleinberger, E. (2000). Advice taking in decision making: Egocentric discounting and reputation formation. *Organizational Behavior and Human Decision Processes, 84*, 260–281. doi: 10.1006/obhd.2000.2909

Chapter 13

An International Student in the United States: A Case Study of Communication Theory of Identity

Yu Lu, Ph.D., *University of Texas Medical Branch*
Peter J. Marston, Ph.D., Communication Studies, *California State University, Northridge*
Michael Hecht, President, *REAL Prevention LLC*

Identity has been a significant concept for well over a hundred years and a focus of empirical research in the social sciences since the late 1970s, especially with the development of Social Identity Theory by Henri Tajfel and John Turner (1979). In the intervening years, with the rise of multiculturalism, gender and queer studies, and intersectionality, identity has become an even more important and prominent topic. In the field of communication studies, one of the most established theories of identity is Michael Hecht's Communication Theory of Identity (CTI), a theory that, while consistent with most previous social scientific conceptions of identity, is distinguished by the central role it assigns to communication (Hecht, 1993).

Traditional theories of identity involve communication in two ways: first, as interpersonal and social processes that may be important in *creating* identity, and, second, as a means of *expressing* identity. CTI, on the other hand, views communication as a *constituent*, or basic, component of identity, thereby conceptualizing identity in a way that extends beyond strictly psychological structures and into embodied, relational, and social behaviors. CTI has been studied empirically and related to a variety of relational and cultural contexts and a range of communication outcomes, including communication and relationship satisfaction, topic avoidance, communication appropriateness and effectiveness, and feelings of being understood (e.g., Jung & Hecht, 2008; Kam & Hecht, 2009).

Four Frames of Identity

CTI posits four frames of identity—that is, four ways in which individuals interpret their identity in relation to the social world. These frames are the personal frame, the enacted frame, the relational frame, and the communal frame. The *personal frame* consists of our self-concept or self-image: those beliefs and attitudes we hold toward ourselves. These would include beliefs about our personality, character, skills, fortune, and limitations, as well as our assessments of, and dispositions toward, these various qualities (the latter being what is commonly called self-esteem). Since this frame exists at the level of an individual's psychology, it is the most consistent with traditional conceptions of identity.

The *enacted frame* consists of one's communication and other social behaviors. As noted above, CTI contends that identity exists not only in our self-concept, but also in our actual behaviors–that is, *part* of our identity is the way we behave, most importantly in our communication. These behaviors may be patterned and relatively consistent (e.g., always polite, predictably late) or they may be exceptions to such patterns (e.g., had too much to drink at a holiday office party and yelled at a coworker). In either case, these behaviors are how we enact ourselves and, therefore, are part of our identity.

Unlike the personal and enacted frames, the *relational frame* is co-constructed or negotiated with others. It consists of the social roles and relationships that we initiate, define, and maintain through social interaction. The relational frame contributes to identity in four ways. First, our self will be conceived and presented differently depending on who we are around or the relationship we are in. Thus, an adolescent's sense of self and their communication are likely to be quite different when relating to friends than when relating to parents or employers. Second, we may internalize the ways others think of us, as when a bullied child begins to see themselves as worthless or weak. Third, people typically will, at least partially, *define* themselves in terms of relationships (e.g., a parent and their child, a minister and their congregation). Fourth, our relationships, themselves, may develop identities that are jointly created, as when a dating relationship becomes "a couple" or when business partners enter into legally-defined, contractual relationships.

Finally, the *communal frame* consists of collective identities that are produced, socially and culturally, and that help to connect or bond social groups. For example, when one invokes "the African-American experience," one is invoking a communal frame of identity. Communal frames may be most commonly associated with a variety of racial, ethnic, national, gender, and sexual identities, but may also be associated with generational identities (e.g., baby boomers, millennials), subcultural identities (e.g., punks, hackers), and even professional identities (e.g., community organizers, police officers). It is also important to note that communal identities may be shaped by cultural stereotypes that may not agree with an individual's self-identification with social or cultural groups. For example, a priest may accept the expectation that he be especially pious and circumspect, even though he, himself, may view clergy as quite human in their temptations and failings.

The Interpenetration of Frames

Another important aspect of CTI is that it does not conceive of these four frames of identity as discrete, separate entities. Rather, each of these frames may interpenetrate the others and characteristically do. Interpenetration involves two basic relations. First, elements of the various frames may overlap. For example, we may have a self-image of being efficient and competent (personal frame), and we may have a history of performance reviews at work that note these very qualities (relational frame). Second, the elements of various frames may influence one another. For example, our identification with a particular gender or sexual orientation (communal frame) may lead us to join organizations or attend events promoting associated rights and political interests (enacted frame).

What is key about interpenetration is that these relations do not subordinate one frame to another. Consider the interpenetration of the personal and enacted frames. While our communication clearly affects our own self-concept, it is equally true that our self-concept leads us to communicate in some ways rather than others. Thus, while these two frames undoubtedly interact, it is not possible to say one is merely part of the other; rather, they interpenetrate. For example, a young man who does not speak up in class may view himself as shy or introverted and this aspect of his self-concept will, in turn, likely influence his choices of when and when not to speak. Similarly, the positions from which we negotiate our relational identity will typically begin with the beliefs and attitudes that comprise our self-concept, but the very process of such negotiation will influence, in turn, these very same beliefs and attitudes. For example, a romantic partner may view themselves as being a supportive listener, but conversations and conflicts in their relationship are likely to influence—and perhaps confirm—this perception. Finally, communal identities are not simply aggregates of individuals' personal, enacted, and relational frames, but trends and patterns in the latter frames undoubtedly influence the communal frame. For example, we see political shifts and strategies in LGBTQIA movements that both reflect and shape self-concepts, communication, and relationships within this community—and with the larger culture.

Identity Gaps

As the preceding discussion of the interpenetration of frames demonstrates, the various frames of identity will typically include elements that are consistent and, perhaps, mutually confirming. But this is not always the case. When elements of the various frames are inconsistent or even contradictory, we have what CTI designates as an *identity gap*. For example, a personal-enacted identity gap may arise if we view ourselves as kind and sensitive, but frequently find ourselves in interactions where our communication results in hurt feelings or embarrassment. A personal-relational identity gap may occur when we view ourselves as capable and proactive, while our parents or spouse treat us as though we are quite the opposite. An enacted-relational gap will exist in most cases when a partner in a monogamous relationship is unfaithful. Similar identity gaps may exist among all of the frames.

To date, six identity gaps have been studied empirically: the personal-enacted, the personal-relational, the personal-communal, the enacted-relational, the enacted-communal, and the communal-relational (Jung & Hecht, 2004; Kam & Hecht, 2009; Phillips, Ledbetter, Soliz, & Berquist, 2018; Urban & Orbe, 2010). In these studies, identity gaps have been associated with various negative communication outcomes, as well as different, but predictable, thematic experiences among social groups, such as immigrants and first-generation college students. For example, Kam and Hecht (2009) found that personal-enacted identity gaps experienced by college students with their grandparents (e.g., when college students do not communicate with their grandparents in a way that is consistent with who they are) have a negative impact on their communication satisfaction and relational satisfaction with the grandparents. Among a group of Korean immigrants, Jung and Hecht (2008) found that personal-enacted identity gap and personal-relational identity gap were linked to higher level of depression.

A CTI Case Study

What follows is a three-part case study and application of CTI based upon the experiences of a Chinese in the United States: one of the co-authors of this chapter, Yu Lu.

Part One: What is my name?

As a Chinese in the US for over 10 years, name has always been a struggle for me. This started during college when I was back in China. In the first class I had with an American Peace Corps teacher, our class activity was to assign everyone an English name to be used for the rest of the semester. I was one of the few students who did not have one and found myself quite lost in coming up with a new name in just a few minutes. Many Chinese simply picked an English name that is similar to their Chinese name pronunciation. For example, a friend named "Lin" called herself "Lynn." However, my name, "Yu" (which is virtually impossible to pronounce using the phonemes in standard English), though quite common as a Chinese name, does not have an easy match in English. I became one of the few students who did not have an English name for the class. However, when I knew I was coming to the US to study, I was determined that I was finally going to adopt an English name. Not only because I thought everyone should have one (as I had often heard) but also because native English speakers had difficulty in pronouncing my name. One day, I sat down with a dictionary of English names, and, randomly turning to a page, chose "Nina."

When I arrived in the US, and I would introduce myself, I would say my Chinese name, but tell people they could call me "Nina" if they preferred. For a while, people called me by either name, but I began to hear a lot of complaints from my American friends that they felt impolite when calling me "Yu," because when they pronounced it (incorrectly) as "you," it sounded like "Hey, you, come here!" I found myself always apologizing for my name and one day, I decided I was going to go by "Nina" and "Yu" would only exist on paper. My professors, classmates, and friends all knew me as "Nina" from then on. Of course, it took me a while to recognize that people were calling me when they said "Nina." I occasionally was asked about my Chinese name, as some friends wanted to know my "real name," but they often end up giving up and go back to "Nina."

I was quite content with my English name until my first week in my Ph.D. program. I had introduced myself as "Nina" to my cohort and, one day, one of them asked, "Do any of you know a person named Yu Lu? I saw the name on one of the assigned office desks but don't know who that is." I had to explain that Yu was my Chinese name and my cohort was all very surprised that I had two names. Later, my advisor, learning of this situation, said, "you should use your own name." I had to explain to him the difficulty Americans experience in pronouncing my name and the complaints I had heard. He replied, "you should still use your own name. It's others' responsibility to learn to pronounce your name correctly, not yours to make up a new name for them. This is over-accommodation (a term from Communication Accommodation Theory, defined as excessive adaptation to communication partners, Giles, Coupland, & Coupland, 1991)."

This conversation really struck me. As a matter of fact, "Nina" truly did not mean anything to me but my Chinese name symbolizes a lot. It is a combination of my mother's (Yu) and father's (Lu) family names and all of my cousins from my mother's side have the same given name (same pronunciation, different character/writing), because we want to show our strong attachment to our mothers' family and our grandparents. Yu also means "the radiance of jade," which reflects my parents' hopes for me. Plus, it is the same name as a famous Chinese military general and strategist of the Three Kingdom period (~200 AD), one of my favorite historical figures. I would, of course, prefer "Yu" over "Nina" when there was a choice. My years of experience in the US had changed my perception that all foreigners have to have an English name because I knew that many did not have one. However, I felt an obligation to make life easier for Americans who knew me.

Now, I introduce myself as "Yu Lu" to anyone I meet for the first time. Many people would refer to me as "Yu" and most still pronounce it as "you," but they know to switch to "Yu Lu" for clarification when it becomes confusing. I still get jokes about my name (e.g., "Thank Yu [you]") or hear stories about people getting confused in conversation because of my name, but no more complaints. It is possible that all the complaints I had perceived in the past were not really complaints, but reflections of my own ambivalence about my name. I still use my English name "Nina," but only when I order coffee from Starbucks!

CTI Analysis

In this first example of "What is my name?," we observe all four identity frames. The Chinese name, "Yu," and what it symbolized for Yu, was part of her personal identity, and the action of taking on the English name, "Nina," and introducing herself with that name, were examples of the enacted identity. Relational identities that played important roles in the name case included how Yu was expected to take an English name by her Peace Corps teacher and the feedback she received about her name (e.g., from her Americans friends, from her advisor). Finally, the communal identity involved in this case was the social expectation of everyone having an English name (although, as Yu later realized, this expectation was not shared by everyone in the group).

What is perhaps most pronounced and important in this example are the identity gaps that emerged upon her adoption of the English name, "Nina." These gaps became the driving force behind many of Yu's decisions. For example, a personal-enacted identity gap existed when Yu identified with her Chinese name, but decided to take on an English name, which she initially had difficulty recognizing when people called her by that name. Although she chose a new English name as part of her personal identity, she did not predictably respond to it, creating a gap between her personal identity and her enacted identity. A relational-enacted identity gap arose when Yu's American friends struggled with the pronunciation of her Chinese name and the attendant confusion with the English pronoun "you."

This gap was also apparent when Yu's advisor expressed disagreement with her choice to adopt an English name. The gaps Yu experienced with her American friends were the reason she initially adopted an English name and the gap Yu experienced with her advisor made her reconsider this enacted identity, which led to her decision to revert to her Chinese name.

There was also a communal-enacted identity gap. When Yu did not take on an English name during her class with the Peace Corps teacher, she experienced a gap because she believed it was a "rule" (or common practice) for Chinese students to adopt an English name. By taking on the name "Nina," this gap was eliminated. As shown in these examples—and consistent with CTI—identity gaps, or inconsistencies, among identities are typically experienced negatively and individuals are often motivated to take actions to reduce the gaps. Social scientists have often posited that there is a tendency for individuals to seek consistency (Feldman, 2013), whether among their thoughts (personal identities) or between thoughts and behaviors (personal and enacted identities). In addition, a drive to fit in, or conform, suggests that people prefer communal identities to be consistent with their own personal, relational, and enacted identities (Feldman, 2013). Of course, as we all know, people are not always consistent, nor do they always conform. In fact, some people actually value the opposite. Remember the American philosopher Ralph Waldo Emerson's phrase "a foolish consistency is the hobgoblin of little minds" that, for some, has become a personal credo.

Part Two: Who are my friends?

The first event I attended at my American university was the International Orientation, which was organized to provide basic information about living and studying in the United States. I especially wanted to meet people from other countries because it would be a good opportunity to practice English and to learn about different cultures. This also was a cultural expectation among Chinese students. One well-known story in China is about how a Chinese student who had been in the United State for several years never learned English but learned to speak Cantonese (a dialect of Chinese spoken by a large number of Chinese immigrants in the United States) because he interacted only with other Chinese. Everyone laughed at this story, but we also knew the story was typical. Many educators in China, in fact, use this story to persuade students to interact more with Americans, to make our study abroad experience more worthwhile. My parents told me the same thing—that I should try to fit in, make American friends, watch American media, etc. That was my plan, but things do not always go according to plan. Before I knew it, I was already sitting with a couple of other Chinese students and planning activities together after the orientation. It turned out that, at the orientation, everyone was looking for people from their own countries. I guess it is our nature, in a place thousands of miles away from home, surrounded by foreign-looking strangers, to seek something familiar.

So, while my first attempt of making non-Chinese friends failed, I was not going to stop there. Luckily, I had signed up to live in the dormitory and paid for the meal plan at the university cafeteria, which gave me a lot of opportunities to meet with all kinds of people. I usually would go to the cafeteria with my Chinese friends and we would run into other friends (Americans and other international students) and end up eating all together at a large dining table. This became my pattern, and it was interesting when one day I happened to go to the cafeteria by myself and everyone was asking me where my Chinese friends were. I truly enjoyed interacting with my new friends. It was easy to make international friends because all of us were equally eager to meet new friends. On the other hand, experiences with Americans were mixed. I made a few American friends who were very friendly, and we hung out on many different occasions. There were also unpleasant experiences when Americans were reluctant to speak with me, perhaps because I would have to ask them to repeat themselves or explain phrases they used. This made me so self-conscious of my English that I felt bad when I had to interrupt a conversation by asking for clarification or when others had to ask me to repeat what I said because of my incorrect pronunciation. I took others' suggestions to watch American media to learn English. I was also lucky to have a few good friends who were very patient with me and my English improved over time.

Still, these unpleasant experiences remained a topic of conversation among my friends and eventually I realized that sometimes it was not just because of my English but also others' expectations of my English because I am Chinese. A Korean-American friend who grew up in the United States and did not speak any language other than English told me a story that clarified this. When she went shopping at the mall one time, a shopkeeper approached her and spoke very slowly and used lots of hand gestures because the shopkeeper thought she did not speak English. When my friend replied in clear English, the shopkeeper was shocked to find out she was a native speaker. I certainly have experienced many similar situations. There were many friendly Americans who would smile at me, but we would have little conversation. Or sometimes I would go to the grocery store and the person at the counter would have lively conversations with all other customers before and after me, but turn into complete silence with me. I found the explanation later, when I was teaching an Intercultural Communication class; one student talked about how he really wanted to make friends with some Arab students living in his dormitory and to get to know their culture, but he hesitated to initiate the conversation because he was unsure if these Arabic students would consider it appropriate and was worried that they might not speak proper English. My solution was to be more active and initiate conversations. My English was not perfect and people would know that I am not a native speaker, but at least they would not need to worry that I do not speak English at all.

CTI Analysis

In this example of "Who are my friends?," all four identity frames again can be observed. These include personal identity of Yu being a Chinese/International student in the United States and enacting that identity through her efforts to make English-speaking friends and to improve her English. Another enacted identity was her habit of being with her Chinese friends. Multiple relational identities are also present. For example, there was the relational identity formed by others' (e.g., educators and parents) expectations of Yu making American friends or her assumed inability to speak English effectively. Also, there was the relational identity based on Yu's friendship with other Chinese students; she was viewed as a member of the Chinese group and, therefore, expected to go to the cafeteria with the other Chinese students. Another relational identity was the way her assessment of her proficiency in English was influenced by her interactions with others (i.e., she became conscious and uncomfortable with her English because of conversational difficulties). Finally, Yu arrived in the United States with the communal identity from Chinese culture that Chinese students studying abroad interact mostly with Chinese, and she was fighting this communal identity by making English-speaking friends. She also experienced communal identity from the American culture that Asians do not speak proper English and do not want to engage in conversations, and she tried to fight this communal identity by taking initiatives in conversations.

As CTI suggests, identity frames do not operate in isolation, but interpenetrate. We can see in this example that Yu's enacted identity of hanging out with her Chinese friends was observed by others and later ascribed to her as a relational identity (i.e., when she went to the cafeteria without them). We also see an interesting case of Yu's personal identity in disagreement with the communal identity. By definition, communal identity is the collective identity produced socially and culturally, which can be viewed as generalizations about a group of people based on their characteristics, behavioral patterns, and the like. The communal identity of Chinese students in the United States is that they mostly hang out with other Chinese students. This may be generally true because many Chinese students do behave like that. However, Yu had a personal identity that is inconsistent with this communal identity, and, in her eyes, her enacted identity and relational identity were reflected in her efforts to meet and develop friendships with non-Chinese students. This example highlights the important contribution of CTI to expand the idea of identity to not just how we see ourselves, but also how others see us. The rich complexity of relational identities plays out in this narrative as Yu negotiates among the identities of International Student, Chinese, friend, and student. They interpenetrate in complex ways with each other and with others' ascriptions about them (e.g., the shopkeeper who assumed someone of Korean heritage was a non-native English speaker). These interplays of relational identities are even more pronounced as we turn to the final section and Yu's student-teacher relationships.

Part Three: When do I speak?

Having grown up in the teacher-centered educational system in China, pursuing higher education in the more student-centered system in the United States was a challenge. Like many other Chinese students, I found participating in class the biggest issue. I was surprised to see lively discussions in American classrooms and especially shocked that some American students would speak up without their professors' permission, sometimes even interrupting professors during lecture. In China, teachers lecture and students take notes. A "good" student does not speak unless the teacher asks for answers to questions. If students have questions, they know they should wait until after class. If they really want to ask the question, they have to raise their hand, speak only when—and if—permission is given by teachers. I had a high school teacher that never gave me permission to speak even though he saw my hand raised, and so I had to ask my questions after class. Like many other students from Asian cultures, it took quite some time to get used to the idea that class discussion is not only allowed, but encouraged. Whether I was able to participate in discussion was another story.

Not used to speaking up in classrooms, I found it difficult to take notes and participate in class discussions at the same time. In Chinese culture, one should not speak up unless they are sure about their ideas. This is opposite to the American way of "thinking out loud." The Chinese way is to come up with an idea, mentally evaluate the soundness of the idea, and then prepare how to express the idea—all before one speaks. In a class discussion, this can take a lot of time, especially when translating thoughts back and forth between Chinese and English, and many Chinese students, including myself, find that when we are finally ready to speak up, the discussion topic has moved to something else. I still remember my first Health Communication class in my doctoral program, which was one of the classes where 10% of the class grade was participation. I had tried to participate, but because I was completely new to the area of Health Communication, there

*were a lot of times I did not feel confident enough to speak up, but when the pro-
fessor gave the answer to the question we were discussing, I regretted not contributing because my answers were correct. I then found myself facing a dilemma. If
I want to become a good student according to American norms, I should learn to
think out loud, but if I do, I am evaluated negatively according to Chinese norms
because in Chinese classrooms, people who are quick in speaking up are often
seen as class clowns. In the end, I had to follow both norms and learn to switch
between them depending on those with whom I was interacting. This was not an
easy task. After being in the United States for more than 10 years, I am still on
the long journey of practicing my skills in being fluent in both cultures.*

CTI Analysis

In this example of "When do I speak?," we see an interesting case of identity
struggle because of cultural differences. It was clear that cultural norms for the
relational identities, student and teacher, were challenging. At the same time, Yu's
self-identifying as a "good student" (i.e., personal identity) required silence in
China, but participation in the United States, enactments that are clearly at odds.
So, how would Yu enact her student identity? How would others, including both
international and American students, as well as teachers, react to either enacted
identity? How would this affect the student-teacher relational identities and what
would be ascribed to her based on her enactments? Clearly, Yu was faced with a
significant relational dilemma. Should she be a good student by following American communal identities and actively participate in class discussions in American
classrooms or stay consistent with Chinese norms where good students are silent
and actively take notes? What are the costs of each enactment? If she behaved in
ways consistent with Chinese norms she might avoid this identity gap. However,
these behaviors in American classrooms are likely to result in negative evaluations
from teachers and perhaps even grade penalties (i.e., relational identity). This
resulted in Yu's decision to switch her communication style based on whom she is
interacting with: another example of relational identity. In contrast to the previous
example of "Who are my friends?," here we can see how Yu enacts an identity that
is consistent with the communal identity of the culture she is immersed in so that
she is perceived as a good student by her teachers. This, again, reveals the interpenetration of the identity frames. Yu's personal identity of being a good student
was defined by the communal identity of what describes a good student, reflected
by the enacted identity of class participation, and influenced by the relational identity established by her teachers' feedback. Yu's experiences, in fact, reflect the gaps
experienced by many international students (Jung, Hecht, & Wadsworth, 2007).

Conclusion

In this chapter, we have explained and illustrated the Communication Theory of Identity in order to demonstrate its heuristic value in theory and practice. CTI is intended not only to promote deeper understandings of communication, but also to encourage more effective communication. Think about the frames of identity implied in a chapter such as this one. What identities did you enact in the process? Do you have international friends or peers with whom you share experiences similar to the ones Yu describes? If so, did that lead you to a certain relational identity (e.g., friend of a certain international student)? What if your student identity is enacted by being quiet, but taking detailed notes, only talking to your teacher one-on-one outside of class? If you are an American-born and educated student, how did that make you feel about your own enacted student identity? And, if you are the teacher, reading this, what sort of enactments did you prepare for your next class? If the chapter led you to think about these types of questions, then CTI spoke to you, your identities, and your experiences.

Discussion Questions

1. What are the personal, enacted, relational and communal identities that are most important to you?

2. What are the relational identities that the people you like ascribe to you?

3. What are the biggest identity gaps you experience? Where do they occur?

4. If you were to change one thing about your identity, what would it be?

REFERENCES

Feldman, S. (2013). Cognitive consistency: Motivational antecedents and behavioral consequents. Cambridge, MA: Academic Press.

Giles, H., Coupland, J., & Coupland, N. (Eds.) (1991). Contexts of Accommodation. New York, NY: Cambridge University Press.

Hecht, M. L. (1993). 2002—A research odyssey: Toward the development of a communication theory of identity. *Communication Monographs, 60*, 76–82. doi: 10.1080/03637759309376297

Jung, E., & Hecht, M. L. (2008). Identity gaps and level of depression among Korean immigrants. *Health Communication, 23*(4), 313-325. doi: 10.1080/10410230802229688

Jung, E., & Hecht, M. L. (2004). Elaborating the communication theory of identity: Identity gaps and communication outcomes. *Communication Quarterly, 52*(3), 265–283. doi: 10.1080/01463370409370197

Jung, E., Hecht, M. L., & Wadsworth, B. C. (2007). The role of identity in international students' psychological well-being in the United States: A model of depression level, identity gaps, discrimination, and acculturation. *International Journal of Intercultural Relations, 31*, 605-624. doi: 10.1016/j.ijintrel.2007.04.001

Kam, J. A., & Hecht, M. L. (2009). Investigating the role of identity gaps among communicative and relational outcomes within the grandparent–grandchild relationship: The young-adult grandchildren's perspective. *Western Journal of Communication, 73*(4), 456–480. doi: 10.1080/10570310903279067

Phillips, K. E., Ledbetter, A. M., Soliz, J., & Bergquist, G. (2018). Investigating the interplay between identity gaps and communication patterns in predicting relational intention in families in the United States. *Journal of Communication*, 1–22. doi: 10.1093/joc/jqy016

Tajfel, H. & Turner, J. C. (1979). An Integrative Theory of Intergroup Conflict. In W. G. Austin & S. Worchel (Eds.), The Social Psychology of Intergroup Relations. Monterey, CA: Brooks-Cole.

Urban, E. L., & Orbe, M. P. (2010). Identity Gaps of Contemporary U.S. Immigrants: Acknowledging Divergent Communicative Experiences. *Communication Studies, 61*(3), 304-320, doi: 10.1080/10510971003757147

Chapter 14

Theories of Self-Efficacy: The Case of Registering to Become an Organ Donor

Katy A. Harris, MS, *University at Buffalo, the State University of New York*
Thomas Hugh Feeley, Ph.D., *University at Buffalo, the State University of New York*

We sometimes find ourselves in situations that require action on our part in the face of adversity. In such situations, we may feel confident that we can do what is needed to overcome the adversity or we may believe we are unable to make it happen and must accept the negative outcomes of inaction. For example, a lifelong smoker may feel that she simply does not have the willpower to kick the habit and is forced to deal with the potential negative health consequences of smoking or deny their existence altogether. Perceiving ourselves as capable of certain actions is a crucial determinant to whether or not we attempt to handle such situations. The belief in our own capability is our perceived *self-efficacy*, a term formally defined as a belief in our ability to organize and execute a particular course of action to successfully manage prospective situations (Bandura, 1977). One key element of self-efficacy is that our perception of self-efficacy is unique to a given situation (Bandura, 1980; Maibach & Murphy, 1995). For example, we may perceive ourselves able or competent when asked to conduct statistics on a given research project but less competent if asked to write the results from these analyses. Thus, self-efficacy is higher with conducting statistics than it is with my writing skills. When asked about our self-efficacy regarding multiple behaviors, we could claim to be efficacious at certain behaviors, but entirely incapable at other behaviors (Bandura, 1997). One implication of this is a hesitancy to enter situations where one's own self-efficacy is lower than expectations.

According to Bandura (1997), self-efficacy may be affected by (at least) four factors. The first factor, *mastery experiences*, refers to the mastery of the behavior through actually engaging in the experience previously. This can vary from person to person, as some people have the opportunity to engage in certain behaviors more often than others (Bandura, 1997). A simple example in relation to organ donation is registration to become a deceased organ donor, a process that involves the signing of a donor registry. If you have done it once, you will likely be able to do it again when you renew your driver's license because you know what you have to do (i.e., sign the card) and you know what you're signing (agreeing to donate organs under specific circumstances). The second factor relates to *vicarious experiences*. One's self-efficacy can be enhanced by viewing modeled behaviors, either in person or via the mass media (Bandura, 1997). A modeled behavior refers to someone else correctly enacting the target behavior, and as a result the individual may resolve, *They did it, so maybe I can do it, too*. For example, I may see myself as weak at media theory, but after seeing my friend ace the graduate seminar I may gain confidence in my ability to perform well in the course also.

Third, *direct social influence* potentially impacts perceptions of self-efficacy. We often rely on relevant social connections when making self-evaluations (Bandura, 2001). If someone else believes we can do something and communicates this belief to us, we are more likely to feel that way as well. This is why it is so important to provide positive reinforcement to individuals who are known to lack self-confidence in a given area.

Finally, *physiological factors* play a role in our self-efficacy as well. Our beliefs about our physiological abilities impact self-efficacy perceptions. In relation to organ donation, many believe they cannot donate because they are too old or too sick for their organs to be of any use. Alternatively, some claim the "ick factor," where the idea of transplantation doesn't set well with them (Morgan et al., 2008).

Self-efficacy is a core construct of a larger theoretical concept called Social Cognitive Theory (SCT; Bandura, 1997). According to the social-cognitive framework, communication occurs via two pathways, either directly, by informing, motivating, or guiding individuals, or indirectly, through social media (Bandura, 2001). Rather than existing as reactive and passive individuals, people are agentic, and develop and change through social systems. These social systems lead to the determinants of health-related decisions and behavior—the knowledge of health risks, perceived self-efficacy to exercise control over health behaviors, outcome expectations regarding various health habits, health goals, and the perceived facilitators and socio-structural impediments to engaging in the behaviors (Bandura, 2004). Self-efficacy affects our behavior both directly and indirectly (Bandura, 2012). The goals we set for ourselves are directly influenced by self-efficacy; if we believe we can do something, we can set a goal to do it. Our *outcome expectancies* are also determined by our own self-efficacy, which includes physical, self-evaluative, and social factors. Self-efficacy helps us navigate socio-structural factors as well; if we possess self-efficacy, we overcome issues, whereas without self-efficacy, we come to see our goal as futile. Each of these factors, in turn, influences ultimate behavior, alongside simple efficacy toward the behavior.

Theorizing and Studying Self-Efficacy in Health Communication Research

Bandura (2004) describes self-efficacy in the health promotion domain as both an indirect and direct determinant of behavioral intention. Self-efficacy has received much attention in the health subfield of communication (Bandura, 2012; Maibach & Murphy, 1995) and has been built into more extensive theorizing about our health-related behavior to address how to boost one's self-efficacy and how self-efficacy ultimately impacts our decisions.

One such approach, the Health Belief Model (HBM), posits that health behaviors are based on four constructs: the *severity* and *susceptibility* perceived, *benefits of action*, and *barriers to action*. First, we consider the perceived *severity* (i.e., *How harmful would it be if I do not change my behavior?*) of a threat and how *susceptible* (i.e., *How likely is this threat to happen to me?*) we are to a threat in relation to action or inaction on our part. Second, we consider if we can take action or not based on perceived benefits or barriers in relation to action or inaction (Glanz Rimer, & Viswanath, 2008; cited in Zhang et al., 2017). Self-efficacy comes into play when considering our beliefs about our ability to take action or not. If we perceive ourselves as efficacious in engaging in a recommended health behavior, we can overcome the perceived barriers.

Two related approaches incorporate self-efficacy, alongside threat perception, as a determinant of whether a response is positive or maladaptive: Protection Motivation Theory (PMT) and the Extended Parallel Processing Model (EPPM) (Rogers, 1975; Witte, 1994). Similar to the Health Belief Model, PMT and EPPM propose that previous evaluations of one's self-efficacy regarding a given behavior can influence reassessment of self-efficacy after message exposure (Maloney, Lapinski, & Witte, 2011). Specifically, after exposure to a fearful message, recipients assess their perceived self-efficacy, alongside response efficacy, susceptibility, and the severity of the threat (i.e., *Would this outcome significantly impact me?*). In the case of fear appeals, a message aiming to persuade someone to consent to organ donation should not heavily focus on the circumstances in which one may become a donor (i.e., brain death), as the threat perception (e.g., how likely one is to be in that situation) would likely overshadow any self-efficacy information in the message.

In these approaches (HBM, EPPM, PMT), self-efficacy moderates the success of a given health message; that is, increases in self-efficacy lead to increased intention to engage in the recommended behaviors. When applying these approaches to communication situations, it is important to consider how each approach incorporates self-efficacy to ensure that the message is actually touching on self-efficacy. Self-efficacy may be measured using several techniques (see Maibach & Murphy, 1995). The most basic way to ask someone about their efficacy perception uses a yes/no answer format (e.g., *"Can you accomplish this task?"*). A more granular method involves rating one's perceived self-efficacy along a scale. Self-efficacy questions that ask the participant to rate his/her self-efficacy capture the more subtle differences that a yes/no answer choice cannot. Self-efficacy scales that measure efficacy using multiple questions with multiple answer choices exist for a wide range of behaviors because a single measure of self-efficacy is meaningless. In fact, the concept of generalized self-efficacy or trait self-efficacy (i.e., beliefs about one's general capabilities at accomplishing general tasks or goals) has been studied with little support (Bandura, 2012; Maibach & Murphy, 1995). Maibach and Murphy (1995) claim that a proper measurement of self-efficacy will inquire about (1) the specific behavior or class of behaviors, (2) the situational domain of the behavior, and (3) the time frame of the behavior.

Fear appeal theories and approaches (e.g., EPPM) make predictions using perceived self-efficacy as one of two types of efficacy relevant to fear appeal processing (Maloney et al., 2011), where the measurement of efficacy indicates the nature of the coping (e.g., Will the recipient accept the message recommendations or negatively react to the message?) (Armitage et al., 2001). The commonly used scale to assess responses to fear appeal messages, the Risk Behavior Diagnosis Scale (Witte, Cameron, McKeon, & Berkowitz 1996), asks six efficacy questions, broken down further to three self-efficacy and three response-efficacy questions (as well as six threat-related questions) (see Witte et al., 1996, for the full questionnaire and validation study). Six items of perceived efficacy assess one's perceptions of his/her own ability to use the message recommendations (e.g., *I am able to do this*) and perceived response efficacy (e.g., *This behavior is effective in protecting me from harm*). Using simple calculations, one could determine the likelihood of message rejection versus message acceptance by subtracting the threat score (combining severity and susceptibility ratings) from the efficacy score. A positive number indicates danger control (i.e., intention to engage in recommended behaviors) because that means efficacy beliefs overcome the level of fear and the recipient perceives himself/herself as capable of action, whereas a negative number indicates that the participant does not feel that he/she could engage in the recommended behavior because the efficacy is too low in relation to the barriers presented by the threat (for more information, see Maloney et al., 2011).

Bandura (2012) has criticized some popular methods of measuring self-efficacy. Scales that utilize neutral (i.e., "neither agree nor disagree with this statement") values, such as a '3' on a '1' to '5' scale, misinterpret the way self-efficacy works in his conceptualization of the theory. In Bandura's (2012) view, self-efficacy can only be conceptualized as an increasing concept with a minimum low point. Midpoint answers on '1' to '5' scales (or '0' to '10,' '1' to '7,') should then indicate moderate self-efficacy, rather than undetermined or unidentifiable self-efficacy. A neutral or unidentified level of self-efficacy, in Bandura's (2012) view, means nothing. No perception of self-efficacy intuitively indicates low self-efficacy. Additionally, the multiple theories that incorporate self-efficacy, and similar concepts, lead to overlapping of terms and ideas. In a review of studies using related concepts, such as perceived behavioral control (e.g., Ajzen, 1991), Bandura (2012) found that after self-efficacy, adding many other concepts did little to further explain behaviors.

Careful attention to how questions are worded, and what is truly being asked, is crucial to explain how self-efficacy affects our health decisions. As exemplified many times, health behaviors, and the associated decisions, rely on varying contexts of self-efficacy that need attention to the factors influencing these self-beliefs. In the context of organ donation, there are three types of donors (living donors, cardiac death donors, and brain death donors) and, thus, self-efficacy may vary in consenting to donate related to each method of donation. The remainder of this chapter touches primarily on brain death donation through understanding one's self-efficacy to donate. Before doing so, however, a brief background on the medical crisis of the donation is in order.

Self-Efficacy in Action: Increasing the Organ Supply

Since the first successful kidney transplant in the 1950s in South Africa, the advances in transplantation are nothing short of medical marvels. Individuals live longer and healthier lives through organ transplantation. In many cases, identifying a donor is the only means of survival for individuals on the national waiting list. The number of Americans who are in need of an organ donor increases yearly due to high incidence of diabetes, increase in hepatitis C, and other common health conditions that cause one to need an organ transplant (Department of Health and Human Services, 2018). This increase, however, has not been met with an increase in the number of organs available for transplant. For example, there are currently nearly 116,000 individuals on the national waiting list for an organ transplant (United Network for Organ Sharing, 2017) and, in 2016, 33,610 organs were transplanted. Every deceased donor can donate up to eight organs and the typical donor contributes nearly three organs for transplant (Department of Health and Human Services, 2018). Thus, there is a great need to increase the number of individuals willing to consent to donation.

Self-Efficacy: The Secret Ingredient

Research in health communication has identified two primary ways that self-efficacy has been used to drive campaigns to increase the number of individuals who formally register their consent through a dedicated state portal (usually through Motor Vehicles transactions): through campaigns to increase self-efficacy and through message testing. When an individual is identified for transplant eligibility, the local organ procurement organization (OPO) is contacted, and the OPO representative consults with state records to see if the patient has consented to donation. If a patient has not communicated his or her consent, the next-of-kin must provide consent for the patient. Thus, it is in the best interest of donation, and for the patient, if his or her wishes are made known while s/he is living.

The challenge for increasing the number of individuals on the state registries is to communicate to them about how to donate organs and what it means to be an organ donor. As one can readily see, these two challenges are isomorphic with Bandura's (1977) concepts of *efficacy expectations* and *outcome expectations*. However, campaigns typically address outcome expectations first, then efficacy expectations second. In reality it is important for individuals to first learn what it means to donate and how one becomes a donor before addressing how one registers to donate.

The biggest obstacle is identifying unique and impactful ways to educate the general public about donation so that they understand how to sign the registry and why it matters to do so in the first place. Two examples bring this obstacle to light. Few individuals have cause to actively seek information about donation and likely ignore campaign ads if they happened upon them during media perusal. Understanding this, campaigns have used the workplace and the university to bring the message to employees and students (e.g., Morgan et al., 2008; Feeley, Anker et al., 2010). The use of peers to deliver the message promoting donation has worked in strengthening the self-efficacy among non-registered individuals. Peers or models carry greater credibility in delivering the message about donation (Feeley et al., 2009).

In a campaign using university students, Feeley, Anker and colleagues (2010) featured student-to-student campaigns to provide brief educational modules to students before asking peers to become registered donors. The idea was that student-to-student delivery methods would show students' greater efficacy with regard to how one registers and also indicate its importance in registering one's consent. Students learn from other students how one registers and the value of registration (see also Feeley et al., 2009).

A second campaign sought to increase patients' self-efficacy to discuss living donation in a sample of individuals in need of a liver donor in New York State (DeLair et al., 2010). To do this, DVDs and brochures were produced, using testimonials and survey data from former living liver donors who recently underwent transplantation. Direct messaging from actual donors provided a more impactful message and data indicated that patients' self-efficacy increased after exposure to the intervention on a measure of self-efficacy related to living donation (e.g., "I know enough about living donation to discuss it with close friends and family"). The outcomes of this study demonstrate how the factor of *direct social influence* is important at increasing self-efficacy; this message strategy was effective because actual donors shared their own stories.

Self-efficacy is, at its core, a theory of social psychology, and seeks to understand decision-making around important health and social decisions (see Feeley et al., 2009). However, it becomes relevant to communication scholars, as practitioners seek to increase individuals' self-efficacy so that they see themselves as able to enact a given behavior (e.g., registering their consent to donate) and the value of doing so (e.g., so their family understands their position if incapacitated). Usually, strategic messaging, combined with education campaigns, is the primary method used to influence self-efficacy levels in a targeted population (for a review, see Anker et al., 2016).

Related to the necessity of message targeting, communication research has sought to better understand what messages serve to better strengthen self-efficacy in the general population. One study compared narrative appeals to statistical appeals and found narratives to engender most positive message reactions in a sample of undergraduate students (Feeley, Marshall, & Reinhart, 2006). Stated differently, stories about donor cases were better received by individuals when compared to reading pallid numbers and statistics about the donation shortage. As Bandura (1997) explains, our self-efficacy is influenced by media, and we learn through *vicarious experience*; narrative formats are commonly used for vicarious learning in health communication.

A subsequent three-study analysis (Reinhart, Marshall, Feeley, & Tutzauer, 2007), compared the use of gain-framed messages to loss-framed messages in the context of organ donation. A gain-framed message, for example, highlights the benefits associated with being a potential donor, such as the lives saved; whereas loss-framed messages would emphasize the costs of not becoming a donor.

Results indicated that gain-framed messages invoked significantly greater message reactions. In fact, loss-framed messages (i.e., messages detailing the losses that might accrue from *not* donating) engendered psychological reactance in students, whereby receivers perceived manipulative intent on the part of message senders. Thus, positive messages about the gains or benefits from donation appear more persuasive when seeking to increase others' self-efficacy toward enrolling to become a donor, a finding in line with several theories incorporating self-efficacy. For example, messages developed based on fear appeal theories (e.g., PMT, EPPM) must not over emphasize the threatening or loss-related information because the efficacy manipulation may not be successful if fear or negative affect is too high.

In a 2010 study by Anker, Feeley, and Kim, the authors directly tested self-efficacy as a potential mediator in the attitude-behavior relationship in the context of donation. The literature has identified positive attitudes toward organ donation in the general public (Feeley, 2007; Gallup, 2012), but these positive attitudes have not directly translated into high registration rates across the United States. The authors proposed that individuals who are low in self-efficacy to donate would be less likely to register. Using a five-item measure of self-efficacy (e.g., "I would be able to overcome fears about donation that I might have in order to sign the registry"), Anker et al. (2010) found a mediational relationship, in that positive attitudes predict higher self-efficacy to donate which, in turn, predicts registry status. When self-efficacy is added to the model, the direct relationship between attitudes and behavior is nonsignificant, providing evidence for mediation. To promote registration, communication practitioners would benefit by targeting self-efficacy to donate in those who feel positively toward organ donation.

Conclusion

The concept of self-efficacy is a powerful theoretical ally when attempting to understand decision-making in not only health contexts, but in everyday life. Self-efficacy is especially important in decisions that are difficult to change. In these cases, individuals may perceive they cannot undertake the required action for one reason or another and may also see completion of the action to be futile in the end. Increasing individuals' self-efficacy can serve to increase the likeliness one changes their outlook on undertaking the targeted behavior.

Increasing self-efficacy in particular health contexts, such as organ donation, is a problem that communication scientists and practitioners must address according to the specific theory utilized when designing a health campaign or message. For example, according to the approaches such as Social Cognitive Theory, or the Health Belief Model, self-efficacy is a determinant of one's *outcome expectancies*.

Since these expectancies may include beliefs about the potential benefits or the losses in relation to one's behavior, it may be best to design a message or campaign with a focus on overcoming aversive outcomes one believes is associated with organ donation (i.e., target beliefs such as, *it is too difficult for me to register while I'm at the DMV, or I can't register because it's too unsettling to think about organ donation*). Such messages may simultaneously help us gain *vicarious experience*, which is expected to influence self-efficacy via demonstration of a target behavior. In the case of organ donation, communication practitioners could create a campaign which involves a demonstration of specific behaviors related to becoming a donor, such as physically signing up or discussing organ donation with family members.

Message designers may also reemphasize the importance of registering, such as when one renews their driver's license, to individuals who previously agreed to donate. In the years between license renewals, new information may have altered one's attitudes and beliefs about organ donation, or they may have not given much thought to the concept of donation. Messages targeting previous registrants should thus emphasize the *mastery experience* one has; they have signed the card once before, and thus have the ability to do so again. Such messages may also elaborate on the *physiological factors* related to engaging in the behavior. In this example, emphasizing one's ability to engage in an action completed at least once before. Additionally, messages that target previously registered organ donors may encourage registered donors to engage in *direct social influence* by encouraging their social networks to become organ donors as well (see, for example, Morgan et al., 2008 and Feeley, Anker et al., 2010).

If one is designing a message based on Protection Motivation Theory, or the Extended Parallel Processing Model, such a message would need to tailor the self-efficacy information so that it helps the recipient overcome any fear or negative emotion initially aroused in the message. A fear appeal, for example, could go too far in emphasizing losses associated with donating or not donating (e.g., through overemphasizing preventable deaths or overemphasizing one's own mortality and the conditions of brain-death donation). It is thus up to the message designer to carefully consider their audience's beliefs about organ donation, determine which of the factor(s) is likely to influence self-efficacy in the specific context, and effectively direct attention to the positive self-efficacy information in the message (see, for example, Reinhart, Marshall, Feeley, & Tutzauer, 2007).

To conclude, in the context of organ donation, the general task is to increase self-efficacy by showing individuals the ease of donating, which may overcome their physiological beliefs (e.g., *it is too difficult for me to go and register*), or their lack of experience (e.g., *I can't register because I don't know how*), and to emphasize the potential life-saving value of registering one's consent in the unlikely event one becomes eligible to donate.

Discussion Questions

1. In what context would you consider yourself low in self-efficacy? Given the definition of self-efficacy, how might you increase your self-efficacy if you wished to do so?

2. What is the difference between efficacy expectations and outcome expectations? Provide an example to illustrate this difference.

3. Name three or four factors that potentially influence one's level of self-efficacy in a given context. Which one, do you think, is most important in influencing self-efficacy levels?

4. How have theories of self-efficacy been used to explain why individuals elect to (or not elect to) register their consent to be an organ donor?

REFERENCES

Anker, A. E., Feeley, T. H., & Kim, H. (2010). Examining the attitude–behavior relationship in prosocial donation domains. *Journal of Applied Social Psychology, 40*(6), 1293–1324.

Anker, A. E., Feeley, T. H., McCracken, B., & Lagoe, C. A. (2016). Measuring the effectiveness of mass-mediated health campaigns through meta-analysis. *Journal of Health Communication, 21*(4), 439–456.

Armitage, C. J., & Conner, M. (2001). Social cognitive determinants of blood donation. *Journal of Applied Social Psychology, 31*(7), 1431–1457.

DeLair, S., Feeley, T. H., Kim, H., del Rio Martin, J., Kim-Schluger, L., LaPointe Rudow, D., Orloff, M., Sheiner, P. A., & Teperman, L. (2010). A peer-based intervention to educate liver transplant candidates about living donor liver transplantation. *Liver Transplantation, 16*(1), 42–48.

Bandura, A. (1977). Self-efficacy: Toward a unifying theory of behavioral change. *Psychological Review, 84*, 191–215.

Bandura, A. (1980). Gauging the relationship between self-efficacy judgment and action. *Cognitive Therapy and Research, 4*, 263–268.

Bandura, A. (1997). *Self-efficacy: The exercise of control.* New York: Freeman.

Bandura, A. (2001). Social cognitive theory of mass communication. *Media Psychology, 3*(3), 265–299.

Bandura, A. (2004). Health promotion by social cognitive means. *Health Education and Behavior, 31*, 143–164.

Bandura, A. (2012). On the functional properties of self-efficacy revisited. *Journal of Management, 38*(1), 9–44.

Department of Health and Human Services. (2018). Retrieved from https://www.organdonor.gov/index.html

Feeley, T. H. (2007). College students' knowledge, attitudes, and behaviors regarding organ donation: An integrated review of the literature. *Journal of Applied Social Psychology, 37*(2), 243–271.

Feeley, T.H., Anker, A.E., Watkins, B. Rivera, J., Tag, N., & Volpe, L. (2009). A peer-to-peer campaign to promote organ donation among racially diverse college students in New York City. *Journal of National Medical Association, 101*, 1154–1162.

Feeley, T.H., Anker, A.E., Williams, C.R., & Vincent, D.E. (2010). A multi-campus classroom intervention to promote organ and tissue donation. In E. Alvaro & J. Siegel (Eds.). *Applied psychology and organ donation: Implementing and evaluating health behavior interventions*. Mahwah, NJ: Lawrence Erlbaum Associates.

Feeley, T. H., Cooper, J., Foels, T., & Mahoney, M. C. (2009). Efficacy expectations for colorectal cancer screening in primary care: Identifying barriers and facilitators for patients and clinicians. *Health Communication, 24*(4), 304–315.

Feeley, T. H., Marshall, H. M., & Reinhart, A. M. (2006). Reactions to narrative and statistical written messages promoting organ donation. *Communication Reports, 19*(2), 89–100.

Maibach, E., & Murphy, D. A. (1995). Self-efficacy in health promotion research and practice: Conceptualization and measurement. *Health Education Research, 10*(1), 37–50.

Maloney, E. K., Lapinski, M. K., & Witte, K. (2011). Fear appeals and persuasion: A review and update of the extended parallel process model. *Social and Personality Psychology Compass, 5*(4), 206–219.

Morgan, S. E., Stephenson, M. T., Harrison, T. R., Afifi, W. A., & Long, S. D. (2008). Facts versus 'feelings': How rational is the decision to become an organ donor? *Journal of Health Psychology, 13*, 644–658.

Reinhart, A. M., Marshall, H. M., Feeley, T. H., & Tutzauer, F. (2007). The persuasive effects of message framing in organ donation: The mediating role of psychological reactance. *Communication Monographs, 74*(2), 229–255.

Rogers, R. W. (1975). A protection motivation theory of fear appeals and attitude change. *The Journal of Psychology, 91*(1), 93–114.

United Network for Organ Sharing. (2017). Retrieved from https://unos.org/

Witte, K. (1994). Fear control and danger control: A test of the extended parallel process model (EPPM). *Communications Monographs, 61*(2), 113–134.

Witte, K., Cameron, K. A., McKeon, J. K., & Berkowitz, J. M. (1996). Predicting risk behaviors: Development and validation of a diagnostic scale. *Journal of Health Communication, 1*(4), 317–342.

Zhang, X., Baker, K., Pember, S., & Bissell, K. (2017). Persuading me to eat healthy: A content analysis of YouTube public service announcements grounded in the health belief model. *Southern Communication Journal, 82*(1), 38–51.

Chapter 15

Lauren's Job Interviews: A Case Study for Nonverbal Expectancy Violations Theory

Andrew S. Rancer, Ph.D., *The University of Akron*
Heather L. Walter, Ph.D., *The University of Akron*

The Theory

We are sure that you have experienced a situation where someone has behaved or communicated with you in a way that you did not expect. For example, perhaps you were talking with the owner of a dry-cleaning store about a problem with the cleaning of a garment. This is the first time you have ever spoken with this individual. In addition to carefully touching and examining your shirt or blouse, the owner repeatedly grabs your arm and touches your hand. After a few of these touches, you begin to feel uncomfortable and attempt to minimize these touches by moving away from the proprietor and decreasing your verbal communication with him. You have just experienced a "violation" of expectancies regarding the use of touch among strangers.

Judee Burgoon (1978, 1983, 1985) and Steven Jones (Burgoon & Jones, 1976) originally developed Nonverbal Expectancy Violations Theory (NEVT) to explain the consequences of changes in distance and personal space during interpersonal communication interactions. Nonverbal Expectancy Violations Theory was one of the first theories of nonverbal communication developed by communication scholars and has been continually revised and expanded. Today, the theory is used to explain a wide range of communication outcomes associated with violations of expectations about verbal and nonverbal communication behavior. Although the name of the theory was later shortened to simply Expectancy Violations Theory, because the focus of this chapter and case study is on the *nonverbal components* of expectancy violations theory, we have chosen to label the theory, Nonverbal Expectancy Violations Theory (NEVT). Nonverbal Expectancy Violations Theory has generated much interest and research over the last 40 years.

Assumptions of Nonverbal Expectancy Violations Theory

According to Nonverbal Expectancy Violations Theory, several factors interact to influence how we react to a violation of the type of nonverbal behavior we expect to encounter in a particular situation (Burgoon & Hale, 1988). Several key elements are contained in the theory. According to Burgoon, Guerrero, and Floyd (2010), "...a combination of communicator, relationship, and context factors, such as one's sex, age, personality, relational familiarity, cultural similarity, status, liking, physical setting, formality of the interaction, and conversational topic, all feed into what is expected for a given interchange" (p. 268).

Nonverbal Expectancy Violations Theory first considers our *expectancies* or *expectations*. We have expectations about our and others' normative or appropriate behavior and communication according to the situation, the context, the environment, and the communicators involved in the interaction. Through social norms, we form "expectations" about how others should behave nonverbally (and verbally) when we are interacting with them. If another person's behavior deviates from what we typically expect, then an expectancy violation has occurred. Anything "out of the ordinary" causes us to take special notice of that behavior. For example, we would notice (and probably be very uncomfortable) if a stranger asking for directions stood very close to us. Similarly, we would notice, and, again, probably feel somewhat uncomfortable, if our significant other stood very far away from us at a party. A violation of our nonverbal expectations is unsettling and can cause emotional *arousal*.

We learn expectations from several sources (Floyd, Ramirez, & Burgoon, 1999). First, the culture in which we live shapes our expectations about types of appropriate or "normative" communication behavior, including nonverbal communication. Some cultures (often referred to as "contact cultures") tend to exhibit more eye contact, more frequent touch, and have much smaller personal space zones than cultures referred to as "noncontact" cultures.

The *context* in which the interaction takes place also affects expectations of others' behavior. A great deal of eye contact from an attractive other may be seen as inviting or even exciting if the context of the interaction is in a social club. However, the same nonverbal behavior may be seen as threatening, or even terrifying, if that same behavior is exhibited in a sparsely populated subway car late at night. Depending on the context, "a caress may convey sympathy, comfort, dominance, affection, attraction, or lust" (Burgoon, Coker, & Coker, 1986, p. 497).

The meaning attached to a particular communication behavior may also depend on the characteristics of the individuals involved in the interaction. The nature of the relationship between the two communicators controls how they (especially the receiver) feel about the violation of expectations. If we "like" the person who is engaging in the violation (or if the person is a high-status other, has high credibility for you, gives you positive feedback, and/or is seen as very physically attractive to you), the violation may be seen positively. However, if we "dislike" the source (or if the person is a lower status other, has low credibility for you, and gives you negative feedback), we seem to prefer more "ordinary" nonverbal behaviors, which conform to social norms, and the violation may be seen negatively. That is, if a stranger continually "smiles" at you while you are seated in an adjacent booth at a restaurant, that nonverbal behavior may be perceived as either a positive or negative violation of expectancies depending upon whether your view that stranger as attractive, credible, or generally likeable, or not. According to Nonverbal Expectancy Violations Theory, this is called *communicator reward valence*, an element that influences our reactions to a violation. Clearly, in Western culture, excessive smiling at a stranger is usually not considered normative behavior. As such, if someone you do not know smiles excessively at you, then arousal has been stimulated and a nonverbal expectancy violation has occurred.

However, if you view this "stranger" as attractive and credible, you may "valence" that expectancy violation behavior (i.e., excessive smiling) as positive. *Valence* is the term used to describe the evaluation of the behavior. Certain behaviors are clearly negatively valenced, such as being subjected to a rude or insulting gesture (i.e., someone "flips you the bird" or rolls their eyes at you in a nonverbal message of condescension). Other behaviors are positively valenced (i.e., someone signals "V" for victory after a touchdown or "thumbs up" for your new sweater). Some behaviors are ambiguous. For example, imagine that you are at a party and a stranger to whom you are introduced unexpectedly touches your arm. Because you just met that person, that behavior could be confusing. You might interpret the behavior as affection, an invitation to become friends, or as a signal of dominance. Nonverbal Expectancy Violations Theory predicts that even an "extreme violation of an expectancy" might be viewed positively if it was committed by a highly rewarding communicator (Burgoon & Hale, 1988, p. 63).

In addition, our personal experiences also affect expectancies. Repeated interactions condition us to expect certain behaviors. If our usually cheerful roommate suddenly stops smiling when we enter the room, we encounter a distinctly different situation than we expected. Nonverbal Expectancy Violations Theory suggests that expectancies "include judgments of what behaviors are possible, feasible, appropriate, and typical for a particular setting, purpose, and set of participants" (Burgoon & Hale, 1988, p. 60).

Thus, the "nonverbal expectancy violations" theory suggests that it is not just a matter of the nonverbal behavior violations and the reactions to them. Instead, who is doing the violation matters greatly, and must be accounted for in order to determine whether the violation was seen as positive or negative.

The Case of Lauren's Interviews

Lauren was excited that, in the final month of her senior year at State University, she had three interviews set to take place in two weeks. If these interviews went well, it meant having a job before graduation and an easier transition into the workforce. Her parents would be so happy to know that all the time and money spent on school would already be working in her favor. Three interviews in two weeks meant a good deal of preparation and research, but Lauren was up to the task. She would be ready with answers to likely questions and focused on asking intuitive questions of her own that indicated her knowledge of each company. Lauren's major, Communication Studies, helped her become aware of the behaviors that would make a good first impression. Prepared, ready, excited, and even a little anxious, Lauren began the employment interview process.

Interview 1

Lauren arrived at Allied Marketing early, dressed tailored and professionally in her interview suit, and ready to go. The receptionist asked her to wait for a few minutes while Ms. Allison Hobbes, VP of Human Resources at Allied Marketing, was getting ready. After 20 minutes, Ms. Hobbes arrived in the reception area, nodded hello to Lauren, and motioned for her to follow. Lauren wasn't given an indication of whether she should call her Allison or Ms. Hobbes. It was difficult for Lauren to keep up, as Ms. Hobbes walked briskly through the building, seemingly uninterested in whether Lauren was still there. Lauren heard a cell phone vibrate, and Ms. Hobbes glanced at it. Then, without explanation, Ms. Hobbes stopped walking to send off a response before continuing down the hall. Ms. Hobbes opened a conference room door and motioned for Lauren to sit at one end, while Ms. Hobbes set herself up on the other. There was more than five feet of physical distance between them, and Ms. Hobbes had yet to even make any eye contact with Lauren.

Ms. Hobbes began the interview. Her questions must have been written in her notes, because she never really lifted her eyes off the page. She asked easy questions, ones that Lauren had anticipated. However, Lauren was unprepared for how emotionally distant and awkward this felt. Lauren tried to make a connection with Ms. Hobbes, animating her voice and seeking eye contact, but Ms. Hobbes's behavior was difficult to read. Lauren made an attempt at a harmless joke to lighten the mood, but was met by a dismissive interruption heading to the next question. Despite several well polished answers, Lauren was beginning to think that she was failing miserably at this interview. Ms. Hobbes was giving no indication that she liked, or was interested in, Lauren as a candidate for this position.

As the interview went on, Lauren became a bit withdrawn. It was uncomfortable to participate in this conversation. The dialogue they were speaking seemed reasonable, but the communication between them felt cold and uninviting. Ms. Hobbes stayed focused on her notes, breaking only to check her watch or phone. Lauren got the feeling that conducting employment interviews was not one of Ms. Hobbes favorite tasks, and that the process was taking up precious time away from being elsewhere. With little facial expression or other signs of positive feedback, Lauren concluded that this just wasn't going well.

Lauren left confused and worried. What had she done that had caused the interview to go so wrong? While the position at Allied was a good entry-level opportunity for Lauren, she was certain that there was no chance she would be offered the job, and even if she was, it didn't seem like the right place for her. Lauren was determined to approach her other two interview opportunities in a way that would not repeat today's experience. She really hoped that her other interviews would be different.

Interview 2

Despite Lauren's confidence taking a hit from the first interview, she had thrown herself into the preparation needed to get through the second one. Arriving at Banks & Bumble, Lauren was anxious, but ready. Upon checking in with the receptionist, Lauren was taken directly to the office of Ms. Brenda Jones, Director of Training & Development for Banks & Bumble, Inc. Ms. Jones stood up and came over to shake Lauren's hand and welcomed her to have a seat. Lauren sat down and the conversation began.

The interview was smooth, but challenging. Ms. Jones asked about Lauren's experiences at school and in her part-time jobs. Lauren was able to share some brief stories that showed her competence and interest in Banks & Bumble. Ms. Jones made regular eye-contact with Lauren and nodded her head, showing interest when Lauren spoke. Lauren learned a great deal about what Ms. Jones was looking for and the position seemed to be a good fit for her. Quickly, Lauren began to believe that this company and job would be a great place to start her career, and potentially offer her growth. While there were parts of the job that weren't ideal, like the fact that the company expected all salaried employees to work 45–60 hours each week and to travel to Detroit once a month for team meetings, Lauren was still excited to consider this opportunity and, even before she was done with the meeting, Lauren consciously hoped that she would hear from Banks & Bumble soon.

Ms. Jones completed the interview and offered Lauren a quick tour of their facility. Along the way, Ms. Jones kept a steady pace, walking side-by-side with Lauren, and pointing out departments and workspaces. As they passed employees in the hallways, Ms. Jones smiled and nodded or said hello. And when they got back to the reception area, Ms. Jones showed Lauren pictures of Mrs. Banks and Mr. Bumble, the company's owners, just as Mr. Bumble was coming through the door. Ms. Jones introduced Lauren and they exchanged a few pleasantries before Mr. Bumble had to run off to a meeting, and Lauren was able to thank Ms. Jones and say goodbye.

Interview 3

After two such different experiences, Lauren didn't know what to expect when she entered Del Labs at precisely 1:00 p.m. for her third interview. She certainly wasn't expecting Ms. Paula Cooks, Director of Human Resources for Del Labs, to be waiting at the front door for her. But there she was looking out the window and holding the door open to let Lauren in. The greeting was effusive and overwhelming, as Mrs. Cooks immediately introduced herself, shaking Lauren's hand and then patting her upper arm. Lauren felt more like a visiting family member than an interviewing job candidate. While it seemed a bit over the top, Lauren was encouraged by the obvious interest the interviewer was taking in her.

Ms. Cooks told Lauren to call her Paula, and asked Lauren if she would like something to drink. Lauren declined, and they walked past the receptionist's desk into a small work room. Paula sat next to Lauren, and turned her chair, which was just about 18 inches away, to look at Lauren while they spoke. Paula asked some expected questions and leaned in, nodding, while Lauren answered. Several times, Paula asked a question and leaned forward and pat Lauren on the arm or shoulder. The breaking of Lauren's personal space felt intrusive, and yet Lauren got the feeling that Paula liked her and was excited to have her join *Del Labs*. Unless, of course, Paula was this friendly with everyone. It was hard to tell. Paula spoke with confidence and knowledge, showing a great love for the company, the work she did, and interest for Lauren to join them.

As the conversation progressed, Lauren started to feel exhausted. Keeping up with Paula's intense energy was reassuring but somewhat overwhelming. Paula offered to show Lauren around the building and proceeded to give a tour that included stopping at several workers' desks to introduce Lauren. Each stop included some niceties and indicators of close worker relationships. Paula made a point to hug one coworker as they continued the tour and put her arm around another to emphasize his importance to the company.

Paula finally returned Lauren to the front door, saying goodbye and waving away Lauren's outstretched hand to shake and, instead, reached over and gave her a little hug. As Lauren stepped out into the parking lot, she tried to shake the feeling that this position might be exhausting; not because of the job itself, but due to working for Paula. While she seemed like a kind and competent boss, Paula would clearly be a very different supervisor than what she had experienced in the past.

Analysis: Elements of Nonverbal Expectancy Violations Theory in Lauren's Interviews

Lauren's experiences demonstrate three very different communication styles by the women that interviewed Lauren, and each have implications concerning Nonverbal Expectancy Violations Theory. Her first interviewer, Allison Hobbes, demonstrated nonverbal indicators of emotional distance. Allison kept a physical distance, failed to make eye contact, and didn't use active listening behaviors. Her second interviewer, Brenda Jones, seemed to demonstrate typical and expected nonverbal behavior during the interview process. Brenda used active listening techniques, used touch and gestures appropriately, and kept the relationship positive and professional. The third and final interviewer, Paula Cooks, demonstrated nonverbal behaviors indicative of someone who presumes a closer relationship than expected. As a result, she used touch and body orientations which deviated considerably from what we would expect to encounter on an initial employment interview. Both Allison's and Paula's behaviors are examples of nonverbal expectancy violations. While they did so in differing ways, and to differing results, they both used nonverbal behaviors that were surprising, given the situation, and violated the expectations that Lauren had for a professional interview. Below we will examine, in more specifics, some of the elements of the theory that are demonstrated through Lauren's interviews.

As Lauren was learning in her classes and experiencing in her work life, certain nonverbal (and verbal) behaviors came to be expected. Professional work circumstances are subject to norms, or expected behaviors, that come to be considered as "normal." When Lauren met with each of the interviewers, she may not have been acutely aware of all of the nonverbal expectancy violations that were taking place, but they did create "arousal" in her. That is, Allison's behavior was contributing to a distancing climate, while Paula's behavior was contributing to an overly close one.

Each time Allison or Paula used nonverbal behavior that violated an expectation, Lauren bristled a little and was surprised by the violations. Her reactions were perfect examples of emotional arousal discussed earlier in the chapter. If you go back to the descriptions of each interview, you can count numerous violations to Lauren's expectations that left her feeling that something was off or unexpected. As a result, these behaviors colored Lauren's entire experience at each interview.

It is important to consider the context of the instances of nonverbal expectancy violations, because each behavior, in and of itself, does not always constitute the same emotional arousal. In Lauren's interview with Allison, the fact that Lauren liked the company, and wanted to be liked, left Lauren particularly bothered by the distancing nonverbal behavior Allison was displaying. Lauren interpreted these behaviors as an indicator of dislike or that Lauren had done something wrong. The nonverbal expectancy violations in this case were disturbing and concerning to Lauren, and she placed a negative reward valence on the experience. By contrast, in Lauren's interview with Paula, there were some positive reward valences evident. While Lauren's emotional arousal told her it was unexpected and uncomfortable for Paula to demonstrate such closeness inappropriately, Lauren was also flattered by the possibility that this was an indicator of Paula's interest in her for the job. It wasn't until the context revealed that Paula's tendency to violate nonverbal expectancies with touching and physical closeness was something she did with everyone that Lauren realized the behavior was not as meaningful as her initial reactions led her to believe.

Discussion Questions

1. As you reflect back on Lauren's experiences, can you identify the nonverbal violations exhibited by either Allison or Paula? What about Brenda?

2. Was the interview with Brenda devoid of any nonverbal expectancy violations?

3. What is the threshold in an interview context for certain nonverbal expectancy violations before we are surprised into some emotional arousal?

4. Are we able to accept certain violations of our expectations because of our desire to fit into the situation or, in Lauren's case, to get the job?

5. How would these nonverbal violations have been different in a different context: (a) What if these were descriptions of first dates or meetings with someone you have known for a long time? (b) Does the gender of the interviewer and or interviewee change expectations; if so, how? (c) Does the context change our nonverbal expectations and therefore impact the way we perceive the violations?

REFERENCES

Burgoon, J. K. (1978). A communication model of personal space violations: Explications and an initial test. *Human Communication Research, 4,* 129–142.

Burgoon, J. K. (1983). Nonverbal violations of expectations. In J. M. Wiemann & R. P. Harrison (Eds.), *Nonverbal interaction* (pp. 77–111). Beverly Hills, CA: Sage.

Burgoon, J. K. (1985). Nonverbal signals. In M. L. Knapp & G. R. Miller (Eds.), *Handbook of interpersonal communication* (pp. 344–390). Beverly Hills, CA: Sage.

Burgoon, J. K., Coker, D. A., & Coker, R. A. (1986). Communicative effects of gaze behavior: A test of two contrasting explanations. *Human Communication Research, 12,* 495–524.

Burgoon, J. K., Guerrero, L. K., & Floyd, K. (2010). *Nonverbal communication.* Boston, MA: Allyn & Bacon.

Burgoon, J. K., & Hale, J. L. (1988). Nonverbal expectancy violations: Model elaboration and application to immediacy behaviors. *Communication Monographs, 55,* 58–79.

Burgoon, J. K., & Jones, S. B. (1976). Toward a theory of personal space expectations and their violations. *Human Communication Research, 2,* 131–146.

Floyd, K., Ramirez, A., Jr., & Burgoon, J. K. (1999). Expectancy violations theory. In L. K. Guerrero, J. A. DeVito, & M. L. Hecht (Eds.), *The Nonverbal Communication Reader* (2nd Ed., pp. 437–444). Prospect Heights, IL: Waveland Press

Chapter 16

A Few Good Laughs at a Funeral? Incongruity Theory of Humor Communication

Rachel L. DiCioccio, Ph.D., *University of Rhode Island*

Humor communication is omnipresent in our everyday lives. A universal communication tool, we demonstrate humor with our family and romantic partners, with our friends and coworkers, and sometimes even with those we have just met (DiCioccio, 2015). Humor is a complex mechanism that has the potential to engage, entertain, shock, and even horrify others all with the same message (DiCioccio, 2012). When used purposefully, humor communication can influence the direction and state of an interaction, and impact, in the long term, the quality of an interpersonal relationship and the satisfaction of the partners involved (Martin & Lefcourt, 1983). Understanding the intricacies of humor, and how it works to elicit a desired response, is valuable not only to those who study this communication phenomenon, but to all who strive to use humor appropriately.

What is humor communication and how do we characterize this multifaceted tool? Researchers have conceptualized multiple definitions of humor, all of which recognize humor "...as a communicative act that can serve single or multiple cognitive, emotional, and relational functions" (DiCioccio, 2013, p.53). Therefore, as a communicative act, humor can potentially contribute to the goal-fulfillment and maintenance of an interpersonal relationship. Several definitions are key in illuminating the enactment of humor communication. Martin (2007) extrapolates from a variety of definitions that humor is a "broad term that refers to anything people say or do that is perceived as funny and tends to make others laugh, as well as the mental processes that go into both creating and perceiving such an amusing stimulus and also the affective response involved in the enjoyment of it" (p. 5). Defining the prosocial and positive enactment of humor, Booth-Butterfield and Booth-Butterfield (1991) suggest that humor includes "intentional verbal and nonverbal messages and other forms of spontaneous behavior that elicit laughter, chuckling and taken to mean pleasure, delight and/or surprise, in the targeted receiver" (p. 206). Taking a more encompassing perspective that serves to integrate the communication, psychological, and sociological dimensions of humor, Lynch (2002) argues that, "...humor is a message sent by an individual or group with psychological motivation, but this humor message is also dependent upon the interpretation by another individual or group, which takes into account the social context and functional role of humor within that context" (p. 430). Finally, in their synthesis of humor theory, Rancer and Graham (2012) situate humor as a social phenomenon and underscore that the power and influence of humor reside in the necessary and negotiated interpretation that takes place between relational partners. Collectively, these definitions highlight the purposive nature of humor and the notion that humor communication requires mutual engagement between interactants. Appropriately delivered and interpreted, humor between partners is like a well-choreographed dance. Sources strive to create and elicit a particular response with their humor use, and receivers recognize and appreciate the humor delivered. When accomplished successfully, humor reflects a collaborative activity that has a direct impact on the climate and quality of an interaction (DiCioccio, 2013).

So how does one successfully produce, express, and interpret humor communication? Extant humor research has produced numerous theories, models, and explanations about the production and appreciation of humor. However, since the early conceptualization of humor, one widely recognized and employed theory of humor is Incongruity Theory (Koestler, 1964). Incongruity Theory uses a cognitive lens to explain how we create, interpret, understand, and appreciate a humorous message (Rancer & Graham, 2012). Incongruity Theory suggests that "...humor is the product of the juxtaposition of contrasting or dissimilar concepts...[and] when confronted unexpectedly with a message that is incongruent with our expectations, the contradiction can be seen as humorous" (DiCioccio, 2015, p. 37). Simply put, humor resides in what is unforeseen and surprising. It is the recognition and enjoyment of the unexpected, absurd, ironic, or ludicrous that defines one's humor appreciation.

Defining Incongruity Theory

The universal nature of humor transcends individual and cultural differences situating it as a central aspect of the human experience. In all its forms, Incongruity Theory has endured as the dominant theoretical explanation for the experience of humor communication. "It [incongruity] is widely considered to be one of the most important concepts, if not the most important, as to the description and explanation of the humor process" (Forabosco, 2008, p. 45). Since the time of Aristotle and, more definitively, the Renaissance, the notion of incongruity, and the element of the unexpected, have been recognized as a part of creating and relishing in the humor experience (Attardo, 2014). In his encyclopedia entry characterizing the philosophy of humor, Moreall (2014) notes that although not formally termed humor, both Aristotle and Cicero allude to what makes us laugh and the contemporary concept of incongruity. "Aristotle said that one way for a speaker to get a laugh from an audience is to create an expectation and then violate it...[and] Cicero said that in jokes we often expect one thing but something else is said" (p. 568). Theorists like Eysenck (1942) and Koestler (1964) introduced more concrete explanations for distinguishing humor from nonhumor that recognize humor as resulting from the violation of what we expect and hold to be true. This conceptualization evolved into the formal Theory of Incongruity introduced by Berlyne (1969; 1972) in the early 1970s.

Whereas other humor theories focus on the emotional and social aspects of humor, Incongruity Theories collectively serve to illuminate the cognitive process that defines the recognition and appreciation of humor. Taking a cognitive approach to understanding humor focuses on analyzing the structural components of humorous stimuli and the ways they are processed (Ruch, 2008). The incongruity perspective argues that one's critical thought process, which recognizes the juxtaposition of two concepts that are usually far removed from each other, is the key determinant in defining humor (Martin, 2007). Through identifying and appreciating the odd contrast created by the connection of two mismatched ideas, humor is discovered and we are amused. According to Martin (2007) "...[Incongruity] Theories suggest that the perception of incongruity is the crucial determinant of whether or not something is humorous: things that are funny are incongruous, surprising, peculiar, unusual, or different from what we normally expect." (p. 63). The concept of incongruity aligns with our understanding of experiencing the element of surprise. At the core, perceptions of incongruity and surprise both depend on a divergence from what is anticipated, and, together, they can conceptualize what constitutes humor communication. While surprise defines the emotional component of the humor exchange, incongruity articulates the cognitive aspect of the humor process (Attardo, 2014).

Shultz (1972) and Suls (1972; 1983) adjusted the original conception of incongruity to include a resolution component as part of the cognitive process. This problem-solving approach to humor comprehension views humor interpretation as a two-step process: perception plus resolution (Martin, 2007). Upon receiving the initial message or setup of the joke, the listener anticipates a particular ending to the story or punch line. When a counter-ending is presented, the listener is caught off guard and must work to make sense of the incongruity. If the contradiction can be resolved, humor and amusement ensue. If the contradiction cannot be resolved, however, the listener is left confused by the incongruity, rather than entertained (Martin, 2007; Rancer & Graham, 2012). For example, American comedian and television late-night host Stephen Colbert said, "So, if I am reading this graph correctly [pause], I'd be very surprised" (Galef, 2011). Colbert sets us up with the first phrase for his interpretation, then, instead of his interpretation of what the graph shows, follows with a surprising comment about his ability to interpret what a graph shows. We are then able to resolve the clash of our existing framework of logic, which is satisfying. As Galef (2011) notes, we have to find the "appropriate interpretive framework" (p. 1).

Debate continues, though, as to the necessity of the resolution aspect of humor interpretation. Research consistently underscores that incongruity is a necessary element to designate an exchange as humorous. Even though it is a required element of a humorous message, incongruity, by itself, does not always guarantee humor (Martin, 2007; Ruch, 2008). Some incongruities are just not funny. Although a distinct inconsistency is present, the result may be shock, horror, disappointment, or disgust (Ruch, 2008). For clashing ideas to be perceived as humorous, a key parameter is the contextual or relational lens through which they are viewed (Martin, 2007). Thus, if a relational quality such as a relational history between interactants is absent or the context deems the use of humor as inappropriate, no one responds with chuckles or laughter.

The family context is primed for the examination of humor. Our family is the central place where we learn how to create and appreciate humor. "Families provide our first, earliest, and ongoing engagement with humorous communication" (Ketrow, 2012, p. 158). For most of us, the family unit provides a safe space to engage in humor-learning through the necessary trial and error process, and teaches us how to successfully express and interpret humorous messages. Our family is the perfect setting for us to hone our humor creation, delivery, and interpretation skills for the entirety of our life span. The following case study uses the context of a family funeral to elucidate the complexity, subtlety, and nuanced aspects of incongruity humor.

A Funeral Is No Time to Laugh...Or Is It? A Case Study of the Use of Humor

The Wilsons are the epitome of an incredibly close family. This large, but tight-knit group, of grandparents, aunts, uncles, and cousins, has always placed a huge emphasis on the family unit and there is no question that they cherish their family time. When the children were little, Sunday dinner was the family norm. Every week, the entire group would convene at "Gram's and Papa's" house;

fifteen cousins ran around and played, while the adults ate, caught up, and told stories. This was always a valued family routine. The experience of being raised in this type of culture underscored the significance of maintaining strong interpersonal connections with family. This upbringing also accentuated cohesion as a key way to rally family support and stability. Humor has always been a mainstay at any Wilson gathering. Entertaining, and making each other laugh and sometimes gasp, was, and is, the centerpiece of these family interactions. In the Wilson family, children learn early that humor is not only important, but also essential, in dealing with any and all aspects of life.

Claire and Alice are the only two girls in the cousin clan and they are just one year apart in age. To say they have always been inseparable is an understatement. Since early childhood, Claire and Alice have had a mutual understanding of, and appreciation for, the world around them. They "get" each other and appreciate their shared family experience. Giggling and playing "school" as young children gave way to giggling and sharing secrets as teenagers. And now, as adults with families of their own, they are more like sisters than cousins. They confide in each other, give support, offer advice, and, of course, still giggle during their weekly conversations.

Unfortunately, this weekend, the Wilson family is gathering for a somber occasion: a funeral for their family member, Aunt Maria. As expected, family members have traveled from all over the country to be together. All the cousins, including Claire and Alice, are present to celebrate the life of their aunt. The following exchange takes place as the family mourns and prepares to bury Aunt Maria.

The funeral home is crowded. Many friends and coworkers have come to say good-bye and pay their respects to the Wilson family. Claire and Alice have spent the day greeting folks along with the rest of their family.

Alice: Hello, Mrs. Roth. Thank you so much for coming.

Mrs. Roth: Oh, Alice, Claire…I am so sorry for your loss. Your Aunt Maria was such a wonderful woman…smart, funny, the best cook ever, and one of my dearest friends. And, of course, she was ALWAYS impeccably dressed!

Claire: So true. She was the best…in every way. She loved you very much and you were no doubt her best friend. I loved that one story she would always tell about your cross-country fiasco when you were in college.

(All three women chuckle).

Mrs. Roth: Oh my gosh! That was a crazy trip! Your aunt got us so lost, driving in circles for hours. She had the worst sense of direction…but at least she looked good behind the wheel!

Alice: She always looked good! Our entire lives, she was always dressed to the nines and had her hair coiffed just right. Case in point (*Alice and Claire both make a silly ta-da gesture toward the coffin*)…she even looks good today…on this day!

(*The cousins smile at Mrs. Roth and all three quietly start giggling*).

Mrs. Roth: Yes, I know! I should be so lucky to have my hair ever look that good! Only Maria could pull off looking this good at her own funeral!

(*They all laugh and embrace one more time before Mrs. Roth moves on to talk to the next family member*).

15 minutes later

Claire: Are you staying overnight after the funeral tomorrow, or are you flying out right after?

Alice: We are going to stay one more night and head home in the morning.

Claire: Yeah us too. (*Claire nods her head.*) Ohhh Boyyy (*said slowly in a low deep voice*)…look who's here…Aunt Helen and those damn shoes have arrived! I wasn't sure "they" (*using air quotes*) would make yet another grand appearance!

Alice: Of course the shoes would make the trip…they are a well-traveled pair of kicks. Ugly as hell, but well-traveled!

Claire: I never doubted that Aunt Helen would wear the shoes. I just figured they'd be confiscated by airport security for being a threat to fashion! Weapons of mass offense!

Alice: (*Trying to laugh as quietly as possible, Alice struggles to get the sentence out*). Oh, my gosh, we are soooooo horrible!

Claire: So are those shoes! Aunt Maria would just die if she knew that her beloved sister Helen showed up wearing those heinous shoes!

(*Both women are trying hard to hold in their laughter but this inevitably results in a very noticeable display—torsos shaking, red cheeks, and tears streaming down their faces. Both cousins turn away from each other, avoiding eye contact, hoping to discourage any more outbreaks of laughter*).

Saturday morning—family and friends are seated in the church for Aunt Maria's funeral mass. The priest steps up to the pulpit to deliver the eulogy.

Father Mark: I am honored to eulogize Maria Wilson today. She was a committed parishioner and a very dear friend of mine. This church, filled with her family and friends, speaks volumes about the person she was. She was a loving and devoted sister and aunt and she was a loyal and close friend to so many. I have a ton of stories I want to share today about her work with at-risk youth and her volunteer work at the pediatric center to paint the picture of Maria's life. Of course, a more accurate portrait would also include all the tales of her crazy gambling escapades and her love of 30-year-old scotch! Ba-dum bump! (*Father Mark laughs as he gestures playing the drums. He is the only one who laughs while the rest of the church is silent*).

Father Mark: But I digress. So Maria started her volunteer work at the East Coast Hospital …

(*As the priest continues to speak, Alice and Claire give each other wide-eyed looks.*)

Claire: (*She leans into Alice and whispers*). So if I go before you, promise me you'll hire a funnier priest to deliver the stand-up at my funeral. It would kill me if this guy delivers my eulogy!

(*Alice quietly snickers while blotting her nose with a tissue to cover her smile and suggest she's sniffling, while Claire gives a wide-eyed goofy smile*).

Alice: Of course (*She whispers while tucking her chin in and raising her eyebrows*). I'll see if I can book Seinfeld or Chappelle to give yours.

Claire: (*Mouthing the words and winking*) Thank you.

Both cousins give huge smiles, snicker softly, and squeeze each other's hands before returning their attention to the rest of the funeral mass.

Taking a Closer Look at the Success and Failure of Incongruity Theory

The funeral of a family member serves as the unique backdrop to examine humor communication. Collectively, the interactions described demonstrate the use of humor to manage and cope during a time of significant grief and sadness. The exchanges depicted in this case study delineate four different prosocial interactions. Each example reflects the use of incongruity to deliver and interpret humor communication. Interpreting incongruity includes both the obvious that we recognize immediately, followed by an element that jars our sensibility and causes us to step back and reconsider what was said. Several qualities influence how the juxtaposition of incongruous elements is recognized as humorous. These conditions can range from general social norms that define appropriateness to those based on contextual circumstances or relational history. The following analysis identifies four examples of incongruous humor, explains the contextual and relational conditions that define whether and how incongruous interaction is perceived as humorous, and points to the factors that contribute to its success or failure.

The first exchange takes place among Alice, Claire, and Mrs. Roth. There is a high level of familiarity and ease among the cousins and family friends as they greet each other and exchange messages of comfort. Two levels of humor reside in this first example. First, Alice remarks that her aunt always looked good, even on the day of her own funeral. This most obvious example of incongruity is suggesting a person can "look good" when dead. These two notions—looking good and being dead—are contradictory. Generally accepted social norms dictate that, although an odd statement to make, this comment is appropriate for the situation. It is normative at most American funerals to comment about the physical appearance of the deceased. That is why making such an incongruous comment is widely accepted, appreciated, and can be entertaining. Because of this, it is possible that other mourners at the funeral could have overheard the statement and also be amused, without having any inside knowledge of the story or connection with Alice, Claire, and Mrs. Roth. The second layer of incongruity in this exchange is the notion that one would want to have the same circumstance as a dead person. When Mrs. Roth remarks that she wishes to be so lucky as to have her hair look as good as that of the deceased aunt, she implies just that. According to Martin (2007), although unexpectedness is an element of incongruity, research shows that sometimes a more predicted and anticipated ending can be funnier. The cousins (Alice and Claire) find Mrs. Roth's statement funny because they, essentially, anticipate the punch line that follows their setup about how well their aunt dressed and the care she took with her hair, especially "today, on this day." Because Alice and Claire know and appreciate the longtime friendship between Mrs. Roth and their aunt, they easily recognize the humor in Mrs. Roth's declared hair envy. Here, humor resides in the relationship among these three communicators and their relational knowledge about the deceased.

The second humorous exchange occurs between Alice and Claire and demonstrates the influence of relational history on the interpretation of incongruity. Upon realizing that another family member (Aunt Helen) has arrived at the wake, Claire comments that the "damn shoes…[made] yet another grand appearance!" The humor that follows between the two cousins centers on a sustained, inside joke, and reflects the cousins' shared appreciation of the story and its continuation. There are multiple examples of incongruity in this exchange that, together, serve to underscore the cousins' closeness, as well as help them manage their current emotional state around the death of their aunt. Incongruity is used in an obvious way by anthropomorphizing and inflating the importance of the ugly shoes. In her first comment, Claire recognizes the shoes as stand-alone entities, suggesting they are also attending the wake regardless of Aunt Helen. Claire continues to exaggerate the significance of the shoes by equating them to weapons of mass destruction. The implication is that although the shoes will not kill you like a real weapon, their offensiveness is just as deadly. Both of these statements recognize a well-established frame of reference for the cousins. Clearly, they have a long-running joke between them about Aunt Helen's ugly shoes and often return to this story as a way of maintaining their connection. According to Ketrow (2012), humor is a strategic tool that allows for both the maintenance and evolution of family relationships. It is comforting for the women to fall back on a joke they have been enjoying since their youth as a way of dealing with the current situation and moving forward. The interaction concludes with Claire suggesting that "Aunt Maria would just die" if she knew Aunt Helen wore the ugly shoes to her funeral. This statement, unlike the others we have discussed, is far more open to interpretation. The incongruity may be accepted in one of two ways. First, this statement could be seen as appalling and cringe-worthy. Second, it could be seen as funny. While others might be offended and view this comment as a flippant remark, Alice, because of her relational history with Claire, knows how to interpret the incongruity. In this case, the interpretation is the product of relational context (very close cousins), as well as the shared circumstance (coping with grief).

The third example of incongruity humor takes place at the funeral service when a Roman Catholic priest delivers the eulogy for Aunt Maria. The humor statement made by Father Mark illuminates how context and perceptions of appropriateness influence the interpretation of incongruity between source and receiver. Father Mark attempts to integrate humor into Aunt Maria's eulogy when he states "a more accurate portrait would also include all the tales of her crazy gambling escapades and her love of 30-year-old scotch!" Generally, a eulogy honors or lauds someone who has died. Thus, the speaker would offer positive descriptions or impressions, such as information about the deceased's contributions as a volunteer. Father Mark contrasts these ideal attributes with Aunt Maria's more scrupulous qualities. The construction of this statement clearly depicts incongruity and, therefore, from Father Mark's perspective, demonstrates the successful integration of humor in the eulogy. From the receiver's perspective, there are several contextual issues that influence the interpretation of the incongruent statement and the perception of humor. The first contextual issue is the appropriateness of including flaws and less attractive qualities to remember and celebrate a loved one. Although there is a clear contrast in Father Mark's statement that is unexpected and might catch the listener off guard, in this case, the listeners are mourning and suffering from a significant loss. Therefore, the situation places an additional, emotional lens for deciphering the incongruity. This explains why the church is silent after the priest makes the joke; their grief and somber mood supersede the humor that potentially resides in the comparison. Additionally, the incongruity presented by "who" is delivering the statement also determines it as nonhumorous for these receivers. While it might be conceivable that the statement would be seen as humorous if a family member had delivered it, the unexpected comment coming from a priest is incongruent, but also inappropriate. From the receivers' point of view, Father Mark violates the priestly behavior of always seeing the good in others and keeping a parishioner's secrets. The notion that only a family member can make light of a deceased loved one further explains the silence demonstrated by the church following the priest's remarks. The receivers' determination of nonhumor in this situation constitutes an example of the context level of incongruity trumping the content of the message. Fortunately for our priest, Carrell (2008) defends theorists who believe that incongruity exists regardless of any condition that has been stipulated in the chapter previously. In other words, the appropriateness of the comment does not influence if it represents a humorous statement. Furthermore, if humor fails, responsibility for the failure falls on the audience, rather than on the creator of the joke.

The final example of incongruity humor in this case study returns to a communication exchange between the two cousins, Alice and Claire. At the end of the case, Claire reacts to Father Mark's attempt at humor. Rather than making an outright derogatory comment about the priest, she instead mocks him, and his attempt at humor with her own incongruent demand: "hire a funnier priest to deliver the standup at my funeral." The humor in this statement resides in the fact that priests are not analogous to standup comedians and we certainly don't hire them, or anyone for that matter, to deliver one's eulogy. Claire concludes by saying, "it would kill me if this guy delivers my eulogy!" The suggestion here is that a eulogy delivered by Father Mark could make being dead even worse. The absurdity of this statement is obvious, but also appropriate, given the enormity of Father Mark's earlier failed attempt at humor. The silence that follows Father Mark's "Ba-dum bump" is so uncomfortable that it warrants being labeled "worse than death" and that is just what Claire's joke indicates. The mutual recognition and appreciation of this statement as humorous is derived not only from the cousins' relational history, but also the conditions of a relative's funeral and the uncomfortable topic of death and dying. This last humorous exchange reveals the integration of content, context, and relational history used to interpret incongruity humor.

The unique context of a family funeral provides a valuable situation to explore and critique the use and interpretation of incongruity humor. In this setting, the use of humorous communication takes on multiple functions: to cope, to relieve stress, to reminisce, to grieve, to connect, and to reconnect. The incongruities exemplified in the exchanges among Alice, Claire, and Mrs. Roth, and the speech from Father Mark, illustrate the importance of moving our scrutiny of humor beyond the simple joke into the complexities created by relationships and situations. Thus, the exploration of this case study highlights how and why incongruity humor can be used and how and why it is deemed a success or failure.

Discussion Questions

1. What allows Mrs. Roth to know that her odd "I should be so lucky..." comment will be interpreted as humorous by Claire and Alice?

2. In the shoe exchange between Claire and Alice, what nonverbal cues are employed by Claire? How do they help convey the humor of the exchange?

3. Why might Alice interpret Claire's "Aunt Maria would just die" statement as derogatory and inappropriate?

4. What contextual factors influence the interpretation of Father Mark's eulogy statement?

5. When the source and receiver's perceptions of a potentially humors statement don't align, who's interpretation determines how it is characterized?

REFERENCES

Attardo, S. (2014). Incongruity and resolution. In S. Attardo (Ed.). *Encyclopedia of Humor Studies Vol. 1.* (pp. 383–385). Los Angeles, CA: SAGE Publication.

Berlyne, D. E. (1969). Laughter, humor, and play. In G. Lindzey & E. Aronson (Eds.), *Handbook of social psychology* (2nd ed., Vol.3, pp. 795–852). Reading, MA: Addison-Wesley.

Berlyne, D. E. (1972). Humor and its kin. In J. H. Goldstein & P. E. McGhee (Eds.), *The psychology of humor: Theoretical perspectives and empirical issues* (pp. 43–60). New York: Academic Press.

Booth-Butterfield, S., & Booth-Butterfield, M. (1991). The communication of humor in everyday life. *Southern Communication Journal, 56,* 205–218.

Carrell, A. (2008). Historical views of humor. In V. Raskin (Ed.). *Primer for Humor Research.* (pp. 303–332). New York, NY: Mouton De Gruyter.

DiCioccio, R. L. (2012). Humor as aggressive communication. In R. L. DiCioccio (Ed.). *Humor communication: Theory, impact, and outcomes.* (pp. 93–108). Dubuque, IA: Kendall Hunt.

DiCioccio, R. L. (2013). Make me laugh, make me listen: Using humor to accomplish interpersonal influence. In C. J. Liberman (Ed.). *Casing persuasive communication.* (pp. 51–65). Dubuque, IA: Kendall Hunt.

DiCioccio, R. L. (2015). We could sure use a laugh: Building hope and resilience through humorous communication. In G. A. Beck, & T. J. Socha (Eds.). *Communicating hope and resilience across the lifespan.* (pp. 34–52). New York, NY: Peter Lang.

Eysenck, H. J. (1942). The appreciation of humor: An experimental and theoretical study. *British Journal of Psychology, 32,* 295–309.

Forabosco, G. (2008). Is the concept of incongruity still a useful construct for the advancement of humor research? *Lodz Papers in Pragmatics, 4.1, Special Issue on Humour,* 45–62.

Galef, J. (2011, February 14). "That's funny..." Incongruity in humor, art, and science. Retrieved from http://www.3quarksdaily.com/3quarksdaily/2011/02/paradigm-shifts-in-art-humor-and-science.html

Ketrow, S. M. (2012). Humor in families: A crucible of humor and communication. In R. L. DiCioccio (Ed.). *Humor communication: Theory, impact, and outcomes.* (pp. 157–174). Dubuque, IA: Kendall Hunt.

Koestler, A. (1964). *The act of creation.* London: Hutchinson.

Lynch, O. H. (2002). Humorous communication: Finding a place for humor in communication research. *Communication Theory, 12,* 423–445.

Martin, R. A. (2007). *The psychology of humor: An integrative approach.* Burlington, MA: Elsevier Academic Press.

Martin, R. A., & Lefcourt, H. M. (1983). Sense of humor as a moderator of the relation between stressors and moods. *Journal of Personality and Social Psychology, 45,* 1313–1324.

Morreall, J. (2014). Philosophy of humor. In S. Attardo (Ed.). *Encyclopedia of Humor Studies Vol. 2.* (pp. 566–570). Los Angeles, CA: SAGE Publication.

Rancer, A. S., & Graham, E. E. (2012). Theories of humor. In R. L. DiCioccio (Ed.). *Humor communication: Theory, impact, and outcomes.* (pp. 3–10). Dubuque, IA: Kendall Hunt.

Ruch, W. (2008). Psychology of humor. In V. Raskin (Ed.). *Primer for Humor Research.* (pp. 17–93). New York, NY: Mouton De Gruyter.

Shultz, T. R. (1972). The role of incongruity and resolution in children's appreciation of cartoon humor. *Journal of Experimental Child Psychology, 13*(3),456–477.

Suls, J. M. (1983). A two-stage model for the appreciation of jokes and cartoons: An information-processing analysis. In J. H. Goldstein & P. E. McGhee (Eds.), *The psychology of humor: Theoretical perspectives and empirical issues* (pp. 81–100). New York: Academic Press.

Suls, J. M. (1972). Cognitive process in humor appreciation. In P. E. McGhee & J. H. Goldstein (Eds.), *Handbook of humor research, Vol.1: Basic Issues* (pp. 39–57). Oxford: Pergamon Press.

Chapter 17

Truth Default Theory and Cases of Political and Academic Lie Detection

Timothy R. Levine, Ph.D., *University of Alabama, Birmingham*

Truth Default Theory (Levine 2014) is a bold and ambitious new theory that offers a communication perspective on deception and deception detection. TDT is bold and ambitious because it seeks to offer a new and improved understanding of deceptive communication that departs sharply from previous theories in its premises, focus, structure, and predictions. The perspectives offered by many of TDT's predecessors (e.g., Paul Ekman's thinking about leakage and Interpersonal Deception Theory) are rejected and TDT claims broader application, enhanced predictive power, and more logical and empirical coherence than other theories of deception. In short, TDT strives to set a new agenda for how deceptive communication is understood and researched. It offers a communication approach with its focus on humans as social beings existing in social groups and interacting with one another. With regard to lie detection, it focuses attention on what is said (message content), rather than nonverbal cues. TDT also specifies which aspects of interaction matter most in lie detection.

Why Theory? Why TDT?

To understand the need for TDT and its importance, three considerations are especially relevant. The first relates to the importance of the topic: deception. Second, we need to consider why having a good theory is important. What value does good theory add and what makes a good theory good? Third, once criteria for theoretical worth are established, we can then compare TDT to its rivals to assess if there is a need for a new theory in the first place and, if so, the extent to which TDT offers improvement. Each of these three considerations is discussed in turn.

At the outset, I must confess a somewhat cynical view of academic rationales for the importance of some topic of study or another. I have often joked that if you need to explain why something is important, maybe it isn't. Rationales for important topics are often statements of the obvious. Surely, readers will recognize the importance of important topics. More seriously, making a rationale implies that a rationale is needed. Lots of important discoveries and insights began with curiosity. I'm not sure that a reason beyond curiosity is even needed. I just do not accept that an anticipated, practical payoff is a prerequisite for scientific inquiry. Maybe importance is better assessed by historians looking back in time. Impact is best gaged with hindsight.

This said, the practical payoffs of research on deception and deception detection are many and obvious. Catching criminals, preventing terrorism, and not being scammed are but a few. But if you accept TDT, there is a much deeper rationale. TDT not only strives to improve lie detection in a variety of contexts and across human cultures. TDT also has something to say about human nature and the critical role of communication in human life. And beyond the substance of the theoretical stance, TDT further strives to demonstrate the power of good theory in social science. As was noted in the opening paragraph, TDT is bold and ambitious. TDT hopes to (a) be a role model for doing social scientific theory, (b) exemplify the power of good theory, and (c) place the academic discipline of communication at the cutting edge of social scientific theory construction.

An especially valuable social scientific theory needs to score well on at least five qualities. First and foremost, a theory needs empirical adequacy. The theoretical claims and predictions need to correspond with our knowledge of the world and the findings generated by research. Good theoretical arguments rest on premises that are true. And, when a good theory makes a new prediction, that prediction turns out to be correct. Further, predicted findings must replicate when tested again. In short, good social scientific theories are works of nonfiction and provably so (within the limits of social science). Theories need to provide an accurate reflection of reality. They need verisimilitude.

Second, theories need to be coherent. All the presumptions and claims of the theory need to be logically consistent with each other. No element of a theory can preclude another part of the same theory. Obviously, valid theories don't self-contradict. But equally important, theories need to be coherent in another way. They need to bring coherence to facts that otherwise lack coherence. Theories bring order to research findings. They offer a way to make sense of otherwise disjointed or inexplicable facts. Theories provide explanations both for why the facts are what they are and for how various facts fit together into a bigger picture.

When combined with empirical adequacy, this second type of coherence is a big part of the value theory provides.

Third, an often underappreciate feature of good theories is that they provide prioritization. They tell us what is important and what we should be looking at. In understanding any given phenomenon or topic, there are any number of variables that might be relevant. Rather than a random search and trial and error, theories point us in a direction. Theories tell us what is important and what isn't. Good theories direct us to the critical considerations and navigate us clear of dead-end research and piles of conceptual clutter.

Fourth, good theories trail blaze new discoveries. I have already established that theories have a coherent logic that set priorities. Following the implications of that logic (if it is sound) can lead to new ideas that no one ever thought to research and to new and previously untested predictions. It is difficult to have a new idea that turns out well. If you try to think of a new idea from scratch, chances are either (a) someone already thought of it and you are reinventing the wheel (so to speak) or (b) it really is new and the reason no one did that before is because it's a bad idea. But, theory gives us a disciplined way to arrive at new insights. Other people didn't think of the new idea before because they didn't have the theory to guide them and (to the extent that the logic and empirical adequacy of the theory are sound) the new ideas are likely to have merit because the theory that led to them had merit.

Finally, theories provide us with generality and a solution to the problem of induction. The problem is that standalone empirical findings are always finite. That is, findings reflect the particular time, place, sample, and method of the research that produced them. There is no methodological remedy. You can randomly sample from a population, but you can't randomly sample (with sufficient sample sizes) time, cultures, languages, and/or specific design features (like question wordings or experimental inductions). Empirical findings just can't achieve generality. This is the problem of induction. But, theory allows bounded generality. Theories provide claims that always hold within the specified boundary conditions where the theory applies. So, rather than trying to do the impossible task of making a valid generalization with finite data, we can do research designed not to make generalizations, but to test the theory-specified generalizations. We use our research findings to test theory, and we use our theory to make generalizations. Theories provide generality that we can't obtain otherwise.

Now that criteria for evaluating theory have been articulated, let me briefly mention TDT's notable predecessors: Ekman's ideas (Ekman, 2009; Ekman & Friesen, 1969), Four-Factor Theory (Zuckerman, DePaulo & Rosenthal, 1981),

Interpersonal Deception Theory (IDT, Buller & Burgoon, 1996), and the Cognitive Approach (Vrij, 2015). Although each of these various theories makes different predictions, they all share a common logic I call "Cue Theory."

The logic of a cue theory goes like this:

1. Lying and honest communication are psychologically different experiences.

2. The psychological differences between honesty and lies are signaled behaviorally by leakage, clues, and/or cues.

3. Deception can be detected, albeit indirectly and probabilistically, by the observation of the behaviors (leakage, clues, and cues) produced by the psychological states differentiating honesty and lies, given certain boundary conditions.

That is, certain psychological states—such as emotions, arousal, cognitive effort, and strategic efforts to appear honest—mediate and explain the link between lying/honesty and behaviors that signal lying. The psychological state(s) specified vary from cue theory to cue theory. For example, Ekman emphasizes emotions. Liars might feel fear of detection or guilt about lying and these deception-produced emotions might be revealed in microfacial expressions that leak these emotions and reveal the act of lying. Vrij's thinking, in contrast, posits that lying is more cognitively demanding than honesty and, therefore, liars might provide fewer details in their verbal statements. Different cue theories also specify different boundary conditions. For Ekman, lie stakes are crucial. The emotions linked with deception are only expected for lies of consequence. In Vrij's cognitive approach, the links between deception and cognitive effort need to be boosted by providing additional load by, for example, asking a person to explain events in reverse time order (Vrij et al., 2008). So, different cue theories posit different mediators and moderators. But they all share a common, logical structure and the common prediction that the key to deception detection is the observation of specific behaviors deriving from psychological states that differentiate honest and deceptive messages.

My main objection to the various cue theories is empirical adequacy. In my reading of previous research, the various cue theories have all been empirically falsified. Cue theories are what Ferguson and Heene (2012) label "undead theories." They can be shown to be false and should be dead, but they still dominate thinking and research, despite their empirical shortcomings. Meta-analysis clearly shows that the behavioral cues specified by various cue theories are, at best, weak and inconsistent (DePaulo et al., 2003). Worse still, for cue theories, there is a negative correlation between the amount of evidence and support (Bond, Levine & Hartwig, 2014). That is, the more research that investigates any given cue, the weaker the support. If that were not enough, meta-analysis also shows that the moderation and mediation specified by various cue theories does not align with research findings (Bond & DePaulo, 2006; Hartwig & Bond, 2014; Levine, Blair & Carpenter, 2018). Because of the theory-data mismatch, various cue theories lack empirical adequacy and fail to provide a coherent account of the facts. TDT strives to do better, and I believe there is much data consistent with my claim that TDT enjoys better empirical support than other deception theories (see Levine, 2014; 2015 for reviews).

TDT Summarized

TDT is both modular and propositional. TDT is comprised of 13 standalone modules that are integrated into a coherent framework with 14 propositions (see Levine, 2014, for a brief summary; a full explication will be provided in a forthcoming book). Here is a brief version.

The core idea is the "truth-default." The truth-default is a cognitive state characterized by passive belief of incoming communication. That is, the truth-default is a state of mind in message receivers. As the default, it is the starting place. We start out on the presumption that others' communication is honest and we do this unless we have reason to do otherwise. We just believe others. Skepticism, suspicion, and recognition of deception can happen, but these require prompting by some "trigger." Absent a sufficient potent trigger, the idea that a message might be deception just does not come to mind.

In TDT thinking, humans are social beings down to our core. Our survival, both as individuals and as a species, rests on coordination and cooperation with our fellow humans. This coordination and cooperation requires effective and efficient communication. Effective and efficient communication requires a truth-default, or something very much like it. If we typically doubted what others said, learning would be impaired and cooperation would be tenuous. The truth-default facilitates communication and, thus, provides us with a huge advantage. But it involves a tradeoff. We become vulnerable to deceit, at least in the short term (before we ostracize, shame, and/or discredit known liars). But what we gain from efficient communication vastly outweighs the negative consequences of occasionally getting duped. Further still, we have developed deception prevention systems, like socialization and religion, to discourage deception, and we have social networks to out liars and warn others upon the discovery of deceit.

According to TDT, deception is infrequent, relative to honesty, and it is not normally distributed. Most people are honest most of the time and most lies are told by a few prolific liars (Serota & Levine, 2015; Serota, Levine & Boster, 2010). Further, most deception is motivated and occurs in predicable situations

(Levine, Kim & Hamel, 2010). Because deception is infrequent relative to honesty and because deception occurs in particular situations, the truth-default leads us to correct beliefs most of the time. Passive belief works well most of the time. We presume others are honest. Others really are honest. So, all is good.

The truth-default can be overridden. Trigger events can lead people to abandon the truth-default and scrutinize communication for potential deception. According to the theory, trigger events include (a) a projected motive for deception, (b) behavioral displays associated with dishonest demeanor, (c) a lack of coherence in message content, (d) a lack of correspondence between communication content and some knowledge of reality, and/or (e) information from a third-party warning of potential deception.

Once a trigger is sufficiently potent to overcome the truth-default, people try to actively ascertain if the communication in question is honest or deceptive. According to the theory, reliance on cues or demeanor (constellations of behavioral cues) leads to inaccurate truth-lie discrimination that is only a bit better than mere chance. More accurate lie detection, however, is possible through (a) evidence-based fact-checking, (b) consideration of plausibility of contextualized communication content, (c) examination of potential motives for deception, (d) certain active approaches to questioning, and (e) persuading people to honestly confess their lies and admit the truth (see Levine, 2015 for a review of the evidence).

The Backstory

The story of how TDT became a theory started with my good friend and coauthor Steve McCornack. A young Steve got suckered, bigtime, by an unscrupulous and devious girlfriend. Inspired (or traumatized?) by the experience, Steve did his undergraduate thesis on deception detection in romantic couples (McCornack & Parks, 1986). His big findings were that the closer the relationship, the more confident people were in their judgments of their partner, and this led to truth-bias, which blinded lovers to their partners' lies. I got to know Steve when he became a new professor in the program where I was doing my Ph.D. I heard his job talk and thought his work was really cool. I became his research assistant for the last two years of my graduate work. The first experiment we did together (McCornack & Levine, 1990) tested if we could overcome a couple's truth-bias by prompting suspicion. The short answer turned out to be "no." While nonsuspicion-primed participants believed their partners 80% of the time, those in the high suspicion condition were still truth-biased, believing their partner two-thirds of the time. Suspicion significantly reduced truth-bias, but it did not eliminate it or create a lie-bias. The take home message for me was that truth-bias was really powerful. I became curious about why. What was up with truth-bias?

My thinking, way back then, was heavily influenced by the work of Kahneman and Tversky on judgmental heuristics (e.g., Kahneman, Slovic & Tversky, 1982). It wasn't until much later, when I read Gigerenzer (2000), that this would change, and TDT would take shape. The take-home message of the Kehneman-Tversky work is that humans are biased decision-makers who rely on quick decision rules that lead to predictable errors. This seemed to fit truth-bias findings so well. Truth-bias was called a "bias" after all. Surely it reflected some sort of flawed thinking.

The first break in that line of thinking came as a result of a confrontation with a graduate student (Hee Sun Park, who is now a Professor and an ICA fellow) when I was a young professor. She made an argument that we came to call the "veracity effect" (Levine, Park & McCornack, 1999). She said, at least given the way researchers had designed deception detection experiments, truth-bias could not lower accuracy as we had previously thought. Researchers, she noted, set up their experiments so that there were always an equal number of truths and lies. Truth-bias, she argued, made people worse at detecting lies, per se, but it also made people more likely to get truths right. Given the 50-50 ratio of truths and lies in previous experiments, she argued, the improvements in the accuracy for truths and declines in correct judgments for lies would cancel out. Truth-bias would only reduce accuracy (scored across truths and lies) when lies were more pervasive than truths.

This raised the question of lie prevalence outside the lab. If honesty was the norm, then truth-bias was not a bias at all, but actually a tendency that made good sense. This idea fit with Gigerenzer's more general critique of Kahneman and Tversky: that when heuristics are understood in the context in which they are used, they make us better, not worse, decision-makers.

Another critical piece of the puzzle was provided by Hee Sun Park a few years later. She thought that cue theories were a thing of the lab, not how people really detect lies. She came up with a very simple study. We could just ask people to think of a time when they detected a lie and ask them how they did it. When we did this, we found that most lies were detected after-the-fact, based on either some type of evidence or the liar just confessing the truth (Park et al., 2002). Few lies were detected in real time based on behavioral cues. Thus, when the meta-analytic findings challenging cue theory came out (e.g., DePaulo et al., 2003; Hartwig and Bond, 2011; 2014), I was already skeptical of cue theory logic.

The early truth-bias findings, the nuance added by the veracity effect, and findings regarding how people really detect lies collectively provided the main initial building blocks for TDT. These became modules in what would eventually become TDT. Then, a series of meta-analyses came out about cues and deception detection accuracy (Bond & DePaulo, 2006, 2008, DePaulo et al., 2003) that provided some hard facts that seemed to hold up nicely across studies. I began trying to think of what a framework might look like that could/would account for all of the findings. When I got an idea, I designed an experiment to test it. When the idea worked out, I tested it again to make sure it held up. My thinking was that I needed to be a sure as I could of the facts so that I was building on a solid empirical foundation. Gradually, I came to see that the various findings fit together in a way that made sense. I read more. I did more and more research. And, TDT gradually took shape.

TDT has been a 30-year project. It began with a job talk by a new professor that got me thinking. It got pushed along by some insightful students and coauthors (people like Hee Sun Park, Pete Blair, Kim Serota, Rachel Kim, and David Clare) and lots and lots of findings. Initially, each new finding led to more (and new) questions, rather than satisfying answers. But I kept following up. After a while, a picture starting taking shape. I started anticipating findings better, and I worked to formalize the predictions. Once the basic logic was created, that logic led to new predictions to test. Once I got the modules mostly nailed down, I started writing about the bigger picture. When the book-length version of TDT is published, the theory will be fully explicated to my satisfaction and the data will be integrated and sufficiently summarized. While there will surely be many lose ends and adjustments, I (at least for now) think that the hard part is done and the theory is ready for the academic public.

I hope TDT both catches on and is (mostly) well received. I'm happy with citations the 2014 article version is generating. Surely there will be criticism. Other scholars may seek to modify TDT and bend it to their needs and vision. I really hope some graduate students find it useful and maybe even inspiring. I'm quite curious to see it all play out. Generally, I'm cautiously optimistic about TDT's future. But even if no one ever reads this chapter, TDT is totally ignored, or some huge flaw is uncovered, I'm pretty good with it all. I've had a blast creating TDT. I like what I came up with and I feel a deep sense of accomplishment. TDT showcases who I am as a communication scientist. It satisfies my sense of craft. I see TDT as bold and ambitious, perhaps even audacious. But in science, data is the arbiter and time will tell if TDT holds appeal and has verisimilitude.

Practical Implications for Communication

TDT holds many practical implications for human communication. First and foremost, trust is usually a good thing. According to TDT, truth-bias isn't really a bias in any pejorative sense. We need to believe other people for communication to function. Further, because deception is both infrequent and predictable, the truth default works quite well most of time. Chronic suspicion and skepticism work against efficient and effective communication. Suspicion is even bad for our health (Cacioppo & Patrick, 2009).

Not only is trust good, but sowing distrust is socially destructive and dangerous. If we need trust in others' communication for social coordination, then eroding that trust harms social functioning. From the perspective of TDT, the rise of fake news, alternative facts, and the like increase the frequency and potency of triggers, make the truth-default less functional, and facilitate confrontation, rather than cooperation. This, I think, is not good.

TDT offers a much better approach to lie detection. Consider first, does the person have a reason to lie? If not, it is a good bet they are honest. Next, listen to what people say and try to understand what is said in context. If possible, fact-check. Things that check out are probably true, while statements that contradict known facts should be suspect. If you can't fact check, consider plausibility. You can also ask questions to obtain answers that can be fact-checked or at least that give you a better feel for plausibility. Finally, sometimes liars can be persuaded to come clean and tell the truth. Research has shown that these suggestions improve lie detection (Levine, 2015). In summary, trust people until you have a good reason not to. Then follow TDT's advice for improved lie detection.

Some Cases

The 2016 US Presidential election and its aftermath provide challenging cases for understanding deception and the public's understanding on honesty. According to politifact.com fact checking, 50% of Clinton's statements were scored as true or mostly true while only 12% were rated as false or "pants on fire." Alternatively, 17% of Trump's statements were scored as true or mostly true compared to 47% that were rated as false or "pants on fire." Yet, many Americans viewed Trump as the more trustworthy of the two. How could this be? The answer I think has much to do with what I call demeanor. Deception motives also come into play. Clinton came off as a careful politician. She was often "stiff" and seemed to choose her words carefully, especially in contrast to Trump. Clinton's demeanor (constellations of intercorrelated cues) was closer to the folk wisdom (but not reality) regarding how dishonest people act. Trump, in contrast, said many outlandish things. On the surface, saying politically incorrect things did not seem to be in his own interests as a politician. It was unpoliticianlike. This, I think made him seem more authentic and honest to many people. He did not appear to have a motive for deception (at least from the standpoint of conventional political objectives).

Since the election, *The Washington Post* has been fact checking Trump's statements (Kessler, Rizzo & Kelly, 2018). During the first 100 days, President Trump averaged 4.9 false claims per day. By August 1, 2018, the average had increased to 7.6 false claims per day. On September 13, 2018, his average was up to 8.3 lies per day. On September 7, 2018, President Trump made 125 false or misleading statements in a mere two hour period. Yet some segment of citizens still seem to believe him.

From the perspective of TDT, fact checking is the best way not to get deceived. If you know the truth (or at least have some strong factual evidence), you can assess statements as to how well they align with the evidence. Being false, however, does not mean that a statement is a lie. False statements might stem from misinformed or delusional sources who genuinely believe the false things they say. But deceptive intent aside, an informed audience is less likely to get fooled. This is even more the case for a well informed audience with strong critical thinking skills. In TDT, evidence and critical thinking matter, not the ability to decode non-verbal cues and read demeanor.

The next case takes us from the political to the academic. In 2016, a psychologist named Aldert Vrij published an essay on baselining as a method of lie detection (see Vrij, 2016). Baselining is a strategy where a would-be lie detector observes cues and demeanor during honest (baseline) communication and compares those to cues and demeanor to communication where deception is suspected. This might make sense according to some cue theories. We can see if there are behavioral changes or not between, for example, answers to innocuous baseline question and questions about a crime where the person is a suspect or witness.

In reading the Vrij (2016) article, a particular passage caught my eye. Here is the quote: "Although the baseline lie detection method is frequently advocated in interrogation techniques and frequently used [citation provided], it has received virtually no attention from researchers. I could find one published study [self citation to a 2014 article]" (p. 1113). Before continuing, let me ask you, what is the take-away message from that passage?

Now, here is some more information. There was a program of research in the 1980s by Miller and his students looking at the baselining strategy (e.g., Brandt, Miller, & Hocking, 1980; 1982). By 2006, ten years before the Vrij claim, baselining research was summarized in a well-known and often cited meta-analysis

(Bond & DePaulo, 2006). That meta-analysis summarized results of 31 studies (prior to 2006) involving prior exposure to baseline information and 21 studies testing baseline exposure head-to-head against no prior exposure controls. Thus, I knew the claims of "virtually no attention from researchers" and one "one published study" were objectively false. When there are more than 20 prior studies that are summarized in meta-analysis, clearly there has been substantial prior interest and many published articles.

However, a claim being false does not make it deceptive or a lie. Let's consider first, would a reader who didn't know the literature be misled? The answer must be yes. A reasonable user of the English language would conclude that there was little prior research on the topic, and that Vrij was the originator of that research (i.e., he was a coauthor of the one previously published study). Next, how about motivation? Does Vrij gain something by hiding the truth? Here I think the answer is yes, too. He might be credited with the original research. Finally, we should ask, did he know about the prior research or might there be an honest mistake. One thing we could do is use citation software to see who has cited the original Brandt et al. works. As it turns out, Vrij has cited those older studies in the past. So, at least he knew in the past that they existed. Further, the only way he could not know was if he was unaware of the content of work he claims to have authored. The claims of virtually no attention and just one prior study appear to be outright lies. They are objectively false, they are misleading if accepted at face value, they are self-serving, and there is evidence that the maker of the false claims almost certainly had to know the claims to be false.

What these cases have in common is that that they highlight the role of evidence, fact-checking, and communication content in deception detection. Cues and demeanor can impact who is believed, but not if they should be believed.

Summary and Conclusion

TDT is a different kind of communication theory and a different kind of theory of deception. TDT differs from most other communication theories in at least two ways: modularity and its abductive roots. Some communication theories are model-based and can be diagramed with a flow chart or a series of causal pathways. Other theories have a formal propositional structure with assumptions and deductive derivations. Still other communication theories are more abstract and provide frameworks or viewpoints, rather than specifying falsifiable predictions. To my knowledge, TDT's modular constructions is quite unusual among communication theories.

It seems to me that TDT's modular structure provides at least two big advantages over nonmodular theories. First, I think it greatly expands applicability and usability. Scholars can use only the module(s) that fits their particular interests or focus. Researchers interested in deception motives can use the deception motive module, while those interested in deception detection through interrogation can use the diagnostic utility and/or expertise modules. Second, if it turns out that there is a flaw in one module or another, that module can be adjusted, or even abandoned, without necessarily bringing the other modules down.

A second aspect of TDT that sets it apart from many other communication theories is that it was derived through abductive reasoning (see Haig, 2005 or Rozeboom, 1997 for descriptions of abductive theory building). Rather than starting with assumptions or speculation, TDT started with findings. It grew from efforts to provide a coherent explanation from otherwise disorganized, but empirically solid, facts. It underwent an iterative process of refinement based on initial data and repeated conceptual replication. This process of development, I believe, gives TDT an advantage in terms of empirical adequacy and coherence. These are what TDT was optimized for in development. Therefore, when push comes to shove in hard empirical comparisons with alternative theoretical predictions, TDT is a good bet to come out on top.

TDT is also quite different from other deception theories in numerous ways. TDT sees truth-bias as an advantage and an evolutionary adaptation, rather than a bias and a product of flawed reasoning. TDT sees deception as infrequent, rather than as ubiquitous. TDT downplays the role of nonverbal or linguistic cues. Attention to cues and demeanor impairs accuracy in TDT. Sender variability matters more in TDT than receiver variability. Detection rests on contextualized content, rather than cues. TDT turns attentions to issues like deception motives and truth-lie base-rates, rather than lie stakes, medium of communication, mere extent of interactivity, or cognitive load. In short, TDT is both structurally and substantively different from other deception theories.

In the world described by TDT, most people are mostly honest most of the time, and people most often believe other people most of the time. In fact, the idea that communication might be deceptive usually does not come to mind. When it does come to mind, something triggered it. While people certainly do lie and deceive others from time to time, they do so for predictable reasons. Parents everywhere teach their children that is wrong to lie, and every major human culture and religion discourages deception. This is hugely important because humans need to learn things from other humans. Humans need to cooperate with others. Humans need to build relationships with others. All this requires that communication is honest and can be trusted. The truth-default that is functional is required for efficient and effective communication among individuals and the creation of functioning societies.

TDT rejects the logic of cue theories of deception detection. There is no mechanism or process specified in TDT that suggests a reliable link between deception and any specific nonverbal or linguistic behavior across individuals. To the contrary, TDT predicts that the use of cues pushes accuracy down toward chance levels. Instead, TDT specifies fact-checking content, the use of evidence, content understood in context, context-specific questioning strategies, consideration of motive, and persuading honest admissions as the paths to improved lie detection. Indeed, TDT-guided research has recently produced and replicated some of the most impressive levels ever reported in deception detection research (e.g., Levine et al., 2014).

In conclusion, TDT offers a new and different take on deception in human communication. It seeks not only to change how deception is understood, but also to expand our understanding of how to approach theory in the field of human communication.

Discussion Questions

1. Do you think everyone has a truth-default?
2. What are the strengths of Truth-Default Theory?
3. Of the qualities that are important in evaluating a theory, which of them is the most important?
4. What makes TDT a theory?
5. TDT rejects cue theory logic. Do you agree?
6. What is the main premise of TDT?
7. What are some other triggers beside those mentioned in TDT?
8. What do you think are the best ways to detect deception?
9. Discuss why many voters trusted Trump over Clinton. Why isn't fact checking enough?
10. Pick a claim that is currently in the news. How would we know if it was a lie?

REFERENCES

Bond, C. F., Jr., & DePaulo, B. M. (2006). Accuracy of deception judgments. *Personality and Social Psychology Review, 10*, 214–234.

Bond, C. F., Jr., & DePaulo, B. M. (2008). Individual differences in judging deception: Accuracy and bias. *Psychological Bulletin, 134*, 477–492.

Bond, C.F., Jr., Levine, T.R., & Hartwig, M. (2014). New findings in nonverbal lie detection. In P.A. Granhag, A. Vrij, & B. Vershuere (Eds.), *Deception detection: Current challenges and new directions* (pp. 37–58). Chichester: Wiley.

Brandt, D. R., Miller, G. R., & Hocking, J. E. (1982). Familiarity and lie detection: A replication and extension. *Western Journal of Speech Communication, 46*, 276–290.

Brandt, D. R., Miller, G. R., & Hocking, J. E. (1980). The truth-deception attribution: Effects of familiarity on the ability of observers to detect deception. *Human Communication Research, 6*, 99–110.

Buller, D. B., & Burgoon, J. K. (1996). Interpersonal deception theory. *Communication Theory, 6*, 203–242.

Cacioppo, J. T., & Patrick, W. (2009). *Loneliness: Human Nature and the Need for Social Connection.* New York: W. W. Norton.

Chan, M. (Nov., 2, 2016). Donald Trump more trustworthy than Hillary Clinton, poll finds. *Time.* http://time.com/4554576/donald-trump-trustworthy-hillary-clinton/.

DePaulo, B. M., Lindsay, J. J., Malone, B. E., Muhlenbruck, L., Charlton, K., & Cooper, H. (2003). Cues to Deception. *Psychological Bulletin, 129*, 74–118.

Ekman, P. (2009). *Telling lies.* New York: W. W. Norton.

Ekman, P., & Friesen, W. V. (1969). Nonverbal leakage and clues to deception. *Psychiatry, 32*, 88–106.

Haig, B. D. (2005). An abductive theory of scientific method. *Psychological Methods, 10*, 371–388, https://www.politifact.com/personalities/donald-trump/ https://www.politifact.com/personalities/hillary-clinton/

Ferguson, C. J., & Heene, M. (2012). A vast graveyard of undead theories: Publication bias and psychological science's aversion to the null. *Perspectives in Psychological Science, 7,* 555–561.

Hartwig, M., & Bond, C. F., Jr. (2011). Why do lie-catchers fail? A lens model meta-analysis of human lie judgments. *Psychological Bulletin, 137,* 643–659.

Hartwig, M., & Bond, C. F., Jr. (2014). Lie detection from multiple cues: meta-analysis. *Applied Cognitive Psychology, 28,* 661–676.

Kessler, G., Rizzo, S., and Kelly, M. (Aug. 1, 2018). President Trump has made 4,229 false or misleading claims in 558 days. *The Washington Post.* https://www.washingtonpost.com/news/fact-checker/wp/2018/08/01/president-trump-has-made-4229-false-or-misleading-claims-in-558-days/?utm_term=.c8275f8b6e5f

Kessler, G., Rizzo, S., & Kelly, M. (Sept. 13, 2018). President Trump has made more than 5,000 false or misleading claims. *The Washington Post.* https://www.washingtonpost.com/politics/2018/09/13/president-trump-has-made-more-than-false-or-misleading-claims/?utm_term=.a929915d9739&wpisrc=nl_fact&wpmm=1

Levine, T. R. (2014). Truth-default Theory (TDT): A Theory of Human Deception and Deception Detection. *Journal of Language and Social Psychology, 33,* 378–392.

Levine, T. R. (2015). New and Improved Accuracy Findings in Deception Detection Research. *Current Opinion in Psychology, 6,* 1–5.

Levine, T. R., Blair, J. P., Carpenter, C. J. (2017). A critical look at meta-analytic evidence for the cognitive approach to lie detection: A re-examination of Vrij, Fisher, and Blank (2018). *Legal and Criminological Psychology, 23,* 7–19.

Levine, T. R., Clare, D., Blair, J. P., McCornack, S. A., Morrison, K., & Park, H. S. (2014). Expertise in deception detection involves actively prompting diagnostic information rather than passive behavioral observation. *Human Communication Research, 40,* 442–462.

Levine, T. R., Kim, R. K., & Hamel, L. M. (2010). People lie for a reason: An experimental test of the principle of veracity. *Communication Research Reports, 27,* 271–285.

Levine, T. R., Park, H. S., & McCornack, S. A. (1999). Accuracy in detecting truths and lies: Documenting the "veracity effect." *Communication Monographs, 66,* 125–144.

McCornack, S. A., & Levine, T. R. (1990). When lovers become leery: The relationship between suspicion and accuracy in detecting deception. *Communication Monographs, 57,* 219–230.

McCornack, S. A., & Parks, M. R. (1986). Deception detection and relationship development: The other side of trust. In M.L. McLaughlin (Ed.) *Communication Yearbook 9.* Beverly Hills, CA: Sage.

Park, H. S., Levine, T. R., McCornack, S. A., Morrison, K., & Ferrara, M. (2002). How people really detect lies. *Communication Monographs, 69,* 144–157.

Rozeboom, W. (1997). Good science is abductive, not hypothetico-deductive. In L. L. Harlow, S. A. Mulak, & J. H. Steiger (Eds.) *What if There Were No Significance Tests?* (pp. 302–352). New York: Psychology Press.

Serota, K. B., & Levine, T. R. (2015). A few prolific liars: Variation in the prevalence of lying. *Journal of Language and Social Psychology, 34,* 138–157.

Serota, K. B., Levine, T. R., and Boster, F. J. (2010). The prevalence of lying in America: Three studies of reported deception. *Human Communication Research, 36,* 1–24.

Vrij, A. (2015). A cognitive approach to lie detection. In P. A. Granhag, A. Vrij & B. Verschuere (Eds.), *Deception Detection: Current Challenges and New Approaches* (pp. 205–229). Chichester, UK: Wiley.

Vrij, A. (2016). Baselining as a lie detection method. *Applied Cognitive Psychology, 30,* 1112–1119.

Vrij, A., Mann, S., Fisher, R. P., Leal, S., Milne, R., & Bull, R. (2008). Increasing cognitive load to facilitate lie detection: The benefit of recalling an event in reverse order. *Law and Human Behavior, 32,* 253–265.

Zuckerman, M., DePaulo, B. M., & Rosenthal, R. (1981). Verbal and nonverbal communication of deception. In L. Berkowitz (Ed.), *Advances in experimental social psychology* (Vol. 14, pp. 1–59). New York: Academic Press.

Chapter 18

Validating Women and Their Miscarriage Experiences: An Application of Confirmation Theory

Maria Brann, Ph.D., MPH, *Indiana University-Purdue University Indianapolis*

Individuals have a basic human need to be confirmed or validated (Buber, 1957; Laing, 1961; Sieburg, 1985). This need is met through verbal and nonverbal communicative acts (Dailey, 2008; Ellis, 2000; Sieburg, 1985). Ellis (2000) defines confirmation as a transactional process individuals use to communicate with others that lets them feel endorsed, recognized, and acknowledged as valuable, significant individuals. Confirmation "encourages communication so that individuals can explore, develop, and process their thoughts and feelings" (Dailey, 2006, p. 437), which has been shown to have numerous constructive outcomes. For example, confirmation has been positively associated with an individual's well-being (Reis, Sheldon, Gable, Roscoe, & Ryan, 2000) and relational satisfaction (Gottman, 1994).

Specifically, confirming messages allow recipients to feel acknowledged and can cultivate an individual's feelings of value and connection to others (Dailey, 2010; Sieburg, 1985). Individuals' personal development is fostered through confirming messages that validate an individual's sense of self (Dailey, 2010). Confirmation, then, is similar to person-centered messages that substantiate and legitimize individuals' unique experiences. This is particularly beneficial for supportive communication that can utilize confirmation to facilitate sensemaking by allowing individuals to elaborate, process, and understand their experiences (Burleson & Goldsmith, 1998).

Not surprisingly, Confirmation Theory originated in the interpersonal communication context (Laing, 1961; Watzlawick, Beavin, & Jackson, 1967), demonstrating the significance of confirmation in relationships with romantic partners (e.g., Cissna & Keating, 1979; Dailey, Romo, & Thompson, 2011) and families (e.g., Dailey,

2006; Ellis, 2002). It has been extended to other relational contexts as well to show value in academics (e.g., Ellis, 2000; Goodboy & Myers, 2008), sports (e.g., Cranmer & Brann, 2015; Cranmer, Brann, & Weber, 2017), and health (e.g., Dailey, McCracken, & Romo, 2011; Dailey, Romo, & McCracken, 2010). Nearly all relational contexts can benefit from confirming communication. Therefore, understanding and utilizing Confirmation Theory may lead to more satisfying relationships and better outcomes (e.g., mental health).

Confirmation Theory

Because individuals have a fundamental need to be validated to personally develop, Confirmation Theory suggests that confirmation is essential for individuals to recognize their true identity (Buber, 1965; Laing, 1961). The focus is on the relational quality of the communication, not necessarily the specific content of the messages (Sieburg, 1976; Watzlawick et al., 1967). When individuals use confirming messages, they demonstrate that they value the person, what s/he says, and the interaction or relationship. Confirmation typically involves positive interactions that lead to feelings of acceptance and helps create and maintain a positive relational environment. Confirming communication fosters active engagement and leads to a greater understanding not only of oneself, but also of the relationship between the individuals (Schrodt & Ledbetter, 2012). Conversely, disconfirmation illustrates negative regard for another person and can involve disparaging or indifferent comments, which leads to feelings of nonacceptance (Dailey et al., 2010; Sieburg, 1985). This allows individuals to assess how they are regarded by others and to assess the emotional tone of the relationship.

Understanding the relationship is key, as this may help individuals make sense of their own identities and experiences. For example, when assessing confirming messages, it is important to note what all is being confirmed. Beyond the individual and the relationship, Watzlawick et al. (1967) argue that individuals confirm or disconfirm themselves with their responses. They note that individuals reveal intrinsic aspects of themselves (i.e., self-definitions) when they communicate. Therefore, when assessing oneself and the message being communicated in the interaction, it is important to note that the confirming, or disconfirming, messages being communicated may be a more accurate reflection about the person communicating. For example, a seemingly supportive statement of "you'll be fine" when someone confides about how s/he is feeling actually negates the person's feelings by not allowing the person to connect with the other person and share those feelings. This may lead to the individual questioning her/his ability to assess her/his feelings and experiences (Dailey, 2006).

Although confirmation's goal is positive affect for an individual who receives this type of communication, confirming messages can differ in many ways. For example, confirming messages can vary in intensity, quantity, and quality, or by their function (Laing, 1961). Sieburg (1985) suggested that confirming messages include three types of responses: recognizing, acknowledging, and endorsing. Recognizing another person's existence is the most fundamental act of confirmation, which includes verbal and nonverbal engagement with the person. Acknowledgment communicates interest in another person by listening and directly responding to another person's thoughts and feelings. Endorsement communicates acceptance of another person's self-experience and is the strongest type of confirmation. This can include agreement, praise, or even nonverbal confirming responses such as eye contact. Similarly, disconfirming messages can be categorized into three types of responses: indifferent, impervious, and disqualifying (Sieburg, 1985). Indifference denies existence and involvement of communication and is evidenced by silence, interruptions, or inappropriate nonverbal responses that do not allow an individual to continue with her/his comments. An impervious response denies another's self-experience through distorting another's self-image, emotional expressions, or evaluations. Finally, disqualification inhibits communication through the use of ambiguity or irrelevant or tangential responses, which acknowledge the person's communication but shifts the direction of the conversation. Beyond the typology, however, additional research conceptualizes confirmation along a continuum from confirming to disconfirming, thereby suggesting that all responses have some degree of confirmation (e.g., Cissna & Sieburg, 1981).

Acceptance and Challenge

Although typically associated with acceptance, confirmation involves more than just demonstrating that people are accepted for who they are, but also that they are seen and valued for what they can become (Buber, 1965). Therefore, confirming messages often involve more than just acceptance, but also include an element of challenge to encourage individuals in novel ways. Acceptance is typically conceptualized as positive regard, or attentive and affectionate communication (Dailey, 2010), whereas challenge messages involve communicative behaviors including asking questions and "coaching others through their emotions" (Dailey, 2010, p. 595). Confirming messages of acceptance provide validation and security, whereas challenging messages communicate that individuals are capable of achieving a greater potential (Dailey et al., 2011). These confirming messages of acceptance and challenge allow individuals to feel engaged with, and connected to, others (Cissna & Sieburg, 1981; Seiburg, 1976), usually helping to create and maintain a positive relational environment. Confirming communication fosters active engagement and leads to a greater understanding not only of oneself, but also of the relationship between the individuals (Schrodt & Ledbetter, 2012).

Communicating about Miscarriage

Miscarriage (i.e., fetal loss before the 20th week of gestation) is one of the most common health complications experienced during pregnancy with as many as 25% of known pregnancies ending in miscarriage (American Pregnancy Association, 2017). This can be particularly traumatic for women, especially those who desired the pregnancy. Miscarriage has been associated with numerous negative outcomes, such as anxiety and depression (Brier, 2004; Swanson, 2000). However, some of these related consequences can be alleviated through supportive communication (Brann, 2015a). Because women often blame themselves or, at a minimum, often feel uncertainty about the miscarriage experience and newly forming identity, communication with a woman about her pregnancy loss should focus on validating her and her loss. As she is attempting to make sense of her loss through communication (Brann, 2015b; Shapiro, 1993), confirmation can help facilitate the sensemaking process (Burleson & Goldsmith, 1998). Confirming communication can benefit not only the woman who experienced the loss, but also those who interact with her, as it has been noted that communicating about miscarriage has the potential to change relationships with partners, family members, and friends (Brann, 2015b).

"You Can Get Pregnant:" A (Dis)Confirming Conversation[1]

The sun was shining and, although the April breeze was a bit brisk, Samantha was eager to get out of the office and take a walk with her close colleague and friend, Beth. They had just exited an exceptionally long meeting and Samantha needed to clear her head as she was having trouble focusing at work. Once outside and quickly down the sidewalk, their conversation began.

Beth: Are you okay?

Samantha: No, I am not okay. Today is the day I was due from my first miscarriage, and I just miscarried again last week. And I'm sitting in these useless meetings with people talking about things that don't really matter, and I'm about to lose it.

---

[1] The case presented is based on the narratives of 66 women who recalled a memorable conversation they had with someone about their miscarriage experience. Messages are actual statements made during interactions. All names are pseudonyms.

Beth (looks straight ahead as they walk down the sidewalk and after a long pause): Oh, Samantha, I am so sorry that you are going through this.

Samantha: Thanks. It's just hard.

Beth: I know. At least you know you can get pregnant.

Samantha: What?

Beth: The good news is that you know you can get pregnant. It could be worse, like if you were infertile and couldn't even get pregnant. And it's a good thing that it happened now before you had to actually go through labor or something. You know, everything happens for a reason.

Samantha: Well, I guess so, but it still hurts.

Beth (looking down at her phone): I know. Like I said though, you know you can get pregnant, and even though it must be hard, everything happens for a reason so you just have to believe that this is God's will.

Samantha: Maybe so, but I still don't understand why it happened.

Beth: You know stress can cause miscarriages. You had those migraines last week. Maybe the next time you get pregnant, you should take some time off of work or have me help you with your projects so you aren't so stressed.

Samantha: Maybe

Disconfirming communication masquerading as confirmation.

Although Beth's likely intent was to provide support to her friend, her attempts at confirmation were not successful. The content of most of her messages may initially be perceived to be confirming, but when assessed more closely, the quality of the communication was not confirming (Sieburg, 1976; Watzlawick et al., 1967). She began by offering condolences, but even when communicating sympathy, it was for the situation and not specifically about the loss of a child. She initially tried to show acceptance by being attentive to the topic and affectionate with her condolences. Beth attempted to validate the situation by having Samantha "look at the bright side" by noting that at least Samantha could get pregnant, things could be worse, and there was a reason for the situation. However, Beth actually invalidated the loss Samantha was experiencing by doing so. What initially appeared as confirming actually disconfirmed Samantha's experience and hindered her from sharing more information in an effort to process, and make sense of, what was occurring (Dailey, 2006). This was evident by Samantha's decreased communication and hedging throughout the conversation.

Beth was *impervious* to Samantha's attempts to discuss her loss when she trivialized the loss by not necessarily acknowledging it and instead kept focusing on Samantha's "good news" of her ability to get pregnant. She was *indifferent* to Samantha when she nonverbally showed disinterest by glancing at her phone or not making eye contact. Finally, when Samantha attempted to discuss her pain, Beth provided a *disqualifying* response by not addressing her concern and, instead, stated that everything happens for a reason (that it was God's will) and then moved on with the conversation.

As noted by Dailey (2006), by negating Samantha's experience and not allowing her to share and process her experience, Samantha likely began to question not only her experience, but herself and her relationship with her friend as well. Beth's comments are not uncommon, as these types of attempts at confirming messages have been echoed by multiple women (MacGeorge & Wilkum, 2012). Furthermore, although said comments are expressed with the intent to be helpful, they are actually, at a minimum, unhelpful and more likely hurtful (Gross, 2006). Additionally, Beth attempted to challenge Samantha to achieve her potential of becoming a mom by letting her know that she is capable of becoming pregnant and in the future she can help the process by being proactive to reduce stress (which, although it was an attempt to be helpful, is actually perpetuating unsubstantiated information about the correlation between stress and miscarriage). When Beth suggested a reason for the miscarriage (i.e., stress) and a solution (i.e., accept help at work to reduce stress), it was likely her attempt to acknowledge the reality of the situation and provide what she viewed as a helpful response that would connect the women, but instead blamed Samantha for something that she had no control over.

"It's Okay to Feel What You Are Feeling:" A Confirming Conversation

What if, on that same sunny afternoon, Samantha and Beth's conversation during the afternoon walk went something like this:

Beth: Are you okay?

Samantha: No, I am not okay. Today is the day I was due from my first miscarriage, and I just miscarried again last week. And I'm sitting in these useless meetings with people talking about things that don't really matter, and I'm about to lose it.

Beth (gently touching Samantha's arm): Oh Samantha, I am so sorry that you lost your baby.

Samantha: Thanks. It's just hard.

Beth: I don't know what you are feeling because I've never been through this, but I remember what my aunt said when she went through it a few years ago. She said that she didn't know how much it could hurt.

Samantha: Yea, she's right. I didn't know either, but it does.

Beth: I'm here for you and although I have no idea what you're going through, I will support you in any way that I can. It is hard for me to understand how painful that can be for a mother's heart, but this is a safe space so please know that you can talk to me about it anytime.

Samantha: Thanks, that means a lot. I'm just trying to figure out why this is happening to me, and I'm feeling kind of guilty because I was a little relieved the first time it happened because we didn't think we were ready for a family yet, but now we really wanted this baby so I'm sad, but also angry at myself.

Beth: I don't know why it is happening, and it is perfectly acceptable to feel all the things you are feeling. Have you talked to your midwife about how you are feeling?

Samantha: No, not yet.

Beth: Okay, well if you want to talk more about it with me, I'm here to listen.

Beth hugs Samantha before they turn around to head back to work.

Confirming communication. This conversation also illustrated elements of acceptance and challenge, but it was done with actual confirmation instead of disconfirmation masquerading as confirmation. To begin, Beth *recognized* Samantha and her baby when she expressed condolences. When Beth offered condolences to Samantha, she stated how sorry she was for the loss that she was experiencing, not an ambiguous situation. She confirmed her experience by nonverbally communicating her attention and affection through appropriate touch and did not make comments that turned the focus away from Samantha's loss (Dailey et al., 2011). Beth *acknowledged* Samantha's feelings and uncertainty and then even challenged Samantha by asking questions and trying to help her work through her emotions (Dailey, 2010). Beth illustrated her *endorsement* of Samantha by agreeing with her uncertainty, mixed emotions, and plan to talk more when she was ready. Unlike the first scenario in which Samantha felt dejected and unsure about her experience or how to move forward, the second scenario allowed Samantha the opportunity to process her experience, communicatively, with Beth to help her make sense of what happened, explore her feelings, and determine how to move forward.

Implications

Applying Confirmation Theory to interactions, particularly encounters that could benefit from supportive communication (Burleson & Goldsmith, 1998), is useful for understanding how receiving confirmation has the potential to influence an individual's attitude, emotional state, and behavior (Dailey, Crook, Glowacki, Prenger, & Winslow, 2016). This could prove to be useful in multiple contexts. As noted by Dailey (2006), confirmation should enable open discussion, as confirming responses validate different perspectives and encourage exploration of thoughts and feelings. This can offer therapeutic opportunities for individuals dealing with emotional, mental, and physical health concerns. The open dialogue and exploration of multiple perspectives can also enable more effective intercultural communication as previous instructional communication research suggests that confirmation behaviors transcend cultures (Goldman, Bolkan, & Goodboy, 2014).

Confirming interactions should assist individuals in building skills in expression, clarification, and defense of their perspectives. Thus, it is clear that constructs of Confirmation Theory should be applied in school and work settings to encourage learning, creativity, and productivity. By engaging in a conversation that encourages individuals to explore emotions and more fully develop their own perspectives, individuals should experience a greater sense of self-efficacy when communicating with others. This can be beneficial when formulating new friendships and partnerships. Additionally, gaining greater confidence allows individuals to communicate more effectively, and utilizing accepting and challenging messages provides individuals with tools to be more effective at persuasion, encouragement, and support (Dailey et al., 2010).

Because confirmation encourages communication that allows individuals to explore and process their thoughts and feelings, whereas disconfirmation hinders communication by invalidating the person's messages, it is important to characterize confirming messages not only as validation, but also as promotion of active engagement and communication between individuals (Dailey, 2008). This is important for productive and healthy relationships. Extending this perspective will allow for more effective communication patterns among relational partners, family members, colleagues, and others in everyday interactions in multiple environments, including home, work, school, healthcare, and sports.

Discussion Questions

1. What are other specific verbal and nonverbal communicative responses Beth could have used to confirm (i.e., recognize, acknowledge, and endorse) Samantha's miscarriage experience?

2. What are possible outcomes to receiving disconfirming responses when sharing personal experiences with someone else? For example, how might Samantha feel about herself, her situation, and her relationship with Beth after the first interaction?

3. Why is it important to not only accept but also challenge others when offering confirmation during an interaction? What might those messages sound like during a health-sensitive conversation such as the case presented in this chapter?

4. Recall an interaction you've had with someone about an emotional, mental, or physical health concern. Describe the confirming and/or disconfirming messages exchanged during that conversation. How did those messages affect the conversation and the relationship between you and the other person?

REFERENCES

American Pregnancy Association. (2017). *Miscarriage*. Retrieved from http://
www.americanpregnancy.org/pregnancy-complications/miscarriage.html

Brann, M. (2015a). Nine years later and still waiting: When health care providers'
social support never arrives. In R. Silverman & J. Baglia (Eds.), *Pregnancy
loss: A narrative collection* (pp. 19–31). New York, NY: Peter Lang Publishing.

Brann, M. (2015b). No time to grieve: Losing my life's love and regaining my
own strength. In M. Brann (Ed.), *Contemporary case studies in health
communication: Theoretical & applied approaches* (2nd ed., pp. 23–34).
Dubuque, IA: Kendall/Hunt.

Brier, N. (2004). Anxiety after miscarriage: a review of the empirical
literature and implications for clinical practice. *Birth, 31*, 138–142.
doi:10.1111/j.0730-7659.2004.00292x

Buber, M. (1957). Distance and relation. *Psychiatry, 20*, 97–104. doi:10.1080/0033
2747.1957.11023080

Buber, M. (1965). *The knowledge of man*. New York, NY: Harper & Row.

Burleson, B. R., & Goldsmith, D. J. (1998). How the comforting process works:
Alleviating emotional distress through conversationally induced reappraisals.
In P. A. Andersen & L. K. Guerrero (Eds.), *Handbook of communication
and emotion: Research, theory, applications, and contexts* (pp. 245–280). San
Diego, CA: Academic Press.

Cissna, K. N., & Keating, S. (1979). Speech communication antecedents of
perceived confirmation. *Western Journal of Speech Communication, 43*,
48–60. doi:10.1080/10570317909373953

Cissna, K. N., & Sieburg, E. (1981). Patterns of interactional confirmation and
disconfirmation. In C. Wilder-Mott & J. H. Weakland (Eds.), *Rigor and
imagination: Essays from the legacy of Gregory Bateson* (pp. 253–282).
New York, NY: Praeger.

Cranmer, G., & Brann, M. (2015). "It makes me feel like I am an important part of this team": An exploratory study of coach confirmation. *International Journal of Sport Communication, 8,* 193–211. doi: 10.1123/ijsc.2014-0078

Cranmer, G. A., Brann, M., & Weber, K. D. (2017). Quantifying coach confirmation: The development and preliminary validation of the coach confirmation instrument. *Communication & Sport, 5,* 751–769. doi: 10.1177/2167479516660037

Dailey, R. M. (2006). Confirmation in parent-adolescent relationships and adolescent openness: Toward extending confirmation theory. *Communication Monographs, 73,* 434–458. doi:10.1080/03637750601055432

Dailey, R. M. (2008). Assessing the contribution of nonverbal behaviors in displays of confirmation during parent-adolescent interactions: An actor-partner interdependence model. *Journal of Family Communication, 8,* 62–91. doi:10.1080/15267430701573599

Dailey, R. M. (2010). Testing components of confirmation: How acceptance and challenge from mothers, fathers, and siblings are related to adolescent self-concept. *Communication Monographs, 77,* 592–617. doi:10.1080/03637751.2010.499366

Dailey, R. M., Crook, B., Glowacki, E., Prenger, E., & Winslow, A. A. (2016). Meeting weight management goals: The role of partner confirmation. *Health Communication, 31,* 1482–1494. doi:10.1080/10410236.2015.1089398

Dailey, R. M., McCracken, A. A., & Romo, L. K. (2011). Confirmation and weight management: Predicting effective levels of acceptance and challenge in weight management messages. *Communication Monographs, 78,* 185–211. doi:10.1080/03637751.2011.56468

Dailey, R. M., Romo, L. K., & McCracken, A. A. (2010). Messages about weight management: An examination of how acceptance and challenge are related to message effectiveness. *Western Journal of Communication, 74,* 457–483. doi:10.1080/10570314.2010.512279

Ellis, K. (2000). Perceived teacher confirmation: The development and validation of an instrument and two studies of the relationship to cognitive and affective learning. *Human Communication Research, 26*, 264–291. doi:10.1111/j.1468-2958.2000.tb00758.x

Ellis, K. (2002). Perceived parental confirmation: Development and validation of an instrument. *Southern Communication Journal, 67*, 319–334. doi:10.1080/10417940209373242

Goldman, Z. W., Bokan, S., & Goodboy, A. K. (2014). Revising the relationship between teacher confirmation and learning outcomes: Examining cultural differences in Turkish, Chinese, and American classrooms. *Journal of Intercultural Communication Research, 43*, 45–63.

Goodboy, A. K., & Myers, S. A. (2008). The effect of teacher confirmation on student communication and learning outcomes. *Communication Education, 57*, 153–179. doi:10.1080/03634520701787777

Gottman, J. M. (1994). *What predicts divorce? The relationship between marital processes and marital outcomes.* Hillsdale, NJ: Lawrence Erlbaum Associates, Inc.

Gross, J. (Ed.). (2006). *About what was lost: 20 writers on miscarriage, healing, and hope.* New York, NY: Plume.

Laing, R. D. (1961). Confirmation and disconfirmation. In *Self and others*, (pp. 98–107). London, United Kingdom: Tavistock Publications.

MacGeorge, E., & Wilkum, K. (2012). Predicting comforting quality in the context of miscarriage. *Communication Reports, 25*, 62–74. doi:10.1080/0893 4215.2012.719463

Reis, H. T., Sheldon, K. M., Gable, S. L., Roscoe, J., & Ryan, R. M. (2000). Daily well-being: The role of autonomy, competence, and relatedness. *Personality and Social Psychology Bulletin, 26*, 419–435. doi:10.1177/0146167200266002

Schrodt, P., & Ledbetter, A. M. (2012). Parental confirmation as a mitigator of feeling caught and family satisfaction. *Personal Relationships, 19*, 146–161. doi:10.1111/j.1475-6811.2010.01345.x

Shapiro, C. H. (1993). *When part of the self is lost: Helping clients heal after sexual and reproductive losses.* San Francisco, CA: Jossey-Bass.

Sieburg, E. (1976). Confirming and disconfirming organizational communication. In J. L. Owen, P. A. Page, & G. I. Zimmerman (Eds.), *Communication in organizations* (pp. 129–149). St. Paul, MN: West Publishing Co.

Sieburg, E. (1985). Confirming and disconfirming response in families. *In Family communication: An integrated systems approach,* (pp. 189–219). Boston, MA: Allyn & Bacon.

Swanson, K. M. (2000). Predicting depressive symptoms after miscarriage: A path analysis based on the Lazarus paradigm. *Journal of Women's Health and Gender-Based Medicine, 9,* 191–206. doi:10.1089/152460900318696

Watzlawick, P., Beavin, J. H., & Jackson, D. D. (1967). *Pragmatics of human communication.* New York, NY: Norton.

Chapter 19

The Beard Buster: Applying the Theory of Independent Mindedness to the Barbasol Company

Theodore Avtgis, Ph.D., *Medical Communication Specialists*
Corey Jay Liberman, Ph.D., *Marymount Manhattan College*

Introduction

If you have ever worked in an organization where you have been fearful of communicating to/with those in hierarchically-superior positions, believe us: you are not alone. The more important questions, however, are why employees are fearful of upward communication and what can be done to increase the likelihood of what Spencer (1986) calls employee voice and what Kassing (1997) calls dissent. This chapter will focus on a theory, the Theory of Independent Mindedness (Infante, 1987a; Infante, 1987b), that has been used as a guiding framework to answer the previous queries. The chapter will begin with a brief overview of the Theory of Independent Mindedness, inclusive of its major claims and the links that it makes among intentions to communicate with superiors and (a) argumentativeness, (b) verbal aggressiveness, and (c) communicator style. You will then read a case study about *Barbasol*, an Ohio-based manufacturing organization responsible for the creation, distribution, and sales of its shaving products (i.e. razors, shave cream), whose culture and employees might open the path for effective superior-subordinate communication. Finally, the chapter concludes with an explanation of how, specifically, the case study can be understood and analyzed through the lens of independent mindedness. By the conclusion of this chapter, you will better understand how organizational conditions (i.e. the organization's culture), coupled with individual trait characteristics (i.e. argumentativeness, verbal aggressiveness), combine to create the context necessary for upward, superior-subordinate communication.

Theory of Independent Mindedness

Historically, organizational communication has borrowed, significantly, from other disciplines, in the development of quality theory, focused on communication aspects of organizational life. In fact, it was W. Charles Redding, known widely in the literature as the father of organizational communication, who questioned why the social processes and practices linked to organizations and organizing so often lacks a focus on *communication* (see, for example, Redding, 1966). The Theory of Independent Mindedness (TIM) can be thought of as one of the first true organizational communication theories, using exclusively communication constructs. This is in contrast to other organizational communication theories that have drawn largely from other disciplines, such as economics, business, and psychology, among others. Originally developed by Infante (1987a, 1987b), the main argument undergirding the Theory of Independent Mindedness is that if the members of an organization are going to learn from its mistakes, the necessary prerequisite variable becomes willingness to communicate (see McCroskey & Richmond, 1990, for an overview). In other words, employees must be desiring to voice concerns up the hierarchical ladder so that change-makers (who, according to this theory, are also change-seekers) are communicatively aware of employee issues. For example, if an employee is discontent with her pay or with the strategies adopted by her boss to deliver negative feedback or the dress-code policy or unfair treatment of gender, upward communication, with the hope of organizational, institutional change, is necessary. So…what increases the likelihood of willingness to communicate?

According to the Theory of Independent Mindedness, one of the major assumptions is based on the idea of cultural congruity. That is, for any organization to be successful, the culture of the organization (microculture) needs to be congruent to the larger culture within which it operates. This cultural coordination can be seen in other organizational theories, such as Ouchi's (1981) Theory Z (see Avtgis, Rancer, & Liberman, 2012), which, in short, argues that the most effective organizations are those with employees working within a cultural context that is supportive, that endorses collective decision-making practices, and that promises the opportunity for shared voice. American culture, as framed in the Constitution of the United States, is predicated on the freedom of speech and individual rights. The Theory of Independent Mindedness assumes that these rights should also be afforded and fostered within organizations. Framed as a corporatist theory, the Theory of Independent Mindedness is believed to result in increased employee motivation, satisfaction, and productivity (Infante, Rancer, Avtgis, & MacGeorge, 2017).

If you stop to think about it for just a brief moment, this certainly stands to reason. Assume that you are currently employed by an organization who utilizes cross-departmental teams as a strategy for brainstorming its new beverage products. In this organization, those in hierarchically-superior positions have no interest in hearing the dissenting ideas of those in more subordinate positions. As a result, since you are oftentimes silenced, and your ideas are oftentimes tabled and/or ignored (even if fruitful), your inclination to talk about this is impinged. Compare this with the organization that not only wants to hear about these issues, but actively promotes the communication of dissent and discontentment, perhaps even fostering an organizational environment inclusive of 360-degree feedback (see, for example, Fairhurst, 2008). In which of these two organizational contexts are you likely more willing to be motivated, satisfied, and productive? These three terms (all of which find homes in the industrial/organizational psychology literature) are difficult to operationally define, and their scope extends well beyond this chapter, though it is likely that the answer to this question would be the second organization mentioned. Why? Because it promotes independent mindedness and the opportunity for organizational change.

The theory further assumes that all employees have an active voice in decision-making processes at all levels of the organization (Infante et al., 2017). Part of such processes includes a robust exchange of communicating ideas and perspectives in organizational operations. Returning to the example provided earlier, assume that all organizational constituents are involved in the decision to create, market, and brand a new cola beverage. From a marketing perspective, many important questions must be raised. Who is the target market for this new beverage? What is the key point of difference that makes this cola more attractive (and better) as compared to its competition? What will be this product's price point? Where will this product be placed and how will it be advertised? Without introducing members of the sales team and the marketing team and the design team and the advertising team and the development team into this discussion, the likelihood of forthcoming failure is heightened. As such, the exchange of ideas becomes that much more important. This is among the major, overarching claims of the Theory of Independent Mindedness, and, again, is why it is thought of as one of the first "truly" communicative theories within the organizational communication micro-field.

However, the Theory of Independent Mindedness, given its corporatist nature, is unlike the organizational theories that have been developed in eastern cultures (i.e. Japan, China), in that eastern theories deemphasize individual pursuits of power and status. Instead, the Theory of Independent Mindedness advocates pursuits of power and status that differentiate people from one another. In fact, such differences should be emphasized, as they are part of the larger American culture (Avtgis & Rancer, 2007). This is where there seems to be a fusion between McGregor's Theory X (command and control as a form of management) and McGregor's Theory Y (fusion of individual and organizational goals), again producing the theoretical correlation between the theory of Independent Mindedness and Ouchi's Theory Z (see McGregor, 1960). The Theory of Independent Mindedness is a radical departure from the more control-based and power-based theories that advocate that management act *upon* employees, as opposed to act *with* employees (Ewing, 1982; Infante et al., 2017). Instead, the theory assumes that control and power are fluid in nature and can move in any given relational direction at any given time. As such, and key to the theory, subordinates lower on the hierarchical chain of command can become more powerful in certain social instances. That said, however, power and control need to be expressed in prosocial ways in order for them to be positive organizational attributes. How are power and control used in prosocial ways? Research indicates that in order to achieve this "prosociality," competent communication skills should be manifested and/or socially developed. According to the literature, the three communication traits that most heavily influence the degree to which an organization will achieve independent mindedness are argumentativeness (Infante & Rancer, 1982), verbal aggressiveness (Infante & Wigley, 1986), and communicator style (Norton, 1978).

Argumentativeness is believed to be a constructive trait defined as a "tendency to present and defend positions on controversial issues while attempting to refute the positions that other people take on those issues" (Infante et al., 2017, p. 85). Argumentativeness is believed to bring about many organizational benefits, such as organizational dissent (Kassing & Avtgis, 1999), increased job satisfaction (Infante & Gorden, 1985), and proactive conflict resolution strategies (Martin, Anderson, & Sirmangkala, 1997). Verbal aggressiveness is considered a destructive trait that reflects a tendency to attack the self-concept of people instead of, or in addition to, their positions on issues (Infante et al., 2017, p. 86). The use of verbal aggression within the organization has been linked to several destructive outcomes, such as employee inattentiveness, increased levels of unfriendliness, and lower levels of satisfaction (Infante & Gorden, 1989), as well as a tendency to use ineffective and inappropriate organizational dissent strategies (Kassing & Avtgis, 1999). In short, as Infante and Gorden (1987) contend, "an organizational communication climate which emphasizes argumentativeness and de-emphasizes verbal aggressiveness facilitates the generally uncompromising desire for freedom of speech by individuals in American society" (p. 74). Combining these two, aforementioned, variables, employees who are high on the argumentativeness continuum, and low on the verbal aggressiveness continuum, bring about the ideal social context for independent mindedness.

The third trait that comprises the Theory of Independent Mindedness is communicator style and reflects "the way one verbally and paraverbally interacts to signal how literal meaning should be taken, interpreted, filtered, or understood" (Norton, 1978, p. 99). There are 10 distinct styles of communication, comprised of the following: dominant style (communicating in a way that takes charge of a situation), dramatic style (communicating in a way that either understates or overstates information), contentious style (communicating in a combative or antagonistic way), impression-leaving style (interacting in a way that is memorable), animated style (frequent use of nonverbal gestures/behaviors), relaxed style (communicating in a way that lacks anxiety or tension), open style (communicating in an extroverted and spontaneous way), attentive style (communicating in a way that gives other people the impression that you are listening to them), precise style (communicating in a way that is exact and detailed), and friendly style (communicating in a more intimate way) (see Norton, 1978, for an extended discussion of these styles). Of these 10 dimensions, particular combinations of these styles can create either an affirming communicator style (i.e. communicating in ways that validate the self-concept of another person) or a non-affirming communicator style (i.e. communicating in ways that threaten other people's self-concepts). An affirming communicator style, for example, is likely to manifest itself when certain communication styles are employed (i.e. relaxed, open, attentive, friendly), while a disconfirming communicator style is likely to emerge when other styles are discursively produced (i.e. dominant, dramatic, contentious, animated).

Independent mindedness is believed to be achieved when an organization can instill (a) high levels of argumentativeness, (b) low levels of verbal aggressiveness, and (c) an affirming communicator style with employees at all levels of the organization. Table 1 describes the various trait profiles associated with independent mindedness, linking these three independent variables together. It is important to note that independent mindedness should be considered on a continuum, rather than as a simple dichotomy. In the end, the Theory of Independent Mindedness describes and predicts how the use of employee voice can serve to assist or hamper organizational communication and organizational productivity.

COMMUNICATION TRAIT PROFILES OF THE THEORY OF INDEPENDENT MINDEDNESS		
Profile	Trait Level	Outcome
ONE	High Argumentativeness	High Employee Commitment
	Low Verbal Aggressiveness	High Employee Satisfaction
	Affirming Communicator Style	High Employee Productivity
TWO	High Argumentativeness	Moderate Employee Commitment
	Low Verbal Aggressiveness	Moderate Employee Satisfaction
	Nonaffirming Communicator Style	Moderate Employee Productivity
THREE	Low Argumentativeness	Lower Employee Commitment
	Low Verbal Aggressiveness	Lower Employee Satisfaction
	Affirming Communicator Style	Lower Employee Productivity
FOUR	Low Argumentativeness	Lowest Employee Commitment
	High Verbal Aggressiveness	Lowest Employee Satisfaction
	Nonaffirming Communicator Style	Lowest Employee Productivity

Source: Infante et al/*Contemporary Communication Theory, Second Edition*/2017

The Case of the Beard Busting Barbasol Company

This case study centers around the *Barbasol* company, which manufactures shave cream and razors for men (*Barbasol*) and women (*Pure Silk*). Founded in 1919 by Frank Shields, the *Barbasol* brand quickly became nationally known. To this day, each *Barbasol* can of shave cream still contains the red, blue, and white colors reflective of the classic spinning poles located outside barbershops throughout the United States. When these spinning poles were activated, they signaled to customers that the barbershop was open. Efforts to market the *Barbasol* brand were not lost on Shields, who was able to convince perhaps the greatest baseball player of all-time, Babe Ruth, to endorse the product. The product quickly became popular with the American people. The *Barbasol* brand prides itself on being an American company that employs American workers. The only manufacturing plant for the entire company is located in Ashland, Ohio.

The company is employee-focused and provides constant training for its employees and management. This includes training, strategic planning, production innovation, safety protocols, economic status and initiatives of the company, and many other aspects of the business and operations. If one were to witness a day-to-day operation of the plant, he/she would experience a seamless power structure, where every employee knows his/her role and the impact of this role on the entire organization. The company also offers generous perquisites to its employees, which include a monthly, catered lunch, shirts that are embroidered with the company name and the employee's first name (styles of the shirts vary), and four bottles of shave cream (their choice between *Barbasol* or *Pure Silk*) per month. These management practice initiatives are representative of a company that values employee involvement, commitment, and tenure. For example, leaders from their corporate headquarters will regularly visit the facility to inform employees of upcoming strategic plans and actively seek employee input at all levels.

Based on some recent gossip, Ronald, an entry-level manufacturer, began to get nervous. He had only been working for *Barbasol* for roughly two months (a bit over seven weeks) and he recently learned that three of his coworkers (Nancy, Jefferson, and Lester) were all fired since he arrived at the Ashland plant in June. Of course, for legal purposes, Alexander, Ronald's boss, was not allowed to say why the three were fired, other than the 'it was time for them to go' speech, with which most blue-collar workers were all too familiar. But Ronald was scared. He had been through four jobs in the last two years and he wanted this one to be more permanent. Although he was at his previous organization of employment for 16 months, he was only with the two prior for a total of four months. It was not that Ronald was not a good or hard worker. In fact, it was just the opposite. He worked his absolute tail off. He earned 'Employee of the Month' honors four months (out of the 16 that he was there) at his last job, which was working at a manufacturing plant for an electronics company. He was always on time. He never took a lunch break so that he could accomplish more in less time. He never called out sick. His coworkers loved him. His boss loved him. It was just that he had enough. His only occupational flaw is that he gets bored after a while and needs a new adventure.

But, according to Ronald, things at *Barbasol* were different. For some reason, he could see being there for the long haul. Perhaps it was the friendliness of his coworkers. Perhaps it was the overall culture of the organization. Perhaps it was the relationship that he had cultivated with Alexander. Perhaps it was his interest in Felicia, the woman who worked in Accounting. Perhaps it was living so close to Ashland, Ohio, and having such a quick commute to work. Perhaps it was his paycheck. Perhaps it was a combination of all of these. Whatever the reason(s), he needed to know what he could do in order to avoid the fate of Nancy, Jefferson, and Lester. What could he do? How could he proceed? After speaking with several of his coworkers, he had an idea. If only he knew what he was doing well, specifically, so that he could continue doing these things. And if only he knew what he was doing poorly, so that he could do them differently. In other words, how about monthly feedback reports? He knew that not everyone in the company would be onboard. After all, who wants to know if they are doing poorly? But what about only offering this feedback to people who wanted it? In fact, this, too, could come across as something rather positive: that Ronald truly cared about his work and wanted to hone his skills. It was time to speak with Alexander about his idea, so he decided to give him a quick phone call to set up a meeting.

At *Barbasol*, although they do use e-mail for purposes of correspondence, Ronald still believes that other forms of interactive media (i.e. telephone), and even that now-antiquated form of communication, face-to-face dialogue, are much more prudent. So...Ronald called Alexander at 12:20pm on a random Thursday afternoon.

Ronald: Hey there, Alexander...this is Ronald...how goes things???

Alexander: Ron...my man...things are good...how are you?

Ronald: Things are great...just having lunch...enjoying the day...you know.

Alexander: I thought that you do not eat lunch, Ronny?

Ronald: Who said I don't eat lunch? If I did not eat lunch, I would weight 142 pounds...not 241 pounds.

Alexander: That is true, indeed.

Ronald: I eat. I just do not take a lunch break.

Alexander: Ahhhhhh.

Ronald: So...the reason for my call is that I want to discuss something kind of important.

Alexander: Oh no...is everything OK, Rony???

Ronald: Yes...everything is fine. I was just hoping that I could...well...borrow your ear for a moment.

Alexander: How about tomorrow morning...before the day begins... say...7:15am???

Ronald: Ahhh...perfect...thank you, sir!!!

Alexander: Sir? The last time I heard that I was in history class...and the teacher was talking about Sir Walter Raleigh. I don't even remember who he was. I just remember the name.

Ronald: That is great!!! Thank you, kindly, and I will see you in the morning.

Alexander: Have a great afternoon, Ronny.

Ronald: You too, Alexander.

That evening, Ronald knew that he could speak with his friends (not connected to *Barbasol*), as well as those from within the company, for advice. For strategy. Instead, however, he chose to have an early dinner, after a long day at work, watch a few episodes of *The Big Bang Theory* on *TBS*, and call it a night. Before he knew it, his alarm went off, and it was 6:00am. He had his normal breakfast (bacon, egg, and cheese on a croissant), coupled with his everyday ingestion of two cups of coffee. He was ready. He jumped in to his 2010 Toyota Camry, drove the [roughly] nine miles from Jeromesillve to Ashland, and anxiously awaited the meeting with Alexander. Although they were more friends than anything else, Ronald was still nervous, uncertain how his boss would respond to his request. Well…he was about to find out. He knocked on Alexander's office door and, upon hearing the 'come on in' response that followed, Ronald entered.

Ronald: Good morning, Alexander.

Alexander: You know what is funny about that saying, Ron? You just expect that someone is going to say 'good morning' back. However, I always wondered whether or not it was more of a question than a greeting. As in 'are you having a good morning?' Like 'good morning so far?' I have always wanted to answer that with a yes or a no. I guess that is why folks from the south say 'morning' instead of good morning. They frame it as a sentence instead of a question. Do you get my drift?

Ronald: Only you could start the day, at 7:15, with something smart and something funny at the same time.

Alexander: Did you expect anything less, my friend? How was your night?

Ronald: Not bad. Pretty laid back. Nothing crazy. You?

Alexander: I was dragged to see my daughter's dance recital. I mean, I love her to death. Please do not get me wrong. But I had to miss the game for this. The Indians were playing the Yankees. But she did great and it was very sweet.

Ronald: That is very nice. Very nice indeed.

Alexander: So, what can I do you for?

Ronald: Well…first…thank you for seeing me…I really do appreciate it.

Alexander: You know our policy here. Open doors mean open roars.

Ronald: No, no, no…no roaring today.

Alexander: I know…I was just playing. You are not a roarer anyway. Or at least I have not seen it yet.

Ronald: I do, however, have a suggestion.

Alexander: OK…fire away.

Ronald: As you may or may not know...I do love it here. Very much. Better than any other job I have had in a long time.

Alexander: See...this sounds like the preface to the 'I am leaving *Barbasol*' speech.

Ronald: Haha. No. But, since I have been here, there really has been little (if any) feedback in terms of my performance. Now I know that I will have an evaluation after six months, but I kind of feel that this might be too far away.

Alexander: Wow...most people would do anything not to have to be evaluated. To just slide by under the guise of darkness at it were.

Ronald: Well...that might be true for some. But not for me. I think that we, at *Barbasol*, would be much better off if we were given feedback more often.

Alexander: Does everyone feel this way?

Ronald: I have not spoken to everyone. In fact, I am coming to you on my own here. It might be a selfish thing, but maybe it is just me who is asking for this. It is just that...well...I have been at other places...other organizations...other companies...where people leave...honestly...they are fired...and we are not told why. But we all know why. It is because they screwed up. They did it this way when they were supposed to do it that way. Or they did it that way when they were supposed to do it this way. Or they spoke to Individual X when they were supposed to speak to Individual Y. I don't want to be this person.

Alexander: You do know that this is going to take a lot of time to put into practice. I also fear that most of the people that you work with are going to be against this. I also think that managers...those who are going to have to do this overseeing and reporting that you desire...are going to find this overly-obtrusive and time-consuming.

Ronald: If we think about it as a gain, rather than a loss, for *Barbasol*, and for all of those people it employs, I really, really, really think that it could be a great thing here.

Alexander: I will tell you what, Ronny. I will bring this up at our next monthly meeting.

Ronald: OK.

Alexander: I will not let anyone know that it came from you. I will let them know that it came from me. Or that I read some recent article in the *Harvard Business Review* about the link between employee feedback and increased productivity or motivation or something like that.

Ronald: OK.

Alexander: I think that if others are onboard, we can definitely make this happen. And if not, meaning that it gets shut down like a Cleveland Browns running back getting the ball, fourth-and-goal from the one-yard-line, then perhaps you and I can figure out a plan.

Ronald: Alexander…that would be amazing. And I know that you think that I am crazy about desiring feedback. Especially if this feedback means that I will be told that I need to be doing a better job. But, in the long run, I think that it will be great…and serve us all (including you) well.

Alexander: I really appreciate your willingness to come speak with me about this today. It truly says something about your character and workmanship. You are awesome, Ronald.

Ronald: Thank you, sir. Just one more question.

Alexander: Absolutely. Shoot.

Ronald: Was that the first example of feedback…or do I need to wait until the monthly meeting?

Both Alexander and Ronald laughed and they got up from their seats, walked to the office door, and gave each other a handshake. It was going to be a good Friday ahead at the *Barbasol* company.

Application of the Theory of Independent Mindedness

When considering the *Barbasol* company, and the case study employed here, through the lens of the Theory of Independent Mindedness, one can easily see how the principles of the theory are being applied and incorporated into the organization's culture. First and foremost, it is important to shed light on the idea of cultural congruity (mentioned at the start of the chapter). The practices of those at *Barbasol* reflect the free speech principles and self-determination reflective of the larger, individualistic culture of the United States. Simply put, the microculture of the organization is highly correlated with the cultural values of the macroculture. Through the constant feedback loop involving employees at all levels of the organization, employee voice is constantly being sought and encouraged. Whether it is the individualized employee wellness program, celebration of employee birthdays, or other significant events, the culture exudes a level of care and concern for each organizational member. In fact, members are cross-trained so that any one employee has the skill set versatility to fill in where needed. For example, employees are trained on how to operate on the production line, as well as shipping, receiving, and best practices regarding occupational safety (i.e. driving tow motors, operating hand trucks).

In addition, when looking closely at the dialogic exchange between Alexander and Ronald, it is clear that there is a link between the *Barbasol* culture and the larger culture in which the organization is embedded: a key argument of the Theory of Independent Mindedness. Although possibly hesitant, Ronald felt both the desire and power to communicate both his distaste for the status quo of job feedback (or lack thereof), as well as his desire for organizational change. Hesitancy, however, is likely more the norm than the exception when it comes to superior-subordinate communication. After all, one might be uncertain as to how the target of such dissent will receive the information, and the dialogic exchange is likely to stir up emotions. That said, however, from the perspective of this theory, it was the cultural congruence that provided the social context necessary for the communication of upward disagreement.

Second, as you will likely recall from the front end of this chapter, argumentativeness is a key variable predicative of independent mindedness. It is important, here, to remember that argumentativeness is a positively-valenced attribute of organizational communication. In other words, proposing and creating dissenting and opposing viewpoints is the only way to bring about organizational change. At *Barbasol*, the training in encouraging active employee voice can be demonstrated in the constant feedback-seeking cycles in which management engages with employees at all levels of the organization. These interactions often include discussions of personal matters, such as family and relationships, as well as popular culture, such as music and sports. It is not uncommon to hear debates about football teams or musical artists throughout the day, with a perpetual focus on the collective mission. In fact, the organization has musical theme days (i.e. classic rock, country), where music is played throughout the warehouse, and it is common for employees to be singing loudly, sometimes in unison, to any given song. According to the Theory of Independent Mindedness, the ability to exercise such free speech, as evidenced in the *Barbasol* culture, has resulted in low turnover rates, employees embracing company initiatives, and a family-type working environment.

As can be seen in the conversation between Alexander and Ronald, argumentation did manifest itself. The controversial issue, of course, was whether or not there exists a need to deliver more routinized feedback to employees. On the one hand, Ronald explains that it would help him (and, by association, his fellow coworkers), as he would know what he was doing well and how he could keep up his good work practices. Such feedback would also indicate where Ronald needed to improve, ultimately having both individual-level and organizational-level benefits. On the other hand, Alexander explains that it would be overly cumbersome to provide such routinized feedback, and it is likely, according to him, that other managers would find this extra work to be more burdensome than rewarding. Again, however, because of the social context conducive for independent mindedness (i.e. cultural congruity and argumentativeness), the social interaction was, in the end, largely productive.

Third, research on aggressive communication informs us that when people seek to increase argumentative behavior, there is not necessarily a decrease in verbally aggressive behavior, as they are two separate and distinct constructs (Rancer, Whitecap, Kosberg, & Avtgis, 1997). However, the organizational practices outlined in this case study speak to the creation of an organizational culture that does not value verbally aggressive behavior. In fact, the cultural expectations at *Barbasol* are that employees will regulate their aggression during any and all social encounters. By instilling voice, and encouraging positive expressions of dissent, constant interaction among all members of the organization is emphasized. Further, a mural-sized mission statement, located in the breakroom, highlights the family focus of the organization and emphasizes philanthropic causes that are centered on issues related to children. Such practices are connected to positive relational and organizational outcomes (see Avtgis, et al., 2012), which includes a reduction in the practice of verbal aggression. If there are verbally aggressive exchanges, they are used in a way that strengthens the bonds between employees (see, for example, Martin, Dunleavy, & Kennedy-Lightsey, 2010). For example, two employees with a strong, positive relationship may have a communication exchange that includes the following correspondence:

Employee A: Hey...are you going to work *AT ALL* today???

Employee B: I haven't made up my mind yet!!!

Such exchanges serve to concretize the relational bond and add to a positive organizational culture. However, it should be noted that there is no intent to "hurt" the other person because of such communication exchanges.

In addition, when looking at the verbal exchange of messages between Alexander and Ronald, it is clear that neither employs verbally aggressive communicative moves. After reading the transcript, one can easily see how verbal aggression could have seamlessly entered into the exchange. On the one hand, Ronald, the subordinate, letting his superior know about an organizational practice that he deems rife with issues, could clearly use heated debate strategies. On the other hand, Alexander, the superior (at least by hierarchical position), after receiving data that he needs to perhaps alter his way of providing and delivering job feedback, could have also become upset and angered. However, it is clear that neither turned his [potential] emotions into aggressive communication. According to the Theory of Independent Mindedness, it would have resulted in an unfruitful communicative exchange. Why? Because, as Infante and Wigley (1986) remind us, there is a striking difference between argumentativeness and verbal aggressiveness. Specifically, they claim that argumentativeness involves "presenting and defending positions on controversial issues while attacking the positions taken by others on the issues," whereas verbal aggressiveness is "attacking the self-concept of another person instead of, or in addition to, the person's position on a topic of communication" (Infante & Wigley, 1986, p. 61). Neither Alexander, nor Ronald, verbally attacked the other. They steered clear of verbal aggressiveness and, instead, let argumentativeness serve as the catalyst for communication.

Finally, communicator style is a key variable for the Theory of Independent Mindedness. In short, it is important for one to deliver his/her message in an affirming way. That is, communicating in a way that validates the self-concept of the other person (Infante et al., 2017). In this case, it is clear, in leaders' practices, that they value employee input and do so using an affirming communication style. Such communication practices, when coupled with encouraging dissent and the valuing of feedback (i.e. argumentativeness), result in an equal exchange of information through which power structures and other organizational practices are maintained in a manner that is consistent with respect for the self-concept of each individual. The concepts of argumentative and aggressive communication are, thus, moderated by whether or not a person chooses to use an affirming versus a non-affirming communication style. Such affirming communication practices transcend 'on the clock' interactions to include communication during breaks, company outings, and the like. Such practices seek to concretize the concept of open and honest communication between and among all employees within the organization.

Looking, again, at the discourse between Alexander and Ronald, one can make the valid argument that among the reasons for the effectiveness of the exchange between the two is because of the stylistic nature, or undertone, of the conversation. Being relaxed, friendly, and attentive not only increased the likelihood of Ronald bringing forth his recommendation, and the ease of so doing, but also increased the likelihood that Alexander took the feedback constructively, rather than as a personal affront or attack. Looking back to the chapter's table, it is no wonder that Profile One is most likely to create high employee commitment, high employee satisfaction, and high employee productivity: because high argumentativeness and low verbal aggressiveness is coupled with an affirming communicator style.

Conclusion

In their pivotal article about the Theory of Independent Mindedness, Infante and Gorden (1987) speak about a "chain of reasoning" (p. 78) that provides the organizational context necessary for effective, upward communication. In so doing, they argue that it is the organization's culture, embedded within a larger, macro-culture, which, in turn, makes argumentativeness both acceptable and endorsed, devoid of verbally aggressive language (and paralanguage), producing independent mindedness and the opportunity for organizational change. This case study has shed light on the practical implications of the Theory of Independent Mindedness and, again, reminds one of the role that theory plays in our everyday, communicative lives. In the end, the Theory of Independent Mindedness is an effective and valuable theory that can help explain a myriad of different organizational communication phenomena. This theory is a *true* communication theory, as it is comprised of the three communication predispositions of argumentativeness, verbal aggressiveness, and communicator style. Parsimony, as mentioned in this book's introduction, is one of the basic communication theory-building tenets, reminding us that a theory should be stated as simply as possible, yet should, at the same time, be overly explanatory. The Theory of Independent Mindedness has certainly demonstrated its utility as a tool for researchers to parsimoniously assess and interpret quality, and non-quality, communication within organizations: and its use is getting us one step closer to understanding the prerequisites necessary for effective superior-subordinate communication.

Discussion Questions

1. Explain how the concept of cultural congruity influences organizational productivity, employee morale, and employee satisfaction.

2. If you were a trainer of new employees for the Barbasol organization, how would you train them consistent with the Theory of Independent Mindedness?

3. If you were a manager in the Barbasol organization, how would you implement the tenets of the Theory of Independent Mindedness on a daily basis?

4. If you were a consultant to a company wanting to utilize the Theory of Independent Mindedness, how would you communicate the basic approach to instituting such an effort?

Although the Barbasol company is a real company, the case study illustrated here was fictional

REFERENCES

Avtgis, T. A., & Rancer, A. S. (2007). The theory of independent mindedness: An organizational theory for individualistic cultures. In M. Hinner (Ed.), *The role of communication in business transactions and relationships: Freiberger beitrage zur interkulturellen und wirtschaftskommunikation: A forum for general and intercultural business communication* (pp. 183–201). Frankfurt, Germany: Peter Lang.

Avtgis, T. A., Rancer, A. S., & Liberman, C. J. (2012). *Organizational communication: Strategies for success*. Dubuque, IA: Kendall Hunt.

Ewing, D. (1982). *"Do it my way or you're fired": Employee rights and the changing role of management perspectives*. New York: John Wiley & Sons.

Fairhurst, G. T. (2008). Discursive leadership: A communication alternative to leadership psychology. *Management Communication Quarterly, 21*, 510–521.

Infante, D. A. (1987a). Aggressive. In J. C. McCroskey & J. A. Daly (Eds.), *Personality and interpersonal communication* (pp. 157–192). Newbury Park, CA: Sage Publications.

Infante, D. A. (1987b, July). *Argumentativeness in superior-subordinate communication: An essential condition for organizational productivity*. Paper presented at the annual American Forensics Summer Conference of the Speech Communication, Alta, UT.

Infante, D. A., & Gorden, W. I. (1985). Superiors' argumentativeness and verbal aggressiveness as predictors of subordinates' satisfaction. *Human Communication Research, 12*, 117–125.

Infante, D. A., & Gorden, W. I. (1987). Superior and subordinate communication profiles: Implications for independent-mindedness and upward effectiveness. *Central States Speech Journal, 38*, 73-80.

Infante, D. A., & Gorden, W. I. (1989). Argumentativeness and affirming communicator style as predictors of satisfaction/dissatisfaction with subordinates. *Communication Quarterly, 37*, 81–90.

Infante, D. A., & Rancer, A. S. (1982). A conceptualization and measure of argumentativeness. *Journal of Personality Assessment, 46*, 72–80.

Infante, D. A., Rancer, A. S., Avtgis, T. A., & MacGeorge, E. L. (2017). *Contemporary communication theory.* Dubuque, IA: Kendall Hunt.

Infante, D. A., & Wigley, C. J. III. (1986). Verbal aggressiveness: An interpersonal model and measure. *Communication Monographs, 53*, 61–69.

Kassing, J. W. (1997). Articulating, antagonizing, and displacing: A model of employee dissent. *Journal of Communication Studies, 48*, 311-332.

Kassing, J. W., & Avtgis, T. A. (1999). Examining the relationship between organizational dissent and aggressive communication. *Management Communication Quaterly, 13*, 100–155.

Martin, M. M., Anderson, C. M., & Sirimangkala, P. (1997, April). *The relationship between use of organizational conflict strategies with socio-communicative style and aggressive communication traits.* Paper presented at the annual meeting of the Eastern Communication Association, Baltimore, MD.

Martin, M. M., Dunleavy, K. N., & Kennedy-Lightsey, C. D. (2010). The instrumental use of verbally aggressive messages. In T. A. Avtgis & A. S. Rancer (Eds.), *Arguments, aggression, and conflict: New directions in theory and research* (pp. 400–416). New York: Routledge.

McCroskey, J. C., & Richmond, V. P. (1990). Willingness to communicate: Differing cultural perspectives. *Southern Communication Journal, 56*, 72–77.

McGregor, D. (1960). *The human side of enterprise.* New York, NY: McGraw-Hill.

Norton, R. W. (1978). Foundation of a communicator construct. *Human Communication Research, 4*, 99–112.

Rancer, A. S., Whitecap, V., Kosberg, R. L., & Avtgis, T. A. (1997). Testing the efficacy of a communication training program to increase argumentativeness and argumentative behavior in adolescents. *Communication Education, 46*, 273–286.

Redding, C. W. (1966). The empirical study of human communication in business and industry. In P. E. Ried (Ed.), *Frontiers in experimental speech communication research* (pp. 47–81). Syracuse, NY: Syracuse University Press.

Ouchi, W. G. (1981). *Theory Z: How American business can meet the Japanese challenge.* Reading, MA: Addison-Wesley.

Spencer, D. G. (1986). Employee voice and employee retention. *The Academy of Management Journal, 29,* 488–502.

Chapter 20
Genderlect Theory:
Applications to Public Relations

Roxana D. Maiorescu-Murphy, Ph.D., *Emerson University*

Defined as "a strategic communication process that builds mutually beneficial relationships between organizations and their publics" (Elliott, 2012), the public relations process revolves predominantly around the practitioners' communication skills that enable the development and maintaining of relationships with outside stakeholder groups, such as consumers, journalists, and government officials, as well as internal groups, such as employees, shareholders, and executives. The public relations industry is dominated by women, yet most of the leadership positions are held by male professionals (Mundy, 2016; Sha, 2013; Vardeman-Winter & Place, 2017). In addition, women have remained significantly underpaid compared to their male colleagues (Dozier, Sha, & Shen, 2013; Hazleton & Sha, 2012; Sha, 2013). While a multitude of factors may inform these imbalances, the Genderlect Theory can provide a paramount explanation: women and men communicate differently. Women communicate to build relationships, which could explain why an industry like public relations, which revolves around relationship management, is dominated by female professionals (Maiorescu, 2016). Men communicate to gain or maintain status, which makes their speech more assertive, a possible explanation for salary and promotion negotiation (Leibbrandt & List, 2014).

Yet, the Genderlect Theory goes beyond shedding light on the dynamics extant in the public relations industry to inform the very practice of the profession. For example, professionals coach leadership teams to enable high-quality relationships between employees and managers, perform "issues scanning" to ascertain the problems that consumers and activist groups may raise with regard to a company's products or business operations, assist organizations in responding to crises, and are in charge of social and traditional media communication (Theaker & Yaxley, 2017). In their many functions and endeavors to build and maintain relationships, practitioners face gender dynamics and divergent communication styles. Hence, an understanding of the Genderlect Theory becomes relevant for effective public relations. This chapter provides an insight into the Genderlect Theory and highlights its practical applications. The next sections detail the main tenets of genderlect and provide practical applications. At a later stage, the chapter discusses concerns with regard to the applicability of the theory.

Communicating for a Goal vs. Communicating for Relationships

As an instructor of communication, I have oftentimes been asked by my students to apply a theoretical lens and interpret their text message exchanges. It seemed as though the empirical research behind the concepts discussed in the classroom prompted them to confidently test and experiment with theories in an effort to address the challenges of college life. My communication degree, albeit with a public relations focus, had suddenly transformed me into a relationship guru. I vividly remember an April morning and the pressure I was under to finish a manuscript submission by the deadline. As I was giving my manuscript a last-minute facelift, a student entered my office. Looking dejected, she held out her smartphone and asked me to read the "terrible text" that her boyfriend had just sent her. "It's over," she said. "It's all over." As a committed teacher, I left my work behind and read the message in a heartbeat. "Happy birthday." It was the most refreshing break that I could have taken from my research. "You need the Genderlect Theory," I responded, and found it hard to stifle a smile. Deborah Tannen's Genderlect Theory (2013) provides a superb insight into the misunderstanding of the preceding birthday wishes. Men communicate for a goal; women communicate to maintain relationships. While my student perceived the message as distant, cold, and therefore an indication of a possible breakup, her boyfriend's goal was to wish her a "Happy birthday." Probably caught up in a busy morning, he left out the communication context that she was expecting; what plans did he have for her special day?

My mind was put at ease a few days later, when I was informed that the situation was under control and that the Genderlect Theory did, indeed, help to address it. This example represents an effective illustration of the nexus of the Genderlect Theory: men's and women's communication styles are so divergent that they can be easily classified as different dialects (Tannen, 2013), hence the name of the theory, "Genderlect." Yet what triggers these divergent communication styles? Gillian (2003) argues that men and women are socialized differently; these differences emerge from childhood, as girls begin to play cooperative games and boys competitive ones. In time, this socialization engenders different perspectives and women emphasize interconnectedness, while men value hierarchies, rules, and independence (Griffin, 2014). Consequently, women engage in rapport talk, which is symmetrical and effective in making connections and forming close bonds, while men communicate asymmetrically to deliver information, win arguments, and/or demand attention (Tannen, 2013).

Let's assume Richard Roe is the director of research and development (R&D) at a pharmaceutical company in New York City. He convenes a 2:00 p.m, meeting with his 40 subordinates. Richard arrives on time, hands out copies of the meeting's agenda, and addresses his team: "Good afternoon, everyone. Four important points to discuss today. Let's get started so we can finish in 30 minutes and resume work." Richard communicates for a purpose. There is no room for superfluous language, as the meeting should be over in 30 minutes and the team should return to work. Jane Doe has been working for Richard Roe for three months. She relocated from Texas. She is new and feels overwhelmed. Her demanding position prevents her from making friends outside the workplace and her colleagues barely talk to one another or to her. She feels it would be nice if Richard at least asked them how they were doing. In this case, Richard's communication meets a purpose, but fails to create relationships between him and employees on the one hand, and among employees on the other hand. Having high-quality relationships with their leader would make the R&D team feel valued, increase their work commitment, and increase their identification with the company's mission, all of which would help to forestall turnover (Cropanzano, Dasborough, & Weiss, 2017). By communicating and relating to employees, Richard would set the tone for a more positive internal culture that derives from increased interactions among employees. In turn, the internal culture would boost employee morale and increase productivity.

Assume Richard Roe retires 10 years later. Jane Doe is promoted to director of R&D. She plans to convene a 30-minute meeting. The meeting will take place on the following Thursday at 1:00 p.m. It is Friday morning, and Jane emails an initial draft of the meeting's agenda to her team. She asks them if there is anything else they would like to discuss and encourages them to edit the agenda, if needed. By Thursday, she notices that her initial discussion points have doubled. She shows up 10 minutes prior to the meeting and talks to her team members. She asks them about their days, their families, their kids, and remembers that Anne had laser eye surgery last week. She approaches Anne to see how it went. It is 1:00 p.m. now and it's time for the meeting to start. With her well-known punctuality, Jane commences the discussion. She wants to get everyone's input about a new product line and ensures that she discusses every additional point on the agenda that her colleagues proposed. The meeting lasts for an hour and 10 minutes. In this case, Jane successfully maintains relationships with her subordinates by relating to them;

she knows them on a personal level, she respects and values their opinions, and makes sure that everyone's voice becomes part of the decision-making process. Jane communicates to connect and bond, which in turn enables her to trigger a collaborative, internal culture, as employees feel comfortable sharing information. In addition, they enjoy spending time at work, they deeply trust Jane, and they do not mind working overtime if she asks them. After all, she is a team player and works overtime, too, if needed to make her department succeed. However, Jane's relationship management approach is time-consuming. The meeting lasted more than it should have and her constant requests for employee input leaves both her and her team less time to focus on the actual research behind the new product line.

Which communication style is more effective? Richard's *report talk* enables him to meet business objectives, but leaves employees demotivated, less committed, and more inclined to try their luck on the job market. Conversely, Jane's *rapport talk* is generating employee loyalty and increased commitment, but requires extensive time that could be used to meet business goals. Public relations practitioners would recommend that the two communication styles be blended. (Maiorescu, 2016; Tannen, 2013). A leader should communicate both to achieve a goal and to build relationships. They would ask Jane to delegate employee feedback to the public relations department. The public relations department would send out the meeting's agenda and suggest employee feedback. Jane would then be informed of her colleagues' recommendation and would be advised to prioritize them. She should continue to show up a few minutes before the meeting starts to maintain relationships with her coworkers. However, five minutes would likely suffice. Jane should communicate why certain points did not make it to the agenda and attempt to address them through other means, such as delegating responsibility to her personal assistant. By acknowledging which points could not be addressed and discussing how she plans to tackle them at a later time, Jane values her colleagues' feedback, their high-quality relationship continues, and the meeting becomes less time-consuming. In sum, both report and rapport talk are equally valid and one should draw from both in order to be effective in the workplace and beyond (Tannen, 2013).

Facing Conflict vs. Avoiding Conflict

Because men communicate for status, they see an opportunity to gain respect and recognition even when faced with a conflict (Tannen, 2013). Conversely, women are inclined to avert it, as they perceive that it may negatively impact their already-established relationships (Tannen, 2013). Consider *Wells Fargo's* cross-selling scandal that erupted in 2016 and revealed over 3.5 million fake accounts that employees opened in an effort to meet unrealistic sales goals imposed by management (Egan, 2016; 2017). In September 2016, *Wells Fargo's* CEO John Stumpf testified before the Senate Banking Committee and admitted to his company's wrongdoing, but refused to step down, despite repeated calls (Egan, 2016). From the perspective of the Genderlect Theory, his gesture can be interpreted as an attempt to redress the company in order to regain respect. Successfully managing the crisis to restore consumer trust represents an opportunity for status reaffirmation. In a crisis similar to *Wells Fargo*, public relations professionals would advise the executive board on the possible implications of the CEO's resignation. John Stumpf did eventually resign in October 2016, which, from a public relations perspective, sends an important signal about the company's intention to distance itself from the past and start anew.

Conversely, the Genderlect Theory indicates that women may be likely to avoid crises altogether (Geier, 2015). In 2015, the United States Environmental Protection Agency (EPA) revealed that Volkswagen sold around 11 million cars that passed emission tests through a "defeat device," which was installed during tests in an attempt to avoid environmental legislation (Geier, 2015). Referring to the scandal, Eileen Naughton, *Google UK's* managing director, made the following statement:

> Imagine a woman engineer…knowingly tricking that technology…when it's not allowable by law…I believe women have different ways of taking risks…of ruminating…before they jump to conclusions (Sanghani, 2015).

Her statement implies that women leaders may have averted the crisis as a result of their concern for others, which is an important tenet of the Genderlect Theory. In addition, a crisis negatively impacts relationships with consumers, probably to the point to which the damage is irreparable. Hence, women focus on avoiding conflicts and could potentially avoid corporate scandals (Geier, 2015). Eileen Naughton's statement implies that women leaders would have communicated clear rules and set strict ethical expectations or, if employees had engaged in unethical behavior, the crisis would have been promptly addressed and the consumers informed in due time. Consequently, from a public relations perspective, the actions of female leaders (concern for consumers and a focus on maintaining their trust) represent effective means to retain corporate reputation and can save companies from the negative impact of a scandal on business operations.

Justice in Context vs. Justice as Fairness

Interestingly, when faced with a conflict, past research has found that a woman's response is context-dependent. For women, justice tends to be enmeshed in personal relationships (Gillian, 2003), while for men, decision-making remains independent of connecting and bonding. When faced with a conflict, women's decisions are more likely to be made after an in-depth discussion with the parties involved, while a man's approach is more likely to involve a discussion after they have proposed a resolution (Griffin, 2014). Suppose William Bruce is a team leader in a call center. The call center has strict rules with regard to employee punctuality. Sally Hudson has been working as a customer care representative for nearly a year. She is a college student who works to support herself. She has always been punctual, but, now, the final exams are taking a toll. She oversleeps. William Bruce gives her an official warning and reinforces the rules; if she is late once more, she loses her job. Sally explains her situation in detail, and William tries to be empathetic: "Sally, it is tough, and I am sorry you are going through this, but we have rules, and they apply to everyone. There is nothing I can do. You have to be here on time." Sally shares the discussion with her colleagues. They understand her, yet they are content; while William reinforces the rules so drastically, they perceive him as fair, in contrast to their former manager, Anne, who they believe was playing favorites. Anne seemed to overlook tardiness and bend the rules for those in college, employees with kids, and whoever else she felt was struggling outside of the workplace. While those employees loved her, college graduates and single employees felt they carried the call center on their shoulders.

In this hypothetical example, public relations practitioners recommend applying the rules consistently and within a relationship framework (Shore et al., 2011). Specifically, while William should reinforce the policies, he should actively listen to Sally's concerns, rather than dismiss them. In many cases, we find that employees feel that their concerns are addressed if their leaders solely listen, and nothing more. In addition, William could find an alternative schedule for Sally that enables her to more efficiently juggle between final exams and customer service. An effective strategy that William can enact is to ask Sally for solutions: "What do you think would work best for you in terms of your schedule?" By asking Sally directly, William maintains a relationship of trust. In addition, it saves him time, as Sally would lay out several possible solutions that they could analyze together. Consequently, it is encouraged that justice, or, more specifically, problem solving, should be approached by a combination of female and male communication (Maiorescu, 2016).

Weak Communication vs. Strong Communication

Studies on genderlect determined that women's rapport talk may be perceived as weak (Zahn, 1989) as a result of several language markers it entails that, while conducive to relationship building, may put women in an inferior position. These elements connote that women tend to put others' needs first (Maiorescu, 2016) and refrain from imposing their views on others (Osoba, 2016). This, in turn, leaves their discourse less assertive than that of men. Tannen (2013) provided several indicatives of weak talk among which hedges ("I guess," "kinda"), hesitations ("ah," "um"), fillers ("like"), disclaimers ("I might be wrong, but..."), qualifiers ("so very much"), and overly polite forms ("I am sorry, if you wouldn't mind, could you please..."). While women's talk is perceived as having aesthetic quality, men's communication style leads to perceptions of dynamism (Zahn, 1989; Mulac et al., 1983). Past research showed that women's talk renders them less confident, less powerful, less attractive, and less aggressive, all of which may lead to stereotyping in the workplace (Goldberg, 2011). Remember Richard Roe and Jane Doe from the preceding paragraphs? Apparently, Richard Roe was forced to retire after the company had faced a crisis. As a result of Richard's communication style, employees failed to share relevant information about the development of a new baby powder called "MaDa." MaDa was launched with a lot of publicity and brought huge profits in the first few weeks, until a Facebook group was created by concerned parents who shared pictures of their babies' rashes. The public relations department brought the consumers' concerns to Richard's attention, who, in turn, asked top management to investigate the matter. It was revealed that egregious mistakes were made in the development of MaDa and that several team members had been aware of the situation before the product was launched. So why didn't they speak up? The investigation revealed that Richard's subordinates feared his leadership style. Because no relationships had been previously established, employees did not trust him well enough to expose their mistakes. They feared losing their jobs. The company held a press conference to respond to the crisis and Richard addressed the media, as follows:

> "We are sorry that we launched a hazardous product into the market and regret the harm we caused. We conducted an internal investigation that revealed that human error led to the development of a product that we have now completely recalled from the market. If we had known this from the start we never would have allowed the launch of MaDa.
>
> We ask parents to visit our official website and submit a request for compensation. Thank you."

Note his strong communication style. While admitting guilt, the strong and assertive statement implicitly defends the company and its management. Concern for others (consumers) fails to emerge as a priority. Compare Richard's response to the one provided by Jane Doe, as journalists asked her a follow-up question:

> "Before I respond to your question regarding the investigation I first want to say how so very sorry we are for all the harm that we have caused. We understand very well that our negligence has put children at risk, and we are

committed to communicating with each and every parent to determine the best solution. While our investigation revealed that MaDa's negative effects are only short-term, we remain fully committed to addressing our mistakes and to regaining the full trust of our consumers. I guess we will have to take a closer look at our structure and determine ways to…um…break down internal siloes so that there will never ever be a situation like this again."

The public relations department analyzed the media coverage and determined that media outlets that cited Jane wrote less negatively about the crisis. They argue that Jane's focus on the consumer and her deep regret for the crisis were the ingredients of a successful crisis response. Indeed, Jane spoke according to what Tannen (2013) refers to as weak speech/rapport talk. She put the needs of others (consumers) first and communicated by taking a relationship management approach to rebuild trust. However, the public relations department recommends that, in the future, Jane stop using language that may lead consumers to feel the company does not control the crisis. (Notice Jane's use of hesitations, such as "um," the hedge "I guess," and the qualifiers "so" and "never ever.") Without these language markers, Jane's statement would have been a mix of weak and strong communication that is especially effective in reestablishing trust in the company, while showing that management is in control of the crisis, takes corrective action, and ensures that the recall is a one-time unfortunate event (Maiorescu, 2016).

Conclusion

In academia, the Genderlect Theory has brought an appreciation of two divergent communication styles and the reconciliation of gender differences. By focusing on the strengths and weaknesses of female and male communication, Tannen's (2013) research informs the public relations practice in areas such as internal and external relationships, leadership, and organizational culture. Above all, if implemented, it has the potential to bring about positive changes for organizations and society: a focus on product safety, efficiency, the well-being of employees, and the promotion of women in the workplace.

It is worth mentioning that researchers are encouraging the study of genderlect in connection with additional variables among which the interactants' cognitive styles, along with the context in which the communication process takes place. Specifically, Elmer (2008) contended that the genderlect theory failed to make allowances for an individual's intraversion/extraversion, and Motschenbacker (2007) argued for the importance of studying the context in which men and women communicate. In a recent a study on Twitter communication of sports journalists, Kaiser (2016) found that, while several tenets of the genderlect were present in the way sport journalists communicated with their followers, women journalists tried to match the online influence of their male colleagues by making use of "professional sports reporting conventions" (p. 772). Consequently, online environments may have the potential to break down traditional gender barriers. In a similar vein, Kunkel & Burleson (1999) found that in the context of comforting communication, both men and women place value on delivering person-centered messages, namely communication that focuses on the "other." Additional studies (i.e., MacGeorge et al., 2004) revealed that the similarities between women and men's supportive communication outweighed the differences. Finally, more research is needed to investigate genderlect with regard to the socialization of children in nontraditional families. We have yet to learn whether, in adulthood, women exhibit an assertive communication style if they were raised solely by their fathers and socialized in a predominantly male environment. Future research should also shed light on the experiences of transgender individuals and their impact on communication styles.

Regardless of the gaps that researchers still need to address in terms of the genderlect, the theory remains of paramount importance for the field of public relations. By shedding light on the divergent communication styles that stem from gender differences, it enables public relations practitioners to successfully develop and maintain relationships with stakeholder groups while navigating possible tensions that may result from miscommunication.

Discussion Questions

1. In your personal and/or professional experience have you encountered differences between female and male communication styles that the chapter has not addressed?

2. Think about your own upbringing. How did it influence your present communication style? Are you predominantly goal-oriented or relationship-oriented?

3. If you were to study the tweets you posted in the past twelve months, would your communication style online differ from how you communicate in

offline settings? If present, what could have triggered these differences? To conduct the analysis, download your tweets (or take screenshots) and save them in a word document. Check every tweet and determine whether it is goal-oriented/assertive, relationship-oriented, or both. Sum up your results. Next time you go out with your friends, try to analyze your communication style. Are you the type of friend who puts the others' needs first or do you tend to be concerned with gaining and/or maintaining status in your group? Do you avoid confrontations or do you enjoy facing them? If you are fascinated by your findings and want to explore the topic more, talk to your communication professor and consider a directed study. You could contribute to the development of the communication field by addressing the present gap in the literature; can the genderlect theory inform online communication?

4. You have just been hired by Apple. You are excited to start your new job. You met your boss, Kathy Williams, during your interview. She was affable but seemed extremely tough. What do you think triggered her very goal-oriented and assertive communication style? After all, you learned in school that women communicate to form and maintain relationships. Would her communication style enable you to grow professionally?

REFERENCES

Cropanzano, R., Dasborough, M. T., & Weiss, H. M. (2017). Affective events and the development of leader-member exchange. *Academy of Management Review, 42*(2), 233–258.

Dozier, D. M., Sha, B. L., & Shen, H. (2013). Why women earn less than men: The cost of gender discrimination in US public relations. *Public Relations Journal, 7*(1), 1–21.

Egan, M. (2016, September 22). Wells Fargo CEO denies orchestrated fraud in accounts scandal. *CNN.* Retrieved from http://cnnmon.ie/2GMkd7e

Egan, M. (2017, August 31). Wells Fargo uncovers up to 1.4 million more fake accounts. *CNN.* Retrieved from http://cnnmon.ie/2vvmNMV

Elliott, S. (2012, March 1). Public relations defined, after an energetic public discussion. *The New York Times*, pp. B2.

Elmer, J. (2008). Genderlect and the MBTI: Creating social coding theory. *ERGO Undergraduate Research Journal, 2.* Retrieved from http://bit.ly/2Ebieut

Geier, B. (2015, September 22). Everything to know about Volkswagen's emission crisis. *Fortune.* Retrieved from http://for.tn/1nPPfjK

Gilligan, C. (2003). *In a different voice. Psychological theory and women's development.* Cambridge, MA: Harvard University Press.

Goldberg, M. (1994). Sex stereotypes as a function of genderlect. *Totem: The University of Western Ontario Journal of Anthropology, 1*(13), 75–79.

Griffin, E. (2014). *A first look at communication theory* (9th Ed.). New York, NY: McGraw Hill.

Hazleton, V., & Sha, B. L. (2012). Generalizing from PRSA to public relations: How to accommodate sampling bias in public relations scholarship. *Public Relations Review, 38*(3), 438–445.

Kaiser, K. (2016). Sports reporters in the Twittersphere: Challenging and breaking down traditional conceptualizations of genderlect. *Online Information Review, 40*(6), 761–784.

Kunkel, A. W., & Burleson, B. R. (1999). Assessing explanations for sex differences in emotional support: A test of the different cultures and skill specialization accounts. *Human Communication Research, 25,* 307–340.

Leibbrandt, A., & List, J. A. (2014). Do women avoid salary negotiations? Evidence from a large-scale natural field experiment. *Management Science, 61*(9), 2016–2024.

MacGeorge, E. L., Graves, A. R., Feng, B., Gillihan, S. J., & Burleson, B. R. (2004). The myth of gender cultures: Similarities outweigh differences in men's and women's provision of and responses to supportive communication. *Sex Roles, 50,* 143–175.

Maiorescu, R.D. (2016). Crisis management at General Motors and Toyota. An analysis of gender specific communication and media coverage. *Public Relations Review, 42*(2), 556–563.

Motschenbacher, H. (2007). Can the term 'genderlect' be saved? A postmodernist re-definition. *Gender & Language, 1*(2), 255–278.

Mulac, A., Wiemann, J. M., Yoerks, S. W., & Gibson, T. W. (1983, July). Male/female language differences and their effects in like-sex and mixed-sex dyads: A test of interpersonal accommodation and the gender-linked language effect. In *Second International Conference, Social Psychology and Language, Bristol, England.*

Mundy, D. E. (2016). Bridging the divide: A multidisciplinary analysis of diversity research and the implications for public relations. *Research Journal of the Institute for Public Relations, 3*(1), 1–28. Retrieved from https://bit.ly/2l5yNgc

Osoba, J.B. (2016). Genderlect as discourse in Yoruba movies. Crossroads. *A journal of English studies, 1,* 31–47.

Sanghani, R. (2015, October 21). Google boss: 'Volkswagen scandal wouldn't have happened if more women were in charge.' *The Telegraph.* Retrieved from http://bit.ly/1GvfHaN

Sha, B-L. (2013). Diversity in public relations: Special issue editor's note. *Public Relations Journal, 7*(2), 1–7.

Shore, L. M., Randel, A. E., Chung, B. G., Dean, M. A., Holcombe Ehrhart, K., & Singh, G. (2011). Inclusion and diversity in work groups: A review and model for future research. *Journal of Management, 37*(4), 1262–1289.

Tannen, D. (2013). *You just don't understand. Women and men in conversation.* New York, NY: HarperCollins.

Theaker, A., & Yaxley, H. (2017). *The Public Relations Strategic Toolkit: An essential guide to successful public relations practice.* New York, NY: Routledge.

Vardeman-Winter, J., & Place, K. R. (2017). Still a lily-white field of women: The state of workforce diversity in public relations practice and research. *Public Relations Review, 43*(2), 326–336.

Zahn, C.J. The bases for differing evaluations of male and female speech: Evidence from ratings of transcribed conversation. *Communication Monographs, 56,* 59–74.

Chapter 21

Thinking About Interpersonal Relationships and Social Penetration Theory: Is It the Same for Lesbian, Gay, or Bisexual People?

Jimmie Manning, Ph.D., *University of Nevada, Reno*

"Just got off the worst date of my life," the first text said, followed immediately by another. "THE. WORST."

"Should I call?" I responded. Almost immediately after sending the text, I got a call.

"You wouldn't believe this guy!" she said, not even offering a hello.

"What happened?"

"He told me his entire life story with lots of personal information," she responded. "He kept giving me details about things I did *not* need to know!"

"Like what?" I asked, not ready for the answer.

"For starters," she said, "he asked me if I had an STD. Uncomfortable, right? So I'm sitting there, saying nothing in response, my mouth probably hanging wide open, and he starts to tell me about every STD he's ever had!"

"What?" I asked, more than a bit shocked.

"Then," she said, "he goes into some conspiracy theory about how he thinks his dad really died from an STD. Then he tells me the story of his dad, how his dad was an alcoholic, intimate details about his parents' fights… and then, you won't believe this, Jimmie…"

"What?" I asked, wondering how things could get any worse.

"He started crying! Right in the middle of the restaurant." She let out an exasperated sigh. "I didn't know what to do, so I gave him my napkin."

"Oh no," I responded, trying to hold back my laughter and be supportive.

"But wait! Then he starts apologizing and asking me if I saw him as 'womanly'!"

"Do you?" I couldn't control my laughter at this point.

"Yes! He told me that his last girlfriend emasculated him, and so now he felt guilty about crying."

"So what did you do?" I asked, trying to imagine how I would respond to such an awkward situation.

"I pretended to get a text from my parents who needed help," she responded.

"But your parents live in Kansas!"

"He doesn't know that," she told me. "And he never will. I am 100% ghosting out on this guy. Too much, too soon, no way."

Although no theory can eliminate every awkward moment, the theory that is the topic of this chapter, *social penetration theory*, can help to explain why what happened on the date described at the beginning of this chapter was so uncomfortable. Moreover, the theory helps to predict the outcome of the first-date conversation described by the woman there: that a relational partner—defined in this chapter as one of two or more people who interact in or with the potential for a relationship—decided to terminate future communication and stop the relationship development process. According to social penetration theory, relationships have four stages that people can go through as they become more intimate with each other (Altman & Taylor, 1973). Soon in this chapter, each of the four stages will be described and explained in detail. Although social penetration theory has four stages, in many relationships—such as the relationship in the story that opened this chapter—people do not go through all four stages to fully develop what they, or others, might call a relationship.

Specifically, my friend felt overwhelmed on the date by the amount (breadth) and intimate nature (depth) of the information she was learning. A good understanding of social penetration theory could have helped both her and the man she was dating to better understand what was happening in the situation; in response, they both could have had the opportunity to adjust their communication practices to make the date more comfortable. Specifically, if the man on the date knew social penetration theory, then he would understand that too much personal information too soon can make the other person in the conversation feel uncomfortable. As a result, it is less likely that the relationship will continue to develop. As for my friend: Even though knowing the theory probably would not allow her to stop her date from disclosing so much personal information, it could have helped to calm her as she realized why the communication that was occurring made her feel so uncomfortable. Although her story involves romantic social penetration, the theory can also be applied to friendships or social relationships, and examples of how it applies in those situations will be provided later in this chapter. For most relationship types, social penetration theory offers many practical implications for understanding relationship development.

Social Penetration Theory, Interpersonal Communication, and Relationship Development

Social penetration theory was developed by Irwin Altman and Dalmas Taylor and presented in the now-classic book *Social Penetration: The Development of Interpersonal Relationships* in 1973. Although social psychologists by training, the theory they presented relied on interpersonal communication practices as much as, if not more than, the psychological processes that occur when relationships are developed. Altman and Taylor's (1973) presentation of social penetration theory details three functions regarding relationship development. Specifically, the theory describes how *relationships advance through stages of penetration and depenetration*; helps to explain how *people psychologically respond to interpersonal communication in each stage*; and helps to predict whether *a relationship will advance (or not advance) based on the communication within a given stage*. Each of these three elements are explored in deeper detail here.

Describing Relational Progression: Four Levels of Information Sharing

One key aspect of Altman and Taylor's (1973) social penetration theory is how it examines the information shared by people who are forming a relationship. Specifically, they distinguish among four different levels of information that might be shared by people forming a relationship. To explain each of these four levels of information, they use onions as a metaphor. Specifically, they discuss how, similar to an onion and its layers of skin, layers of information are peeled away by relational partners as they interact. Each level of information that is peeled away in a relationship, similar to when peeling away the layers of an onion, becomes more intense in nature (Taylor & Altman, 1987). The first of these layers, *surface-level information*, includes a person's most basic, easily accessible attributes, such as skin color or gender. For the most part, surface-level information includes things that people can learn simply by looking at another. Going to a second, deeper level, *peripheral-level information* is the information that most people typically feel free to share in any general social circumstance. For example, most people do not mind sharing their first name or what city they are from when they first meet a person. Such information has to be disclosed, meaning that it is not surface level, but it is also fairly easily shared, meaning that it does not go to the third, intermediate level.

This *intermediate-level information* includes topics or details that are not always readily shared, but that also are not the most private of information. For example, someone might not immediately introduce themselves as a Beyoncé fan, but at the same time, revealing such a fact would not be highly personal. At the same time, it is more unique (and perhaps more personal) than simply sharing a name. Finally, the fourth and final category of *central-level information* is considered to be highly private and typically is shared only when someone feels close to another person or that the source is especially trustworthy. In the story that opened this chapter, my friend's date was disclosing a lot of central-level information about him and his family, whereas on many first dates, information tends to be surface, peripheral, and, if things are going well, intermediate.

Further Describing Social Penetration Theory: Four Stages of Relational Development

Although personal information is important, it only accounts for about 21% of talk between relational partners (VanLear, 1987). That means people also use other forms of interaction—including other conversation topics as well as *how* people communicate—to grow closer. Altman and Taylor (1973) account for some of these aspects of relational development by describing four stages that relationships go through as they move from being more superficial in nature to being close and familiar. The first of these stages, *orientation*, typically happens when two people are strangers. This stage involves little to no personal sharing. As one example that relates to how social penetration theory applies to friendship, two men might both be sitting in a Chicago park watching their children play:

Cody: Isn't this great weather?

Lemar: I hear that! I've been working too much. It's nice to spend some time with my kids.

At this point the two men have shared little information about each other. They both have confirmed that they are probably fathers, that they both have a day off from work, and that they are enjoying the weather. These same topics—family, work, and how one spends free time—*could* be considered personal if talked about in depth. However, the nature of initial interaction typically means that these kinds of topics will only be explored at the surface and peripheral levels.

If the two fathers continued to talk, they might go into the intermediate level and learn that they are both Cubs fans:

Lemar: You know, since I moved here, I've been wanting to go to a game. You ever go?

Cody: Just once—but I've been wanting to go again!

This kind of inquiry—one that begins to go deeper into a person's interests and explores common interests—moves the relationship into the second stage of social penetration theory: *exploratory affective exchange*. The question Cody asks Lemar digs deeper into an intermediate-level topic, yet, at the same time, it also leaves the question open to a variety of responses. If Lemar responded with, "We should go sometime!" that would take the interaction even deeper into exploratory affective exchange stage. As these examples suggest, the exploratory affective exchange stage involves talk about more or extended topics, and perhaps at a deeper level. However, those topics are still not as highly personal in their exploration and might even be tentative or even cautious in nature.

As the two men continue to meet up at the parks and have conversations while their children play—and eventually go to Cubs games, introduce their domestic partners to each other, and have social outings—they will almost certainly move into the *affective exchange stage*. In addition to increased disclosures at the intermediate and even central levels, they might also recognize their friendship through direct affective statements. These can be indirect remarks ("I'd like to introduce you to my good friend Lemar!") that indicate a relationship or affection as well as more direct statements ("Cody, I just wanted you to know that I've enjoyed having you as a friend."). Such affect can also be demonstrated nonverbally (such as greeting one another with a combination handshake/side-hug) or through the roles played in each other's lives (such as one friend inviting another to be his child's godfather). Although many friendships fully mature at the affective exchange stage, some of the best friendships might move into the fourth and final stage, *stable exchange*, where communication is generally open at all levels and where both partners feel quite comfortable with revealing lots of central information.

It is important to consider that social penetration is not a guide for how relationships *should* progress, but, rather, is a description of how they *tend to* progress (Carpenter & Greene, 2016). In most cases, a social relationship will never go beyond the orientation stage and will involve only surface or periphery information. The truth is that people only have so much time, emotional energy, and relational resources to share, and so many relationships will be social, while only a few will move to the later stages of social penetration theory to become deeply personal relationships. It is also important to consider that relationships are not necessarily bad because they do not progress through these steps in order (Mongeau and Miller Henningsen, 2015). Although advancing too quickly might be uncomfortable and undesirable for some—just as it was for my friend who had the bad date described at the beginning of the chapter—some will instantly feel comfortable with another person and open up quickly, similar to the two friends described earlier in this chapter who met and interacted with their kids at the park. Many people have some friendships that do not involve much social penetration, and those can be rewarding as well. Again, social penetration theory is not a rule for how relationships *should* progress, but instead helps to describe, predict, and explain how they typically come into being.

Explaining and Predicting Relational Progression: Reciprocity and Rewards

One of the most beneficial aspects of social penetration theory is that it helps to explain why some relationships develop quickly and others do not develop at all. Considering three aspects of interpersonal communication can help to predict whether a relationship will develop or not. First, Altman and Taylor (1973) suggest that interpersonal communication is often most comfortable when it is *reciprocal* in nature. That is, relational partners should be mirroring each other in terms of the breadth and depth of information they reveal. More specifically, *breadth* relates to what topics might be talked about. In the early stages of a relationship, topics are limited and are often less personal. If someone violates that unspoken rule, such as by trying to bring up talk about a topic like politics, it could make a relational partner feel uncomfortable. *Depth*, on the other hand, refers to how intimate talk about a particular topic might become. If someone simply says, "I tend to have opinions about politics," the comment certainly indicates something about a person but, because it does not go into too much detail, does not involve a lot of depth.

However, if a person immediately declared a political party, gave specific opinions of politicians, and belittled people who did not have similar ideological views, then he might alienate a relational partner because it is too much too soon. Rather, in most cases, social penetration would happen more smoothly and perhaps move to later stages if both relational partners are gradually approaching political topics and, based on each other's cues, offering more information. As this all suggests, if one partner tries to broach too many topics and go too deep into those topics too soon, that could violate that sense of reciprocity and make the other no longer want to interact. In relationships that continue into later stages, it is often because partners were picking up on each other's exploratory affective exchange cues and gradually revealing more central-level information.

Beyond reciprocity, Altman and Taylor (1973) also argue that *rewards* often determine interest and need for relationships. Specifically, they outline how every relationship has its costs (efforts or resources put into it) and rewards (the benefits of being in a relationship, such as affection or even tangible resources such as money or gifts). People tend to stay in relationships where the perceived costs are limited as compared to the perceived rewards, especially in comparison to other relationship options they might have (Kelley & Thibaut, 1978). When someone no longer is in a relationship they perceive as rewarding, that might begin a process of *social depenetration*, or the undoing of a relationship. It is important to note, however, that not all aspects of friendship are determined by awards. As Rawlins (2008) notes, sometimes a relationship in and of itself is rewarding; it does not always trace back to a neat equation of costs and rewards.

Disrupting Social Penetration Theory: Sexual Identity and Relationships

Although social penetration theory is quite useful for understanding how relationships develop, it does have its limitations. In their review of the theory, Mongeau and Miller Henningsen (2015) list several critiques, including that the theory is better for understanding romantic relationships than friendships; and that the theory might not do the best at accounting for lesbian, gay, bisexual, and transgender (LGBT) relationships. Often, when critiques are made about a particular theory, scholars then test or explore the theory's limitations using a social scientific research study. For this chapter's case study, qualitative research data are used with empirical analysis to do just that: examine how well social penetration theory accounts for sexual identity. Specifically, the remainder of this chapter will focus on coming out, or "the process by which individuals come to recognize that they have romantic or sexual feelings toward members of their own gender, adopt lesbian or gay (or bisexual) identities, and then share these identities with others" (Rust, 2003, p. 227).

In Adams's (2011) study of coming out, he found that when a LGB person came out to someone, the recipient of the coming out disclosure often felt as if it were strange, as they were hearing something deep and personal about a person they thought they knew so well already. Considering that finding through a social penetration theory lens, it would appear that Mongeau and Miller Henningsen's (2015) critique was warranted; LGB identity might be a factor that makes social penetration theory happen differently. To explore this, I used 290 coming out stories shared by participants for three previous research studies (Manning, 2014, 2015a, 2015b) to do thematic analysis (Braun & Clarke, 2006) related to the following research question: How does social penetration theory appear in stories of coming out? The results of this analysis yielded two relevant themes regarding how social penetration theory might be interpreted in relationships where a LGB person is involved. Each is explained here with data from the study.

Revealing LGB Identity in Newer Relationships: Flexible Information Levels

One key consideration regarding coming out and social penetration theory is that nonheterosexual identity—in the case of this study, a person who is lesbian, gay, or bisexual—was often treated as personal information. However, unlike most personal information in social penetration theory, where what is being shared is more uniformly considered to be at one information-sharing level (e.g., serious illness is almost always considered to be central-level information) for most people, the participants in this study saw their sexual identities as being at many different information-sharing levels based on their personal experiences. Remember, earlier in this chapter you learned that most kinds of information are fairly stable in terms of what level they belonged to in terms of information type. Someone's gender is almost always going to be surface-level information, a name would be considered peripheral-level information, and so on and so forth. Sexual identity in newer relationships, however, might be considered surface-level information, peripheral-level information, *or* intermediate-level information depending on the circumstances, as the examples included here help to illustrate.

"People can usually tell I'm gay": surface-level information. For some LGB people, they explained that it was evident they are gay. As one 21-year old man indicated, "Hello, I have rainbows on every other piece of clothing, I wear makeup, and I am not afraid to use gestures. People already know I'm gay before they even talk to me." Another 21-year old man shared, "Sometimes people don't read me as gay, but I guess I'm a little stereotypical. I'm clean, neat, dress well, and all of that. So usually they know fairly quickly because, I guess because of my appearance." A 40-year old woman shared similar life experience, explaining, "I don't have a wedding ring, my hair is short, I'm thicker—yeah, people probably think, 'Oh yeah, she's a lesbian' and so I don't really have to come out. They already know." For these participants, sexual identity would be considered surface-level information because they feel as if cultural markers of sexual identity indicate who they are even before a first word is exchanged in a new relationship.

"I'm really comfortable with who I am": peripheral-level information. Others, however, said that they did not believe people instantly saw them as lesbian, gay, or bisexual but that, because of their comfort level, it was something they would share fairly quickly. As one 32-year old woman said, "It's not like I go, 'Hi, I'm Roseanna, I'm gay.' But usually I let people know pretty quickly." A 45-year old man shared, "Almost always I try to come out at the beginning of a first conversation with someone. I, I'm proud of who I am and what I've done, and so you could say that it is a form of activism." Others shared stories that were less related to personal-political reasons and that were more matter of fact. As one 25-year-old woman shared, "Yeah, in class introductions or when I work with a new work team or whatever I usually say, 'Yeah, I'm Annie and I come from Lubbock and I'm a lesbian.' I just kind of always put it out there." As these comments indicate, for some it might not be immediately obvious, but their sexual identity is something they share rather quickly and without much hesitation, making it peripheral-level in nature.

"She seemed cool, so I told her": intermediate-level information. Other LGB study participants were more reserved about who they told and saw coming out as more personal in nature. "If I gel with someone, if we're getting more personal about the details we are sharing, then I will just tell her," said one 23-year old man. A 31-year old man shared a similar opinion, noting, "I don't always feel it's any-one's business, and most people can't tell, I don't think, but when I feel closer to someone and we're more than just a work friend or a neighbor, then I'll let them know." A 51-year old woman took a slightly different perspective, saying,

> Sometimes I know telling people you're bisexual can make them uncomfort-able, and so if we are talking about relationships I might even hide that I some-times date women. But when we are closer, and I know they might be less judgmental, that makes it easier to come out to them. I might not go into great details like I would with my best of friends, but I start to let them know that, yeah, I'm bi.

Her explanation clearly highlights the possibility for sexual identity to be intermediate-level information in a social penetration theory process.

Already Close Relationships: LGB Identity as Relational Reorientation

The last few examples examined how LGB identity was perceived as information in newer, still developing relationships. Notably different is when a person comes out as LGB in a relationship that has already fully developed. In the case of these fully developed relationships, many participants reported that they had to readjust to their relationships, almost as if their friends or family members were seeing a new them. As a 32-year old man explained, "After I told my mom, she just looked at me for what seemed like an hour but was probably more like 2 or 3 minutes. Then she cried and said, 'I don't even know you.'" Later, the same participant explained that she did know him better than anyone, but not knowing that one aspect made them both feel more distant in their relationship. A similar experience was shared by a 19-year-old woman, who said, "My friend, she kept saying, 'But we're best friends. We tell each other everything. And now I feel like I don't know who my best friend is.'" As the woman also explained, she felt like she and her friend had to "sometimes go back to step one" to relearn things about each other. "We weren't starting over," she said, "but we were learning new things, especially her about me."

As this suggests, those who are LGB felt as if their sexual identity was being perceived as central-level information that they had to reveal; and that when it was revealed, there were often many relational problems that resulted. Space does not permit these problems to be fully explored in this chapter, but those who are interested should read the work from Adams (2011) or Manning (2015b, 2016) that examine how to make coming out more comfortable for all involved, but especially the LGB person who is making such a vulnerable disclosure. That being stated, coming out was not always a sad event, and, in many cases, people were quite flattered when central-level information was shared. As a 22-year old man said, "My big brother, he was a jock and always, I don't know. I didn't want to tell him. But I did, and—he cried. And he hugged me, and he goes, 'I'm so happy you shared this with me.' And now we're closer than ever."

Conclusion

Social penetration theory generally does a good job of helping people to think about how relationships are formed and how communication—both in terms of information-type (surface, peripheral, intermediate, and central) and interaction behaviors (orientation, exploratory affective exchange, effective exchange, and stable exchange)—is involved. The theory also helps to predict, using costs and rewards, whether or not a relationship will continue to develop. As the case study included here indicates, however, particular relationship types might not be as well represented by the theory and future research might be in order. Specifically, for LGB people, their sexual identities—conceptualized as personal information—might especially be flexible in terms of what information-type they represent in a social penetration process. More research, both about LGB people and social exchange theory in general, will be beneficial to helping everyone consider how their relationships develop. This call for more research is especially important given that most of the literature about social penetration theory was developed in the 1970s and 1980s and much of it without data.

On that note, as one of the creators of the theory asserts in writing up scholarship with two other colleagues, "Human social relationships are characterized by openness or contact and closedness or separateness between participants" (Altman, Vinsel, & Brown, 1981, p. 139). It is important to note that it is not simply the sharing of information, and how slowly or quickly that information is shared, that will build a relationship. As Petronio (2002) notes, the content or meaning of that information is also important. Particular topics or ideas could be seen as unappealing or even disgusting to a conversational partner. Those wishing to apply the theory to their own lives should consider that some information, no matter how it is introduced, could have an impact on social penetration or depenetration. Some of the results of the case study in this chapter help to illustrate that point. The research case study in this chapter—particularly the second theme about LGB coming out leading to a reorientation for the relationship—also helps to illustrate another common critique of social penetration theory. Specifically, many scholars argue it is a theory better-suited to describe how new relationships penetrate and depenetrate (Carpenter & Greene, 2016)—and the examples provided in this chapter certainly bolster that claim.

Discussion Questions

1. Social penetration theory uses the onion as a metaphor for how information is shared in relationships. What are the four levels of information? How are they peeled away through interaction?

2. Social penetration theory examines four levels of closeness in relationships. What are these four levels? Is it bad if we do not get through all four levels in all of our relationships?

3. What does it mean to say that relationships often work when they are reciprocal in nature? How can communication be adjusted or considered in order to make relationships more reciprocal.

4. Does social penetration theory apply to all relationships? Why or why not? And can you list specific relationships where social penetration theory might not apply?

REFERENCES

Adams, T. E. (2011). *Narrating the closet: An autoethnography of same-sex attraction*. Walnut Creek, CA: Left Coast.

Altman, I., & Taylor, D. A. (1973). *Social penetration: The development of interpersonal relationships*. New York, NY: Holt, Rinehart, & Winston.

Altman, I., Vinsel, A., & Brown, B. (1981). Dialectic conceptions in social psychology : An application to social penetration and privacy regulation. In L. Berkowitz (Ed.), *Advances in experimental social psychology* (Vol. 14; pp. 107–160). New York, NY: Academic.

Braun, V., & Clarke, V. (2006). Using thematic analysis in psychology. *Qualitative research in psychology, 3*(2), 77–101.

Carpenter, A., & Greene, K. (2016). Social penetration theory. In C. R. Berger, M. E. Roloff, S. R. Wilson, J. P. Dillard, J. Caughlin, & D. Solomon (Eds.), *The international encyclopedia of interpersonal communication* (pp. 1–3). Hoboken, NJ: Wiley. Retrieved from https://wp.comminfo.rutgers.edu/ kgreene/wp-content/uploads/sites/51/2018/02/ACGreene-SPT.pdf

Kelley, H. H., & Thibaut, J. W. (1978). *Interpersonal relationships*. New York, NY: Wiley.

Manning, J. (2014). Coming out conversations and gay/bisexual men's sexual health: A constitutive model study. In V. L. Harvey, & T. H. Housel (Eds.), *Health care disparities and the LGBT population* (pp. 27–54). Lanham, MD: Lexington Books. doi:10.13140/2.1.1867.8089

Manning, J. (2015). Communicating sexual identities: A typology of coming out. *Sexuality & Culture, 19*(1), 122–138. doi:10.1007/s12119-014-9251-4

Manning, J. (2015). Positive and negative communicative behaviors in coming-out conversations. *Journal of homosexuality, 62*(1), 67–97. doi:10.1080/00918 369.2014.957127

Manning, J. (2016). A constitutive model of coming out. In J. Manning, & C. Noland (Eds.), *Contemporary studies of sexuality & communication: Theoretical and applied perspectives* (pp. 93–108). Dubuque, IA: Kendall Hunt.

Mongeau, P. A., & Miller Henningsen, M. L. (2015). Stage theories of relationship development: Charting the course of interpersonal communication. In D. O. Braithwaite & P. Schrodt (Eds.), *Engaging theories in interpersonal communication: Multiple perspectives* (2nd ed.; pp. 389–402). Thousand Oaks, CA: Sage.

Petronio, S. (2002). *Boundaries of privacy: Dialectics of disclosure*. Albany, NY: State University of New York.

Rawlins, W. K. (2008). *The compass of friendship: Narratives, identities, and dialogues*. Thousand Oaks, CA: Sage.

Rust, P. C. (2003). Finding a sexual identity and community: Therapeutic implications and cultural assumptions in scientific models of coming out. In L. D. Garnets, & D. C. Kimmel (Eds.), *Psychological perspectives on lesbian, gay and bisexual experiences* (pp. 227–69). New York: Columbia University.

Taylor, D. & Altman, I. (1987). Communication in interpersonal relationships: Social penetration processes. In M. Roloff & G. Miller (Eds.), *Interpersonal processes: New directions in communication research* (pp. 257–277). Newbury Park, CA: Sage.

VanLear, C. A. (1987). The formation of social relationships: A longitudinal study of social penetration. *Human Communication Research, 13,* 299–322. doi:10.1111/j.1468-2958.1987.tb00107.

Chapter 22

Language Expectancy Theory: Expectancy Violations of Reverend Billy and the Church of Stop Shopping

Josh Averbeck, Ph.D., *Department of Communication Western Illinois University*

Many of us have seen one person say something and be praised, while another person says the exact same thing and is met with outrage. Such situations make us wonder, "Why do some people get away with saying things that others cannot?" This question is at the very heart of Language Expectancy Theory (LET). LET explains that we have general beliefs about the kind of language certain speakers can use. The theory also explains why certain individuals are able to use unconventional language and still be persuasive. LET has three primary strengths as a theory. First, it is message-focused. Few theories are concerned with the wording of messages and the effects therein. Second, LET can be applied across contexts. Burgoon, Denning, and Roberts (2002) argued that theory building had been context-driven with little applicability beyond the specific context. LET makes specific predictions from a sociocultural perspective, providing broad explanatory power. Third, LET is ripe for new research. Any number of language or expectancy variables could be examined in combination to find the ideal wording for a variety of source characteristics. To demonstrate the strengths of LET, the theory will be explained in greater detail and a case study of Reverend Billy and the Church of Stop Shopping will be presented.

Language Expectancy Theory

Language Expectancy Theory (LET) is a message-based theory of persuasion positing that communicators develop socially or culturally appropriate expectations about how others communicate (Miller & Burgoon, 1979; Burgoon, 1995). There are 17 formal, propositional statements outlining the complexities of the theory (see Burgoon, Denning, & Roberts, 2002). Proposition 1, for instance, states "People develop cultural and sociological expectations about language behaviors that subsequently affect their acceptance or rejection of persuasive messages" (p. 121). Burgoon, Denning, and Roberts (2002) also emphasize the role that credibility plays in proposition 4, "Highly credible communicators have the freedom (wide bandwidth) to select varied language strategies and compliance-gaining techniques in developing persuasive messages, while low-credibility communicators must conform to more limited language options if they wish to be effective" (pg. 123). LET was developed in response to inconsistent empirical findings. Both aggressive *and* unaggressive individuals have been rated as effective, but only certain individuals were effective when using aggressive messages. LET suggests that, rather than focusing solely on the message, the sender of the message has a significant impact on the reception of messages. LET explains why certain individuals can use certain kinds of language and be effective persuaders. Language is defined as a rule-governed system, whereby one may choose to either follow or violate norms. In most transactions, communicators conform to the rules, thereby confirming and reinforcing their normative status. Furthermore, beyond such confirmations, message sources can positively or negatively violate expectations. When an expectation is positively violated (termed an expectancy violation), a source is said to have exceeded the normative bandwidth of expectations in a positive direction within the relevant context. In such a case, the source has pleasantly surprised the receiver and is perceived to be a persuasive and competent communicator. For example, someone with a generally pleasant personality would be seen more positively when he/she avoids swearing when someone drops a book on his/her foot. The avoidance of swearing, even when it seems likely, would be seen as exceeding the bandwidth of expectations. Another form of positive expectancy violation occurs when a low-credibility source conforms more closely to normative expectations. For instance, a grumpy coworker who uncharacteristically says "please" and "thank you" will be more successful in his/her request because the polite language would be a positive expectancy violation. In either case, LET predicts that the persuasive message will result in more favorable attitude or behavior change (Burgoon & Miller, 1971). Receivers are more receptive to messages that include language rated as more positive, appropriate, and expected. On the other hand, expectancies may be negatively violated when an individual either uses language deviating from the norm in a negative direction or when a high-credibility source falls short of normative expectations. By failing to meet the minimal standards for appropriate language, a speaker demonstrates an inability or unwillingness to make one's message worth heeding. For instance, a used car salesperson who tried to tell you a rusty, unattractive, and inoperable vehicle would be a steal at $15,000 is not beyond the negative stereotype of used car salesperson. In such instances, no attitude or behavior change is predicted. Moreover, in certain cases, negative violations may be met with boomerang effects, whereby changes in attitudes and/or behavior will occur in the opposite direction intended by the source. A source can so severely, negatively violate expectations that a receiver may reject the message to the point of doing the opposite. An example of this is when a person asks you to buy a product because it isn't good enough for [insert racial slur]. It is likely you would not buy the product, but you will be likely to encourage others not to use the product either. Finally, LET specifies that when expectations are met, by definition, a confirmation has occurred, whereby the source has communicated within the normative bandwidth of expectations and outcomes should generally trend in a mildly positive direction, although LET predicts relatively little change is likely to occur. Simply meeting expectations does not harm the goal of the sender, but it will not necessarily help either. Most communication meets expectations. Only the unexpected language generates the most change.

Certain social categories are allotted a greater bandwidth than others. Those with normatively high credibility are able to use a wider array of message strategies to be successful in their persuasive goal. For example, Averbeck (2015) found that physicians were able to successfully demand that patients exercise. After receiving the physician's message, participants were more likely to exercise even though they didn't like being told what to do by the physician. They granted the physician a certain degree of credibility and the bandwidth to use such language. Those who are lower in social status tend not be allotted such freedoms. Gender differences have also been observed. Burgoon, Denning, and Roberts (2002) summarize a series of studies that show a gender effect for credibility and expectations. In general, women are rated as less credible and, thus, have a narrower range of appropriate and acceptable language strategies to use in persuasive appeals. Women were rated as less persuasive when they used intense language (very, extremely) in their messages compared to men using similar language.

Expectancies are derived from a variety of sources grounded in social and cultural norms. By observing language behaviors, individuals learn what is appropriate and expected of them, unique behavior patterns are developed and displayed, and specific expectations about individuals may vary slightly from the dominant social and cultural norms (Miller & Burgoon, 1979). Normative expectations are based on a variety of contextual factors. For example, job interviews create unique expectations about language use relative to, say, informal gatherings of friends (Averbeck, 2010). Additionally, the source's personality and relationship with the receiver may contribute to variance in receiver expectations in either positive or negative directions (Burgoon, 1995). Someone in a long-term relationship may be likely to forgive a particularly nasty remark because the relationship is more important than the violation. In other cases, some sources are considered so low in credibility that no positive expectancy violation will result in a persuasive outcome.

It is in this latter source of expectancies that LET has seen a recent resurgence. Determining language expectations from relevant personality variables proves useful to assess the effectiveness of certain language strategies. Averbeck and Miller (2014) predicted expectancy violations based on a receiver's cognitive complexity. A recent study examined one's patient-physician orientation to determine the expectations for controlling language use during doctor-patient interactions (Averbeck, 2015). In both of these studies, a psychological predisposition (cognitive complexity, patient-provider orientation) was used as the basis for language expectations. It may be possible to use a wide array of communication and personality variables as indicators of language expectations. For instance, verbal aggressiveness could predict expected levels of aggressive language from others or taking conflict personally may explain language expectancies during conflict scenarios.

To further demonstrate the utility of LET, a case study of Reverend Billy and the Church of Stop Shopping is presented. Reverend Billy performs as a religious figure by using religious language with hopes that the credibility of a religious leader will encourage people to turn against consumerism.

Reverend Billy

William Talen is a street performer, based in New York City, who goes by the persona Reverend Billy. Since 1998, Reverend Billy has been protesting the expansion of corporate businesses at the expense of local businesses in Time Square. Initially, his performance consisted of wearing a white dog collar, black t-shirt, and white sport jacket, while storming the Disney Store and Starbucks, proclaiming "Mickey mouse is the Antichrist! This is your opportunity to stop shopping and save your souls!" (Talen 1998c) and demanding to know what Starbucks did to the mermaid logo's nipples.

Since 9/11, the focus of his protest evolved and has grown to include environmental justice, racial inequality, and, most recently, deportation of immigrants. Reverend Billy performs as a Southern Baptist preacher that is based on his own complicated relationship with religion (Lane, 2002). What stands out about Reverend Billy is the commitment he makes regarding his appearance as an actual minister through his delivery and word choice (McClish, 2009). He relies on the language style of a preacher to deliver his anticonsumerist message in a way that connects to America's Christian psychology (Quirke, 2016). He refers to the Antichrist, sinning, saving your soul, repenting, and the apocalypse/shopocalypse.

Reverend Billy's performance has expanded to include the Church of Stop Shopping, which is accompanied by a 35-voice chorus. The choir is like any other church choir, except that they get arrested a lot (Quirke, 2016). Reverend Billy's role in the community expanded after 9/11 from local eccentric performer to that of an actual minister providing comfort and support to his community. The Church of Stop Shopping has performed baptisms, weddings, and funerals. In the excerpt below, from a sermon to the Church of Stop Shopping, Reverend Billy names shopping as the source of our collective pain and describes a life of shopping like being in hell.

When you tried to cross 7ᵗʰ Avenue,
just putting one foot in front of the other,
just tax-paying god-fearing little pedestrians...

You look up and there he is... Mickey Mouse.
His smile nearly bifurcates his face. And you realize he isn't really smiling.
You know with horror...
that Mickey hasn't really smiled since 1955.

And you look around at your friends and they quietly burst into flames.
And it occurs to you to ask the question, Am I in Hell?
Oh, children, I know... I know...
Don't you feel the burning? Do you feel the pain?
It registers as a kind of minor happiness. It's shopping. Bless us all. It's shopping.
(Talen 1998b)

Language Expectations of Reverend Billy

Reverend Billy's message to stop shopping would likely be met with great resistance if it were not delivered by a religious figure. To simply anger a customer by attacking him/her for shopping at the Disney Store would not accomplish his goal (Lane, 2002). Becoming the target of customers' anger would only create positive press for the business. Personally attacking the customer would be unsuccessful. Reverend Billy instead shifts the focus from a social choice to a personal choice. The goal of persuading consumers to stop their consumption is one that could succeed on a personal level. To do so, Reverend Billy utilizes the credibility of a religious figure to expand his bandwidth as a persuasive speaker.

The Reverend Billy persona is an appropriation of a minister (McClish, 2009). He is "equal parts evangelist, Elvis impersonator, and Situationist" (Quirke, 2016, p. 2). Reverend Billy is an attempt by Bill Talen to draw upon the established credibility of a social category (minister). Performing as a religious figure affords

Reverend Billy a certain amount of freedom in his messaging. LET explains that expectations are applied to aggregates, rather than specific individuals (Burgoon, Denning, & Roberts, 2002). In other words, social categories are granted credibility. Doctors, religious leaders, and teachers are considered credible. An individual is considered more or less credible simply by being recognized as belonging to certain social categories. Thus, Reverend Billy taps into established credibility for religious figures, even though Reverend Billy may not seem like a credible figure at first glance.

The use of the credibility of the religious figure can be seen in the relationship Reverend Billy has with his community. While he was merely a street performer at first, he became a "genuine" religious figure following 9/11. After tragedies, people often turn to those who can offer comfort, explanations, support, and/or connections to others (Koenig, 2006). Reverend Billy has always encouraged his community to support one another over corporations and choose local business over multinational companies. By asking seemingly silly questions, Reverend Billy asks his audiences to consider what matters most. For instance, when he asks, "In this church we gather to ask the great questions that face us…Is there life after perfect teeth?" he encourages others to look beyond the surface level to find meaningful relationships (Talen, 1999a). It is this underlying message that seems to resonate and increase his credibility.

The language of Reverend Billy is not quite what you would expect from a minister, while seeming to be exactly what you would expect from a minister. He refers to the Antichrist (Mickey Mouse), he is concerned with public decency (Starbucks' mermaid logo), and regularly blesses his congregation. All of his sermons and performances have the language structure of a fundamentalist religious figure who is concerned with your well-being. At the same time, the association of Mickey Mouse as the Antichrist is not what one would expect from a minister.

Reverend Billy is a very charismatic figure and his Church of Stop Shopping promotes their sermons as performances. Several of these performances have won Obie awards for excellence in off-Broadway theater (Village Voice, 2018). When attending a sermon/performance, one may expect to simply be entertained. However, Reverend Billy violates those expectations with the fire and brimstone sermons backed up by the often-arrested choir members. As one visitor explained, "I came away feeling quite exhilarated. And that's the whole point. This show is designed to inspire anyone who already knows all the awful facts to get out and *do* something, individually and collectively" (Hindley, 2010, p. 120).

The exhilaration and motivation felt by the audience is evidence that Reverend Billy is successful in his persuasive attempts. He wants people to change their individual shopping behaviors. He knows he will not be able to change corporations or capitalism. He is very effective at using his credibility to expand his bandwidth of appropriate language. Keeping his language within those appropriate boundaries means his audiences are open to receiving those messages, and he is more likely to be successful.

Conclusion

The case of Reverend Billy demonstrates the broad applicability of Language Expectancy Theory. The use of a high-credibility social status, that of a religious leader, allowed Reverend Billy greater bandwidth to deliver persuasive messages that would have otherwise been rejected. By relying on the established credibility of the religious figure, the Church of Stop Shopping has grown. In order to maintain credibility, the church has offered many of traditional services (baptism, weddings, etc.). LET can explain why such an outlandish figure such as Reverend Billy continues to draw crowds even though the persuasive outcome of his messages is so at odds with the attitudes and beliefs of the general public. The theory may be applied to interpersonal (Averbeck 2010), computer-mediated (Jensen et al., 2013), political (Pfau, Parrott, & Lindquist, 1992), and mass communication (Campo et al., 2004) contexts. The explanatory framework of the theory allows for predictions to be made across situations. Understanding the language expectations for social categories (minister, doctor, corporate executive, etc.) would allow speakers to be more effective in future interactions. There have been many applications of LET to the health context. For instance, Buller et al. (2000) used LET to produce highly effective messages encouraging individuals to take sun safety measures. Klingle (1993) developed health-specific expectations based on LET and found that patient language expectations evolved over time.

While LET's formal propositional framework is thorough, it still offers many fruitful opportunities for new research. For instance, how do people form their expectations? Averbeck (2015) used a predisposition to predict language expectations, but the predisposition does not explain how the expectation was formed. Is it formed through familial interactions, interpersonal experiences, media consumption? Additionally, the theory makes predictions about macrolevel expectations. Yet, we also have our own, specific expectations for certain people and contexts. What happens when those expectations are in conflict? Which expectancy violation is more important and why? Future research could seek to answer these questions.

Discussion Questions

1. Credibility can be complicated. How does Reverend Billy increase and reduce his credibility as a communicator?

2. Why do certain social classes have higher credibility than others? What is an example of a high credibility position/occupation/class? Why is that social class high in credibility?

3. Reverend Billy uses his character to induce positive expectancy violations. Is this positive expectancy violation large enough to persuade people to stop shopping? Why or why not?

4. Can Reverend Billy be too authentic in his language as a religious figure? What could Reverend Billy do to be so close to a traditional religious leader that he is no longer considered credible or persuasive?

REFERENCES

Averbeck, J. M. (2010). Irony and language expectancy theory: Evaluations of expectancy violation outcomes. *Communication Studies, 61*, 356–372.

Averbeck, J. M. (2015). Patient-provider orientation as a language expectancy origin for controlling language in doctor-patient interactions. *Communication Reports, 28*, 65–79.

Averbeck, J. M., & Miller, C. H. (2014). Expanding language expectancy theory: The suasory effects of lexical complexity and semantic complexity on effective message design. *Communication Studies, 65*, 72–95.

Buller, D. B., Burgoon, M., Hall, J. R., Levine, N., Taylor, A. M., Beach, B. H., … Hunsaker, F. G. (2000). Using language intensity to increase the success of a family intervention to protect children from ultraviolet radiation: Predictions from language expectancy theory. *Preventive Medicine, 30*(2), 103–113. http://dx.doi.org/10.1006/pmed.1999.0600

Burgoon, M. (1995). Language expectancy theory: Elaboration, explication, and extension. In C. R. Berger & M. Burgoon (Eds.), *Communication and social influence processes* (pp. 29–52). East Lansing, MI: Michigan State University Press.

Burgoon, M., Denning, P. V., & Roberts, L. (2002). Language expectancy theory. In J. P. Dillard & M. Pfau (Eds.). *The persuasion handbook: Developments in theory and practice* (pp. 117–137). Thousand Oaks, CA: Sage Publications.

Burgoon, M., & Miller, G. R. (1971). Prior attitude and language intensity as predictors of message style and attitude change following counterattitudinal advocacy. *Journal of Personality and Social Psychology 20*, 246–253.

Campo, S., Cameron, K. A., Brossard, D., & Frazer, M. S. (2004). Social norms and expectancy violation theories: Assessing the effectiveness of health communication campaigns. *Communication Monographs, 71*, 448–470.

Hindley, J. (2010). Breaking the consumerist trance: The Reverend Billy and the Church of Stop Shopping. *Capitalism Nature Socialism, 21*, 118–126. DOI: 10.1080/10455752.2010.523138

Jensen, J., Averbeck, J. M., Zhang, Z., & Wright, K. B. (2013). Assessments of credibility in online product reviews: A language expectancy perspective. *Journal of Management Information Systems, 30*, 293–324.

Klingle, R. S. (1993). Bringing time into physician compliance gaining research: Toward a reinforcement expectancy theory of strategy effectiveness. *Health Communication, 5*, 283–308.

Koenig, H. G. (2006). *In the wake of disaster: Religious responses to terrorism and catastrophe.* West Conshohocken, PA: Templeton Press.

Lane, J. (2002). Reverend Billy: Preaching, protest, and postindustrial flânerie. *The Drama Review, 46*, 60–84.

McClish, C. (2009). Activism based in embarrassment: The anti-consumption spirituality of the Reverend Billy. *Liminalities, 5*, 1–19.

Miller, M. D., & Burgoon, M. (1979). The relationship between violations of expectations and the induction of resistance to persuasion. *Human Communication Research, 5*, 301–313.

Pfau, M., Parrott, R., & Lindquist, B. (1992). An expectancy theory explanation of the effectiveness of political attack television spots: A case study. *Journal of Applied Communication Research, 20*, 235–253.

Quirke, S. (2016). *The irreverent Reverend Billy of the Church of Stop Shopping.* (June 2). Retrieved from http://news.streetroots.org/2016/06/02/irreverent-reverend-billy-church-stop-shopping.

Talen, W. (1998a). *The Rev's HEAVY sermon.* Retrieved from http://www.revbilly.com/writings4.html.

Talen, W. (1998b). *The Rev's Sermon from inside the Store.* Retrieved from http://www.revbilly.com/writings3.html.

Talen, W. (1998c). *Disney Invasion #1.* Uncredited video capture. Retrieved from http://www.revbilly.com/archives.html.

Talen, W. (1999). *The Church of Stop Shopping: A Solo Play in One Act.* Unpublished performance text, performed by Bill Talen at the Theatorium and Theatre at St. Clements Church in New York City, May 1999.

Obie Awards (2018). *2000s.* Retrieved from http://www.obieawards.com/events/2000s/

Chapter 23

Verbal Aggressiveness and Frustration-Aggression-Displacement Theory

Charles J. Wigley III, Ph.D., *Canisius College*

What is Frustration-Aggression-Displacement Theory? Berkowitz (1989) reformulated the theory that was originally proposed by Dollard, Doob, Mower and Sears (1939). The Berkowitz reformulation of the theory provides a useful framework for understanding the way that some aggression takes place in workday settings. As employees seek positive rewards and are repeatedly and unexpectedly blocked from reaching those rewards, their frustrations can lead to aggression, especially where the goals are highly valued and the interference in attaining the goals is quite unexpected. Sometimes, this aggression is displaced, i.e., the aggression is verbalized toward someone other than the original instigator of the aggression (much like a driver, eager to reach an important destination on time, expresses road rage against another driver after three other drivers, none of whom is still around, cut the person off in traffic). According to Berkowitz's reformulation, "Frustrations are aversive events and generate aggressive inclinations only to the extent that they produce negative affect." (p. 71). Berkowitz (1989) explained that when an individual is engaged in goal-directed behavior, but is unexpectedly blocked from meeting his or her goal, then the "instigation to aggression" (p. 71) is stronger, especially when the individual perceives the goal as very desirable. Berkowitz (1989) explained (p. 71), "An unanticipated failure to obtain an attractive goal is more unpleasant than an expected failure, and it is the greater displeasure in the former case that gives rise to the stronger instigation to aggression. Similarly, the thwarted persons' appraisals and attributions presumably determine how bad they feel at not getting what they had wanted so that they are most aggressively inclined when they experience strong negative affect." This theory is especially useful in understanding workplace aggression because employees are often prevented from reaching their highly valued personal goals (more remuneration, more sick days, more vacation time, greater personal advancement) by often misunderstood or unclear company policies that are enforced by supervisors.

The first question we need to address is: what is the nature of workplace aggression? Verbal aggression can be found in a variety of workplace settings and in many shapes and forms. The late Professor Dominic A. Infante pioneered a great deal of modern research into verbal aggressiveness, its causes, and its consequences. Much of his efforts were directed toward an improved understanding of how communication functions on a person-to-person basis, including the communication that takes between supervisors and subordinates, as well as coworker-with-coworker. A hypothetical case study illustrating an example of this workplace aggression follows and discussion of some of the ways we might control our own levels of aggression will be addressed.

What are the various forms that verbal aggression may take? Infante (1987, 1995) identified many forms of aggression, including character attacks, competence attacks, background attacks, physical appearance attacks, maledictions (saying bad things about someone), teasing, swearing, ridicule, threats, nonverbal emblems (for example, certain hand gestures), blame, personality attacks, commands, global rejection, disconfirmation, negative comparison, sexual harassment, and attacking target's significant others. While there are other ways that verbal aggression may manifest itself, the eighteen forms reported by Infante appear to be most common.

What causes verbal aggressiveness? Some of the research on verbal aggressiveness (Infante, Trebing, Shepard, & Seeds, 1984) has suggested that some of the primary causes of verbal aggressiveness include psychopathology, disdain for the target of aggression, social learning (see Badura, 1973), and argumentative skill deficiency. Verbal aggressiveness might be communibiologically based in that while aggressiveness itself might not be inherited, the physical characteristics that one inherits might more readily lead to aggressive communication in persons with those characteristics as opposed to others without the characteristics (for a more detailed explanation of the communibiological perspective, see Beatty & McCroskey, 1997).

Are listener characteristics likely to make some individuals feel that they are the subject of aggression? Listener characteristics may play as important of a role in understanding aggression as the characteristics of aggressive speakers. Listener characteristics might lead some people to think that they are the target of verbal aggression, where people without those same characteristics might not perceive the message as aggressive at all. For example, people that are hypersensitive or prone to be ruminators (or brooders) (Anestis, Anestis, Selby, & Joiner, 2009), as opposed to some others, might think that they are the targets of aggression. Communication that is deemed verbally aggressive might trigger a strong verbally aggressive reaction.

Whatever causes aggression and whatever causes some individuals to be more sensitive than others, verbal aggressiveness appears to be a complex topic with, likely, many causes. These causes may vary from one person to another. In spite of its complex nature, however, one useful theory that helps us to understand verbal aggression across people, in general, is Berkowitz's reformulated theory of frustration-aggression. Three key factors in understanding verbal aggression are provocation, frustration, and level of self-focus (the reader may wish to examine Carver, 1979; Carver & Scheier, 1981; Carver & Scheier, 1990; Duval & Wicklund, 1972). Though not explicitly offered as a conclusion by them, this three-part analysis finds its foundation in the writings of Ito, Miller, and Pollock (1996). Accordingly, three questions one might address in examining workplace aggression are (1) was the aggressive employee provoked, (2) was the aggressive employee consistently frustrated over a period of time, and (3) was the aggressive employee sufficiently focused on himself or herself to avoid aggressive behavior? We will consider a typical-hypothetical case of verbal aggression in the workplace and how these three factors might play an important role in explaining the aggression.

What do we know about workplace frustration leading to verbal aggression in the workplace? Avtgis and Chory (2010) identified a number of predictors, outcomes, and correlates of verbal aggressiveness in the workplace. A more contemporary review (Rancer & Avtgis, 2014) has updated this growing area of research. Most of these hundreds of studies focus on correlates of verbal aggressiveness, as opposed to being true causal models. Correlation is, of course, not causation. However, one clear conclusion that stands out from these studies is that workplace verbal aggression, although sometimes thought to be instrumental, is almost always damaging and has a negative impact on morale, productivity, organizational culture, turnover, levels of incivility within organizations, personal health of employees, co-worker relations, and superior-subordinate relations (Avtgis & Chory, 2010). If you wish more details about these problems, you might especially consult Avtgis and Chory (2010) and Rancer and Avtgis (2014) for very well written and exceptionally comprehensive reviews.

However, one study that I would like to highlight of undergraduate student behaviors is particularly insightful and relevant to the hypothetical case study that follows. Undergraduate students were divided into three groups, (1) a control group where participants could achieve their goal, (2) an experimental group where a secret confederate of the researchers kept interrupting and participants were told the secret confederate had a hearing impediment (the nonarbitrary condition where the interruptions served to block goal attainment), and (3) an experimental group where a secret confederate of the researchers kept interrupting and participants received no explanation for the interruptions (the arbitrary condition where the interruptions served to block goal attainment) (Burnstein & Worchel, 1962). In the condition where the interruptions occurred (groups 2 and 3), in private ratings, the interrupters received more criticism from the others than was received in the control group (group 1). Interestingly, in terms of public criticism, none was given to interrupters in the second group, but it was given to the secret confederate in group 3. This study provides some evidence for the idea that frustration resulting from somewhat justifiable causes might lead to lower levels of aggressive response than frustration resulting from less justifiable or nonjustifiable causes of frustration. Let's see how this research might play out in a hypothetical case.

Hypothetical Case Study

Art has been working as a quality control manager in a toy manufacturing plant for a little over four years. Art likes his job. Every Friday, Art meets with five other managers from the manufacturing plant to discuss production issues, such as parts shortages, equipment breakdowns, employee absenteeism, and workplace innovations. The meetings are held by their immediate supervisor, Mary. For the past few weeks, Art has noticed that one of the other managers, Bill, regularly interrupts Art while he is speaking. To make matters worse, Bill never addresses Art personally. Bill never looks at Art, nor acknowledges that Art is even present at the meetings. Art has tried to ask Bill to avoid interrupting him, but Mary always chides Art and says "Settle down" and "Try to get along with your fellow managers." This workplace situation was bad enough, but starting a few weeks ago, Bill began to interrupt Art in order to take credit for Art's innovative ideas. Mary's comments are very upsetting to Art because he believes Mary could get Bill to treat him better and that Mary would reward him for his innovations if she just understood that he was, in fact, the innovator! He dislikes, greatly, her chiding comments and believes that he will lose his job if he continues speaking up. At their last meeting, Art finally proclaimed, "That's it, I've been dismissed long enough! When you two get your act together, let me know!" Then, he stormed out of the meeting.

Practical Implications of Studying Workplace Verbal Aggression

In examining this scenario, it will be helpful to address the three key questions mentioned previously. Was the aggressive employee provoked? Was the aggressive employee consistently frustrated over a period of time? Was the aggressive employee sufficiently focused on himself or herself to avoid aggressive behavior?

Was Art provoked? In this example, Bill provoked Art. By regularly interrupting Art, Bill's behavior was a strong disconfirmation of Art. Bill ignored Art by both failing to acknowledge his presence and input. By doing so, Bill's behavior served as a global rejection of Art. Bill's aggression became manifest not only by his interruptions (an act of commission), but by his failure to even acknowledge his coworker (an act of omission), thereby violating ordinary social protocols. Verbal aggression can manifest itself through actions and, as is the case in this scenario, by one's failing to act in a respectful manner.

There seems to be little doubt that Art was frustrated. He was engaged in goal-directed behavior toward a goal that he highly valued. He wanted to provide uninterrupted input to his supervisor and get recognition and reward for his innovations. Generally, we do not know whether he is a verbally aggressive person. However, we can easily see that he has been frustrated in expressing his ideas and blocked in his efforts to be praised and rewarded by his superior. While his supervisor could have supported his efforts, she chose, instead, to block his efforts toward getting his coworker to avoid interrupting him and wrongfully taking credit for his ideas. It is important to note that Art placed great value on having positive, uninterrupted communication with his supervisor and that her failure of support stood as a significant obstacle to Art benefitting from having his supervisor learn of his innovations.

In the hypothetical scenario, no justification was offered by Bill for Bill's efforts that served to block Art's goal attainment. Reasoning suggests that had Bill justified to Art the way that Bill communicated, then Art might have been less frustrated and, possibly, less likely to express verbal aggression. This conclusion seems to be a reasonable application of the reasoning offered by Burnstein and Worchel (1962).

Was Art sufficiently self-focused to avoid his aggression toward Mary and Bill? Surely Art knew that referring to his supervisor as less than competent ("get your act together") was intended to serve as an injury to his supervisor. It seems rather universally understood that one avoids aggressing against one's supervisor for the purpose of inflicting harm. Now, one might argue that Art's comments were meant to be instrumental and helpful toward getting matters resolved. Such a position seems rather unlikely, however, because a key to keeping one's own verbal aggression in check is to focus on managing one's interpersonal relations (Wigley, 2008; Infante, 1987). Here, it seems unlikely that a competency attack on his supervisor could be seen as a positive step toward managing his interpersonal relationship with her. One could readily imagine a situation where Art would have notified

Mary of the problems he was facing with Bill by sending her a detailed email or, perhaps, requesting a "sit-down" meeting with just the three of them being present. Art clearly had superior, alternative avenues of discourse which would have addressed his problems in a much better way. However, his lack of situational presence, his inability to self-focus and generate alternative solutions for addressing his problems, was so great that be chose the less desirable path of expressing hostility toward his supervisor. Could Art have done a better job of complying with workplace norms? Art must have known that attacking the competency of his supervisor, Mary, was not the kind of response to a workplace problem with Bill that would have been anticipated by Mary. If Art had engaged in a greater level of self-focused behavior, he would less likely have resorted to what might best be described as a workplace tantrum. Ito, Miller, and Pollock (1996) clarify, "Frustration, defined as blocking an ongoing goal-directed behavior, may operate in a manner similar to provocation and serve both as an instigator and an external justification for violating normative constraints against aggression" (p. 63). As noted (Wigley, 2010), "Individuals maintaining higher levels of self-focused attention are, theoretically (according to Ito, Miller, and Pollock, 1996), less likely to resort to verbal aggression as a response to another person because of the generally accepted norm that verbal aggression should be avoided because it is destructive" (p. 392).

Ito, Miller, and Pollack (1996) explained the role of self-focus, "*Self-focus* refers to a state in which a self-regulatory process is initiated, personal standards of appropriate behavior become salient, and attempts are made to comply with these standards (Carver, 1979; Carver & Scheier, 1981, 1990; Duval & Wicklund, 1972)" (p. 64).

Is there hope for better, less aggressive, workplace communication among these three people? Art would benefit from understanding that breaking social protocols might cause him to lose his standing in the company, maybe even his job. Isolated acts of verbal aggression have caused some individuals to lose their jobs. When it comes to workplace aggression, a few bad moments can lead to years of misery and economic suffering. In the scenario, Bill's verbal aggression toward Art might not seem quite so obvious to Mary. Part of Bill's aggression consisted of omissions and might have been outside of Mary's realm of perception. In addition, while it may be true that some individuals regularly interrupt each other in daily conversations, it seems more likely that Mary would be aware of these acts of aggression by Bill (i.e., of his interruptions) than of Bill's acts of omission (i.e., Bill's ignoring of Art).

In his investigation of verbal trigger events (statements by a person that lead to verbal aggression by another), Durbin (2008) found that the top eight most hurtful messages from bosses were character attacks, de-escalation/avoidance, blame, negative comparisons, command, competence attacks, behavior criticism, and threats. When Mary chided Art and said "Try to get along with your fellow managers," she offered a negative comparison of Art (i.e., compared to the other non-chided managers) and used a command function in a negative way. So, Art experienced the interrupting and dismissive communications from Bill and the follow-up hurtful messages from his superior, Mary. At this point, his frustration was so great that he seemed to have hit his "breaking point," leading to his aggressive outburst. Greater self-focus on the negative consequences that will likely follow from his outburst might have served to keep Art's aggression under control.

It should be noted that our general tendency of seeing justified aggression as somehow more socially acceptable than unjustified aggression is rather universal. In fact, the verbal aggressiveness scale (Infante & Wigley, 1986) encourages individuals to report their own level of aggressiveness, especially when they think that their aggressions have been justified. This also suggests that many of us have become desensitized to the very damaging effects of even small episodes of aggression. For example, people often engage in light-hearted teasing of coworkers and think that teasing behavior is humorous and that it serves to build relational bonds between teasers and their targets. By definition, however, teasing is a form of aggression. Although teasers may think of teasing as instrumental in building relationships, the targets of teasing might see the same behaviors as hostile, personally injurious, and damaging. Does teasing an overweight coworker by calling him "chubs" serve to build a relationship or encourage the coworker to lose weight, or, instead, does it lead to hurt feelings and feelings of inadequacy? In the scenario offered, I intentionally chose levels of verbal aggression by Art that seem, on their face, to be rather minor and insignificant. However, just as a tiny germ can cause a great disease, even limited violations of social norms can have dire consequences. Most of us have observed workplace verbal aggression, whether it was name calling, making fun of one's ethnicity by telling so-called ethnic jokes, or one of the harsher forms of aggression (for example, making fun of one's family members), all of which can be very damaging. In a recent study (Wigley, 2013), I found that making fun of a person's individual characteristics is particularly offensive in situations where one cannot easily alter those characteristics. For example, making fun of one's hairstyle (which is easily changed) is considered less offensive than making fun of, for example, one's biological race. This line of reasoning suggests that employees should receive training in how to manage their interpersonal relationships. We should not assume that small levels of verbal aggression are less damaging than higher levels of norm-breaking aggression. Likewise, we should not assume that individuals innately comprehend the distinction between teasing (a typically accepted level of aggression) and ridicule (a form of "aggravated" teasing). To the workplace victims of such aggressions, there may be no distinction at all. Verbal aggression is a voluntary behavior (Infante, 1995) and, to that extent, it is controllable and, in most cases, unnecessary to achieving personal goals as a member of the workforce.

There are many studies examining the role of verbal aggressiveness in a variety of settings. The reader may wish to examine some of the more comprehensive reviews in communication studies literature (e.g., Rancer & Avtgis, 2014; Avtgis & Rancer, 2010; Infante & Rancer, 1996; Hamilton & Mineo, 2002; Wigley, 1998). A number of scholars have examined the role of trigger-events in bringing about aggressive responses (e.g., Wigley, 2010; Durbin, 2008; Berkowitz, 1973; Lawrence, 2006). Other authors have focused on ways of reducing verbal aggression (e.g., Wigley, 2008; Infante, 1988) and how individuals respond to others (e.g., Infante, 1989; Lim, 1990). Quite a few articles discuss measuring aggression (e.g., Infante & Wigley, 1986; Buss & Perry, 1992; O'Connor, Archer, & Wu, 2001; Zuckerman, 1983). One can see that the topic of aggression has been studied for many years because of its widespread nature (Toch, 1969), the damages it causes (e.g., with its hurtful messages, Vangelisti, 1994; Vangelisti, 2007; Wigley, 2006; Young & Bippus, 2001), and the remedies for preventing it. Individuals striving to maintain pleasant and productive work environments can benefit from the extensive research showing that even small levels of aggression can have big consequences. Perhaps the most important lesson we can all learn is that workplace aggression can be reduced if we work to achieve a balanced environment where employees do not feel frustrated and where employees succeed in placing the managing of their relationships with coworkers as a very high priority in their everyday-workplace list of "things to do today."

Discussion Questions

1. Art felt more and more frustrated by Bill as time progressed. At what point should Art have addressed Bill privately and asked him to stop interrupting him? What might Art have said to Bill (please be very specific by writing out a brief script)? Would Art's verbally aggressive comments been less likely after talking to Bill at an earlier point in time?

2. Do you think that Bill knew that he was ignoring Art? If so, what nonverbal behavior might Bill display toward Art in future meetings to assure Art that Bill is listening to him?

3. Was Art's level of frustration his own fault? How do you justify your answer to this question?

4. Think of some work-related situation where you felt frustrated by a coworker or client. Did you "take out" your frustrations on a family member when you got home? Did you ever find yourself then saying something like, "Sorry, I've just had a bad day" to your family member? How might understanding Frustration-Aggression-Displacement Theory help prevent the need to apologize for your displaced aggression?

5. How would you help protect employees from having their goal-directed behaviors frustrated by their coworkers? Would "sit-downs" with individual employees be superior to other methods, such as posting motivational signs? For example, a sign could be posted in the main entrance, "Alone we can do so little. Together we can do so much. —Helen Keller." (Lash, 1996). Could signs that make employees feel less competitive with each other lead to lower levels of frustration because goal attainment would seem to be more based on cooperation and a collective effort than, on the other hand, an individualistic or competitive basis? Can a supervisor encourage communication behaviors that serve to reduce workplace frustrations? How?

REFERENCES

Anestis, M. D., Anestis, J. C., Selby, E. A., & Joiner, T. E. (2009). Anger rumination across forms of aggression. *Personality and Individual Differences*, 46, 192–196.

Avtgis, T. A., & Chory, R. M. (2010). The dark side of organizational life: Aggressive expression in the workplace. In T. A. Avtgis & A. S. Rancer (Eds.), *Arguments, aggression, and conflict: New directions in theory and research* (pp. 285–304). New York: Routledge.

Bandura, A. (1973). Social learning theory of aggression. In J. F. Knutson (Ed.), *The control of aggression: Implications from basic research* (pp. 201–250). Chicago: Aldine.

Beatty, M. J., & McCroskey, J. C. (1997). It's in our nature: Verbal aggressiveness as temperamental expression. *Communication Quarterly, 45*, 446–460.

Berkowitz, L. (1973). Words and symbols as stimuli to aggressive responses. In J. F. Knutson (Ed.), *The control of aggression: Implications from basic research* (pp. 113–143). Chicago: Aldine.

Berkowitz, L. (1989). Frustration-aggression hypothesis: Examination and reformulation. *Psychological Bulletin, 106*(1), 59–73.

Burnstein, E., & Worcel, P. (1962). Arbitrariness of frustration and its consequences for aggression in a social situation. *Journal of Personality, 30*, 528–541.

Buss, A. H., & Perry, M. (1992). The aggression questionnaire. *Journal of Personality and Social Psychology, 63*, 452–459.

Carver, C. S. (1979). A cybernetic model of self-attention processes. *Journal of Personality and Social Psychology, 8*, 1251–1281.

Carver, C. S., & Scheier, M. F. (1981). *Attention and self–regulation: A control theory approach to human behavior.* New York: Springer-Verlag.

Carver, C. S., & Scheier, M. F. (1990). Origins and functions of positive and negative affect: A control-process view. *Psychological Review, 97*, 19–35.

Durbin, J. M. (2008). *Toward the development of a taxonomy of verbal trigger events.* Unpublished master's thesis, University of Akron.

Duval, S., & Wicklund, R. A. (1972). *A theory of objective self-awareness.* New York: Academic Press.

Hamilton, M. A., & Mineo, P. J. (2002). Argumentativeness and its effect on verbal aggressiveness: A meta-analytic review. In M. Allen, R. W. Preiss, B. M. Gayle, & N. Burrell (Eds.), *Interpersonal communication research: Advances through meta-analysis* (pp. 281–314), Mahwah, NJ: Lawrence Erlbaum.

Infante, D. A. (1987). Aggressiveness. In J. C. McCroskey & J. A. Daly (Eds.), *Personality and interpersonal communication* (pp. 157–192). Newbury Park, CA: Sage.

Infante, D. A. (1988). *Arguing constructively.* Prospect Heights, IL: Waveland Press.

Infante, D. A. (1989). Response to high argumentatives: Message and sex differences. *Southern Communication Journal, 54,* 159–170.

Infante, D. A. (1995). Teaching students to understand and control verbal aggression. *Communication Education, 44,* 51–63.

Infante, D. A. & Rancer, A. S. (1996). Argumentativeness and verbal aggression: A review of recent theory and research. In B. Burleson (Ed.), *Communication Yearbook* (Vol. 19, pp. 319–351). Thousand Oaks, CA: Sage.

Infante, D. A., Trebing, D. J., Shepherd, P. E., & Seeds, D. E. (1984). The relationship of argumentativeness to verbal aggression. *Southern Speech Communication Journal, 50,* 67–77.

Infante, D. A., & Wigley, C. J., III (1986). Verbal aggressiveness: An interpersonal model and measure. *Communication Monographs, 53,* 61–69.

Ito, T. A., Miller, N., & Pollock, V. E. (1996). Alcohol and Aggression: A meta-analysis on the moderating effects of inhibitory cues, triggering events, and self-focused attention. *Psychological Bulletin, 120,* 60–82.

Lash, J. P. (1996). *Helen and teacher: The story of Helen Keller and Anne Sullivan Macy*. American Foundation for the Blind.

Lawrence, C. (2006). Measuring individual responses to aggression triggering events: Development of the situational triggers of aggressive responses (STAR) scale. *Aggressive Behavior, 32*, 241–252.

Lim, T. (1990). The influences of receivers' resistance on persuaders' verbal aggressive-ness. *Communication Quarterly, 38*, 170–188.

O'Connor, D. B., Archer, J., & Wu, F.W.C. (2001). Measuring aggression: Self-reports, partner reports and responses to provoking scenarios. *Aggressive Behavior, 27*, 79–101.

Rancer, A. S. & Avtgis, T. A. (2014). *Argumentative and aggressive communication: Theory, research, and application*. Thousand Oaks, CA: Sage.

Toch, H. (1969). *Violent men*. Chicago: Aldine.

Vangelisti, A. L. (1994). Messages that hurt. In B. H. Spitzberg & W. R. Cupach (Eds.), *The dark side of interpersonal communication* (2nd ed.), (pp. 53–82). Hillsdale, NJ: Lawrence Erlbaum.

Vangelisti, A. L. (2007). Communicating hurt. In B. H. Spitzberg & W. R. Cupach (Eds.), *The dark side of interpersonal communication* (2nd ed.), (pp. 121–142). Hillsdale, NJ: Lawrence Erlbaum.

Wigley, C. J., III (1998). Verbal aggressiveness. In J. C. McCroskey, J. A. Daly, M. M. Martin, & M. J. Beatty (Eds.), *Communication and personality: Trait perspectives* (pp. 191–212). Cresskill, NJ: Hampton.

Wigley, C. J., III (2006). The research contributions. In A. S. Rancer & T. A. Avtgis (2006), *Argumentative and aggressive communication: Theory, research, and application* (p. 243). Thousand Oaks, CA: Sage.

Wigley, C. J., III (2008). Verbal aggression interventions: What should be done? *Communication Monographs, 75*, 339–350.

Wigley, C. J., III (2010). Verbal trigger events-Other catalysts and precursors of aggression. In T. A. Avtgis & A. S. Rancer (Eds.), *Arguments, aggression, and conflict: New directions in theory and research* (pp. 388–399). New York, NY: Routledge.

Wigley, C. J., III (2013). *The Malleability-Offensiveness Connection: The role of malleability of a receiver characteristic in accounting for level of joke offensiveness.* Paper presented at the 104th annual meeting of the Eastern Communication Association, Pittsburgh, PA.

Young, S. L., & Bippus, A. M. (2001). Does it make a difference if they hurt you in a funny way? Humorously and non-humorously phrased hurtful messages in personal relationships. *Communication Quarterly, 49,* 35–52.

Zuckerman, M. (1983). The distinctions between trait and state scales is not arbitrary: Comments on Allen and Potkay's "On the arbitrary distinction between traits and states." *Journal of Personality and Social Psychology, 44,* 1083–1086.

Chapter 24

Using the Theory of Planned Behavior to Create Health Change: The Case of University Sleep-Positive Campaigns

Heather J. Carmack, Ph.D., *University of Alabama*
Heather M. Stassen, Ph.D., *Cazenovia College*

The Theory of Planned Behavior (TPB) is designed to identify factors that influence human behavior (Alas, Anshari, Sabtu, & Yunus, 2016). TPB was developed by Icek Ajzen in 1985 as an extension of Fishbein and Ajzen's (1975)[1] Theory of Reasoned Action (Ajzen, 1985, 1988). While initially constructed for use in psychology, the theory has become popular among communication researchers and practitioners. A search for the theory in *Communication and Mass Media Complete*, a research database dedicated to communication research, reveals nearly 250 studies utilizing TPB and over 150 applying TPB's predecessor, the Theory of Reasoned Action. The theory is one of several persuasion theories seeking to understand, predict, and influence individuals' behaviors based on preexisting attitudes. Within communication, TPB is predominantly used to help create, analyze, and understand the influence of communication tactics on an individual's behavior or intention to perform a desired behavior.

Theory of Planned Behavior Examined

The central premise of TPB is that individuals' attitudes about a specific behavior, as well as their perceptions of how others believe they should act, influence their belief in their ability to engage in that specific action. Looking at individual elements, TPB is comprised of five primary components,

---

[1] Fishbein originally proposed the Theory of Reasoned Action in 1967 and worked with Ajzen to develop the theory into what we know today.

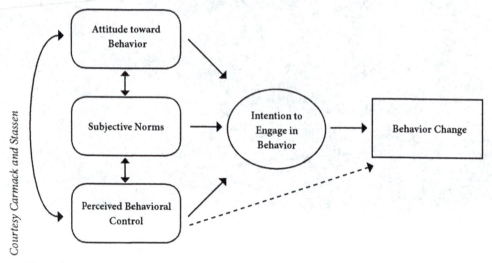

Courtesy Carmack and Stassen

Figure 1

including: (1) attitude toward the behavior, (2) subjective norm, (3) perceived behavioral control, (4) intention, and (5) behavior (see Figure 1). Attitudes, subjective norm, and perceived behavioral control serve as antecedent variables (Ajzen, 1985, 1991), meaning that they work to influence the intention to perform a desired behavior. TPB assumes individuals presented with rational arguments will engage in the desired action (Ajzen, 1985).

Attitude Toward the Behavior

The first determinant, *attitude toward a specific behavior,* "refers to the degree to which a person has a favorable or unfavorable evaluation or appraisal of the behavior in question" (Ajzen, 1991, p. 188). As Ajzen (1985) noted, "the personal factor is the individual's positive or negative evaluation of performing the behavior; this factor is termed attitude toward the behavior" (p. 12). Specifically, it focuses on an individual's beliefs about the outcomes of a given action, and their positive or negative evaluation of those beliefs. For example, a student attempting to persuade her peers to participate in a community clean-up day finds that her peers believe that the neighborhood hooligans will continue to litter and graffiti the neighborhood (outcome belief). Subsequently, they believe that the clean-up day is a waste of time and effort (evaluation of outcome). This leads to an overall negative attitude toward a community clean-up day (attitude toward the behavior).

Subjective Norm

The second antecedent variable identified by Ajzen (1991) is *subjective norm*, which he defines as a "social factor" that "refers to the perceived social pressure to perform or not to perform the behavior" (p. 188). While attitude toward the behavior functions as a personal factor, "the second determinant of intention is the person's perception of the social pressures put on him to perform or not perform the behavior in question. Since it deals with perceived prescriptions, this factor is termed subjective norm" (Ajzen, 1985, p. 12). Social pressure can come from a number of groups, including family, friends, educators, employers, and social organizations, such as church. Importantly, the individual must feel a motivation to comply with those exerting pressure to perform a behavior. Previous research has found that for emerging adults, friends and family members are the most important subjective norm groups (Anderson, Noar, & Rogers, 2013; Andrews, Silk, & Eneli, 2010; Carmack & Heiss, 2018; Moore, Raymond, Mittelstaedt, & Tanner, 2002). Remember the student interested in becoming involved in the community clean-up project? She would be motivated to get involved if she believed her family supported her decision and believed community clean-up was important. She might also consider becoming involved if her friends were also interested and thought it was a good idea.

Perceived Behavioral Control

Finally, intention to engage in a specific action is determined by *perceived behavioral control*, which considers one's belief about the ease or difficulty of doing the specific action. Perceived behavioral control is influenced by a number of internal and external factors, including individuals' belief in their knowledge, skill, discipline, and ability to perform specific actions, as well as support from others and available resources (Kraft, Rise, Sutton, & Roysamb, 2005). Perceived behavioral control is considered the most important of the three determinants (Ajzen, 2011) because it is the only one directly correlated with behavior.

As noted, perceived behavioral control functions as an antecedent to intention, as well as a mitigating factor between intention and behavior (see Figure 1). Ajzen (1985) indicated that behaviors "are controlled by intentions, but not all intentions are carried out; some are abandoned altogether while others are revised to fit changing circumstances" (p. 11). In some cases, intentions not carried into action can be explained by a lack of perceived behavioral control in actually performing the intended behavior. For example, the student involved in the community clean-up has to believe her involvement in the community clean-up can make a difference to the community. If she believes her actions will not have a positive impact on the community, she is less likely to get involved.

Additional Considerations

As TPB has developed, additional determinants have been added, including past behaviors, actual behavioral control, and perceived effectiveness (Ajzen, 2011). These other elements add more dimension to the theory, focusing on actual present and past action, as well as more perceived, long-term outcomes of specific actions. Previous research suggests that actual behavioral control and past behavior may be even more important than the three original determinants (Abraham & Sheeran, 2003; Ajzen, 2011; Carmack & Heiss, 2018; Kor & Mullan, 2011); however, others have cautioned about putting too much emphasis on past behavior as an important element (Bamberg, Ajzen & Schmidt, 2003). Instead, Bamberg et al. (2003) and Cooke and French (2011) suggested that contextualizing past behavior is more appropriate for determining if past behavior is a factor. Take, for example, an individual trying to stop smoking even though she has tried to stop in the past. Past behavior would only consider that she tried to stop in the past. Past behavior context would consider when she tried to stop, what motived her to try in the past, what cessation methods she tried, and what made her unsuccessful. In general, according to TPB, individuals intend to engage in a behavior if they believe the action is positive (attitude), believe others want them to do the action (subjective norm), and believe they will be able to successfully do the specific action (perceived behavioral control), yet research recognizes that other variables are likely at play leading to behavioral intention.

Theory of Planned Behavior in Action

TPB is a popular theory used to study a variety of communication topics, including factors influencing decisions regarding health services (Anderson, Noar, & Rogers, 2013), receiving vaccinations (Britt, Collins, Wilson, Linnemeier, & Englebert, 2015; Hesse & Rauscher, 2016; Yang, 2015), organ donation (Bae, 2008; Bae & Kang, 2008; Park, Smith, & Yun, 2009; Siegel, Alvaro, Hohman, & Maurer, 2011; Sukalla, Wagner, & Rackow, 2017), water conservation, and recycling (Liang, Kee, & Henderson, 2018; Onel & Mukherjee, 2017; Witzling, Shaw, & Amato, 2015).

TPB enables communication researchers and practitioners to craft messages and understand factors that promote healthy habits, encourage socially desirable behaviors, and influence consumer behaviors. TPB has been influential in exploring factors leading to safe sex practices among teens and adults (Guan et al., 2016; Rittenour & Booth-Butterfield, 2006; Sneed, Tan, & Meyer, 2015) and the impact of media and parental communication on children's physical activity and weight (Andrews, Silk, & Eneli, 2010). These studies underscore how antecedents, especially perceived behavioral control and subjective norm, work together to influence behavior intentions. In a study exploring children's intention to use marijuana, Huansuriya, Siegel, and Crano (2014) found that parents' discussing marijuana with their children (subjective norm) and perceived ability to refuse marijuana (perceived behavioral control) led to the intention to not use marijuana. In a study interested in children's physical activity, Paek, Oh, and Hove (2012) found that children's intent to exercise was influenced by their belief that they could engage in physical activity despite temperature and tiredness (perceived behavioral control) and their exposure to a media campaign (subjective norm). Similarly, Zhang et al. (2015) found that social support for physical activity via social media was influenced by individuals' capability to engage in the activity (perceived behavioral control).

TPB has also been utilized to examine consumption behaviors, such as media use and purchasing choices. Many of these studies focus on young and emerging adults. In an increasingly digital era, many of these studies use TPB to understand linkages between attitudes, subjective norms, and behaviors. This research area has examined parental support and mediation of children's media usage (Finke, Hickerson, McLaughlina, Nippold, & Camarata, 2015; Krcmar & Cingel, 2016), Facebook users' posting of edited images (Lowe-Calverley & Grieve, 2018), factors leading to sharing videos on social media (Yang & Wang, 2015), college student intention to use LinkedIn (Carmack & Heiss, 2018), and distracted driving (Buellens, Roe, & Van den Bulck, 2011; Tian & Robinson, 2017). On the other end of the consumption behaviors, researchers have used TPB to examine the underlying antecedents of choice when considering college students' risky credit behavior (Xiao, Tang, Serido, & Shim, 2011), donations to public radio (Kinnally & Brinkerhoff, 2013), and reception of public relations crisis tactics on social media (Kinsky, Drumheller, Gerlich, Brock-Baskin, & Sollosy, 2015). These studies identified many of the nuances of TPB, highlighting how the impact of antecedents change depending on the topic. For example, Dodd and Supa (2015) found that corporate social advocacy, and, in particular, support/opposition of same-sex marriage (attitude) was a predictor of consumer purchase intentions. Conversely, Carmack and Heiss (2018) found that family and friends (subjective norm groups) were strong predictors of LinkedIn use intentions.

Communication scholars have well-established the importance and utility of the Theory of Planned Behavior in influencing individuals' behaviors. Be it credit card use or exercise, the TPB helps scholars and practitioners identify the important attitudes, influencers, and perceived ability that can help them successfully change individuals' actions. Much of this research also demonstrates the effectiveness of the TPB when promoting change in children and emerging adults, such as health communication campaign designers interested in changing emerging adults' behaviors, especially as they transition into a new environment like college.

College life presents a number of new health issues that need innovative solutions. One such health issue is sleep deprivation. The following case study examines university health campaigns targeting sleep deprivation in college students and how the TPB can help in designing effective messages.

The Case of University Sleep-Positive Campaigns

College can be a trying time for young adults; they have to learn how to manage their time without the structures of high school and family. One of the healthy behaviors that students often forego in their academic pursuit is sleep. College students often struggle to get the recommended seven to nine hours of sleep a night, leading to sleep deprivation. In fact, college students report only getting six hours of sleep a night (University of Georgia University Health Center, 2018). Fifty percent of college students report daytime sleepiness compared to 36% of noncollege students (Oginska & Pokorski, 2006), and 70% of college students get insufficient sleep (Lund, Reider, Whiting, & Prichard, 2010). Students who develop too much sleep deprivation experience sleep debt, which is the cumulative loss of sleep (American Sleep Association, 2018). Students accrue sleep debt for a number of typical reasons, such as sleep disorders, sleep disturbances, and social media use (Mark, Wang, Niiya, & Reich, 2016), but also because of reasons affiliated with college life: staying up late or pulling an "all-nighter" to finish assignments, early class schedules, staying up because of a "fear of missing out," and binging on sleep on the weekends (Baltz, 2016). Sleep debt can have serious, negative impacts on college students' academic performance, including decreased GPAs, increased risk of academic failure, compromised learning, and increased risk of depression (Hershner & Chervin, 2014; Regestein et al., 2010).

To combat sleep deprivation and debt, universities across the United States are developing sleep-positive campaigns. These sleep-positive campaigns are designed to encourage students to adopt healthy sleep habits (French, 2012; Lambert, 2017) by recommending that students think about their sleep schedules, extracurricular activities, and their beliefs about napping in order to reduce sleep debt. Along with campaigns, such as University of California-Riverside's "Choose to Snooze" and University of California-Davis' "Be Wise, Shut Your Eyes," universities such as Harvard University, James Madison University, and the University of Miami are also spending millions of dollars to invest in napping pods and napping nooks for students to enact healthy sleep behaviors (Haven, 2013; Kinery, 2016; Munzenreider, 2016). Some universities, like University of California-Davis, are even pairing their campaigns with a free, noncredit, 30-minute napping class students can take to ensure they have a midday respite (Lambert, 2017). So, how could a university design a sleep-positive campaign using the Theory of Planned Behavior?

Theory of Planned Behavior and Sleep-Positive Campaigns

Attitudes. Sleep-positive campaigns are, at their core, attitudinal change campaigns (Corcoran, 2011). In order for students to make changes to their sleeping styles (the behavior change), they must first change their attitudes about sleep, work, and relaxation. These campaigns are designed to raise students' knowledge about sleep and sleep debt, but also to challenge their attitudes about what is considered "normal" college sleep habits. Ask a college student about what is expected in terms of sleep and they will likely tell you that they expect to have long nights, even all-nighters, writing papers and studying. This attitude is fostered even more during midterms and final exams when students expect to be stressed and sleep deprived.

First, sleep-positive campaigns must combat this attitudinal expectation in order to show students the importance of sleep. Campaign messages that communicate information about the dangers of sleep deprivation could have positive impacts, but a successful campaign still needs to combat the underlying attitude about college sleep expectations. These campaign messages might include statistics of students who do not pull all-nighters or stories from students about how they maintain a healthy sleep schedule while still meeting the demands of school.

Second, these campaigns need to change students' attitudes about activities specifically related to poor sleep habits. Changing the major underlying attitude is important, but that will not matter if campaigns do not change students' attitudes about related behaviors. For example, the UC-Davis "Be Wise, Shut Your Eyes" campaign has a specific campaign message about the dangers of using smart phones and laptops at the end of the day. This campaign message states, "Blue light from screens can disturb your circadian rhythm, which regulates sleep" (UCD Student Health and Counseling Services, n.d.). Oregon State University's campaign recommends students rethink their study places, noting that studying in bed is a bad idea because it makes it difficult for students to transition into sleep (Oregon State University, 2018). Sleep-positive campaigns must change these secondary attitudes about related activities in order for the campaigns to be successful.

Finally, sleep-positive campaigns have to challenge attitudes about napping. The perception here is that students who have time to nap in the middle of the day are lazy, not working, or not taking their schoolwork seriously. These assumptions are problematic because research demonstrates that napping can have positive benefits and cut down on sleep debt. Kotaro Aoki, a student at Wesleyan University who naps five days a week, argued, "If you want to achieve anything, you are most likely to be in need of some napping during daytime" (Sayej, 2016). The underlying, negative attitude about napping is connected to perceived understanding of relaxation and expectations for work during the day. Sleep-positive campaigns have to challenge the attitudes about taking breaks in the middle of day as being helpful and important for success, not signs of laziness. In the UC-Davis napping class, students are told, "Your only job is to simply rest and exist" (Lambert, 2017), communicating to students that it is acceptable and beneficial to take a break to rest.

Subjective norm. Campaign designers have to determine the important influencers in students' lives and, more importantly, whose opinions matter. In this case, two groups are undoubtedly important: students and university administrators and professors. Although parents are also important, the proximity of other students and university staff make them important individuals in these campaigns.

First, other students, including friends and roommates, are an important subjective norm group. As noted earlier, friends are perhaps the most important influencer group and they hold sway over students' sleep-positive behaviors. Although friends and roommates are probably supportive of naps, their actions might prohibit students from engaging in other sleep-positive behaviors, such as encouraging them to play video games at night or go for late-night food runs. Students have a "fear of missing out" and friends and roommates may play into that fear in order to get them to engage in activities that contribute to sleep debt. Additionally, finding the right place to nap can be influenced by other students. Other students may be judgmental of students who nap in the library or student union, where napping pods are normally placed (thinking napping should take place in their bedrooms) so getting school-wide support for napping spaces is important.

Second, the university staff, including administrators and professors, need to show support for sleep-positive behaviors. University-sponsored campaigns are a good start because they communicate to the student body that "administrators are not only telling students it's OK to push the snooze button, they're actually encouraging it" (Kinery, 2016). Students who know that their university supports sleep-positive behaviors, such as napping, may be more likely to engage in those behaviors.

Perceived behavioral control. Finally, students have to believe that they have control over their ability to engage in sleep-positive behaviors in order to actually engage in the behavior. Students need to be able to not only envision a life with better sleep, but also have control over their ability to make this happen. The best place to start is with their schedules and time management. What kind of course schedules have students created? What kind of work schedules do they have? Are they able to schedule time for naps? Are they taking on a course load that would allow them to have time to do homework without having to stay up late?

If students do not believe they have a schedule to engage in these behaviors, they will be less likely to act. Students may believe that sleep is important and feel pressure to comply with those encouraging sleep, but may ultimately not engage in the behavior simply because they do not perceive control over their sleep habits.

Summary and Theoretical Implications

The Theory of Planned Behavior allows researchers to investigate how different attitudes, subjective norms, and perceived behavioral control influence individuals' intention to and actual engagement in certain behaviors. In this case, we can see how a number of different and connected attitudes about work ethics, action stereotypes, and experience expectations could help campaign designers create effective messages about sleep. The case study also illustrates the importance of identifying the most influential people in college students' lives in order to persuade them to engage in better sleep practices. Finally, the theory allows campaign designers to show students how they truly can break down decades of problematic assumptions about college and sleep and take control of their sleep health.

As discussed earlier, researchers have begun to test how additional antecedents, such as past action, present action, and perceived long-term outcomes, could also influence behavior. A campaign on sleep-positive behaviors in college students could easily incorporate messages targeting students' current and past napping practices to show students how they can successfully nap in college. Additionally, messages that promote the long-term benefits of positive sleep behaviors, especially linked to future success, could be successful in showing students why engaging in health behaviors now helps them later in life.

This case study also highlights how subject norm groups can have more than just a persuasive effect on individuals' behaviors; they can provide paths to action and help individuals realize their perceived behavioral control. As we noted in our application of perceived behavioral control, universities can help students realize what they have control over. Perceived behavioral control is more than just self-efficacy, or an individual's belief that they can do a certain behavior; it is their belief that they can do the behavior *and* they have control over external forces that help do the behavior. Coverage of the student sleep debt problem and sleep-positive campaigns suggest a number of ways universities can and are helping students, be it with napping classes, sleep pods, or reducing the number of early morning classes offered. Here, universities aren't just an important group; they have the resources to help students see that positive sleep behaviors are possible. Campaigners can work with subjective norm groups to not only create messages that show these groups support positive sleep behaviors, but also to find ways to help students actually do these behaviors.

The Theory of Planned Behavior is just one of many persuasive communication theories which can help individuals change their health behaviors. The key to using TPB to design an effective campaign is to dig deep into identifying not only all the attitudes, subjective norm groups, and perceived behavioral control issues, but also to determine what your target population thinks is most important. A health campaign cannot tackle everything, but a designer savvy in their theory knowledge can determine the most effective antecedents to attempt change.

Discussion Questions

1. Imagine that you are working with the communications office at your college or university to develop a sleep-positive campaign. What elements do you believe should be included in a campaign based on your experiences with students' attitudes toward sleep? If you do not know how students on campus perceive sleep, how might you gather that information?

2. As a student, what factors do you believe lead to a lack of perceived behavioral control regarding sleep? In this example, do you believe that perceived behavioral control has more of an impact as an antecedent variable (leading to intention) or more influence as a mitigating factor between intention and behavior? (See Figure 1)

3. In addition to college faculty and staff as well as peer groups, what influential groups exist that might be able to create a pro-sleep subjective norm? Do you believe there are certain groups that should not be activated as key influencers because students would not have motivation to comply with members of that group?

4. Thinking about the three antecedents, which do you think would be most beneficial in a campaign message to students at your university? What would that message look like?

REFERENCES

Abraham, C., & Sheeran, P. (2003). Acting on intentions: The role of anticipated regret. *British Journal of Social Psychology, 42,* 495–511.

Ajzen, I. (1985). From intention to action: A theory of planned behavior. In J. Kuhl & J. Beckmann (Eds.), *Action control: From cognition to behavior* (pp. 11–40). New York: Springer-Verlag.

Ajzen, I. (1988). *Attitudes, personality, and behavior.* Chicago, IL: Dorsey Press.

Ajzen, I. (1991). The theory of planned behavior. *Organizational Behavior and Human Decision Processes, 50,* 179–211.

Ajzen, I. (2011). The theory of planned behaviour: Reactions and reflections. *Psychology & Health, 26*(9), 1113–1127.

Alas, Y., Muhammad, A., Sabtu, N. I., & Yunus, N. (2016). Second-chance university admission, the theory of planned behaviour and student achievement. *International Review of Education, 62*(3), 299–316.

American Sleep Association. (2018). Sleep debt: Signs, symptoms, and treatments. Retrieved from https://www.sleepassociation.org/

Anderson, C. N., Noar, S. M., & Rogers, B. D. (2013). The persuasive power of oral health promotion messages: A theory of planned behavior approach to dental checkups among young adults. *Health Communication, 28*(3), 304–313.

Andrews, K. R., Silk, K. S., & Eneli, I. U. (2010). Parents as health promoters: A theory of planned behavior perspective on the prevention of childhood obesity. *Journal of Health Communication, 15*(1), 95–107.

Bae, H. S. (2008). Entertainment-education and recruitment of cornea donors: The role of emotion and issue involvement. *Journal of Health Communication, 13*(1), 20–36.

Bae, H. S., & Kang, S. (2008). The influence of viewing an entertainment-education program on cornea donation intention: A test of the theory of planned behavior. *Health Communication, 23*(1), 87–95.

Baltz, J. (2016, April 4). Is sleep deprivation the new college norm? *Huffington Post*. Retrieved from https://www.huffingtonpost.com/

Bamberg, S., Azjen, I., & Schmidt, P. (2003). Choice of travel mode in the theory of planned behavior: The roles of past behavior, habit, and reasoned action. *Basic and Applied Social Psychology, 25*(3), 175–187.

Britt, R. K., Collins, W. B., Wilson, K. M., Linnemeier, G., & Englebert, A. M. (2015). The role of ehealth literacy and HPV vaccination among young adults: Implications from a planned behavior approach. *Communication Research Reports, 32*(3), 208–215.

Carmack, H. J., & Heiss, S. N. (2018). Using the theory of planned behavior to predict college students' intent to use LinkedIn for job searches and professional networking. *Communication Studies, 69*(2), 145–160.

Cooke, R., & French, D. P. (2011). The role of context and timeframe in moderating relationships within the theory of planned behaviour. *Psychology and Health, 26*, 1225–1240.

Corcoran, N. (2011). *Working on health communication*. Thousand Oaks, CA: Sage.

Beullens, K., Roe, K., & Van den Bulck, J. (2011). The impact of adolescents' news and action movie viewing on risky driving behavior: A longitudinal study. *Human Communication Research, 37*(4), 488–508.

Dodd, M. D., & Supa, D. (2015). Testing the viability of corporate social advocacy as a predictor of purchase intention. *Communication Research Reports, 32*(4), 287–293.

Finke, E. H., Hickerson, B., McLaughlina, E., Nippold, M., & Camarata, S. (2015). Parental intention to support video game play by children with autism spectrum disorder: An application of the theory of planned behavior. *Language, Speech & Hearing Serviced in Schools, 46*(2), 154–165.

Fishbein, M. A. (1967). *Readings in attitude theory and measurement*. NY: Wiley.

Fishbein, M. A., & Ajzen, I. (1975). *Belief, attitude, and intention, and behavior: An introduction to theory and research*. Reading, MA: Addison-Wesley.

French, R. (2012, March 5). UC Riverside students encouraged to "choose to snooze". *UCR Today*. Retrieved from https://ucrtoday.ucr.edu/3723

Guan, M., Coles, V. B., Samp, J. A., Sales, J. M., DiClemente, R., J., & Monahan, J. L. (2016). Incorporating communication into the theory of planned behavior to predict condom use among African American women. *Journal of Health Communication, 21*(9), 1046–1054.

Haven, S. (2013, March 3). On-campus nap room proposed at Harvard. *USA Today*. Retrieved from college.usatoday.com/.

Hershner, S. D., & Chervin, R. D. (2014). Causes and consequences of sleepiness among college students. *Nature and Science of Sleep, 6*, 73–84.

Hesse, C., & Rauscher, E. A. (2016). The relationship between family communication patterns and child vaccination intentions. *Communication Research Reports, 33*(1), 61–67.

Huansuriya, T., Siegel, J. T., & Crano, W. D. (2014). Parent-child drug communication: Pathway from parents' ad exposure to youth's marijuana use intention. *Journal of Health Communication, 19*(2), 244–259.

Kinnally, W., & Brinkerhoff, B. (2013). Improving the drive: A case study for modeling public radio member donations using the theory of planned behavior. *Journal of Radio and Audio Media, 20*(1), 2–16.

Kinery, E. (2016, March 7). Napping pods let students doze between classes. *USA Today*. Retrieved from college.usatoday.com/

Kinsky, E. S., Drumheller, K., Gerlich, R. N., Brock-Baskin, M. E., & Sollosy, M. (2015). The effect of socially mediated public relations crises on planned behavior: How TPB can help both corporations and nonprofits. *Journal of Public Relations Research, 27*(2), 136–157.

Kor, K., & Mullan, B.A. (2011). Sleep hygiene behaviours: An application of the theory of planned behaviour and the investigation of perceived autonomy support, past behavior and response inhibition. *Psychology and Health, 26*, 1208–1224.

Kraft, P., Rise, J., Sutton, S., & Roysamb, E. (2005). Perceived difficulty in the theory of planned behaviour: Perceived behavioural control or affective attitude. *British Journal of Social Psychology, 44*, 479–496.

Krcmar, M., & Cingel, D. P. (2016). Examining two theoretical models for predicting American and Dutch parents' mediation of adolescent social media use. *Journal of Family Communication 16*(3), 247–262.

Lambert, D. (2017, December 15). Need a nap? Students regularly fall asleep in this class at UC Davis. *The Sacramento Bee*. Retrieved from https://www.sacbee.com/

Liang, Y., Kee, K. F., & Henderson, L. K. (2018). Towards an integrated model of strategic environmental communication: Advancing theories of reactance and planned behavior in water conservation context. *Journal of Applied Communication Research, 46*(2), 135–154.

Lowe-Calverley, E., & Grieve, R. (2018). Self-ie love: Predictors of image editing intentions on Facebook. *Telematics & Informatics, 35*(1), 186–194.

Lund, H. G., Reider, B. D., Whiting, A. B., & Prichard, J. R. (2010). Sleep patterns and predictors of disturbed sleep in a large population of college students. *Journal of Adolescent Health, 46*, 124–132.

Mark, G., Wang, Y., Niiya, M., & Reich, S. (2016). Sleep debt in student life: Online attention focus, Facebook, and mood. *Proceedings of the 2016 CHI Conference on Human Factors in Computing Systems* (pp. 5517–5528). NY: Association for Computing Machinery.

Moore, J., Raymond, M. A., Mittelstaedt, J., & Tanner Jr., J. F. (2002). Age and consumer socialization agent influences on adolescents' sexual knowledge, attitudes, and behavior: Implications for social marketing initiatives and public policy. *Journal of Public Policy & Marketing, 21*, 37–52.

Munzenreider, K. (2016, February 10). University of Miami students now have $9,000 napping pods to use on campus. *Miami New Times*. Retrieved from www.miaminewtimes.com/

Oginska, H., & Pokorski, J. (2006). Fatigue and mood correlates of sleep length in three age-social groups: School children, students, and employees. *Chronobiology International, 23*, 1317–1328.

Onel, N., & Mukherjee, A. (2017). Why do consumers recycle? A holistic perspective encompassing moral considerations, affective responses, and self-interest motives. *Psychology & Marketing, 34*(10), 956–971.

Oregon State University Academic Success Center. (2018). Get the most out of your naps and sleep. Retrieved from http://success.oregonstate.edu/

Paek, H., Oh, H. J., & Hove, T. (2012). How media campaigns influence children's physical activity: Expanding the normative mechanisms of the theory of planned behavior. *Journal of Health Communication, 17*(8), 869–885.

Park, H. S., Smith, S. W., & Yun, D. (2009). Ethnic differences in intention to enroll in state organ donor registry and intention to talk with family about donation. *Health Communication, 24*(7), 647–659.

Regestein, Q., Natarajan, V., Pavlova, M., Kawasaki, S., Gleason, R., & Koff, E. (2010). Sleep debt and depression in female college students. *Psychiatry Research, 176*, 34–39.

Rittenour, C. E., & Booth-Butterfield, M. (2006). College students' sexual health: Investigating the role of peer communication. *Qualitative Research Reports in Communication, 7*(1), 57–65.

Sayej, N. (2016, April 8). Power napping on campus. *The New York Times.* Retrieved from https://www.nytimes.com/

Siegel, J. T., Alvaro, E. M., Hohman, Z. P., & Maurer, D. (2011). "Can you spare an organ?": Exploring Hispanic Americans' willingness to discuss living organ donation with loved ones. *Health Communication, 26*(8), 754–764.

Sneed, C. D., Tan, H. P., & Meyer, J. C. (2015). The influence of parental communication and perception of peers on adolescent sexual behavior. *Journal of Health Communication, 20*(8), 888–892.

Sukalla, F., Wagner, A. J. M., & Rackow, I. (2017). Dispelling fears and myths of organ donation: How narratives that include information reduce ambivalence and reactance. *International Journal of Communication, 11*, 5027–5047.

Tian, Y., & Robinson, J. D. (2017). Predictors of cell phone use in distracted driving: Extending the theory of planned behavior. *Health Communication, 32*(9), 1066–1075.

University of California Davis Student Health and Counseling Services. (n.d.). Sleep. Retrieved from https://shcs.ucdavis.edu/

University of Georgia University Health Center. (2018). Sleep rocks!…Get more of it!. Retrieved from https://www.uhs.uga.edu/sleep

Witzling, L., Shaw. B., & Amaton, M. S. (2015). Incorporating information exposure into a theory of planned behavior model to enrich understanding of proenvironmental behavior. *Science Communication, 37*(5), 551–574.

Xiao, J. J., Tang, C., Serido, J., & Shim, S. (2011). Antecedents and consequences of risky credit behavior among college students: Application and extension of the theory of planned behavior. *Journal of Public Policy & Marketing, 30*(2), 239–245.

Yang, H., & Wang, Y. (2015). Social sharing of online videos: Examining American consumers' video sharing attitudes, intent, and behavior. *Psychology & Marketing, 32*(9), 907–919.

Yang, Z. (2015). Predicting young adults' intentions to get the H1N1 vaccine: An integrated model. *Journal of Health Communication, 20*(1), 69–79.

Zhang, N., Campo, S., Yang, J., Janz, K. F., Snetselaar, L. G., & Eckler, P. (2015). Effects of social support about physical activity on social networking sites: Applying the theory of planned behavior. *Health Communication, 30*(12), 1277–1285.